Shaping the Discourse

Also from the School of Women's Studies, Jadavpur University

Intimate Others: Marriage and Sexualities in India
Edited by Samita Sen, Ranjita Biswas and Nandita Dhawan

Readings in Gender Studies I
Mapping the Field: Gender Relations in Contemporary India, vol i
Edited by Nirmala Banerjee, Samita Sen and Nandita Dhawan

Mapping the Field: Gender Relations in Contemporary India, vol ii
Edited by Nirmala Banerjee, Samita Sen and Nandita Dhawan

Readings in Gender Studies II
Women Contesting Culture: Changing Frames of Gender Politics in India
Edited by Kavita Panjabi and Paromita Chakravarti

Forthcoming

Readings in Gender Studies IV
Voices and Verses of the Talking Stars
Edited by Madhuja Mukherjee

Readings in Gender Studies 3

SHAPING THE DISCOURSE

Women's Writings in Bengali Periodicals 1865-1947

Edited by

Ipshita Chanda and Jayeeta Bagchi

School of Women's Studies, Jadavpur University

Stree

Shaping the Discourse:
Women's Writings in Bengali Periodicals 1865-1947
was first published in 2014 by STREE,
an imprint of Bhatkal and Sen,
16 Southern Avenue, Kolkata 700 026.
email : streesamya.manager@gmail.com
webpp : www.stree-samyabooks.com

ISBN 978-81-906760-5-2
81-906760-6-9

Rs 550.00

Design by STREE and Krishna Gopal Das,
typesetting by Krishna Gopal Das,
74T Sultan Alam Road, Kolkata 700 033,
and printed at Bengal Phototype Co.
46/1 Raja Rammohan Roy Sarani, Kolkata 700 009.

Published by Mandira Sen for STREE,
An imprint of Bhatkal and Sen,
16 Southern Avenue, Kolkata 700 026.

In memory of Professor Subir Ray Chaudhuri

Note on the Bengali Calendar

The Bengali calendar or Bangla Shan (BS) is a traditional solar calendar formulated by Fatehullah Shirazi on the basis on the lunar Hijri and the solar Bengali calendars. Introduced in 1584, it was dated from the Emperor Akbar's accession to the throne in 1556. The Bengali year is always 593 years less than the year in the Gregorian calendar.

The Bengali months are as follows:

Baisakh (mid-April to mid-May)
Jaishtha (mid-May to mid-June)
Asarh (mid-June to mid-July)
Sravan (mid-July to mid-August)
Bhadra (mid-August to mid-September)
Ashvin (mid-September to mid-October)
Kartik (mid-October to mid-November)
Agrahayan (mid-November to mid-December)
Paush (mid-December to mid-January)
Magh (mid-January to mid-February)
Falgun (mid-February to mid-March)
Chaitra (mid-March to mid-April)

Contents

PART II THE EMERGING 'NEW' WOMAN

Preface

The need for more teaching/learning material in women's studies has been felt for some years now. In our school, in Jadavpur University, we embarked on an M.Phil course in 2000. At that stage, when the direction to be taken in the teaching of women's studies was still quite uncertain, it took several years to frame the syllabus, negotiate the regulation of the university and garner the resources. By 2006, the details had been worked out, and the course had begun to draw interested participants from a variety of backgrounds: not only the expected fresh postgraduates from humanities and social sciences, but also students from physics and medicine, psychiatry and bio-sciences, mature women students returning to the academy with an interest in exploring questions about their own lives and social contexts, NGO workers desiring to learn more about their 'field', and school and college teachers seeking a fresh perspective on their disciplines. Hearteningly, the question of teachers was solved by the collective effort of the entire women's studies' community in the city. Established scholars and young researchers joined forces to teach these classes. An extraordinary energy and engagement vitalized this programme. In time, however, the need was felt to shift gears, towards greater institutionalization.

The context too had changed. The 1990s and early years of the twenty-first century saw a quantum leap in the sheer quantity of literature produced on gender. There was also, more significantly, a major reframing of problems and questions in the field, which needed to be taken into account while conducting teaching the M.Phil course: the syllabus needed re-working and courses needed re-organization. A series of workshops on curricula were held over several months. In 2007, a new syllabus was introduced and the course moved to a semester rather than an annual system.

The burgeoning of writing in the field had prompted the revision of the syllabus; the same factor prompted our thinking about producing readers for the students. The wide array of existing books and articles were not always accessible to students and a need was felt to try and bring some of it together in a form easily accessible to students, who may be returning to the academy after some years, or socially disadvantaged students, who found it difficult to collect and collate the material in print now. Around the same time, there was a move in different parts of the country, encouraged by the University Grants Commission, to introduce Masters' and even Bachelors' courses in women's studies. Indeed, the subject had been included in the National Eligibility Test (NET) for many years, though there had not been very many takers. Most of the established universities revised their undergraduate and graduate curricula to introduce 'gender topics' across humanities and social sciences. In some universities, women's studies is an optional course at the undergraduate level. We are occasionally approached by teachers and students for reading material and by undergraduate colleges for help in applying for women's studies centres. This enormous expansion in teaching—and, therefore, students—demanded a response from us.

We were fortunate that around the same time, the Higher Education Cell of Sir Ratan Tata Trust (Mumbai) at the Centre for the Study of Culture and Society (CSCS, Bangalore) was receiving applications for grants for building resources in women's studies. Their generous grant gave us the opportunity to mobilize resources for not only teaching our own new courses but also to cooperate with other universities and colleges in their endeavours and, most importantly, undertake the urgent task of producing teaching/learning material. It is with their financial assistance that we have been able to prepare these four readers in this series, of which the current one contains translations of women's writings from Bengali. The other two are on contemporary gender issues in India and on questions around culture. This current volume has another source of inspiration. The School of Women's Studies began the Women Writers Reprint Series in 1991. We have now published thirty-six volumes in this series. In these twenty years, however, only one volume of translation has been possible. We are often told that there is an urgent need to publish some of the rich Bengali material in translation to reach a wider audience. This volume is another small step in that direction. We hope that we will be able to bring more translations into print in the next few years.

We realize that the potential readership for this series has been envisaged in perhaps rather too generous terms: spanning undergraduate and research students and their teachers. In this our ambition has been shaped by the paucity of textbooks in the Indian market. This statement needs to be qualified somewhat, because our publishers have already published two very successful volumes in the Theorizing Feminism series that focus on concepts and methodology. Mary John's recent reader has also been a major contribution in this regard. There have been a few more such series by various publishers, many of them of the highest quality and extremely valuable. Given the rate at which women's studies courses are proliferating, however, we need much more and we need them quickly. Hence this effort. At present, this series will include four volumes, but we hope that these will be followed by more in the same vein.

In India today, as in many other regions across the globe, we inhabit a conjuncture of crises. The G-word overshadows all our discourses those who anticipate a shining prospect for India's future and those who prophesize more gloom to come. Without doubt, and even the optimists admit this, we have not been able to manage well the social costs of globalization. We see among large sections of the population distress, deprivation, disparity, and dislocation. At the same time, the leaps in communication technology and the explosion of mass media are changing attitudes and the quotidian lives of many social groups. Our systems and institutions of higher education cannot remain insulated from these developments. Indeed, from within, we feel strong winds of change, but many of us are uncertain as to whether this is an ill wind or whether we are moving in a positive direction. One thing, however, is certain: This is a good time to re-think our higher education, not only in terms of what we teach but how we teach. This series will attempt to straddle the old and the new. These four volumes are a beginning, which we hope will take us in new and as yet uncharted territory. We hope these will be helpful to teachers and students. If they contribute towards the expansion in the field and draw new enthusiasts amongst our midst, they will serve their purpose well.

Samita Sen
Director
School of Women Studies
Jadavpur University

July 2013

Acknowledgements

This collection has been rather long in the making, and along the way, it has accumulated many debts. The translators, who were harried constantly by the editors, deserve our first thanks, because without them, this book would not have been possible. The occasion for this possibility was provided by the Sir Ratan Tata Trust, whose grant to the School of Women's Studies at Jadavpur University has produced this book, along with much other excitement in the last three years. We are grateful for Tejaswini Niranjana's active intellectual support and Rekha Pappu's deft handling of the formalities. We hope that the promises and clarifications made at various stages of our interactions have assumed tangible shape.

Any project of this nature requires strong institutional support, and the university in general and the School of Women's Studies in particular have been with us all the way. We thank the past Vice Chancellor, Professor Pradip Narayan Ghosh, the present Vice Chancellor, Professor Souvik Bhattacharyya, the Registrar Dr. Pradip Kumar Ghosh and Finance Officer Sri Gour Krishna Pattanayak, whose silent but firm presence is behind all that we achieve. All at the School of Women's Studies, Jadavpur University, have contributed their mites in finally finishing the project. We would like, however, separately to thank Samita Sen, as a friend and reader of whatever was proferred in various stages of disarray, rather than in her institutional capacity as Director of the School. Kunal Chattopadhyay was bullied into reading the introduction, and we hope he takes partial responsibility for what finally appears here. No work on Bengali periodicals in the nineteenth and early twentieth centuries is possible without the active and exacting cooperation of Abhijit Sen, currently Publications Officer at Jadavpur University. We have been fortunate to have his constant support, and the critical apparatus as it stands is largely due to his meticulous care.

Anindita Bhaduri, now Professional Assistant at the School of Women's Studies, has meticulously read through the manuscript and helped to check for accuracy. Dr. Shanta Sen has done the rich annotations for the essays. We thank both of them. We are grateful to Chitrarekha Ghosh, who has helped us access the writers' biographies. We are also grateful to the Gokhale Memorial School authorities for allowing us access to the Sarala Ray centenary volume from which the essay by Sarala Ray was translated. The librarians at the archives and library of the Centre for Studies in Social Sciences Calcutta, Bangiya Sahitya Parishat, the National Library, Central Library, Jadavpur University, and the School of Women's Studies Library have helped us as much as they could. We would like to thank the academic and editorial team who were assembled for this book: Rajlakshmi Ghosh undertook the research and Anindita Roy and Mukulika Duttagupta provided editorial assistance. We would also like to thank Stree for their patience and uncompromising exactness, of which all 'their authors' are beneficiaries.

The manuscript has undergone many mutations, and has brought us to a particular stage in our thinking about gender in society, from historical, ideological and functional perspectives. We have 'lived' the manuscript: as women know, life does not remain on hold just because academic work demands priority. Hence it is fit that each of us acknowledges the presence, named or un-named, of our individual friends and family, who have lived through the process with us, whether they agreed with it, were interested in it, or even knew about its unfolding. It would be satisfying to think that Abbas and Sayantan may want to read this particular book some day, and we may consider our work done if they and those of their generation, regardless of gender, find it useful, not only as academic input, but as ways of engaging with gender in society on a day-to-day basis, as the women whose writings collected here did.

INTRODUCTION

I. Women Writing Gender

Ipshita Chanda

This volume comprises translations of essays written by women in Bengali periodicals dating from roughly the last quarter of the nineteenth century until the partition of the subcontinent in 1947. While terms 'woman', 'Bengali', 'nineteenth century', 'Partition' and so on, have been unpacked in detail by many scholars in the field, we have attempted to etch out nuances of the milieu framed by these descriptive terms to explore the process by which the discourse of gender is formed and actualized in society. We do not assume that there is no slippage between the discourse and practice; neither do we assume that each is exclusive of the other. Our premise is that these interlinked activities are part of a process that can be mapped through the intersections of the discursive and practical spaces. This seems to follow from Sandra Harding's conceptualization of gender at multiple levels: as a dimension of personal identity; as a principle of organization of social structures; and as a basis for normative value.[1] Perhaps this may be called a 'literary history' of gender as a category. We have tried to see how this category is constructed through beliefs, reason and emotion, expressed in a particular genre of writing in a specific medium, remaining fluid conceptually. The discourse and practice of gender emerge from their functioning and mutual interactions across time and across social and geographical space, and attempting to map these interactions results in glimpses of visible change. Thus we can offer the reader a sense of change, both in society's thinking processes and in its practice.

The 'women's question', especially in Bengal, has had its share of distinguished commentators and archivists. The outlines of a temporally and spatially situated discourse of gender in society have already emerged and been in currency for twenty-odd years, and engagements with the foundational elements constructing this emergent discourse have also been in currency for a while. The selections have been influenced by these engagements: while the pioneering role of what Padma Anagol has termed 'the Bengal line'[2] is open to imitation and criticism, our concern here is to explore the possibility of an ongoing multi-layered and multi-textured social conversation about women's issues in a particular period. We can discern the dynamics of change in positions and strategies regarding certain issues like women's education, child marriage, widow remarriage, women's seclusion, 'reform', self-help, 'work for the country'. These become political counters in the ongoing struggle for freedom from colonial rule.[3] They cease to remain issues peculiar to the Bengal experience, though many of them arise here. It is not too much to think that the women who wrote in the periodicals, having braved the censure of traditionalists to confess their identities in signed articles, also read what was written in them. This may well be a cause for the change in the dynamics of the local; history also records some changes that were effected here and spread across the country.

The essays, written by women in periodicals beginning from 1865 (when the first essay collected here was published) to 1947 (when the last one came out, form our *rohstoff* material),[4] are read as creating a narrative of the changes in the life practices and beliefs of women writing on issues which they see as crucial to their own well-being. When we refer to the discourse of gender in society, that is what we mean; that these engagements by women at various levels are located and directed towards critique, solution, explication and change. In that sense, the discourse of gender provides the material for a historical narrative. Since we have been able to follow some issues, like the position of the widow, relations between men and women, relations between women themselves, work suitable for women and, of course, education, and capture some sense of dialogue between various positions at a given historical conjuncture, we feel that our effort may allow the reader to understand that a particular 'line', applicable to the entire discursive terrain or even a position arrived at after consideration of writing in particular periodicals in a particular language, would be fraught with risk. This is a period of change and, therefore, debate; it is a period of 'reform', and therefore of conflict between varieties of old and new, as a consequence of contact between cultures, one in a position of political power, and the other subjugated but with a heritage that is still living. The organization of gender and practice, 'performed' in daily social life, is part of this larger change and conflict.

We place the material translated in this book within such a framework. The 'women's question' in the mid-nineteenth century became a public and finally a political issue in tandem with the founding of the Brahmo Samaj, which went some way in proposing/living an alternate way of life for women in what today's theoretical sophistication would label the 'private' and public' spheres.[5] In upper-class and upper-caste Hindu society, confinement of women within the home was a mark of upper-class status, and may have been an aspirational threshold. In many cases, the ancient customs of the Aryans were invoked (Essay 8, *'Abarodhe Heenabastha'*, 'Dire Straits in Seclusion') to decide what was ideal for women. It was assumed that unless otherwise stated, they would be Hindus, and hence inheritors of the glorious Aryan traditions. The Brahmo reformers may not have had to grapple with this inheritance in their own society, but they realized that they had to negotiate these traditions if they wished to effect change on a larger scale. For example, reformers linked education to women's 'crossing the threshold' out of confinement; but they also realized, as we shall try to show, that even if confinement itself was often too contentious an issue for social debate, advocating education for women remained an acceptable strategy for 'reform'. Raja Rammohan Roy, through the Atmiya Samaj founded in 1815, addressed social problems like the *kaulinya* system,[6] the sale of daughters, dowry and caste discrimination. The state of society thus envisaged was one where deep if not radical changes could occur, and education was seen by women who advocated it at the end of the nineteenth century (and the men who legislated it, also, in their own way as a possible means for effecting these changes. The reforms set afoot by Rammohan resulted in the abolition by law, dated 12 July 1832, of the practice of *sati* or *sahamaran*.

There is scope for a long discussion about these two words and their use in contemporary speech and writing and, finally, their translation. Essentially, they refer to the same act, that of the widow burning on her husband's funeral pyre. In one case, the word used has come to be understood as the glorification of the woman 'choosing' to die thus as a chaste wife or 'sati', and in the other, implying the woman's accompaniment of her husband on his funeral pyre, such that they die together, which is what 'sahamaran' literally means. We may have lost many such nuances in translation. Rammohan's own stand against sahamaran was buttressed by arguments from the Hindu *Shastras*. The essay (Essay 5, *'Bharate Nari Hatya'*, 'The Murder of Women in India') however, uses precisely the same Hindu *Shastras* to negate his attempts to establish widow remarriage by holding that this is anathema to the spiritual union that the Hindu marriage entails. The essay is in agreement with his position on the sahamaran issue, but not with his position on widow remarriage. The upper-caste widow's plight was visible to and made visible by the upper-caste reformers in Bengal. Gradually, even in Muslim society, the higher caste of the family was marked by disallowing widow remarriage despite there being no injunction in the Qur'an against it. High-caste Muslims thus also began to follow customs that were brahminical or Hindu in origin, where class gained precedence over community in defining social status.

This spiritualism attributed to the Hindu marriage, with Rammohan's arguments cited as authority, is questioned directly in 1921 (Essay 10, *'Hindu Bibaher Adhyatmikata'*, 'The Spiritualism of Hindu Marriage'). Despite the fact that it is a cause for which Rammohan, a proven crusader for the betterment of women's position in society, is cited as authority, a woman wrote a scathing indictment of this very same claim for spiritualism of the Hindu marriage bond:

> One need not ponder much over where this spiritualism lies. It is obviously vested in that convenient scapegoat, the woman—for whom males, from the revered sage Manu to pre-pubescent schoolboys, have fancied themselves as worthy counsellors and guides. Matters of truth and falsity cannot be judged upon one-sided testimony. Therefore, since one of the parties is rendered voiceless and well-nigh inanimate under this ancient law-giving eminence, how can the real facts about marriage in our country come to light? (Ibid.)

Clearly, the spiritualism of such a marriage is highly questionable, which even the writer of 1885 (Essay 30, *'Hindu Bidhabar Abar Bibaha Howa Uchit Ki Na?'* 'On Whether or Not the Hindu Widow Should Marry Again') did not disagree.[7]

So we may surmise, in both periods, the abolition of widow burning, the condition and remarriage of widows and the abolition of child marriage could be considered together, but their interlinks were differently seen across time in different castes and communities within the same geographical and cultural location. That in itself might show the variety of opinion obtained, which is hardly anything novel. Rather, we may attempt to understand the nature of this variety, and how it led to different political, ethical and personal meanings that shaped the contours of gender discourse across time. We may just mark that we cannot merely categorize this as the 'women's question': it entails a reorganization of society as we know it. Geraldine Forbes says Indian women in the period of reform could not be called 'feminist' in the sense Elizabeth C. Stanton could. The latter emphasized what women could achieve, while Indian women had no coherent vision of what would happen after emancipation.[8] Indeed, Forbes discusses Sarala Devi Chaudhurani, a writer whose work is included in this volume (Essay 52, *'Jogajog'*, 'Communion'), and after analysing the careers of many women like her, concludes that for Indian women, men were not the issue, but custom was. Consequently, it becomes difficult to agree that the 'women's question' rather than gender relations is what preoccupied women in the nineteenth and early twentieth centuries.

On the contrary, we have at least three views about gender relations from women writers of three different socio-religious groups, spanning the entire period. Hindu, Brahmo and Muslim women discuss women's seclusion, women's lack of/deprivation of education and relations within the family, insisting continuously that in order to address what may appear to be the 'women's question', they address what affects the entire social body (for example, Essays 8, 16, 27, 56, 59, 62). Are these attempts at 'reform' rather than challenges to male control and oppression? We find, and will attempt to show from the essays collected in this volume that there is a strategic engagement with male control and oppression, even while the women do not live in what Padma Anagol describes as a 'gender-free' world in the context of western feminist practice.[9] The views collected here may not be a radical vision: however, neither are they a fantasy, because the women who perceive it as such do so through their advocacy of certain strategies to effect change. Let us investigate this in some detail.

In both the essays that we have cited on marriage (Essay 30, 'On Whether or Not the Hindu Widow Should Marry Again', and Essay 34, *'Purush o Nari'*, 'Man and Woman'), separated by thirty-six odd years, the contested ideological ground remains to be the nature of Hindu marriage as described by Hindu *Shastras*. In both cases, the actions that the *Shastras* were called upon to legitimize were subjects of consideration. In the former case, the *Shastras* were used to legislate a particular fate for widows. In the latter, this fate was clearly questioned rather than taken as inevitable. The prescription of the *Shastras* was directly disputed because the way they had been interpreted and implemented in the regulation of social practices was detrimental to woman's dignity, her well-being and her position in Hindu society. Though Essay 30 did not question the *Shastras*, it did call for the close following of its injunctions after proper interpretation.

Both essays argued that the implementation of the *Shastras* by the guardians of society, who needless to say, were men, was detrimental to women's condition and status. The first essay did not question the legitimacy of the *Shastras* thus interpreted and allocated responsibility to those who misunderstood the truth therein. The second, was inclined to question that very legitimacy, exactly because of this same reason: that those responsible for legislating on the basis of the *Shastras*, earlier as well as now, had misinterpreted them, thereby institutionalizing practices that devalued and oppressed women.

These two essays begin by accepting the premise that women's proper place is the domestic sphere which is also the inner house, the *antahpur*, where rules of confinement are observed. The first essay in this volume is a letter written in 1865, by Bibi Taherannesa, from the first class (seniormost) in the Girls' School at Boda. It is addressed to the editor of *Bamabodhini Patrika* on the subject of education (Essay 1, '*Bamabodhini Sampadak ke Patra*', 'A Letter to the Editor of *Bamabodhini Patrika*'). Taherannesa justifies her position that women should be educated by observing that according to the *Shastras* lack of wealth, power or conscience yields chaos, particularly, a woman without knowledge would not know what to do with them. She says: 'The stillborn or dead child causes grief just once, but the foolish untutored child causes such grief that one cannot deny its existence even in one's mind.' This is not very different from the arguments used by Nagendrabala Mustafi (Essay 8, 'Dire Straits in Seclusion'): 'The absence of proper knowledge is the reason why we are becoming so wretched and society looks down upon us.'

In the first instance, the arguments in favour of education would allow women to fulfil the role that society has allocated to them, which the writer does not find necessary to question. In the second, the issue remains the same, but here, added to education is the system of *abarodh*; the confinement of women in the antahpur, if not literally behind veils. In neither case is any established practice governing women's role and image questioned. In the first, the issue of abarodh does not arise in so many words, but that it should form a part of accepted social behaviour for a woman is not disputed. And, in the second, it is named and described as even more oppressive for women if it is coupled with lack of education.

If we are sensitive to this inflection, then we may recognize the difference in form in Essay 10 on spiritualism in Hindu marriage. As we have argued, this essay refuses to use women's better performance of institutionalized roles as an excuse or reason for their being given some rights and privileges, whether it is right to education or the right to survive the husband. Thus we may discern the advent of what we have with increasingly less confidence, termed 'modernity'. An essay written under the pseudonym Banganari (that is, a woman of Bengal), and published in *Bharati* in 1923, argued against women's confinement to the inner house without any advantages of sociability.[10] That it echoes the tone of the writer of Essay 10, 'The Spiritualism of Hindu Marriage', written in 1921 in the same journal, also under a pseudonym, reproduced in Essay 10, seems to indicate the reception of a particular structure of feeling from the West. Both essays depend not upon the *Shastras* but upon logic to explicate the position of women and suggest ways of betterment. The case for women is argued from the vantage point of rationalism, and emancipation is explained on the grounds of being human. The demand seems to be that society should make this confinement bearable, and the argument forwarded is strengthened by making explicit this relation between women's confinement and education. Jane Austen advocated the accumulation of 'inner resources' to her eighteenth-century heroines: perhaps the limit to which the gender question could be taken in the age of rationalism. Banganari writes in 1923:

> The behaviour of the younger members may destroy peace, happiness, discipline and well-being, in a word, the attributes that make a home a home, and often this is precisely the case. Hence, they must learn from a young age to uphold the respect and well-being of the family, and this education is equally necessary for boys and girls. And for all these years, because men are still mired in the past, because they have been given the wrong kind of education in

> this regard, and because, as we have pointed out earlier, they are the powerful group in the family, it is now imperative that they are the ones who should, who must concentrate on being educated adequately in this regard.[11]

The contextualization of the demand for inner resource and its relation to education certainly displayed a broader understanding of education. The spectrum of views about education ranged from those pleas by women in the second half of the nineteenth century who felt it to be the best support for women in confined situations within the home, to Fazilatunnesa, who writes in 1929 (Essay 14, *'Muslim Narir Mukti'*, 'Freedom for Muslim Women') that the only way to withstand the upheavals of the present twentieth century is to acquire education in the fullest sense, not the half-hearted attempts granted to women who go up to primary school and then do not continue. The critique of unfinished education and its consequences for society at large and women in particular are spelt out.

Society is viewed from an informed perspective, from a particular location and presents a full picture in which neither sex is privileged. We may well take this as a powerful argument for a gender-just society. An anonymous Bengali woman wrote in 1921 (Essay 10, 'The Spiritualism of Hindu Marriage'), mentioned earlier, questioning the authority of the *Shastras*; two years later, another Banganari, an anonymous woman of Bengal, in the same periodical, sought to dispel the myths surrounding women's position by likening the woman to the great serpent, the long-suffering giant snake Basuki, bearing the weight of the world and its chaos upon his head:

> The home is not something that the woman alone has to bear upon her head. The weight of it is in fact a part of the mind of everyone who lives there. But because the awareness that it is everybody's burden has not been adequately raised in everyone's mind thus far, in most cases, the home has toppled to one side and is on the verge of wallowing in the mud.[12]

Despite their very obvious differences, especially in time and the formulation of strategy, both essays, philosophical in order to explain the bases of action, and programmatic, in order to offer practical suggestions about actual action, one on spiritualism in marriage and the other on confinement and education, agreed among themselves on broad issues: first, all the authors were in pursuit of the well-being of women, and second, they were in agreement about the misuse and interpretation of the *shastriya* practices or customs by the guardians of society, who happened to be men. They agreed that this misuse facilitated the loss of women's dignity, status and well-being in society. And both essays were also in agreement about the evils that resulted for society at large and women in particular. But read diachronically, the essays reflect a shift in their argument—from laying the blame for women's backwardness on the incorrect interpretation and legislation of existing social norms, customs and scriptures by men who are the guardians of society. The later essays have little trust on any of these, and hold the deliberately erroneous use of various forms of power by men responsible for women's condition. It then becomes difficult to accept that the late nineteenth- and early twentieth-centuries' engagements are about the 'women's question' rather than about gendered relations in society. Indeed, the opposite seems to emerge: that when contemporary women, at least, focused their energy on what appeared to be the 'women's question', the result was that issues considered as 'women's issues' directly confronted the larger society. The system of kaulinya or dowry or sahamaran, subject of reforms meant to improve 'women's position/condition', directly stemmed from gender relations in society, and any change in the 'position/condition of women' would necessarily result in a change in the larger 'social' body itself.

As we have mentioned, some existing social practices, generally seen as belonging to the 'private' sphere of the family and of relationships, became the subject of 'public' debate and discussion when the women's question entered the sphere of legislation.[13] This led to an extension of the 'woman's' question, displaying its relations with every aspect of women's and men's social existence, including their roles as citizens of a modern nation-state with a distinctive culture. Our aim in this collection is to map some trajectories of engagement with the myriad complexities of issues as they arose and were inflected by the changing circumstances in both the larger world and the immediate local context. It is from this perspective that the documentation in this book has proceeded. This may allow us to take a diachronic as well as a synchronic view of issues as they shape and are shaped by the quotidian power relations between classes, castes, genders and communities which cohabit in society across the period spanned by these essays. We study these changes by mapping the positions taken across time and space by women themselves, as represented here through their writings.

The essays are all written in Bengali by women of Bengal. By Bengal is meant undivided Bengal. Often pre-Partition undivided Bengal is referred to as 'Bangladesh' by the writers who wrote before Partition. The division of east and west Bengal posed by Curzon in 1905 and resisted by mostly Hindu Bengalis is not taken into consideration here, though the distinction between Hindu and Muslim societies is consciously maintained by the writers. However, after 1947, these two Bengals ceased to exist politically and juridically as parts of a whole. Indeed, Curzon's move to partition Bengal and thereby effect a division between the Muslim majority and the Hindus, politicized religious identities and introduced some self-consciousness that was articulated in women's writing.

Our first text in this collection (Essay 1, 'A Letter to the Editor of *Bamabodhini Patrika*') as mentioned earlier, is the first and only signed piece of writing by a Muslim woman in a non-Muslim journal.[14] Further access and research may reveal another earlier text in the years to come: but thus far, even in the early twentieth century, there were very few instances of Muslim women writing in Bengali in periodicals published by Muslims, addressing Muslim society.[15] Asghar Ali has shown that this was the case in the earliest periodicals for women published from Lahore and Aligarh as well.[16] In the first period of Urdu journalism, too, women were addressed, but they wrote rarely. We may begin with two questions. First, what led to the education of Taherannesa[17] in the mid-nineteenth century that enabled her to write her letter to the editor?[18] We are told that Abul Kalam Azad and his two sisters were given the same kind of education but their childhood was spent outside Bengal.[19] Sufiya Khatun says in her autobiographical sketch that her parents were from outside Bengal, but she herself was Bengali. Though the details of her BA degree are untraceable, she wrote a number of essays in periodicals and signed off as Sufiya Khatun BA.[20] That, however, was in the second decade of the twentieth century. Do these facts help us to understand why the next text written in Bengali by a Muslim woman, which we are able to access, is Khairunnesa's in 1904 (Essay 22, '*Amader Sikshar Antaray*', 'The Hindrances to Our Education')?

This leads to the second question: what were the factors that led to the silence and hence apparent absence of Muslim women in Bengali journalism in the period when the Aligarh movement had begun?

Particularly, the reign of Sultan Shah Jahan Begum of Bhopal from 1868, and her contribution to the cause of education of both men and women of her community through a donation to the establishment of the seminary at Aligarh and her writing the *Tehzib-e-Niswan-wa-Tarbiat-e-Insaan*, not an essay but an entire encyclopaedia for women detailing all the practical matters that they needed to know about health and daily living, in the nineteenth century seems to be more intriguing.[21] That the Begums of Bhopal were honoured and held up as models for Muslim women in Bengal is evident from essays upon their social impact in some of the periodicals that were published in Bengal. But the instance of Rokeya Sakhawat Hossain did not occur until the early twentieth century among the Muslims in Bengal. Southard points out, 'The social origins of the educated middle class in India, which was a white collar professional rather than an entrepreneurial elite, was different in each province.'[22] But this would apply to a later age. Did this distinction have to do with the gradual assertion of 'Bengaliness' by the *ashraf* class of Bengal's Muslims?[23] In the north and the west of India, the development of Urdu as a language and its position were itself facilitated by the involvement of Anjuman Begumat Hamati-e-Urdu, under the leadership of Shahnawaz Begum of Bhopal in 1909. Was the difference due in some part to the class composition of the Muslim community in Bengal, who formed a sizeable number of the population, but belonged mostly to the peasant class rather than the ashraf class, which in the other parts of India, as mentioned, began to take steps towards reform? We have a detailed consideration of the kind of education that was available for women, as provided by different official and community sources, in Jayeeta Bagchi's contribution in the Introduction II of this volume.

We will turn from this issue with a final question. Rasasundari Dasi, the writer of the first autobiography in Bengali, taught herself to read and write because she wanted to read the scriptures. The primary religious duty of all Muslims, men and women, in any age is to know how to read the Holy Qur'an. However, given that society was controlled by few men, were Muslim women in Bengal guaranteed the 'privilege' of education by their religion unlike their Hindu sisters? In the age before Rokeya's decisive advent upon the scene, Alam tells us there were women like Khairunnesa and Fazilatunnesa who 'came out, breaking the bars of the cage'.[24] Strangely, one is reminded of the visual of Bimala crossing the threshold of the antahpur, coming out into the world, holding her husband's hand, from Satyajit Ray's film of Rabindranath Tagore's *Ghare Baire*. One wonders if that was how Rabindranath imagined it. But one is struck by the difference in the mode of entering the world outside the antahpur that Alam uses to describe the earliest Muslim women of Bengal who received more than the traditional Qur'anic education. It is simultaneously difficult to ask whether this primary requirement of a Muslim that he or she should learn to read the Qur'an as a requisite of faith, was followed in Bengal. And if it were not, why were women deprived of the basic education required to be true Muslims? The women and men who wrote in favour of Muslim women's education and progress into the outside world did not gloss over the fact that they were writing as Muslims: but they were also writing as (or on behalf of) women. It is difficult then to agree that the demand for education in the early period of reform lacked the perspective of gender: it may be added that gendering was a social process, and societies differed in their construction of women and men and the relationships between them. Hence, not only was the demand gendered, but also positioned within the social context, differently for different communities.

Education, and the conditions of its imparting, may be considered in some detail, because parallel to the diachronic history of certain ideas and issues relating to women's place in society, there is the synchronic history of ideas and issues as they affected women who were contemporaries but differently placed. 'Differently placed' is an ambiguous way of posing the matter, but it seems to be the only way to begin an understanding of what Mahua Sarkar has pointed to as the invisibility of Muslim women in the discourse of gender (or for that matter in any discourse) in colonial Bengal.[25] Our attempt is not to make the Muslim woman visible; we would have to admit total failure if that were indeed our aim, for the number of essays by Muslim women in this volume cannot substantiate any such claim. Our attempt is rather to understand, as we have pointed out earlier, the inflections that issues and, as a result, positions and strategies acquire, when located in different castes and communities within the same geographical and/or temporal space.

The first periodical published for Muslim society in Bengal was *Samachar Sabharajendra*, 7 March 1831, edited by Sheikh Alimullah, in both Persian and Bengali. *Tattvabodhini Patrika* from the Tattvabodhini Sabha of the Brahmo Samaj, began publishing in 1837. *Bamabodhini Parika* began in 1863, while the *Abalabandhav* started in 1869. Parallely, in Urdu, *Sharif Bibi* was started in 1893 and the

Huquq-un-Niswan of Sayyid Mumtaz Ali[26] was published in 1898. In the same year, appeared the journal that he started with his wife Muhammadi Begum as editor, *Tahzib-un-Niswan.*[27] All these periodicals were renowned for their championing of the women's cause. The Bengali periodicals were run by members of the Brahmo Samaj that introduced modernity as a lifestyle into Bengali upper-caste and upper-class Hindu society. The Urdu periodicals, published from Lahore, were run by a man educated at Deoband, with close links to the reformist ideals of that madrasa, though his position on the question of women was not exactly welcomed either by the gradualists represented by Sir Syed Ahmed or by the Deobandis themselves. Despite this similarity between the Urdu and Bengali Brahmo periodicals, the championing of women's cause by the Brahmo periodicals and the engagement with Hindu *Shastras* as begun by Rammohan was somewhat different from the position taken by the periodicals, published in the first half of the nineteenth century, directed towards Muslim society and published from Bengal in Bengali. The latter took the view that superstitions and evil customs must be removed from society in the light of the pristine early form of Islam. So it may have been an influence of the *Tahzib-un-Niswan* that by the turn of the century, Syed Imdad Ali, editor of the newly founded periodical *Nabanoor*, published from Calcutta in Bengali, declared, 'Today we respectfully invite every woman confined within our inner house to enhance the radiance of the new light (*nabanoor: noor* is also the light that emanates from the supreme being) by entering the arena of literature.'[28] Years later, this call still echoed in *Saogat* in the annual issue of 1926 (1333 BS):

> As long as women are embroiled and lulled to sleep in the thousand despicable complex bonds of the blind, dark inner house, there will be no freedom for the Bengali Muslim. So, for the good of her offspring, the mother's race in Bengal will have to awaken. Awaken, Bengal's slumbering Muslim women, shrug off your sleep.

By the beginning of the twentieth century, periodicals carried women's arguments for women's rights and position within Islam. They recorded the stages of their participation in negotiations for these rights and positions that contemporary society denied them. Many periodicals contained women's sections: the *Masik Muhammadi* carried *'Mahila Mehfil'* followed by *'Mahila Mahal'*. *Saogat* started in 1918 (mid-November to mid-December, Agrahayan 1325 BS) and renewed in 1926 (mid June-mid-July, Asarh 1333) carried a woman's section called *'Jenana Mehfil'* and in 1929 (1336 BS) published a special issue on women, *Mahila Saogat*. This had been prefigured in the pioneering *Bamabodhini Patrika*, which carried a section called *Bamarachana*. This section comprised women's writings, even if the women sometimes did not sign their names. Thus, though commentators have pointed out that the so-called 'Renaissance' that occurred in Hindu society in the mid-nineteenth century was not replicated in the Muslim society in Bengal until the early twentieth century for specific historical reasons,[29] the fact remained that in both cases, the articulation of the women's question, the description of their plight and the demands and strategies proposed by women for the amelioration of their condition, followed similar patterns. Hindu women found that the *Shastras* allowed them a specific status and position which the male interpreters of the *Shastras* were loath to grant. Gradually, they began to refer to practices and precepts in Muslim society which they deemed more sympathetic, at least from a scriptural point of view, to women. But Muslim women too felt that though the Qur'an *Hadith* allowed them many freedoms, the male guardians of their society did not allow women to enjoy these in practice. In the final analysis, there was a difference in time between the awakening of the two communities to western influences, but the issue related to women's position in society, expressed as 'women's freedom', stimulated responses along similar lines.

We may study one instance from the texts included in this volume. Khairunnesa Khatun (Essay 22, 'The Hindrances to Our Education') says that Muslim women's education needed to be organized in accordance with the tenets of Islam, so that it is disseminated successfully. The Qur'an did not debar women from education, but women would have to be provided schools in the neighbourhood so that they could maintain the rules of purdah in order to attend. Lady Brabourne College, set up in 1930, to meet the needs of Muslim women's higher education, was located in an area where Muslim families lived.

Swarnakumari Devi, writing in 1886, outlines her 'proposal' for the betterment of the widow's lot, suggesting that widows be educated and charged with the education of those women who remained in confinement in the inner house (Essay 17, *'Ar Ekti Prastab'*, 'Another Proposal'). As we have noted, once sahamaran had been declared illegal, there arises what we may well call the problem of widows: their position in society, their economic maintenance, and not the least, their 'morals'.

Spiritual or not, the Hindu widow, saved from the funeral pyre of her husband, seems to have been cut adrift in the deep blue sea of Bengali Hindu society. This is an issue that women thought about and addressed in conjunction with 'education' and 'work' throughout the period. While those intent on preserving Hindu dharma like Shyamasundari (Essay 30, 'On Whether or Not the Hindu Widow Should Marry Again'), refuse to accept remarriage, the problem cannot be denied. So Swarnakumari addresses both this reluctance on the part of Hindu society that claims to follow the *Shastras* and the pressing need for female education in one single move.

The earliest women reformers seemed to understand that the momentous upheavals that would follow when education was imparted to women would lead to a change that would involve the support of a large cross-section of the population. These were women's attempt to articulate their own perspectives and aims specific to their well-being in society. Anagol in her study of nineteenth-century Marathi women's engagement with the existing social discourses in an effort to find their own place and perspective in dialogue with it remarks,

> if one examines Indian women's contributions to the making of modern India in terms of their perspectives and participation in the religious and social reform movement, such a picture is shown to be highly misleading. In fact, if anything, Indian women were not only actively attempting to enter and legitimize their presence within the public sphere, but, more importantly, they were blurring the divide between the two.[30]

She points out that women did not reject what the 1885 writer Shyamasundari Devi repeatedly calls Hindu ideals, but used the strategies of assimilation and accommodation to build separate institutions that were specifically gendered.[31] Thus, the 'religious' and 'social' reforms were for women, at least, political, and overtly so. For example, in the 1920s, when Chittaranjan Das was leading an attempt to introduce 50 per cent reservation for Muslims in the Calcutta Municipal Corporation, Begum Rokeya wrote:

> Sixty-seventy years ago, English education was prohibited even to men. If you studied English, you became a kafer. Now the householders are paying the price for this prohibition. Health, economy, strength, capital, education, every door is closed to the

> Muslim because of his 'inadequacy'. Shouting for fifty out of a hundred jobs in Calcutta Corporation, the Muslim has become part of the 'depressed class' of Indian society.[32]

This brings us squarely into the realm of strategy, and consequently, some sense of concerted 'movement'. Since the 'private' came into the sphere of state legislation, it now formed part of the political sphere, where inhabitants confined hitherto to the private sphere found an opportunity to negotiate their terms. The essays collected here prove that they at least voiced their attempts to do so. Apart from articulating the position of women and analysing it, the strategies were holistic and addressed the gamut of complicated problems that went by the name of the 'women's question': women's confinement to the inner house, education and the problem of widows. The education of women in confinement in the inner houses of Hindu middle-class society was threatened by the government's policy of recruiting English or Christian women as teachers by the colonial government.[33] Upper-class families frowned upon 'foreign' or *mleccha* women entering their inner houses.

The reformist women attempted to work around the prejudices of upper-class society in order to effect some change through education itself. Thus, Khairunnesa's demand for neighbourhood schools in keeping with the tenets of Islam, and Swarnakumari Devi's proposals link the well-being of widows to the education of women in confinement in the inner houses. Both these women directly address the different internal dynamics of their societies, but their objectives are finally similar, and the adjustments they make and the priorities that they choose are dictated by their different dynamics and similar aim. Thus the 'women's question' is in itself far from homogeneous. Apart from the fact that in every community, it begins with considering the condition of women in society and opens negotiations between received and then constructed ideas of reform, progress and 'modernity', the forms of conceptualization and advocacy of practices function as related to the specific community where such conceptualization and practice are sought to be introduced and popularized: one might even say, given the didactic nature of much of the writing, institutionalized.

We may easily see a similarity in argument and position in essays written in the same period, despite locational differences. It appears that despite these differences, the obstructions to women's well-being, position and progress were the guardians of society, a group of men in each community who controlled the institutions and, therefore, the social lives of men and women. The indictment in both cases was of a patriarchal society, though its forms, expressions and consequences were different according to time, place and religion. Both Taherannesa (Essay 1, 'A Letter to the Editor of *Bamabodhini Patrika*') and Nagendrabala Mustafi (Essay 8, 'Dire Straits in Seclusion') had pleaded and counselled men to pay heed to women's plight. Jogindra Mohini wrote an indictment of the polygamous *Kaulinya Pratha* in 1871 (Essay 3 'The Custom of Kaulinya') and pleaded with men to see sense and help women to overcome the obstacles presented by it. Gradually, women no longer felt the need to appeal regularly to men, brother or otherwise. Now the relationship between mother-in-law and daughter-in-law becomes a focus (Essay 31, *'Ekaler Sasuri-Bou'*, 'Mothers-in-Law and Daughters-in-Law in these Times'; Essay 36 *'Badhujiban'*, 'Life as a Daughter-in-Law'). Even when there is no such relationship, women are one another's best allies: an example is Pramilabala Mitra's writing (Essay 33, *'Narir Kartavya'*, 'The Responsibilities of Women') from Gaya in 1915. Such appeals to women in the matter of dowry and the treatment of daughters-in-law attempted to evoke a sense of commonality amongst women, based upon the assumption that women could better their own lot by being sensitive to each other's plight despite their difference in age and power within the family. The so-called 'male'-centred family was thus an object of critique, and the strategy to overcome its domination in shaping women's lives was the realization and practice of solidarity amongst women. These appeals were made not only to women as individuals, because they seem as conscious of their species (*jati* is the word most often used) as of their individual lives, which is their ground for advocating solidarity. Witness the author Pramilabala Mitra's disclaimer (Essay 33, 'The Responsibilities of Women'):

> I hope I am not taken as being dark-skinned just because I am being partial to dark beauty, everyone says that my skin is burnished. In the interests of truth I am not incapable of saying a few harsh things about myself, either.

This essay castigates the desire of mothers-in-law for dowry and fair-skinned brides for their sons, and begins with a tale of a woman who was visibly crestfallen and tense because she had borne a daughter as beautiful as a rosebud, but a girl nevertheless, who would have to be married off. The writer's call is to all women, to rise against their own schooling, feel solidarity and as mothers-in-law, reject such demands. There is a similar call by Sarajubala Basu (Essay 36, 'Life as a Daughter-in-law') to mothers-in-law to remember their own days as daughters-in-law, and show sympathy for younger women in the same situation.

Thus far we have discussed the inflections introduced in the process of discursive formation of gender synchronically as well as diachronically. We may now attempt to understand how changing the conceptualization of certain issues yielded changing strategies of engagement, since one of our proposed goals in this volume is precisely to map change. As an instance, we may consider the issue of education yet again. Education during this period, came to be seen as both training and knowledge, and covered matters ranging from birth control to the building up of inner resources for women who are confined to the home most of the time. Women's desire for betterment, a part of which was the ability to perform their designated roles better, echoes from the earliest of the writings. As we have seen earlier, by the 1920s, confinement does not imply purdah, but the peculiar demands that the family makes on women. Banganari, whose essay's title is *'Griha'*, 'The Home/the Household', makes a clear distinction between what is expected of and allowed to the man, who is a part of a household, as compared to a woman. The range of relationships that both men and women as a 'couple' have extends from in-laws to children. This recalls the 1885 text of Shyamasundari Devi (Essay 30, 'On Whether or Not the Hindu Widow Should Marry Again') who argues that Hindu widows ought not to marry because they are wedded not to any man but to a family. Banganari knows this and her argument is against this very phenomenon: the man's authority is legitimized not by the *Shastras*, but because he is a man. Patriarchy as a social organization allows him, for instance, to seek entertainment outside the home, so he does not feel the stress of family life, whatever responsibilities he has to carry out within it. Banganari's demand is for acknowledgement of this fact and for provision to be made for balancing it out within the fabric of the family: that in her opinion will make the woman's condition more tolerable for women, the family as well as society as a whole. In other words, these demands from women were crafting a set of ideals different from patriarchal society through which, women alleged, the *Shastras* and the Qur'an *Hadith* had been used, often wrongly, to keep women in subjugation.

These ideals, deriving from socio-religious aspects, were not to be operative in what Anagol calls a 'gender-free' world, to which as she describes the western utopian feminists were aspiring.[34] We have noticed the blurred divides between the public and the private, and the emphasis on humanity, but that did not obliterate the feminine identity, even in favour of a homogeneous similarity. Women in the nineteenth century, both in Maharashtra and Bengal, do not appear to have been uncomfortable with their identities and relationships as women. They did not demand the radical abolition of relationships, but made what still seems, in the circumstances, perhaps a more radical demand: a rationalization of relationships towards gender-justice, which would be the basis of an ethics of equality, refiguring relationships between 'man' and 'woman'. Different types of relationships were constantly under negotiation: it was for them and from them that women's existence seemed to demand definition. The 1885 writer, Shyamasundari Devi, had pointed out that the Hindu husband was a *patra*, a vessel, through which the woman's relationship to her marital family was facilitated. This was not the marriage of minds and hearts of two individuals (Essay 30, 'On Whether or Not the Hindu Widow Should Marry Again'). It is because of this, argues Banganari (Essay 34, 'Man and Woman') that the man has taken undue advantage. In *'Griha'*/ Home, 1923 , Banganari again asserts that society controlled by males has institutionalized the male-centric view instead of espousing the open view that all humans had some form of commonality which ought to be respected in all relationships. The demand for education has led women to consider their situation.

Throughout the period, the relations between women and men have been under scrutiny: we have two essays spanning thirty years with precisely this title (Essay 6, *'Streelok o Purush'*, 'Women and Men' and Essay 34, 'Man and Woman'). Such reflections are translated into action to address social injustices perpetrated in the name of gender, be it abandonment of women in marriage or prostitution. So, in a satirical (or extremely practical) vein, a writer in *Bulbul*[35] says,

> Those who create a great commotion of protest on even hearing the word 'divorce' would have done the more intelligent thing if they had staunched the flow of women's education while there was still time.[36]

Education, thus, becomes a problem to those who want to maintain the status quo and the solution for those who want to change it. And, it is from the extension of the scope and aims of education that we find strategies for amelioration of women's sufferings, and concerted efforts in implementing them through solidarity in word and work emerge. Women of enlightened Brahmo families, like the Tagores, make and implement proposals in this direction. We must also note it was emphasized that women and men both had to be educated, and differently in order to fulfil their complementary roles in society, stemming from the belief expressed by these writers that gender-justice was 'human' and desirable.[37] Yet again, the *Shastras*, quoted by Shyamasundari Devi, eulogize the widow's ability to undertake the harsh responsibilities of chastity and *brahmacharya*. Writings around the turn of the nineteenth century do not show any change in the reality of widows, driven to selling their bodies in order to survive. They still require some form of armour to guard themselves from the male guardians of morality who castigate their choice of profession after having barred all other avenues for them to lead lives of dignity. Again, the writers (for instance, Essay 19, *'Bharater Dukhini Bidhaba Streelokdiger Jibika Labher Kato Prakar Upay Haite Pare'*, 'What Means of Livelihood Might There Be for the Poor Widows of India') no longer depend upon the goodwill or the correction of the guardians of society for the betterment of the widow's lot. Their strategies begin with the premise that such ideal circumstances are not obtainable in real life, in contemporary times at least, and so there must be practical solutions to women's problems.

Appeals for solidarity among women, refusal to depend upon men to better their lot and strategies to achieve this end themselves, all this taken together would help make the notion of a 'women's movement' seem coherent. By the 1930s the issue of education is linked to that of 'movement' as well (Essay 59, *'Nari Andolan o Sikshita Meye'*, 'Women's Movement and Educated Women') and to the founding of many organizations by women themselves and by the political parties now admitting women into their ranks.[38] From this vantage point, it would be possible to interrogate some positions that have emerged from the scholarship on women in Renaissance and nationalist Bengal. The existing scholarship does serve to gender the discourse of nationalism by pointing to margins and fragments, animating them through their relationships with an assumed 'continuous centre'. This scholarship, thus, critiques the notion of a 'continuous centre'. The homogeneous category 'woman' that may have operated as a centre in feminist scholarship has been questioned from various vantage points, namely, those of race and class and now of caste and community. Our attempt has been to bring some of these vantage points into dialogue with each other, simply by putting them together for the reader to access simultaneously. We think that when he/she reads them together, the reader will read one against the other, one as an echo of another, one as agreeing or disputing with another. A 'discourse', which is in the most basic sense a conversation inasmuch as it communicates something by expressing it, about the lives and positions of women in society will emerge. This we submit, may be one of the goals of feminist scholarship: to break the linearity of theory with the spontaneity of lived lives.

After reiterating our aim, we may turn to an actual example of our method. For example, nationalism in the essays collected here is inflected by the discourse of 'work', resulting from a history of education and training, which is also documented here in some detail, particularly the feminine idea of work (Essay 41, *'Desher Kaje Banglar Meye'*, 'Bengal's Women Working for the Country'). Swarnakumari Devi's account of the Swadeshi movement, the reasoned condemnation of the violence of some young men, goes so far as to posit that the English ruler's respect must be earned, while protecting the interests of our own: terror makes rule stricter and the people infinitely more vulnerable (Essay 39, *'Rajnaitik Prasanga'*, 'On Politics'; Essay 43, *'Amader Kartavya'*, 'Our Responsibility'; Essay 51, *'Kartavya Kon Pathe?'* 'Which Way Lies Our Responsibility?').

Some readers might consider this as a concession to the English, but we cannot deny that it is a mark of respecting the humanity of the powerful and appealing to it in the only dignified way possible. The writer instead urges that the 'work' of the country should be done with total commitment, violence is not the answer. The notion of work that Swarnakumari deploys here seems to have been derived from the discourse of gender, and enters into the discourse of the nation as *desher kaj*, a term as potent as *desh seva* in Bengali as well as other languages. Reports about women's condition in other lands were common. Women's sections of journals produced by and for Muslim society considered the developments in areas like Turkey and Albania from the point of view of reform of Islamic society through women's progress therein.[39] Locally, they participated through 'work'. The idea of 'work' was distinctly different from 'labour': for women it was 'work in the home', *gharer kaj* in Bengali. This differed from *chakri*: a word denoting a class system. The *chakor* is, in middle-class Bengali and among the classes that emulate them, someone who is paid to work.

An anecdote has it that Vivekananda refused his mentor Ramakrishna's offer of getting him a job in the education system through application to one of the latter's disciples by saying that he would prefer to subsist on the patronage of the Maharaja of Burdwan rather than become a paid servant. Men and women who accepted wages for work were in *chakri*: doing what servants do. *Kaj* on the other hand is not servanthood, though again Banganari is quite cutting in her indictment of this labour of what she calls forced or misplaced love. The 1885 writer, Shyamasundari, had characterized the Hindu wife as 'slave empress of the family' (Essay 30, 'On Whether or Not the Hindu Widow Should Marry Again'). Banganari demands equality on the basis of practical reason.

> The woman is a part of the household, and so on her depends its charm, beauty and well-being, it is true, but the entirety of this beauty, charm and well-being is the responsibility of all who belong to the household as well. And the more importance an individual has within the household, the more does all this depend upon his behaviour. So, in the current circumstances, whatever is generally said, since the man of the house is the chief member of the household, it is upon him that responsibility weighs most heavily. And even if this social organization changes, since the man has always been more powerful, it is upon him that this responsibility will always devolve.[40]

The demand for consideration and sympathy is loud enough here, though in the next generation it is *swadhinata* or freedom that becomes the cornerstone of the discourse, both for women and the nation. It is clear enough that mere participation in the struggle which looked like being won could not guarantee women what they deemed fit for themselves. Leelabati Roy (née Leelabati Nag) engages with Gandhi's views on the proper place and sphere of work for women, and argues against his apparently conservative position (Essay 61, *'Meyeder Upajukta Karmakshetra Ki?'* 'Which Is the Ideal Sphere for Women's Work?') Despite agreeing with him that women are as capable, physically and otherwise, as men, she cannot understand why he should insist on different spheres of operation in some cases, and not differentiate at all in some. The essayist's argument against Gandhi is founded upon her interpretation of equality as ungendered, applying to all regardless of any circumstance.

Work for the country or for economic independence or for more equitable relationships are all forms of work, and in the closing years of our period, as the struggle for independence intensified, all these forms of work occupied women's actions and thoughts as the essays in this volume show. Women wove their desire for freedom as human beings (we often fragment this by substituting 'subjects' or 'selves') into the fabric of the movement for freedom from colonial rule. The concerns of political citizenship included empowerment through knowledge of rights and duties, and organized movement for their realization (Essay 41, 'Bengal's Women Working for the Country'; Essay 48 *'Bharatiya Nari Andolan'*, 'Indian Women's Movement'). Essayists asserted that women must learn what their duties are and how to exercise their rights (essays 28, 29, 44, 45 and 56). Beginning from the very act of representation to the act of legislation, (Essay 46, *'Meyeder Voter Adhikar'*, 'Women's Right to Vote'; Essay 47, *'Bharater Nutan Shasantantre Narir Sthan'*, 'The Position of Women in the New System of Governance in India') Essay 57, *'Narir Rashtranaitik Adhikar'*, 'Political Rights of Women'; Essay 58, *'Amader Katha'*, What We Have To Say') women were present and vocal. It appears from our material and our reading that it would be incorrect to claim that the powerful nation-as-mother and *bhadramahila* tropes or the appropriation of gender by nation suffused all discourses and left no room for any other kinds of engagement in public and private spheres by women. It has been possible to arrive at this thesis by reading from a gendered perspective.

The skewed presence of this perspective in the study of socio-political discourses during the period of the nationalist movement may have led us to believe that there was and could have been one single uniform representation of the 'women's question' in this period. We have tried to identify different groups and communities of women, including the ones who went to jail and wrote in journals as well as people writing with individual contributions. They all shared a common characteristic: they all wrote in Bengali and had access to publication. But because of other differences, those of caste, community and gradually, class (see, e.g., Essay 62, *'Bharater Nari Shramik'*, 'India's Women Workers'; Essay 63, *'Nari Mukti o Ulema Sampraday'*, 'Women's Freedom and the Ulema', and Essay 65, *'Nari o Uparjan'*, 'Women and Employment'), these writers looked at the world differently, though they shared an avowedly gendered rather than a neutered 'human' perspective.

Some of the most unusual views which we sometimes easily mark 'regressive' or 'radical' emerge from the perspective that we have called woman's opinion. Sometimes, they are only a throwaway remark which must be noticed and then read again, for example, Fazilatunnesa's remark in an essay (Essay 14, 'Freedom for Muslim Women'):

> Eden School or Bethune College were not built in one day. What had started with a handful of young students has over a period developed into large centres of education. If Muslim girls did something similar over a period of time, even they could establish two or four schools and colleges and educate other Muslim girls in accordance with the Muslim philosophy of life. Not just that, they may have something like Bethune School, where if they wanted even they could, at least to avenge themselves, say, 'This school will not permit non-Muslim girls'. Only in this way, with immense hard work could Muslim woman achieve freedom in the future, or else, we shall remain deluged in darkness and ignorance till eternity.

Fazilatunnesa was the first female postgraduate in applied mathematics in Dhaka, and she created a sensation by going to college without a burqa (she was stoned). Bethune School opened its doors to Hindu women of good family in 1849; in that context, Fazilatunnesa sees a school exclusively for Muslim girls is telling: whether it is irony or bitterness, it is to be noticed and pondered about. As Salma Raushan-Jahan, writing in *Bulbul*, in 1936 (Essay 58, 'What We have To Say') cites a Hindu 'brother' writing about Muslims:

> When he talks about Muslims, he is looking at only those Muslims who are barbarians intellectually. ... 'Muslims think of themselves as outsiders, colonial conquerors, and we are all aboriginals, natives conquered in this country.' I found this ridiculous ... for the sake of civility could he not have said 'some Muslims think' instead of 'Muslims think', since in reality only some Muslims think, and that too only the office-going Urdu-speaking Muslims?

Renuka Mandal, in 1940 writes about the women's movement in India (Essay 48, 'Indian Women's Movement').

> The Indian women's movement took a definite form after the Second World War. ...The form taken by our nationalist movement in 1905

> did not accommodate women. . . . the revolutionaries of the time had a very hazy view of political freedom, and did not feel the need for a revolutionary women's movement. Hence, women themselves needed to lead the women's movement.

And her solution is:

> . . . the world is still influenced by the philosophy of patriarchal [gender] organization, and in a sense, even regulated by it. Though capitalism has made available the labour of all classes for the benefit of one single class, yet its fundamental truth is that all progressive movements benefit by the structure of capitalist society. The Russian revolution was an expression of the progressive nature of capitalist society. One of the main aims of this revolution was to give women emancipation.

To those of us who live in the world of global capital to use a trendy (or lazy) shorthand, this is puzzling. But it may also be a failure on our part to appreciate the power of ideas, such as education, nation and work. Mechanization may have been almost as potent an idea as liberty, equality and fraternity. Our concern here is merely to point this out as a reason for our attempts to nudge the issues towards conflicting opinions: these were not easily available, and since they have not been documented before, they may seem absent altogether. In this instance, we may say that they are capable, in some number, of problematizing many of the conclusions that we have drawn here. But placed within the context of their times, they provide the outlines of engagement and dialogue. Direct engagement may not have occurred, but opinion formation and expression in the context of contemporary concerns was certainly possible, as the essays by Shyamasundari and Swarnakumari, both written in 1885-86 (Essay 30, 'On Whether or Not the Hindu Widow Should Marry Again' and Essay 17, 'Another Proposal') testify. There are several such groups of essays that seem to be in conversation with one another. The reader's discovery of these dialogues is one of the aims of this collection. There can be several explanations for diverse views, stemming from disagreements about what these connote and how they are structured into a discourse composed of a set of thoughts, proclivities, feelings and ethical positions vis-à-vis society and self that represent 'woman' as a category.

The essays included here appeared in periodicals, and we have deliberately not included any excerpts. We also owe a debt to *Talking of Power* edited by Malini Bhattacharya and Abhijit Sen and *Zenana Mehfil: Bangali Musalman Lekhikader Nirbachita Rachana 1904-1938* by Shaheen Akhtar and Moushumi Bhowmik (English translation, *Women in Concert: An Anthology of Bengali Muslim Women's Writings, 1904-1938*, Stree, 2008), which we see as early steps, necessary for us to be able to take our own.[41] Except for two essays from the latter, translated by Stree earlier, none of the essays published in either of these collections has been retranslated: the attempt has been to increase the range of material available. The collections from original sources made by many scholars have been immensely helpful because of their different rationale for selection, enabling us to access a wide cross-section of the published word.

Perhaps one must also say a word about the translations. They have been, as is clear, done by varied hands, recorded at the end of each. In many cases, when the editors felt that the word conflicted with their reading of the text, they have recorded this change in endnotes. Some endnotes are provided by the authors themselves: we have noted these separately. Some words were differently translated by different people: in most cases the difference has been retained though the original word is the same, because the meaning of the word has been contextualized in the translation. Since another English word was available to convey the sense, it was used and noted.

We may turn, finally, to the writing itself. Essays are a whimsical genre, the moment when Jourdain realized that he thought in prose too.[42] But all the writings collected here cannot strictly speaking be called essays. The letter form, whether to the editor, or to an imaginary granddaughter, which poses the questions of a previous generation to the newly formulated demands of 'today's' women, is defined by the particular reader/listener it is addressing; but in case of the essay, thinking in prose, one has only oneself as audience. All the essays here, then, are not essays, though they may have been printed as such. These are essays by virtue of the fact of not being poetry or fiction and having appeared in a journal. But that is to only record their form and mode of transmission. The essays recount various issues, take various forms, have varied aims and addressees and are accordingly structured differently. Readers will see for themselves the literary dexterity of the essays collected here: the following example comes from an essay that has been quoted a number of times already, but not included in this volume:

> True propriety in a marriage cannot be maintained by one party alone, and the same is applicable to the home as well. Strictures like 'the woman is the beauty and the charm of the home, it is by her efforts that the auspicious progress of the household is possible' are like other strictures of this sort—like drinking poison while pretending that it is elixir; moreover, it is only a fraction of the truth. The woman is a part of the household, and so on her depends its charm, beauty and well-being, it is true, but the entirety of this beauty, charm and well-being is the responsibility of all who belong to the household as well.[43]

The directness of this beginning is striking: the writer does not sacrifice language play (or embellishment, depending upon which critical school the reader is inclined towards) but uses it with great efficiency to initiate her case. The essay as a genre and the periodical as a vehicle are thus used to the full in a literary sense. The gradual suppleness acquired by Bengali as a language is another marked change in this period. Reflected in the great novelists who spanned the period, who perhaps resonated in their readers too, educated women certainly read what these men wrote, and the novelists in their turn made full use of the entire spectrum of the 'women's question' in all its ramifications.

The world of these periodicals allows us one view of the woman's world in contemporary times: more women wrote in periodicals than in other forms of literature. When the nation is placed within this world alongside women's autobiographies or even some women's novels, a dialogue between this world and the characters of women in men's novels may emerge. If the texts resonate together, function as parts of a story or indicate where the tide flowed differently, then taken together they may present a live picture of the period. There is no claim for a complete picture. The values that are ascribed are from this society, but they always seem to be on test by being flaunted in visible detail. Ushaprabha Sen, writing in 1923 (Essay 11, *'Narir Abastha'*, 'The Plight of Women') considers an area where the morals of society are played out and judged: the space of literature. Citing Saratchandra Chattopadhyay's Abhaya, who refuses to live with an abusive husband and proceeds to live with a man of her choice, she points out that if there are men like Abhaya's husband, there cannot but be women like Abhaya as well.

If the *Shastras* that Shyamasundari Devi glorified are the basis of the upper castes' understanding of gender relations in society, we must keep in mind that all women did not think alike; their particular positions depended on their community and caste or class. Ushaprabha offers an alternative, taking a cue from literature, that easily historicizes relations in society:

> Rules and regulations are predicated on the general consensus of a particular moment in the history of a country. Hence society and its norms should keep pace with the changing sentiments of human beings ... (Ibid.).

To reiterate, this collection is an attempt at connecting some views espoused by women and reading them in the context that these connections form. Sometimes the points are adjacent, sometimes they are reached through curves and angles: in time, place, ideology and feeling. Perhaps this implies a rupture, a break in continuity. One of the aims of this volume, however, is to wonder whether the ideas of 'rupture' and 'continuity' are responses to our own need to categorize rather than actually valid theorizations of 'writing' as such and 'women's writing' in particular. Our thesis is modest: we have a collection of writings from a period spanning almost a 100 years in which there were a number of interconnected issues. And though there was basic agreement of aim amongst the writers, we have attempted to preserve also the diversity of opinions and, more striking, of strategies to negotiate existing situations for what is construed as the benefit of women as a class. That there is similarity in wanting a better life, whether in terms of status, position, education or respect for women, is a fact that such collections as ours stress. We have tried to capture some idea of variety within gendered discourse. From that position, it may be possible to understand the process of gendering in time and space, whether it is in the practices or the conceptualization of gender itself. Ultimately, it is within the period and milieu in which these texts were written that we shall have to read them, and it is within these that they will yield to us what they want to say about strategies and conceptualizations.

We are conscious of the effort that must go into this endeavour of translation if the discourse of gender is to be narrativized, with the written word as material. Literary history, then, is also seen as a part of the process of history itself, and we have tried to show how such a history may emerge from readings of a specific literary form. The texts have been selected for the purpose of historiography that will form a context for questions of gender and yield a frame for understanding and engaging with those questions. There may have been very well-known positions taken by eminent men and women at the time, which are generally and justly famous. We have constructed both 'official' and 'counter' history about this time. We have tried to bring together several strands forming the discourse of the social in the period under consideration: the practices of literature, politics, education are all placed in the context of communities, constituted by many overlapping identifications: women, widows, confined women, educated women, Brahmo, Hindu, Bengali, Muslim. We have not ventured to nominate any one of these as subjective thresholds. By this, I mean that we have avoided saying that the writer acted or thought as a woman who was simultaneously a citizen/mother/middle-class person of Bengal. That she was a woman was an overarching, and not the only facet of her 'identity'. We have also assumed that identities function in a web of relations. Specific identifications are sometimes separately articulated and politically used for specific ends. Communities are sometimes confined to these singular identities, but sometimes they spill over into a larger formation within which these identities are seen as limitations, or sources of limitation. The attempt by a male writer to homogenize, and thus limit the identity of the Bengali Muslim as only Muslim is immediately countered by Begum Rokeya, in the 1920s;[44] Salma Raushan-Jahan is also engaged in a similar effort (Essay 58, What We Have To Say). On the other hand, the identity of woman is sought to be formed as a focus for solidarity to ameliorate the condition of the race of women. Sometimes these engagements index religion and class; sometimes gender is the only basis of community. But as the twentieth century proceeds and the idea of both a single Indian nation and its manifest heterogeneity become issues in the struggle against the colonizer and the imagination of a 'free' decolonized society, the essays dealing with the women's condition address the lack that identifies one as a Muslim or as a Hindu woman, in respect to one another and in respect to men of either community, through comparisons and through suggested solutions, the aim being a gender-just society. This is the milieu from which the later writings collected here emerged and were directed towards.

Today the milieu is very different. For one thing, the exclusivity of identity and its aggressive politicization have spiralled through actions and reactions into community and religion becoming suspect. The social organization of gender is informed by another set of contentious debates on various issues, while still grappling with the problems of politicized identities. This is the context in which this book will be read. The proposed reservation for women in Parliament, the law against sexual harassment in the workplace are not women's issues. They may affect women directly, but they do not affect women alone. As Maitrayee Chaudhuri observes, the impact of any ideology can be judged at two levels: the internal logic of the ideas that it foregrounds, and the actual impact of these ideas.[45] The project is to read together a varied selection of writings by Bengali women from different locations in society across a period spanning hundred-odd years from the mid-nineteenth to the mid-twentieth century. The aim is to try to understand the internal logic of the ideas regarding 'woman' as a category during this time, and acquaint ourselves with its impact upon a society which harboured and produced those women.

Notes

1 See the following books by Sandra Harding, *Whose Science? Whose Knowledge? Thinking from Women's Lives* (Ithaca: Cornell University Press, 1992); *Feminism and Methodology: Social Science Issues* (Bloomington: Indiana University Press, 1987); her edited book with Jean F. O'Barr, *Sex and Scientific Enquiry* (Chicago: Chicago University Press, 1987): 1, and *The Science Question in Feminism* (Cornell: University Press, 1986).

2 Padma Anagol, *The Emergence of Feminism in India, 1850-1920* (Farnham, Surrey: Ashgate, 2005).

3 See, for instance, Patricia Uberoi, 'Colonial state helped constitute private domain that Indian nationalists later cherished as free from colonial domination. The colonial state shaped the terrain on which the discourse of reform arose.' *Social Reform, Sexuality and the State* (New Delhi: Sage, 1996).

4 Literally 'raw stuff'; used in genre studies to indicate the real world, from which the material for the plot of a literary piece comes.

5 Rabindranath Tagore, speaking to an audience in China, in 1925, said about his family, one of the best-known among the Brahmos, 'We were ostracized because of our heterodox opinions about religion and therefore we enjoyed the freedom of the outcaste. We had to build our own world

with our own thoughts and energy of mind. We had to build it from the foundation.' In S.K. Das, ed., *English Writings of Rabindranath Tagore*, vol. 2, *Plays, Stories Essays* (Delhi: Sahitya Akademi, 1966): 583. See also Meredith Borthwick, *The Changing Role of Women in Bengal, 1849-1905* (Princeton: Princeton University Press, 1984): 3-25; Krishna Sen, 'Lessons in Self-Fashioning: *Bamabodhini Patrika* and the Education of Women in Colonial Bengal', *Victorian Periodicals Review*, 37, 2: *The Nineteenth-Century Press in India* (Summer, 2004).

6 Sri Jogindra Mohini Basu from Konnagar, *Kaulinya Pratha, Bamabodhini Patrika*, 98, 8 (mid-September to mid-October 1891/Ashvin 1298).

7 The question here is who is the writer? The volume of *Nabajiban* in which this essay is printed lists Shyamasundari Devi as the writer on the contents page. We know it was read out in Savitri Library. Towards the end of the essay, where the excerpt details occurs, we read, 'Now I shall present two excerpts from the essays written by women who responded to the proposal of the leaders of Savitri Library to write an essay on this matter, because I am of the opinion that they are worthy of your attention and discussion.' One of the excerpts is written by Shyamasundari Devi. So, was Shyamasundari Devi the writer of the essay or the excerpt or both? Who read out the essay at Savitri Library? One of the leaders of *Nabajiban*? Are these his words? All these questions must remain in our minds when we read the essays collected here.

8 Geraldine Forbes, *Women in Colonial India, Essays on Politics, Medicine and Historiography* (Hyderabad: Orient Longman, 2005). Conversely, see Samita Sen, *Towards a Feminist Politics? The Indian Women's Movement in Historical Perspective*, The World Bank Development Research Group/ Poverty Reduction and Economic Management Network (April, 2000).

9 Anagol. *Emergence of Feminism in India*.

10 *'Griha', Bharati*, mid-July to mid-August 1923/Sravan 1330 BS.

11 Ibid.

12 Ibid.

13 Though the women's question had always essentially remained a public subject, colonial intervention in this sphere made the Indians feel as if their inner sanctum was being invaded. Besides, the only place where the colonial male felt his superiority was the 'home', and tradition as well as modernity were posited on this feeling that the domestic sphere had to be beyond the control and legislation of the colonizers.

14 There may have been many anonymous ones, which could have well been by Hindu women, and as some have argued, by men. Men were also known to write under pseudonyms in women's magazines; some of

them of course wrote in their own names.

[15] Maleka Begum, *Banglar Nari Andolan* (Dhaka: University Press, 1989); Sonia Nishat Amin, *The World of Muslim Women in Colonial Bengal*, 1876-1939 (Leiden: E.J. Brill, 1996).

[16] Azra Asghar Ali, 1996, 'Recovery of Female Voice through Women's Journals in Urdu in British India 1898-1947', *South Asia: Journal of South Asian Studies*, 21, 2: 61-86; see also her book, *The Emergence of Feminism among Indian Muslim Women 1920–1947* (New York: Oxford University Press, 2000).

[17] She signed herself as Taheran Lecha.

[18] See Ghulam Murshid, *Rasasundari Theke Rokeya Sakhawat Hossain: Nari Pragatir Eksho Bachar* (Dhaka, Bangla Academy, 1997). Murshid tells us that the editor of *Bamabodhini* addressed an open letter to six women whose letters had been received, asking them to provide concrete proof that they were the authors of what they had sent for publication. Published in mid-November to mid-December 1863/Agrahayan 1271 BS issue, what resulted from this letter were not known. But Taheran Lecha's letter was published in mid-February to mid-March 1865/Falgun 1271 BS issue. Murshid's comments on her prose are worth recording. He felt that she was the first Muslim writer to display the effects of Vidyasagar's influence on the construction of Bengali prose. Citing the first Muslim writer of Bengali prose, Khondkar Shamsuddin Muhammad Siddiqui, who wrote *Uchit Sraban Arthat Paramarthik Bhab* (Right Hearing, or the Spiritual Bhava/Orientation) in 1860, draws a contrast between the two styles. But it was impossible to have a school in Boda (whose location Murshid is unable to fix) for girls, far away from the city, to have a school for girls and that too up to the highest, that is, first class. The first school for Muslim girls in Bengal was set up by Begum Ferdaus, wife of the Nawab of Murshidabad, in 1897 in Calcutta; followed by the Suhrawardy School for Girls in 1911, and in 1913, Rokeya founded Sakhawat Memorial School. In 1916, four girls' schools in Midnapore, Asansol, Comilla and Rangpur received government aid. See Sufiya Khatun, *Narir Adhikar o Anyanya*, edited by Sumit Adhikari (Dhaka: Sahitya Prakash, 1999).

[19] Ian Henderson Douglas, *Abul Kalam Azad: An Intellectual and Religious Biography*, edited by G. Minault and C. Troll (Delhi: Oxford University Press, 1993): 37-38.

[20] Sufiya Khatun (1999). This book contains a detailed discussion of the enigma of who Sufiya Khatun actually was, whether she existed at all or not; Bhowmik and Akhtar, in their edited volume fitted *Zenana Mehfil* (Kolkata: Stree, 1998), are undecided about her authenticity and do not

include her essays in their collection; we have included one essay on Hindu–Muslim relations in Bengal, and followed Adhikari's findings in giving biographical notes for the writer.

[21] Siobhan Lambert-Hurley, 'Fostering Sisterhood Muslim Women and the All-India Ladies' Association', *Journal of Women's History*, 16, 2: 40-65. See also Shahryar M. Khan, *The Begums of Bhopal: A Dynasty of Women Rulers in Raj India* (Delhi: Viva Books, 2004).

[22] Barbara Southard, 1993, 'Colonial Politics and Women's Rights: Woman Suffrage Campaigns in Bengal, British India in the 1920s', *Modern Asian Studies*, 27, 2 (May): 397-439.

[23] For a discussion of this issue, see Amin (1996); see also Richard M. Eaton, Who Are the Bengal Muslims? *Essays on Islam and Indian History* (Delhi: Oxford University Press, 2000): 249-75.

[24] Tahmina Alam, *Banglaar Samayikpatre Bangali Muslim Narisamaj* (Dhaka: Bangla Academy, 1998).

[25] Mahua Sarkar, *Visible Histories, Disappearing Women: Producing Muslim Womanhood in Late Colonial Bengal* (Delhi: Zubaan, 2008.).

[26] Sayyid Mumtaz Ali, *Huquq un-Niswan* (Lahore: Dar ul-Isha'iat-e-Punjab, 1898), cited in Gail Minault, 1990, 'Sayyid Mumtaz Ali and *"Huquq un-Niswan"*: An Advocate of Women's Rights in Islam in the Late Nineteenth Century', *Modern Asian Studies* 24, 1 (February): 147-72; Sayyid Mumtaz Ali, 1918, *Tahzib un-Niswan*, (hereafter cited as *TN*), Jubilee Number (6 July): 424-33; Hafiz Jalandhari, 1935, 'Maulvi Sayyid Mumtaz Ali', *TN* (6 July): 607-17 (originally published in 1927 in *Makhzan*, this article was reprinted in *TN* as an obituary). See also Laila Jaman, *Saogat Patrikaar Sahityik Abadan o Samajik Bhumika, 1918- 1950* (Dhaka: Bangla Academy, 1989).

[27] Tahmina Alam, 1998.

[28] Syed Imdad Ali, 1906. *Nabanoor*, 4th year, 4th issue (mid-September to mid-October/Ashvin 1313 BS): 137.

[29] See Amin (1996); Alam (1998); Begum (1989). See also Laila Jaman, *Saogat Patrikaar Sahityik Abadan o Samajik Bhumika, 1918- 1950* (Dhaka: Bangla Academy, 1989).

[30] Anagol (2005).

[31] Ibid.: 220.

[32] Rokeya Sakhawat Hossain *'Rani Bhikarini'*, *Mohammadi*, mid-December to mid-January 1929/Paush 1335 BS [cited in *Rokeya Rachanabali*, edited by Abdul Qadir (Dhaka: Bangla Academy, March 1999/Falgun 1440 BS): 233].

[33] A detailed history of the education of women is documented in Bharati

Ray, *Seams of History: Essays on Indian Women* (Delhi: Oxford University Press, 1995); See also Amin (1996).

34 Anagol (2005): 222.

35 This periodical began publication from 1933 (1340 BS), and was edited by Shamsun Nahar and Habibullah Bahar.

36 Kamaluddin, *'Nari o Purusher Sambandha'* ('The Relationship between Man and Woman'), *Nirbachita Bulbul*, edited by Selina Bahar Jaman (Dhaka: Bulbul Publishing House, and Kolkata:Vishwakosh Parishad, 2005): 554.

37 For views on education, gender and community, see the essays by Fazilatunnesa (Essay 14, *'Muslim Narir Mukti'*, 'Freedom for Muslim Women'), Banganari (1923). *'Griha'*, Bibi Khairunnesa Khatun (Essay 22, 'The Hindrances to Our Education') as well as Indira Devi Chaudhurani (Essay 37, 'What Is the Ideal for Women's Education'). See also, Barbara Southard, 1984, 'Bengal Women's Education League: Pressure Group and Professional Association', *Modern Asian Studies* 8, 1: 55-88.

38 The Congress held a session at Calcutta on 5-7 September 1920; the Nari Satyagraha Samiti was set up in 1922; Bharat Stree Mahamandal in 1910, National Council of Indian Women in 1925 and Nikhil Bharat Nari Sammelan (All India Women's Conference) was formed in 1926. Writing in the first issue of *Mandira* 1, 5, mid-August to mid-September 1938/ Bhadra 1345 BS, Laila Begum reports on a women's conference held in May that same year, a report on the Congress Mahila Sub Committee, its stated aim to 'bring together all the isolated women's sangha/collectives'. A dissenting voice about the involvement of the women's movement in party politics comes, in the same periodical, from Renuka Mandal in 1940 (a translation of which we have included in this volume, Essay 48, 'Indian Women's Movement').

39 See, for instance, Hosna Jahan Chaudhury, 1937, *Abarodh Mukta Albania* (Albania Free of Women's Seclusion) *Bulbul* (Ashvin 1344); see also Laila Jaman (1989) and Alam (1998).

40 *Griha'*, Banganari (1923).

41 A complete list of collections from which we have sourced essays is provided in the bibliographical section.

42 In Moliére's play *Le Bourgeois Gentilhomme*, the hero M. Jourdain is taken aback when he realizes that he talks prose.

43 *'Griha'*, Banganari (1923).

44 See n 32.

45 Maitrayee Chaudhuri, ed., 'Introduction', *Feminism in India, Issues in Contemporary Feminism*, 2 (Delhi: Women Unlimited, 2004): xxv.

II. Education and Gender in Nineteenth-Century Bengal: An Overview

Jayeeta Bagchi

The nineteenth century forms the entry point for modern western education in India. It is needless to say that the journey from 'traditional' to 'modern' was not an easy one. It was fraught with considerable tensions as can be seen in the many debates related to education, especially women's education. The nineteenth-century middle-class Bengali was obsessed with education, but the penetration of western ideas among the Bengali *bhadralok*[1] made it necessary for them to review the notions of 'tradition', as well.

Education did not mean merely literacy. Education meant 'the cultivation of the understanding, the improvement of the moral sense and of good and correct principle.' It was not 'the art of speaking any language correctly but the science of the mind, dependent on no particular pursuit.'[2] It was an attempt to construct a new and different culture related to social and economic power. Culture as constitutive of knowledge would by the second half of the century become so naturalized that it would distinguish the Bengali bhadralok from the so-called lower classes.[3] Tanika Sarkar rightly points out that women's education had much wider social and political implications than the matter of education alone.[4] For women, education would mean literacy plus other accomplishments:'something more', which constituted cultural baggage. As early as in 1818, Rammohan Roy, the first great reformist of the century, took up the issue of women's education while writing against widow immolation. The concept of 'women's condition' in the colonial period stood for the whole notion of the plight of the Indians. Because of this synecdoche, the 'women's question' became the focus of the reformist agenda in India, more specifically in Bengal. 'Scholars of colonial Bengal ... are all concerned with the production of a colonial *culture*. Appearing variously as problems of "modernity", "rationality", or dominant knowledge forms, these studies tell the story of the colonial encounter in Bengal ... either as assimilative, confrontational, or attributive.'[5]

In the late nineteenth century, education, especially women's education, became the fulcrum around which the 'modern' Indian women's identity was created. The bhadralok's agenda was to create a wife companionate, partly based on the Victorian notion of the 'angel in the house' and partly necessitated by the desire to measure up to the western standards of a worthy 'civilized' nation. 'Educating female companions was meant for re-defining the inner and the outer; not creating such a prolongation that the borderlines were merged, creating an arena where sanctities were altercated. The private was to be the reservoir of essential Indian tradition from which men could draw out as and when required. Women were still to be the protectors of unsullied inherited pattern of thought or action.'[6]

To a large extent, the Brahmos spearheaded educational reforms for women, along with cultural-social reforms, through a series of ruptures, initially from the Bengali Hindu elite conservative society.[7] A reformist coterie within the elite persisted with experiments in women's formal education amidst a strong opposition from a conservative section of the Hindu orthodoxy. After the first schism in the Brahmo Samaj, the Nababidhan Brahmo Samaj (New Dispensation) started working towards women's education by welcoming Miss Mary Carpenter in 1864/65. Miss Carpenter's visit to India was aimed at the improvement of women's education which the conservative section of Hindu society shunned because they thought Indian (read Hindu) society was capable of educating its own women with more competence than any person from an alien culture.

What started as a demand for education was inflected and influenced by a larger demand for total, almost radical, social reform. As a serious consequence, two major legal interventions in acts or bills supported or even brought forward by the Brahmos before the turn of the century were the Special Marriage Act (1872) and the Age of Consent Act (1891). This actually meant that girls in the community did not marry as young children, which was meant to ensure schooling before marriage. To some extent, Brahmos did allow their girls to study in formal or non-formal institutions and became patrons of some of the girls' schools. A major contention, however, began with the Cooch Behar Marriage Controversy in 1878. The leader of the New

Dispensation of the Samaj, Keshab Chandra Sen, married off his daughter to the prince of Cooch Behar when neither the bride nor the groom had attained the marriageable age of fourteen and eighteen, respectively, that were agreed upon. Moreover, since the marriage followed Hindu rites and rituals the matter was seen as a case of extreme betrayal, which led to the second schism of the Samaj.

The Hindus, on the other hand, preferred early marriages for their daughters, which meant they barely had any opportunity to experience elementary schooling. But then not even orthodox Hindus were unanimously against women's education. Conformist intellectuals like Radhakanta Deb wanted *zenana* education as against the initial attempts of education by the missionaries in the early nineteenth century. Since proselytization was on the agenda of the missionaries, a resistance towards formal schoolgoing was but natural. The first school for girls was opened in Gouribari, North Calcutta, in 1819 by the Female Juvenile Society under the Calcutta Baptist Mission. Within the next few years, a number of schools for girls were opened by the missionaries. Despite the increase in the number of schools, the bhadralok refused to send their daughters to them and a few progressive, western educated youths introduced the zenana education or non-formal system of education within the private sphere of the household. But soon it was discovered that it was difficult to offer standardized education in this manner. Moreover, getting teachers was expensive and difficult. Respectable teachers were not readily available. By the 1830s, a few Hindu College educated youths were already thinking of a public institution for girls from the respectable families. With this in view Peary Churn Sircar opened a school in Barasat in 1848, and the Bethune School was established the next year.

Education for the Brahmos did aim to turn the traditional woman into an accomplished urban *and* literate woman who would participate socially in refined discussions with her husband as well as exhibit cultural refinement at home and maintain the hearth peacefully.[8] By 1849 the first school for 'respectable' Hindu girls was set up in Calcutta by John Drinkwater Bethune. Bethune School still continues to be one of the premier girls' institutions in Kolkata. This school was patronized chiefly by the Brahmos. In an article entitled 'Women's Education and Bethune School' in 1887,[9] Swarnakumari Devi (1856-1932), a Brahmo, and elder sister of Rabindranath Tagore, wrote that by now men have somewhat understood that if women are properly educated men would be able to live happily and contentedly. Women would be able to become suitable homemakers, companions and mothers. This may serve to clarify the kind of education that was considered 'suitable' for girls.

The first women's organization, called Brahmika Samaj, was set up on 15 July 1865 by Keshab Chandra Sen in Kolkata, where sewing was taught, religious advice was given and women discussed social issues and read articles. Swarnakumari Devi established the Sakhi Samiti in April 1886. The Samiti's work was to increase interaction between women, spread literacy and education among them (*see* Essay 53, *Nari Siksha o Mahila Shilpashram*, 'Women's Education and Vocational Training'). Education, as we have seen, meant also learning household skills along with literacy.

By 1883, Bethune School (and its new wing, the Bethune College) produced the first two female graduates of the entire British Empire: Kadambini Ganguly (1861/2–1923) and Chandramukhi Bose (1860–1944). Kadambini, a Brahmo, studied medicine and achieved a successful medical practice in Calcutta while Chandramukhi, a Christian, went on to become the first woman principal of Bethune College. Kadambini, however, was denied pass marks in the medical final examination because the examiner did not believe that women could be doctors or other professionals. She went to England to get her degree.

An image of the ideal woman emerged sometime in the 1890s: one who happily married the inner with the outer, the private with the public. One who would be musically attuned, good in needlework, expert in cooking and sewing and in maintaining the home. She would be a perfect wife and companion of the husband even within the larger joint family structure. She was expected to flourish with her own personality under her husband's patronage.

In August 1886 an anonymous article in *Bamabodhini Patrika*, '*Streejati o Shilpakarja*' (Essay 18, 'Women and Art') declared that as long as women continued to be given a separate curriculum with an elementary general knowledge, women would remain subordinated to men. Men were given professional education with specialization in one subject; why weren't women too given that kind of specialized education? They were expected to learn the basics of everything and not adept in any field so that they were not able to enter the public arena in some professional capacity. What was being criticized was the whole notion of *abarodh* or women's confinement within the private sphere. By default this then worked as a major critique of zenana education.

Bankimchandra Chattopadhyay wrote his famous essay *'Prachina ebong Navina'* in *Bangadarshan* in 1874,[10] where he with some scepticism laid down the foundations of the navina ('new woman') and the prachina ('traditional woman') as discursive categories. The essential quality that distinguished prachina from navina was *streesiksha* (women's education), he explained. The traditional woman worked at home as an unskilled labourer, the 'new woman's' challenge was to turn the regular uninspiring chores into a skilled occupation; a skill that was needed to be acquired through education. Housework became part of the aesthetic experience of daily life and not merely an activity that had utilitarian value. 'New women' belonged fundamentally to the *abhijata bhadralok* (elite middle class) as against the common working women.[11] The new woman was essentially cultured and polished in her behaviour. It is interesting to note here Bankimchandra's fear of female social mobility. Bankinchandra vehemently criticized the western-educated bhadralok's agenda to turn Panchi, Rami, Madhi into foreign memsahibs. He writes that the babu[12] was turning the traditional woman who laboured at home without question into a lazy superfluous woman, like those of the elite class, devoid of religious piety and without a healthy way of life.

Bankimchandra was not a Brahmo, and strongly rejected the Brahmo urban cultural polish. To say that Panchi, Rami,[13] and so on, would become lazy is again the bhadralok's fear of the transgressive *chhotolok* (lower class). The fact that the gender markers of the lower classes would become ambiguous by gaining education, further added fuel to the fire. The private sphere as the storehouse of 'traditional' culture and religion would then have to be questioned. So, from the perspective of education as facilitator of gendered class mobility, Bankimchandra seems to have found the proper nail on which to bring down the hammer of his strongly articulated criticism.

It *was* education which actually defined the new woman and it *was* part of a middle-class agenda. According to J.H. Broomfield, education was the 'hallmark of *bhadralok* status'. Therefore, it is not surprising that there was actually a very strong resistance to the idea of rural or mass education among the bhadraloks when Campbell wanted to introduce this education policy in the 1870s. Poromesh

Acharya has shown that native elites actively influenced the colonial government in the process of initiating a system of education which was strongly hierarchical in nature.[14]

Later social scientists like Partha Chatterjee depended heavily on Bankim's categorization though navina was replaced by the new woman or *nabya nari* to show the shift in position. According to Chatterjee, the new woman was created out of the 'common woman' by the logic of reversal. The new woman was quite the reverse of the common' woman, who was coarse, vulgar, loud, quarrelsome, devoid of superior moral sense, sexually promiscuous, subjected to brutal physical oppression by males.[15] Borthwick uses the term *bhadramahila* as a companion to *bhadralok*.[16] So, women through the process of *streesiksha* would become the bhadramahila, whose special attribute was being *bhadra* or cultured. *Bhadra* is a word that encompasses both economic and social class here and women were the bearers of both these labels. *Mahila* means woman. The term 'bhadramahila' referring especially to new women was theoretically popularized by Meredith Borthwick. Quite rightfully she remonstrates that the bhadramahila living coevally with the bhadralok is a nineteenth-century idea. While the term 'bhadralok' was widely in use since the nineteenth century for urban middle-class men working in the service sector the term 'bhadramahila' is of a more recent origin. The existence of the bhadramahila cannot be traced before the advent of the new woman.

By the *fin de siècle*, the concept of the new woman had crystallized and the second or even third generations of 'new women' were born. With their distinctive cultural attainments, the 'new women' embarked on creating and re-creating a new social role. I use the word 're-create' cautiously because women were not using it. In fact, it is true that in the early twentieth century the issue of women's education vanished (or rather was banished) from public debate. The debate on women's education was overlaid by more important militant nationalism where the rhetoric was often too male to admit women. (That is not to say that women played no part in militant nationalism.) According to Chatterjee, it happened because of the resolution of the woman's question by the turn of the century. The situation was too complex to admit such a simple resolution. The bhadralok's agenda was resolved. Women's education had become a necessity within the bhadralok class. As far as women were concerned, the question was just being posed. Education was just opening up various new possibilities, opportunities and avenues for women, many of which led to the questioning of the emergent and very bhadralok gender ideology which had 'allowed' women the education in the first place.

Many new women would eventually become educationists in twentieth-century Bengal formally or otherwise. Women like the sisters Sarala Ray (1861-1946), Abala Bose (1864-1951), Sarala Devi Chaudhurani (1872-1946), Swarnakumari Devi's daughter, and others were directly associated with formal academic institutions. Sarala Ray founded the Gokhale Memorial Girls School in 1920; with Abala Bose's enthusiasm the Muralidhar Girls' School was founded in 1919. These institutions are not only functional but are still among the best girls' schools in Kolkata. Abala Bose in fact established almost 200 other schools in various villages of Bengal. In 1925, Abala Bose established the Vidyasagar Vanibhavan to train widows to become teachers in schools since it was difficult to get teachers for all those schools. Sarala Devi Chaudhurani founded the Bharat Stree Sikshasadan in 1930. I would also like to draw attention to those women who were not directly connected to academic institutions. Indira Devi Chaudhurani (1873-1960), Tagore's niece (and Sarala Devi's cousin) wrote and spoke on women's education extensively. She clearly mentioned in one of her articles that she had never been formally a part of an academic institution yet her education and age gives her the right to speak and judge the condition of women's education in Bengal.

Unfortunately, all these women were seen as amateur educationists and, predominantly housewives. Indira Devi Chaudhurani took up Bankim's '*Prachina ebong Navina*' point by point without mentioning it by name to put forward her counter argument in favour of the new woman. Her essay '*Bartaman Streesiksha Bichar*' ('My Opinion on the Present Condition of Women's Education') was written in 1912 (mid-July to mid-August/Sravan 1319 BS).[17] She said women's education had become a part of social life in the last fifty years and higher education for twenty-five. She argued that whatever women have been accused of, namely, lack of religiosity, arrogance, incapability of carrying out housework, lack of health, desire for luxury, selfishness and affinity towards western ways of life could occur only when they were not educated or half-educated. Proper education would ensure that women could go beyond this and achieve much more. So she turned the tables against the coarse rural traditional Indian woman. This is probably the essay she referred to in the beginning of the article, *'Stree Sikshar Adarsha Ki?'* (Essay 37, 'What Is the Ideal for Women's Education?').

Not only then is women's education a way of bettering social life for women and men of a particular class, it may also be suggested as a means of social mobility, in terms of significance if not actual movement.

This generation of new women would take the responsibility of women's education in their hands whether they were involved with formal institutions or not. Sukhalata Rao (1886-1969) was one such example whose mission was to re-create future generations of women in the image of the new woman. Sukhalata belonged to the second generation of the new woman. Kadambini Ganguly was her mother's stepmother. In all the reminiscences about her, Kadambini has been referred to as not simply a successful professional woman but an 'angel in the house'. Punyalata and Sukhalata, her granddaughters, remember how their grandmother used to decorate the house with various art objects collected abroad. While she went to visit her patients she wove lace so as not to pass her time idly. She also attended the religious meetings of the Brahmo Samaj regularly. She was what I would like to call the first generation of the new woman.

We must note that all these categories of urban, modern, Indian, had just about taken shape or were in the process of formation in the early twentieth century. Sukhalata's father and uncles belonged to the first generation of urban settled bhadralok in the family, so Sukhalata and her siblings, cut off from their rural links, were urbane to the core. India as a nation was emerging so the idea of the 'Indian' was simultaneously being consolidated. The formation of the identity of the new women within its boundary introduced the aspect of gender into this process. It is through studying this process that we can say that the new woman had arrived in the urban middle-class milieu and was commonly visible in urban Calcutta.

In '*Adarsha Nari*' (Essay 42, 'The Ideal Woman') written in 1931 in *Bangalakshmi*, Sukhalata singled out a woman's mission as an educationist and indicated her ardour for women's emancipation and protest against child marriage. These are the elements which made Dr. Alice Salomon the ideal woman to be emulated. While women were expected to take care of the public through these efforts, they would also have to be the angel protector of the hearth. Alice's Academy of Social Work was praised because it educated women towards children's upbringing, cooking food, housekeeping, and so on. She mentions Sarojnalini Dutt, as Alice's Indian counterpart, who educated women on the same lines through her social work.[18]

The same year, Nirajbasini Som, reviewing the condition of women's education in Bengal, wrote in the same magazine that 'women are now especially aware of their daughters' education' (Essay 44, *'Bangladeshe Streesikshar Bartaman Abasthar Sankshipta Bibaran'*, 'A Brief Description of the Present State of Women's Education in Bengal'). She no longer thought of women's education as the father's, leave alone the husband's duty. On the other hand, the world of early twentieth-century Bengali fiction (mainly by male authors) is replete with images of the husbands teaching their brides. Rabindranath Tagore's novels *Chokher Bali* (1902-03) and *Ghare Baire* (1916) portray husbands as benevolent teachers, eager to educate their young wives so that they could become better companions or be more presentable to the world. The women whose essays have been translated here narrate a different story.

The mission to educate, create succeeding generations of new women, becomes a part of the new woman's agenda. Sukhalata's aunt and contemporary, Jyotirmoyee Gangopadhyay (1889-1945), remained unmarried to fulfil her life as a teacher in formal schools. Her vociferous recommendation for women's entry into the public sphere not merely to receive the benefits of progress, but also as administrators and executors of law, by default, suggested the need for education (Essay 29, *'Didimar Patra'*, 'Grandmother's Letter').

Sarala Devi Chaudhurani (1872-1946), remained unmarried for a long time until she was assured that after marriage she would be able to continue with her work in the public domain for women's education. In 1907, her insistence on education as the most important public role for women at that point of time is also interesting :

> Make people realize that educating others is a pious act and should be made a part of our daily rituals. ... The utility of a mission is perceived in a two-fold way: as a service to oneself and to others. (Essay 52, *'Jogajog'*, 'Communion').

Sarala Devi was involved in nationalist politics and as such led an active public life. Her decision to take a public post not for financial requirement but to ascertain her right to a profession created a stir not only within the family but also beyond it.

Brahmo women went on to give examples of western women to show that if liberties were to be exercised by educated women, the model ought to be West European liberalism. Conversely, Hindu women tried to emphasize the same point through a revision of tradition and re-reading of ancient texts. It is women's public role which they took up on their own volition, and this, I believe, made them slowly invisible in the stormy debates that characterized the nineteenth-century bhadralok. Men were ready to accommodate angels in the house but when it came to seeing them in public sabha/samiti or meetings and parades it was somewhat difficult to accept. After all, education was meant to secure the private, not bring women out into the public. This was a patriarchal fear of losing control. With Gandhi's advent in Indian politics a new space was created for women in the public sphere without disturbing the whole rhetoric of division of labour and spheres and importance of religion. But as Renuka Mandal and Kamini Roy's essays (Essay 48, *'Bharatiya Nari Andolan'*, 'Indian Women's Movement' and Essay 13, *'Barpan'*, 'Dowry', respectively) show, women were quick to engage with Gandhi's position and take issue with it, as well. Hence, education disappeared from the agenda, not because the women's question was resolved, but because the inevitable happened: having been taught language, so to speak, women now made the fullest use of it in spheres that were hitherto off-limits for them. As a result, the women's question became a larger social 'problem', and generated a dialectic which we, the twenty-first-century Bengali women, have inherited.

Social change wrought by education and the unifying potential of the reformist and nationalist movements is now visible on looking back. For example, though most vociferous women writing during the early twentieth century were Brahmo, yet their Brahmo social identity in public life was slowly being assimilated within the larger Hindu identity. From Sarala Devi Chaudhurani's call to women during the nationalist period, her location within the Hindu community is clear: 'We are the Hindu girls, the daughters of India'(Essay 52, 'Communion'). The rhetoric of militant nationalism was often too Hindu to give space to minorities. Probably the other major reason for this transformation was that the importance of the Brahmo reformism had already run its course.

A late twentieth-century book on the girl child may be useful here:

> In Bengal, a great deal of thinking had gone into the making of the girl child that cannot be neatly polarized into the 'tradition-modernity' or 'inside-outside' dichotomy. Even the Brahmo (reformed Hindu)

> upbringing of the girl child tended to rely on a strictly defined, cleaned up image of the Hindu scriptures, and a whole array of *desaja* (homegrown) ritual practices and proverbs regulated the life cycle of a Bengali girl child.[19]

Following the All India Women's Education Conference held in Poona, Maharashtra, in January 1927, women in Bengal took a significant step by establishing the Bengal Women's Education League in February the same year through a conference held in Calcutta. The following year when the second conference of the League was held it was attended by 300 members.[20] The All India Women's Education Conference soon changed its orientation and hence the name as well. It came to be known as the All India Women's Conference (AIWC) in order to include broader social and political issues. In Bengal, however, the Education League continued as it was and a clear difference of opinion with the AIWC became apparent, though some of the AIWC representatives from Bengal were members of the League. In Bengal, the women's movement continued with education as its focal point. According to Barbara Southard, the list of members included representatives from all leading communities in Bengal, namely, Hindus, Muslims, Christians and even some Englishwomen. Southard does not mention Brahmos separately, but most of the leaders mentioned by her were Brahmos. Though the intellectual leadership of the educational movement still remained in the hands of the middle-class elite of different communities, it was being considered as a movement which had not run its course because the mass was yet to become a part of the movement.

By the early twentieth century, education came to be considered as that touchstone which would help eradicate all gender injustice in society. The single issue of education opened up and was connected to practically everything.

By the early twentieth century, education then became the means through which to achieve empowerment and rights. Here, however, Santa Devi was actually criticizing the education system of the country and its attitude towards aestheticism. Even so, she was certain that education was that essential attribute without which nothing gainful could be achieved.

Finally, I shall end with acknowledging the doubts expressed within the scholarship and in common knowledge, about whether women themselves wished to be uplifted, educated, modernized. Writing in 1904, Khairunnesa Khatun said:

> Men now understand about the need to spread education among all sections of women—the rich, the poor, the *bhadra* and the *abhadras*. Now many of our sisters have understood that too ... why has education not spread among us? ... Without the benevolence of the rich, it will not be possible to educate poor women enshrouded in the darkness of illiteracy. (Essay 22, 'The Hindrances to Our Education').

Khairunnesa's lament throws light on another community in Bengal. Muslim women's education followed a somewhat different trajectory from the majority community's socially more powerful class of Hindus. For some communities, the demand for women's education came from women themselves, partially because those demands began in the early twentieth century when formal educational institutions and elite-educated women were quite widely visible in the public sphere. Hence, Khairunnesa's call to rich Muslims to involve themselves in the education of women is a plea from within for gender justice: a plea that might have gone unheard, but it was not any less eloquent in highlighting women's demand for the amelioration of their condition and their own active role in this process. The effects of education as a tool for empowerment were thus visible by the early twentieth century.

Notes

1 The term *bhadralok* was widely in use since the nineteenth century for urban educated middle-class men working in the service sector under the British Raj. See Sumit Sarkar, *Modern India* (Delhi: Macmillan, 1989); and J.H. Broomfield, *Elite Conflict in a Plural Society: Twentieth-Century Bengal* (Berkeley: University of California Press, 1968).

2 *The Reformer*, 19 September 1831, cited in Benoy Ghosh, ed., *Selections from the English Periodicals of Nineteenth-Century Bengal*, 5 (Calcutta: Papyrus, 1978).

3 See Tithi Bhattacharya, *The Sentinels of Culture: Class, Education and the Colonial Intellectual in Bengal (1848–85)* (Delhi: Oxford University Press, 2005).

4 This is dealt with in detail by Tanika Sarkar, 'Strishiksha or Education for Women', *Words to Win: The Making of* Amar Jiban: *A Modern Autobiography* (New Delhi: Kali for Women, 1999).

5 Bhattacharya, *Sentinels of Culture.*

6 Jayeeta Bagchi, *'Ekaal Kokhon Shuru Holo?'* (When Did This Era Begin?) Mapping Modernity in Women's Discourse in Colonial Bengal', 'Scripting the Nation: Bengali Women's Writing, 1870s to 1960s.' Occasional Paper 9, School of Women's Studies, Jadavpur University, Kolkata.

7 The Brahmo Samaj was founded by Rammohan Roy in 1828. In 1864 under the leadership of Keshab Chandra Sen a schism occurred that gave rise to the Nababidhan Brahmo Samaj. The original Samaj came to be known as the Adi Brahmo Samaj. Later the Sadharan Brahmo Samaj was founded by a radical faction of the Nababidhan Brahmo Samaj through another schism in 1878.

8 There were pro-education voices which talked about same curriculum for men and women. However, other ideas of education were silenced or overridden by this more stronger voice.

9 *'Streeshiksha o Bethune School', Bharati o Balak,* mid-July to mid-August 1887/Sravan 1294 BS: 113-15.

10 Published in *Prabandha Pustak* in 27 April and then was part of *Bibidha Prabandha* (Part I) in 1887.

11 Meredith Borthwick, *The Changing Role of Women in Bengal 1849-1905* (Princeton: Princeton University Press, 1984).

12 Bankimchandra had written a long essay entitled '*Babu*' where he critiqued the decadent absentee landlords and the rising middle class. *Babu* is pitted against the *bhadralok* and has a negative connotation.

13 The names Panchi, Rami and Madhi that Bankimchandra uses reveal that these are non-urban Hindu Bengali women. Even the three letters written by the spurious Chandikasundari Devi, Lakshmimani Devi and Rasamoyee Dasi, as a critique to the essay have Hindu names. 'Devi' was used by upper-caste women whereas 'Dasi' by lower castes. Clearly, these letters were written by Bankim himself and now form part of the essay itself. Urban Brahmos kept more lofty names this was more in keeping with the Brahmo secular ideal.

14 Poromesh Acharya, 'Bengali "Bhadralok" and Educational Development in Nineteenth-Century Bengal', *Economic and Political Weekly*, 30, 13 (1 April 1995).

15 Partha Chatterjee, *The Nation and its Fragments: Colonial and Post-Colonial Histories*, In *The Partha Chatterjee Omnibus* (Delhi: Oxford University Press, 1999).

16 Borthwick, *The Changing Role of Women.*

17 This came out in *Narir Ukti* (mid-December to mid-January 1958/ Poush 1365 BS).

[18] Sarojnalini Dutt (1887-1924), the wife of Gurusaday Dutt, ICS, helped her husband in establishing the Bratachari Samiti. For her social service she was awarded the MBE by George V in 1918. Nari Mangal Samiti founded under her name is still extant, working for women's health, education, industry, for improving women's social and economic condition.

[19] Jasodhara Bagchi, Jaba Guha and Piyali Sengupta, eds, *Loved and Unloved: The Girl Child in the Family* (Calcutta: Stree, 1997).

[20] Barbara Southard, 'Bengal Women's Education League: Pressure Group and Professional Association', *Modern Asian Studies* 18, 1 (1994): 55-88.

PART I

BREAKING THE MOULD

1

BIBI TAHERANNESA

The first published essay written by a Muslim woman is Taheran Lecha/Taherannessa. In fact, before this, the only known instance of a Muslim writer of Bengali prose was Khondkar Shamsuddin Muhammad Siddiqui, who wrote *Uchit Sraban Arthat Paramarthik Bhab* in 1860. Taherannessa signs her letter to the editor of *Bamabodhini Patrika* with the date and the place: Boda Girls' School. There is a place called Boda in West Dinajpur, but the likelihood of having a high school for girls there is remote. Yet Taherannessa signs herself as a student of the First, or highest, class. Her name is spelt in the local spoken language using the 'ch' sound instead of the 'l' and 'n' (for a detailed analysis of her writing and a comparison with Khondkar, see Ghulam Murshid, *Rasasundari Thekey Rokeya Sakhawat Hossain: Nari Pragatir Eksho Bachhar* (Dhaka: Bangla Academy, 1997).

A Letter to the Editor of *Bamabodhini Patrika* (1865)

To a well-wisher of women, the respected editor of *Bamabodhini*,

Great is the supernatural glory of the Supreme Father and ruler of the universe that in order to preserve His own creation, He has fulfilled what He desired by creating both man and woman, thus maintaining the beauty of this world. Of these two *jatis*,[1] let alone following all the rules leading to the progression of all worldly creatures, had one of them not been present, how like an unpopulated forest the world would seem, which is beyond description. Ah! How merciful is the Great One! Not satisfied with giving material resources. He has given the human race the strength of having the means that are capable of achieving all their ends through discipline and organization, by giving them the best and most superior means, the most beneficial joy enhancing the priceless jewel of education, which can yield useful knowledge. The women of this country who lack this gem of education wreak indiscipline in this world of the Great Creator, which is a cause for regret. There is a saying that women are of mean intelligence and excitable; yet they are the mainstay of all practices that maintain the lineage. If their blind lack of knowledge cannot be removed through education, they will fall prey to wrong practices. Because they lack knowledge of proper behaviour towards their parents, husbands and elders, they diminish the glory of the Creator, the health of their children and their own health. The *Shastras* say that in youth, wealth, power or the lack of conscience can be the root of meaningless chaos.[2]

If women lack knowledge, what havoc may they wreak when they come into contact with this? If we consider it, then there is no limit to the low acts that can be done by the ignorant. To be ignorant in this material world is a disadvantage, if women are supposed to maintain the lineage without proper knowledge. The stillborn or dead child causes grief just once, but the foolish, untutored child causes such grief that one cannot deny its existence even in one's mind. Women's minds enlightened by knowledge, thereby facilitating the nurturing of their families with discipline and propriety, could be a cause for their own and their families' happiness, which can hardly be exaggerated. If they were educated, they would be able to behave decorously towards their parents, husband, children and elders. If the son were educated, the way in which he would illuminate the reputation of his lineage would make his life worthwhile. Similarly, if the daughter were also educated, and took the right path, she would bring radiance to the lives of the natal and the marital families. Could there be any doubt about that? There are many examples of this amongst the ancient women of this land; Lilavati,[3] Khana,[4] Shabari[5] and others. As everyone knows, such women gained fame because of their knowledge and its influence, and they were a source of light to their natal and the marital families. Ah! If on this ephemeral earth, all women were educated and followed the path of dharma, then what a joyous place this sorrowful earth would become merely thinking about it causes one to be happy. O civilized men of this land, do not remain neglectful of educating women. If you really want to see the earth a happy place, then make the effort to adorn your women with the ornament of education.

Translated by Ipshita Chanda
Department of Comparative Literature, Jadavpur University

'Bamabodhini Sampadak ke Patra', *Bamabodhini Patrika*, mid-February to mid-March 1865/Falgun 1271 BS, bhag 1 (part 1), khanda 2, sankhya 19 (no. 19), pp. 275-77.

Notes

1 A traditional system of social stratification in India, used both in the sense of race and caste. Translated in English as 'caste', a social hierarchy unique to India, based on heredity that determines its members' prestige, occupation, place of residence and social relationships. Perceived as endogamous, social relations between members of different jatis were severely limited and formalized in the nineteenth century. Difference between social strata is maintained through differential access to prestige and economic resources, and membership is completely ascribed by birth. However, anthropologists and historians believe that there was mobility within the caste system throughout the ages.

2 *Shastras* refer to Hindu scriptures; a broad umbrella term that includes a huge range of literature from the Vedas, Upanishads, *Puranas, Smritis* and *Sutras* refer to a category of texts rather than a particular text.

3 Lilavati was a woman mathematician from the early medieval period; the daughter of the celebrated astronomer and mathematician Bhaskara of Maharashtra in the twelfth century. His famous work *Lilavati* is said to be actually composed by his widowed daughter.

4 Popular sayings/proverbs attributed to a female astronomer named Khana or Kshanavati in old Bengali and relate to astronomy and astrology, often with special reference to agriculture. Unfortunately, no specific data is available about her life.

5 A female forest ascetic in the epic *Ramayana*. Shabari represents perfection secured through unflinching devotion to spiritual guides, waiting for Rama's arrival for many years. Her enlightenment points to the possibility of deliverance of low-caste women.

2

EKTI BHADRAMAHILA

No biographical details about the author could be found.

Bengali Women and the Issue of Freedom (1871)

Wise men easily realize that the women of our country, owing to their lack of freedom, have been turned into inanimate objects. They cannot meet any wise men or visit any great place as they are kept confined in the same place, where they meet the same people. There are learned men in many places who could advise them well, which would benefit them in this world and the next. They could visit these places for the same purpose.

According to many great men of this age, camaraderie has not yet developed between men and women. In such circumstances, how can women move out of their houses and enjoy such freedom? For me this statement does not appear justified as I do not feel that by getting on well with their husbands, who are their nearest ones, or with other men who are their friends and relatives, their dignity could in any way be damaged. Women cannot be a part of the Brahmo Samaj and take part in the meditations of the *Param Brahma*, the Supreme Being, with their relatives, neither can they enter school premises and to quench their thirst for knowledge. They can only lead their lives like the caged cuckoo, fluttering to and fro within their enclosed space. This has curbed their intelligence and has reduced them to flames smouldering beneath the ashes. In the past, queens like Savitri,[1] Rukmini[2] and Draupadi[3] were able to fulfil their dharma and were also knowledgeable. They visited many places on their own, which instead of harming them actually helped them, as one would expect. If a woman steps out of the four walls of the house, does she lose her good character? Had it been true then all European women would be unchaste. But most of them are dutiful, educated, faithful and qualified, something unimaginable to achieve for women of our country, even in their dreams! Who will not be overwhelmed reading about the lives of such dignified women worthy of respect? And now, we have to judge how these women adorned the female species and why our sisters in Bengal have always been living under deplorable conditions. The women of this country do not possess even 1 per cent of the qualities of an European woman.

We can well understand that the lack of freedom has led to the calamitous condition of the women of Bengal who from their birth till death are reduced to the existence of caged birds and beasts.[4] Alas! When will the light of freedom illuminate the hearts of women and clear away the darkness of subjugation? The great and wise men of today's civilized society wish to grant freedom to their wives[5] but the fear of social ostracism causes this hope to remain latent in their hearts and wane with time. The constant confinement of women within the four walls of the house has made their apprehension of the outside world a part of their personality. Thus if they have to go out of the house or talk to friends they feel that it would be as terrifying an experience as death.

Men have complete supremacy over women; they will do as they please, women will not be allowed to interfere in any way. How amazing! What can be more pleasurable to men than to find to their educated, liberated wives fulfilling the duty of looking after their families conscientiously and with care, and also being appreciated by people all over the world? He, who is our Father and has created us, has not discriminated between men and women and has shown equal mercy or retribution to all. One cannot say that the women of our country will ever be able to break the firm chains of subjugation that bind them. I had thought that educated broadminded wise men would dispel the sorrow-filled darkness and free women from bondage, that they would redress the sorrows of women and put them upon the first steps of the golden stairway of emancipation. But my wish-fulfilling creeper has not borne fruit and I doubt that this will happen in future.

O Almighty Creator of the Universe, Supreme Lord! How much longer will Your daughters suffer the agony of the prison, how much longer will You leave Your weak daughters to live like animals? O merciful Great Father! Have pity! Turn Your merciful gaze on the sisters of our country. In Your presence whom else will they turn to? Whom will they pray to when You are their Father, their shelter and support. Now I can only weep before You, You are our Father, our only support. We are like the thirsty chatak bird awaiting Your drops of mercy. Lead the great men of our country from the darkness of their delusions.

Translated by Prajnamita Dasgupta
Department of Comparative Literature, Jadavpur University

'Bangadeshiya Mahilaganer Swadhinatar Bishay', Bamabodhini Patrika, mid-May to mid-June 1871/Jaishtha 1278 BS, bhag 7 (part 7), sankhya 94 (no. 94), pp. 62–64.[6]

Notes

1 According to Hindu mythology, Savitri was the only daughter of Ashwapati, the king of Madra. After severe penance, Ashwapati was blessed by Sun-Goddess Savitri and a very powerful daughter was born to him who was named after the goddess. Nobody was willing to marry such a powerful woman. Hence, Savitri chose Satyaban, the son of Dyumatsen, the king of Salya, as her husband.

2 The most prominent and principal wife of Krishna, ruler of the Yadava clan, allies of the Pandavas in the battle of Kurukshetra as described in the *Mahabharata;* she is also considered as the avatar of Lakshmi.

3 She is the wife of the five Pandava brothers in the epic *Mahabharata,* written by Veda Vyas. This is one of the instances of polyandry found in Indian literature. Her public humiliation by the Kauravas, cousins of the Pandavas, over the dispute regarding the extent of the kingdom, resulted in her inciting her husbands to take revenge. Though this was not the only cause of the epic 18-day battle between the Kauravas and Pandavas, it is also referred to as an instance of a woman's wrath.

4 The word used is Bangladesh, which refers to undivided Bengal up to 1947 in all the essays in this collection; and not to the nation-state that came into being in 1971.

5 The word used in Bengali was *paribar*, which literally means family. *Paribar* is often used to refer to 'wife' in Bengali.

6 The article carries no author's name. The term *bhadramahila* refers to a lady of a genteel background, of the educated, generally middle and upper classes. Also see, Introduction II.

3

JOGINDRA MOHINI BASU

No biographical details about the author could be found.

The Custom of *Kaulinya* (1871)

Education is progressing in our country, without doubt, but no one is thinking of the customs related to *kaulinya*.[1] These customs are making the country a place of debauchery and many *kulin* virgins succumb to unbearable tortures. My heart is torn asunder when I think of the terrible plight of the kulin girls. Alas! They have to bear the horrors of widowhood all life-long; they never see their husbands, and must live in their natal homes just because their husbands had visited them only once at the time of marriage and left them thereafter. Alas! What a terrible and wrong custom Ballal Sena introduced,[2] which has led the country to fall low enough to practice foeticide. Alas! When shall Bengal be progressive enough to discard this evil custom, and when shall these unfortunate women be adorned with education and dharma, becoming free of their eternal agony? If a kulin brahmin marries fifty women and then is devoured by time, all those women would have to bear the pains of widowhood. Alas! As a result, the country is ensnared in sin. Hence, until this land is freed from this evil custom, Bengal will not be able to move forward on the path of progress. Alas! Thinking of those young kulin widows, who have had no material notion of their husbands, which tough heart will not melt? How would these girls obey the harsh customs of chastity and austere rituals of widowhood? They are unable to adhere to these ruthless customs and become enmeshed in the great sin of debauchery. This makes this happy land of Bengal seem like a land of sorrow. O great and glorious men who wish their country well and want to be of use to it! Please take extra care so that this horrible custom is eradicated and our motherland is freed of sin. Take care to uproot the thorny tree of this ancient evil custom from this land: how would the plight of your sisters ever end, otherwise? O great merciful God! These grief-stricken weak women have no other way of overcoming their distress except your mercy.

Translated by Ipshita Chanda
Department of Comparative Literature, Jadavpur University

Bamarachana: 'Kaulinya Pratha', Bamabodhini Patrika, mid-September to mid-October 1871/Ashvin 1278 BS, bhag 8 (part 8), sankhya 98, (no. 8), pp. 196.

Notes

1 A form of hierarchy amongst the upper castes, instituted from the eleventh century in Bengal by Adisura, where a section of the brahmins (custom also followed among the kayasthas) possessed special attributes, *gunas*, which endowed them with a prized higher ritual rank that could be passed down through lineage. Thus marriage to a kulin male brought valued higher status to the bride's family, who in doing so followed hypergamy, marrying their daughter into higher status. Kulin daughters, however, could only marry kulins, and were not permitted hypogamy, marrying someone of lower status. The marriage system amongst kulins permitted a male to marry many women in return for dowry. The women often remained in their natal families, perhaps meeting their husbands just a few times or not at all in their lifetimes. Child marriage meant that often very young kulin girls were married off to elderly kulins, who would die shortly, leaving them to the very severe rigours of orthodox widowhood. Some of these brides remained virgins and yet became widows.

2 Ballal Sena became ruler of a large part of Bengal province in AD 1158, succeeding his father Vijayasena, who established the dynasty, wresting land from the Buddhist Pala rulers. He was responsible for reorganizing the caste system and establishing the practice of kulinism among brahmins, kshatriyas and vaishyas in Bengal. Ballal Sena practised a tantric form of Hinduism, and as a brahmin Hindu ruler opposed Buddhist Senas. He was succeeded, probably around AD 1170, by his son.

4

SRIMATI MAYASUNDARI

Around the 1870s, Srimati Mayasundari wrote in journals like *Bangamahila* and *Sadharani*. Very little is known about the author. The original article carried the term 'Srimati' before her name.

Is Birth as a Woman a Bane? (1875)

It is unfortunate to be born as a girl child in Bengal. If the Lord hadn't given us patience to cope with our problems, we cannot tell what would have happened. From birth we are deprived of good fortune; even our parents and relatives are unhappy about us. The father, who wished for a boy, expresses his disgust at being the father of a girl child. We are unable to understand what prevents us from being the apple of his eye. If one says the money spent on the marriage of a girl is a huge sum, it cannot be denied that the money spent on a boy's education is an equally huge amount. One can easily give a boy superior status by saying that his education will reap rewards by his earning and the care that he would provide for his old parents; on the contrary, a girl is going to drain the wealth of the house by taking away all that her parents had in the form of dowry. Is the girl to blame for all this, or is society responsible? During the marriage of the son, the father extorts from the bride's family. So why wouldn't the same father suffer during his daughter's wedding?

Girls do not receive education in a systematic way. Though the seeds of education are slowly taking root in their minds, yet society is responsible in preventing their growth. Even though they are sent to schools, they do not receive much education. By the time they are in their tenth year they have to leave school as they get married and are expected to settle down with their families. These little girls have no idea what bringing up a family means! But they are expected to do so forsaking their basic education! Their routine revolves around their husbands, remaining engulfed in the folds of their saris and keeping silent for the benefit of their husbands and for their own self-respect. If the husband is willing to allow her to continue with her education, she might do so for some time till she gives birth to her child. So it is well understood that she is able to pursue her dreams till she begins to mother a child. She is not allowed to see anything, even the famous Howrah Bridge that has been recently constructed. She only gets to hear about it which can be a distortion of facts as there can be a conflict between what is seen and what is reported. If they are not able to attain education and gain first-hand knowledge through seeing and knowing what is happening, their existence becomes futile. But it would be wrong to say that they are completely unhappy in their family life.

Translated by Soma Mukherjee
Delhi Public School

Bamaganer Rachana: 'Nari Janma Ki Adharma?' Bangamahila, mid-July to mid-August 1875/Sravan 1282 BS, khanda 1 (vol. 1), sankhya 4 (no. 4), pp. 93–94.

5

ANONYMOUS

The Murder of Women in India (1882)

When the British triumphed over Sindh and established their kingdom, Sir Charles Napier, a famous general, was entrusted with the task of administration.[1] Soon after taking charge, Sir Charles Napier learnt that the inhabitants of Sindh murdered their women on flimsy pretexts. He immediately devised a means of inflicting rigorous punishment as a preventive. Out of fear of punishment, the people adopted an artifice. After murdering the women, they would spread the rumour that they had committed suicide. This vexed Napier intensely and made him promulgate a declaration broadcast in 1847. We translate it below, which will enable readers to understand some of the miseries that women in India have faced.

> Attention, all inhabitants of Sindh. The government has repeatedly asked you not to kill your womenfolk. When the British triumphed over your country, this crime was widely prevalent amongst you. The religion of your conquerors considers the assassination of women as a deadly sin.[2] Who has the power to defy their rule? Fate has abundant wretchedness stored for those who are brave enough to challenge their laws. ... O people of Sindh! Inhabitants of Baluchistan![3] You are the disciples of Muhammad! Did not your Prophet ask you not to kill women?[4] By killing women not only do you defy our religion but also your own. The government will not

> allow this. For this reason, the government has begun to punish the murderers of women and this sinful act has gradually been abated. However, some people amongst you are such fools that they think it is easy to deceive the British. After strangling their women, many people have spread the rumour that the deaths of these unfortunate women who have supposedly hanged themselves are suicides. Do you think that the government believes you and thinks that all these women have really committed suicide? Do you believe that you can cheat the government through this kind of deception and that the government will condone the assassinations of so many women without opposition? If you really believe this, then it is necessary to teach you how erroneous your belief is. You must know that if you still associate yourself with this sin, you will face immense torment. You are being informed officially that if any woman in any village is found dead, the entire population will be subjected to a heavy fine and this fine will be forcefully extracted. The government will dismiss the sardar, the head of that village. All relatives of the husbands of the dead women who live within this entire state, extending to Karachi, will be arrested. And you all will be subjected to such perils that after this the news of a woman's suicide will cause you to tremble. The day such an event takes place will be an ominous one for the people of that place. You all know that whatever I am saying is quite justified, as in Sindh, the news of women committing suicides was not heard of before legal punishment was implemented to prevent the murders of women. However, this year, it has been observed that many women have been hanged to death. Their relatives and near and dear ones have spread the news that they have committed suicide. Fie on their husbands! Fate has intense pain in store for them because the British government can never be deceived by such sinners. They will end the lives in harsh toil. All these murderers will be sentenced to transportation and their pleas will not reach anyone's ears.

Readers, what do you feel after reading this declaration? Alas! To prevent the premature deaths of the unfortunate and helpless women of this country, what attempts were made by an English ruler! He was a general. His business was only to kill human beings. But heart cried out for the women of this country though their own relatives did not cry for them. The killing of women was always prevalent among the Muslims. It goes without saying that where polygamy and severe offences take place routinely, there is possibility of much oppression of women in the inner apartments without any outsider coming to hear about it. Those people who have stepped into the fort of the Muslim emperors of Agra must have seen a dark room situated under the ground. Even to this day huge gallows may be seen in this room. It was said that whenever the emperor was infuriated with one of his innumerable wives, she was hanged in this room. Who can count the number of helpless women whose lives have ended like this![5] Today, has the murder of women been completely eradicated from this country? We have heard of many incidents from different places that while attempting to chastise the daughter-in-law, the husband or the in-laws have killed her. Later they have tied a rope around her neck and made an uproar that she has committed suicide. Thus, so many barbaric incidents have happened within this society that one's desire to give voice to proposals for the emancipation of the daughters and daughters-in-law of Bengal still remains.

Translated by Mrittika Ghosh
Department of Comparative Literature, Jadavpur University

'Bharate Nari Hatya', Bamabodhini Patrika, September 1882/Bhadra 1289 BS, kalpa 2, bhag 4 (part 4), sankhya 212 (no. 212), pp. 143–45.

Notes

1 General Sir Charles James Napier (1853), was the British Army's Commander-in-Chief in India. His major contribution was the conquest of the Sindh province which is now Pakistan.

2 The religion of the conquerors was Christianity. According to Christianity, the seven deadly sins are wrath, greed, sloth, pride, lust, envy and gluttony.

3 At the time of Napier's arrival, Sindh, covering an area about the size of England and Wales, was not yet part of British India, though its rulers all had treaty obligations to the East India Company. Sindh, with a population of about a million, was predominantly Muslim. Its rulers were Baluchis of the Marri tribe—the Taipurs—who had seized control of the country in 1783 and divided it into three states: Khairpur (upper Sindh), Hyderabad (lower Sindh) and Mirpur. The rulers of these states, the Amirs, were nominally under Afghan sovereignty, but for some years no tribute had

been paid. In 1839, the Amirs had reluctantly signed new treaties with the East India Company in connection with Lord Auckland's plans for his Afghan campaign. The Amirs, who were not strong enough to resist British demands, had to permit the occupation of a part of their territory by Company forces and allow the use of river Indus for the conveyance of stores en route to Afghanistan.

4 The Prophet criticizes the ill treatment of the girl child, including expressing sorrow at its birth, in the Qur'an, Surah 16, ayat 58-59.

5 Writing on Napier's discovery of female murders in a Muslim-ruled and Muslim-domainted area, the writer seems to limit the practice of polygamy and female murder to Muslims alone. The stereotyping of Muslim men as promiscuous because of religious sanction given to polygamy, fits in with this popular myth, accentuated by stories of the secret debauched life led in harems. In fact, polygamy was prevalent among Hindus as well, and murder could well have resulted amongst them too.

6

KRISHNABHABINI DAS

Krishnabhabini Das (1864-1919) was encouraged immensely by her husband, Debendranath, to study and become educated. She was the first Bengali woman to go to Europe. Extremely impressed on seeing the liberties of European women, she wrote '*England-e Bangamahila*' under a pseudonym (1885). Immediately after its publication, however, it was banned because of the writer's radical thoughts on the issue of women's freedom. In 1909, she volunteered to work with the Bharat Stree Mahamandal. Giving up her comfortable life, she chose to walk barefoot, like most women then, on the streets of Calcutta, wearing a khaddar sari, encouraging and requesting the *purdahnashins* or women in purdah to get educated. It was because of her efforts that the Mahamandal opened up three more branches where Bengali, English, geography, history, sewing, handicrafts, mathematics, music and the playing of musical instruments were taught. In 1916, she established a home for widows. She was selected as an examiner at the Calcutta University, though she was never formally educated.

Women and Men (1890)

As old customs and practices of this changing nineteenth century are fast disappearing, various new manners and customs are being adopted in the social behaviour of every civilized country. But there is nothing like action and resultant reaction in the foundations of human society because of the great agitation among the educated and the civilized about the status of women and the relationship between the natures of women and men. For a long time, everyone was content to think that the relationship between women and men was determined by nature, and no one dared to debate about or intervene into such a serious matter. But for some years now, everyone is quite ready to debate the subject, as they do about old customs and manners freely and without fear. There is now a remarkable excitement in every civilized nation about the roles and rights of women in society, and, as a result, different ways of developing women's education have been initiated everywhere. In many countries, women have been given the right to become doctors or clerks, and laws regarding women and marriage too have been amended. This new life of women even in India is the outcome of this great agitation, which shows that the status of women in the world has greatly improved from what it was.

Although other women and their well-wishers have succeeded in making those advancements work, terribly harmful counter-views are still obstructing the path to our improvement. No one knows how many conflicts and arguments, how much time and labour are still needed to cross that hurdle to make women equal to men. Men's hatred or mockery about women's education and development has disappeared, or is disappearing, but it is being replaced by great hostility. Such animosity will not be permanent, surely. As women and men are bound in a natural relationship by mutual attraction, there is no doubt that in the end the truth of their mutual relations and companionship rather than unnatural antagonism will prevail between them.

Three questions immediately come to mind while discussing this subject. One, in every culture and society, from the past until the present, what kinds of professional posts have women held? Two, what are the reasons—natural and unnatural—why they have held or are holding these posts? Three, does a progressive, prosperous and happy society still want women to follow old rituals and customs, considering that this is the best (it has to offer), or does it want to bring about equality of position and relations among women and men?

When we look at the history of the entire race of women till the present, we see that at all times, in every family of every nation, women have been and still are subjugated by men. Barring one or two, all women, are completely owned and dominated by more powerful men. Although a progressive society works very hard for the benefit and development of women, the general populace and women themselves believe that they deserve such subjugation. They are the property of their male relatives in their own families, therefore, it is their sole duty to live and work according to the wishes, tastes and dictates of these men. ...

Our second question: Why is it that historically, women throughout the world, have been and still are entirely dependent on men? Honour, worship, laurels, virtuous and civilized practice—we can cover it up by assigning any name to it—but who can deny such subordination? Unless we acknowledge the fact that women are genuinely inferior to men, no explanation of such worldwide and permanent subjugation of women is possible. ... But there is no proof in the world that the race of women is really inferior to the race of men, and that women are entirely devoid of masculine virtues. There is indeed dissimilarity between them, but that is akin to the difference between the left and the right hands. With practice it is possible to do equally well with the left hand everything that the right hand does ... the slight supremacy of the right hand cannot be denied. And because of this little difference, a woman's hands are shackled with heavier chains in the workplace. Apart from that, even if such differences did not exist, the arrangement of duty decreed by nature—the duty to bear children and nurture them for a long time—clearly explains why women are always subjugated by men and are entirely dependent on them for food and shelter. ... How much longer are women to be deprived of every right in life and society simply because they are the 'females' of the species? Let us see how we can justifiably answer this third question.

The foremost aim of humankind is to proliferate and maintain the species. Thus in an uncivilized and barbaric phase of any society, the contention that women are entirely subjugated by men because of their frailty and their inability to protect their own children is absolute and final. To survive in those conditions, humankind decides on supremacy and subjugation on the basis of physical power alone. But as the human species becomes more cultivated with the development of civilization and education, it depends less on physical power and develops laws to protect the lives, property and rights of the strongest and the weakest members alike. The more a society is uniformly civil, the more it is able to treat the strongest and the weakest without any bias. Although the primary task of human beings, like the baser creatures is to propagate their species and to protect it, this is not their only task; rather the primary task is to attain that dignified life in which human beings find corporeal pleasure trifling enough. The mind along with the body is also necessary to help fulfil those divine and dignified wishes of the Almighty who is not content with only providing human beings with bodies, as he has done for animals.

And it should also be kept in mind that no race has spread its domination or has been considered great merely and solely because of its physical power. A race can become better than another only by virtue of mental ability and ethical sense. ... Humans have mastered the world by virtue of knowledge and intelligence, and compelled the most powerful animals to obey and serve them. ... A race that is more ethical and clever becomes more powerful than the others. Look at religion, philosophy, science, literature and art—physical power is not relevant and here are the finest examples of human achievement.

Such arguments strengthen the belief that women are deprived of every right in society and are dominated by men not because of their physical powerlessness but by their mental inferiority. Now, we should verify how much of this is really true.

If we take the extreme point of view regarding the subject (since people generally tend to take such extreme views) and say that each woman is inferior to each man, then such natural shortcomings do seem quite dreadful. ... Between each member of the race of women and that of men in the world, there is no such difference of inferiority. Only if we take an average account of their vices and virtues, men are found to be greater than women. But when we take the examples only of individuals we find that many women are undoubtedly better than the average man, and some women are exceedingly better than men, barring a few saints. People always say that women by nature are incapable of deep thought, judiciousness and prolonged mental exertion, and they are unimaginative and devoid of any sense of humour as well. The lives and works of famous women amply prove that such accusations are quite baseless. ... No judicious or unbiased person will deny that the reason why women have not been fully equal to men is because they lack intelligence. When we see everywhere how much pain, suffering, mockery, inconvenience, encumbrance and insult women have to put up with in their struggle with men in life, the fact that they have stepped over those social and physical barriers to compete evenly with men clearly demonstrates the extent of their intelligence and capacity of thought.

There is also a great difference of opinion regarding the spiritual and moral equality between women and men. Though many people concede the superiority or equality of women in those two areas, in practice they endorse views of women's incapability. People say, on the one hand, that the disposition of women is much more virtuous and pure in comparison to men's, and that is why they stand to lose their purity and virtue, becoming inferior when they join regular work and rub shoulders with men. On the other hand, it is said that women are devoid of high moral virtues, and therefore, they need to be ruled by powerful, virtuous and benevolent men to assist in the preservation of society and religion. Now, we should try to find out which of these two suppositions is correct. ...

According to the notion that women by nature lack courage, truthfulness, honesty, benevolence, greatness and high virtues, and their hearts are filled with the basest qualities of deceit, meanness, conceit, jealousy, affectation and vindictiveness. ... It has to be admitted that comparing the permanently free life of men with the permanently confined life of women, on an average, women have a greater inclination towards those vices. ... If the conditions are reversed we will find that women's greater addiction to those vices is due to faults of circumstance alone, and are not inherent in womankind. Like women, men's hearts too are equally filled with those vices, but the hallowed air of freedom always sweeps them away. Compared with men in general, women are found to be inclined towards greater virtues with dignity in a country where the lives, belongings, comfort and high opinion of both the races are upheld with equal care. What does that prove?

Moreover, conceit and maliciousness, meanness of heart and mind are attributed only to women. If both men and women were to live in the same condition, they would have had those vices in equal share. In every country and in every historical time, men have been banished from their normal course of life and from the right to pursue knowledge because of imprudence or religious despotism; and in those times and in those places we find that along with the women of their class, worthless and idle men are also equally full of those vices. And not only that, in many civilized and free countries too, among equally educated women and men, the latter are found to be more addicted to vices in most cases.

And now we will look at the opinion that ascribes, instead of special vices, many special qualities to women. Foremost among those qualities is modesty, and, in addition to that, the qualities of tenderness, shyness, self-effacement, quick-wittedness, ingenuity and devoutness too can be counted. But if we examine them closely as before, it is clearly perceived that though women are said to be qualified with those virtues, these are not naturally intrinsic to them. Many people must have noticed that when they were young, the female and male siblings both were equally shy and modest, but while the sister is lauded for it the brother is ridiculed. That is why the boy shakes it off before attaining adulthood and the girl conserves it lovingly. So when we see modesty and shyness in adult women, we tend to think it is their special virtue. Moreover, among brutish races where men do not care for modesty, the womenfolk are entirely devoid of that quality, and this proves that such quality is not intrinsic to women. On the other hand, in families where men are extremely sensitive about women's modesty and religiosity, it is considered as the principal virtue.

Tenderness and its companion, kindness, are part of men's lives too. And as women always have to care for the various aspects of their limited living space, they are far more habituated to quick considerations and better tastes. Many people must have noticed that if a man, out of miserliness or because of being without a wife, is compelled to keep track of the small details of life continuously, he too like women would readily become accustomed to quick thinking and sensitivity. ... These traits are seen in the noblest persons of both the races. And we cannot admit that devoutness is a special quality only of women since so far only men have been the originators and preachers of all religions. Wherever there is any religion that is worshipped with respect, belief and adulation, men have monopolized it and have never entrusted it to women. But most of the time, women are found to be more believing and more inclined towards addiction to a religion that is false and superstitious, and that is because they are utterly banished from the developments of knowledge and science in a civilized world. With the development of scientific knowledge, when previous beliefs and conceptions are found incompatible, the mind discards them to adopt or establish newer modes of religion according to need.

Consequently, it can be said that in the usual sordid, limited and unchanging life of women, religion acts as a window to the brighter outside world. Only through that window does the spirit perceive the light of the outer world; and the spiritual and mental life which is not satisfied with mere food, clothes and golden ornaments tastes the pure air of a genuine life. Unfortunately, the miserable condition of women makes the only outlet in their lives an all-important one, which they defile and besmirch by superstitions and misconceptions.

By comparing women and men with regard to their intellect, devoutness and moral sense, we can clearly perceive that the characteristic traits of both are similar. But from the dawn of civilization, women and men have led completely different lives. Educated differently, they have adopted different habits, are encouraged to work differently and thus have become skilled in different fields of work, and this is why the phrases and concepts—'man's work', 'woman's work', 'male virtue', 'female virtue'—have become so firmly entrenched in our minds.

However, it is our duty now to review the enduring and immutable difference between women and men—the biological condition imposed on women by nature to bear children and engage in motherly duty. According to nature, women will bear and nurture children, and men will protect women and children and provide support for them. Motherly duties keep women confined to the home, therefore duties in the outer world fall on men.

And so we see that where women's subservience and dependence have continued long and unchanged in primitive societies and families, where women have always been neglected and hated as they are merely 'females', where men have behaved in a recklessly wanton manner guided by a desire to relieve their own duty only by marrying the women off with complete disregard to their mental and moral consent, there has never been any argument ever about mutual relations, duties and rights of women and men in society.

The practice of making married women dominate over unmarried women, and banishing redundant women from society by any means possible, is but another name for the same primitive and uncivilized practice. The idea that there is no need for women except as a requirement for men is born out of that primitive conception, resulting in crimes of multiple marriage and female infanticide in Africa and in our country too. And because of that same idea, noble European women, until recently, were forced to adopt a celibate life in a convent.

By comparing women and men we can see quite well that the evidence for women's physical, mental and moral degeneracy is not substantive enough to deny them their social and other general rights. Now let us look at the customs, laws and arguments, both for and against this ancient and longstanding arrangement. First, the political and legal argument: while there are different opinions about other subjects, in this case, everyone's point of view is the same.... Granting women rights and freedom equal to men means going against nature and inviting a terrible upheaval in society. To counter this argument we can say without fear that nature can safely be left alone to defend itself. The developments of society always depend on discarding aged and iniquitous customs and adopting newer ones in their place. It seems rather harsh that only those strictures regarding women remain uncertified and unchanged. ...

And now we have to face the arguments that speak against the concept of women's equal rights in the working place. People who are against it say that if the sweetest, purest and most tender woman is allowed to compete with men for arduous work in the struggle of life, she will lose her sweetness, tenderness and purity. The charming lyricism of courtship between women and men too will vanish, giving rise to a harsh rivalry between them, instead of the courtesy and tenderness of the powerful towards the powerless. Women will definitely slip further down in that terrible rivalry.

But it seems that people who argue in such a way tend to think of a handful of women they know personally rather than thinking about women in general. They tend to consider as models for all womankind that small number of women who sit peacefully in their mansions surrounded by servants and attendants and ... even the gentlest wind seems frightened to blow over their tender bodies. Is it not more worthwhile to banish such imaginary women unfit for life's struggle from thought, and to thank God by acknowledging the fact that womanly tenderness, purity and sweetness are not made up of such evanescent and brittle material that they cannot remain intact unless kept in a glass showcase? All things considered, it seems that the apprehension of women's greatest danger does not come from the easy and moderate ways of a free life and hard labour, but instead from idleness and lack of employment in the complex mechanism of a subservient life.

We shall now discuss what common people think about women. They think of women as an extremely inferior race, which exists solely for the use and benefit of men. ... The reason for this general hostility is women's permanent and successive subservience down the ages from primitive times. This idea is circulated in every society, among every class of people; it pervades high literature of every race and the music of the lowly classes; and this superiority–inferiority complex has become so deeply entrenched in people's minds that one never finds it astonishing or extraordinary. ... And women too, habituated as they are, participate in this chant about their inferiority. The Italian poet, Leopardi, accuses women by saying that they hate great poets or learned men if they are ugly or disabled.[1] And a famous German philosopher has stated that it is useless to expect anything from women since they have long hair and short intellect. In Sanskrit literature too there is no dearth of songs and poems that speak of women's inferiority and weakness. We feel ashamed reading these comments of poets and learned men, but they also make us laugh because it is men rather than women who care for brainless beauty. Few women feel kindly towards handsome men without virtues. Although it is true that due to their long subservience women have lost much of their virtuous qualities, poets and philosophers should not have called all womankind inferior by looking at one or two discrete examples. Moreover, it cannot be denied by anyone that women have reached this lowly state only because of men's fabricated accusations against them; and hatred towards women has increased because of this habit of marking them as inferior.

The most dangerous and terrible barrier against equality in society and rights for women is the barbaric and odious notion that women exist only for men and they have no other purpose in life except to fulfil that specific objective. We can see that this idea is so deeply rooted among barbaric and uncivilized races that they are even unable to think that women are not born only for men's benefit. Traces of this antediluvian belief are seen even among races in Europe famed for their civilization and civility. In the course of this single essay it is quite impossible to describe in detail the perpetual occurrences of the terrible, distressful, dark and sad events engendered by men's domination of women. But we can clearly perceive that this beastly idea about women has been so detrimental to people in every country, in all the temperate, torrid and frigid zones, in all civilized and barbaric societies that women are first taken as generally inferior, so every right and property are denied to them, and then throughout life, their bodies, minds and souls are exploited only for the sensual satisfaction of licentious and wayward men. This is why unless the belief that women are equal to men, or even superior rather than inferior, takes firm root and unless men wrench out from their minds the despicable ideas of women that they grow up with, they would not learn to respect women. Until the belief that women do not exist only for men's use becomes ingrained in people, no one would be able to save humankind from this dangerous and dreadful sickness.

From all these comparisons and discussions of vices and virtues of women and men, noted above, we conclude that women's minimal natural inferiority conjoined with motherly responsibility have bestowed on men the right to rule and dominate both the races. But women's inability is not so severe as to earn them complete banishment from all social and general activities, or to deny them the rights held only by men. One might ask, 'If that conclusion is correct, and, considering women's minimal natural inability, if the artificial barriers and hindrances created by rules and regulations directed towards women are abolished, what would be the benefit for women and society attained by the new changes?' While answering this question it should be our primary duty to keep in mind the disparity between present outcome and future consequence. It will take many generations to completely transform women's familial, social and general state of life. Even the famous Greek philosopher, Plato, did not think it possible to form a stable human society without slaves. We too cannot clearly envisage a beautiful and developed human society where women will stand on an equal footing with men and will enjoy the same set of rights. But it seems certain that with time the new changes will become strong and durable by the unrestricted application of natural rules with freedom for all, and this new order of society would be stronger and safer than the present one, as its basis would depend not on wilful and artificial difference but on natural difference between women and men.

There will be some present results, however, from the new changes. Women will be roused from their intellectual slumber if they are allowed all kinds of education and general work. Women in decent families who are rendered helpless by the absence of their husbands or fathers will be able to earn professionally to support themselves and their children. And if they are able to earn their upkeep from decent occupations, thousands of widows will not readily forsake their faith for monetary greed. When the master of a family is sick, or unable to work, he is extremely saddened by the sorry state of his helpless wife and children; but if his wife is educated enough to earn money by working as a doctor, or teacher, or clerk, or matron, the dying husband's heart would not be laden with distress for the future, and his family would not suffer from poverty in his absence. And if women are trained from a young age to do regular work, their families would become more disciplined and virtuous.

It cannot be doubted too that if the labour and working capacity of both women and men come together, humanity will be able to achieve much more. As competition will become unfettered and free, only the most capable will be selected for top jobs, so all work will be done more perfectly. But, then, we should also ask whether society would need to pay an additional premium for such profitable methods. That is because many people are apprehensive that if women and men compete with each other equally in every kind of work, their natural and mutual attraction will be abolished. And when that happens, people will no longer respect matrimonial bonding, or they will lose any desire for marriage. Moreover, as women will get individual and social recognition even without the sanction of marriage, they will refuse to be burdened by a conjugal bond. But it is easier to dispel these apprehensions from our minds because these are baseless. If the present state of human nature does not change, its physical and moral power of attraction will always make men and women come together, and there will never be any longstanding rivalry or opposition between them. As we specifically notice in these discussions about women, the number of men taking sides for women is almost equal to the number of women, and an equal or larger number of women take the side of men, which is against themselves. And all those people who oppose the genuine development of womankind by saying, 'We want to transform women into men,' will find it reassuring to know that if nature is left alone to do its own work it will do so quite prudently, so that there will never be any unnatural change or hostility between women and men, and women will never be transformed into men.

Just as familial bonding is the basis of civilized society, according to a special social rule, marriage, the bond between women and men for life, is also the foundation of family. This is why, like the power of human language, it is also uniquely human; therefore, as long as human society exists, marriage too shall exist. As human civilization becomes more developed, the foundational bonds of family too will become rigid and pure. Society itself will hate the sinful relations and beastly attitudes that cause so much mischief and chaos. If women are allowed this new and genuine freedom, there is a possibility that it would initially be misused, since the vices and weaknesses that have become habits for women as a result of centuries of artificial and unjust fetters would not go away soon. They would have to be uprooted painfully and with punishment as part of a natural momentum. ... Although it would momentarily be painful, ultimately it would produce eternal happiness.

Our earnest beliefs that when women and men would help each other equally in every sphere of life with equal distribution of duties and rights, when a moral sense would depend not on the complexes of superiority or inferiority of the races but on a rightful and natural morality, when women and men would truly understand the meaning of virtue and respectability, then we could hope to see society purged of rubbish. Only then would the human family move forward with determination and dignity from brutish barbarism towards a triumph of human sensibility. Then finally would humankind would be able to enjoy heavenly and eternal happiness instead of evanescent and mortal pleasure.

Translated by Somesh Roy
Department of English, Alipurduar College

'Streelok o Purush', *Bharati o Balak*, mid-Feb to mid-March 1890/ Falgun 1296 BS.

Also available in *Krishnabhabini Daser Nirbachita Prabandha*, edited by Aruna Chattopadhyay, (Kolkata: Dey's Publishing and School of Women's Studies, Jadavpur University, 2004) pp. 13–24.

NOTE

1 Giacomo Leopardi (1798-1837), a famous poet, scholar and philosopher whose scholarly and philosophical works and lyric poetry place him among the great writers of the nineteenth century.

7

NAGENDRABALA MUSTAFI

Though Nagendrabala Mustafi (1877-1906) could only complete her primary education, her interest in languages encouraged her to master Oriya, English and Sanskrit. She began writing poems from the age of twelve. Her essays were regularly published in periodicals like *Navya-Bharat, Sahitya, Bamabodhini Patrika, Birbhumi, Purnima, Janmabhoomi, Anandabazar Patrika,* and so on. She was awarded the title 'Saraswati' for her book *Amiyagatha* and the *Adhyakshagana Puraskar* by the Hare Prize Essay Fund for *Premgatha.*

A Necessary Appeal (1894)

In Hindu society, women have no right to choose their husbands. The girl must be married off to the man who is decided upon by her close relatives, like her father, brothers and uncles. No one considers whether the man, who will be holding the hands of this hapless girl, on whom her entire life depends—her happiness, hopes, beliefs everything—and with whom she will be jumping into life's tribulations, and spending her whole life with him, is someone whom she likes. This is the custom of our society! Prior to the marriage, none takes a special interest, even once, to understand whether or not the prospective groom and the bride like each other, several families get devastated by subsequent marital clashes. Marriage is a tough task. Man leads a new life after his marriage. The lives of both the husband and the wife should become one in marriage. They must lead their lives together very cautiously. How many persons know how to unite their lives? How many achieve it? He who has been able to attain it is blessed with heavenly pleasure. But it is very difficult for two persons to live together without experiencing any problems. To achieve this, two qualities are necessary—love and care. A happy marriage depends upon the mutual exchange of love and care between the husband and the wife. But how many couples know how to share these precious emotions which, nevertheless, are not easy to share? Only the fact of being married to each other does not make the sharing of love and care any easier. If a couple can achieve it, their lives would not be burdened by the daily tedious and trivial misunderstandings. Only a couple who mutually admire each other and is a source of comfort for each other can share such emotions. So I think the couple must consider whether they are suitable for each other before marriage. But to determine whether one is suitable for the other is not easy, as none knows if what is preferred by one is actually liked by the other.

The moon is forever beautiful to the gaze,
But is it ever so pleasing to Nalini's eyes?

The bride may not like the groom who is selected by her guardians. Her heart silently burns without anybody's knowledge. Hence, the sense of likes and dislikes is different for everyone. Hearts do not beat in the same way. The way an individual knows his or her own self, cannot be the same as others understand him. So whether there will be a compatible conjugal relationship between them is something that a couple must understand before their marriage. As couples do not have the right to take such difficult decisions, countless families are devastated owing to marital clashes. If the husband had the right to choose his wife, there would not have been so much unhappiness in life—the couple, through mutual love, could have enjoyed conjugal bliss and appreciate the meaning of life.

Alas! in this distressed country and afflicted society, will those happy days, when Aryan women like Savitri,[1] Damayanti[2] and Bhadra[3] had the right to choose their husbands on their own, ever return? Will Hindu society see those blessed days come back again? We pray earnestly to the Almighty so that we may get those fortunate days back to us. When He accepts our earnest appeals, families shall no longer be ruined by marital discords.

Translated by Sanchayita Paul
Department of English, North Bengal University

'Prayajaniya Prarthana', *Bamabodhini Patrika*, October 1894/Ashvin 1301 BS, kalpa 5, bhag 3 (part 3), sankhya 357 (no. 357), pp. 191–92.

Notes

1 For details, see Eassay 2, n 1.

2 A mythological character, she was the daughter of Bhima, king of Vidarbha. King Bhima and his wife pleased sage Daman by their worship and Damayanti was born to them by his blessings. She was extremely beautiful and chose the very talented and handsome Nal, son of Birshen, king of Nishadh, as her husband.

3 In Hinduism, Bhadra is a goddess of the hunt and one of Shiva's servants.

8

NAGENDRABALA MUSTAFI

Eassay 7 offers a note on the author.

Dire Straits in Seclusion (1895)

We do not consider the practice of purdah that is prevalent for women in our country as something good. This practice is the root of all our miseries; the reason behind our pitiful condition. We are entrapped in the cage of purdah just as a bird is locked within the confines of the cage. Consequently, our mental faculties are getting weaker by the day, and our minds are failing to bloom in the light of knowledge. Life cannot move ahead on the path of progress unless one acquires proper knowledge. In the absence of the right kind of knowledge, this rare and valuable human life is spent in a condition worse than that of animals. We have been trapped in a cage ever since infancy; how then would we acquire the right kind of knowledge? ...

If some good-hearted person kindly takes the initiative to guide our trivial lives towards betterment, all quarters of society start castigating that person. As a result, the person abstains from continuing with the task. ... Can the bird sing the virtues of Hari without ever hearing them sung by someone else? The bird needs to be tutored in the name of Hari so that it can sing his virtues. Purdah hinders our education. We need to be taught about society so that we can acquire proper knowledge.

The mind is trained by education. ... It is only the proper kind of knowledge that makes the human heart whole. The absence of such knowledge is the reason why we are becoming so wretched and society is looking down upon us. Alas! If only society would once take the pain of trying to know the reason behind such a deplorable state and initiate steps to rectify it, then we would no longer be required to bear the humiliation of being looked down upon. Had society felt even the slightest degree of kindness towards us, we could then identify ourselves as being descendants of the Aryan race. Our lives too would then be as sacred and glorious as those of the Aryan women. Such was their prowess that they could willingly participate in battles and behead their enemies. The flesh and blood of the Aryan women constitute our bodies as well. How then were they more powerful and stronger? And why are we so weak? Is not society the only reason? At that time society did not try keeping women as tamed birds within the confines of a cage. Hence, they were in possession of proper knowledge, and courage and could perform accordingly. Had they too been subjected to purdah like us, their noble lives too would have been spent in a deplorable condition. Sisters! Come, let us pray to our Father, Lord of the Lords, so that we can free ourselves from this rigid grip of purdah. We certainly will overcome this awful state by His grace, and our lives too will be as respectable and fulfilling as those of the Aryan women.

Translated by Suvradip Dasgupta
Department of Comparative Literature, Jadavpur University

'Abarodhe Heenabastha', *Bamabodhini Patrika*, May 1895/Baisakh 1302 BS, kalpa 5, bhag 4 (part 4) sankhya 364 (no. 364), pp. 30-31.

Note

1 Hari is another name of Krishna worshipped as a reincarnation of Vishnu, the principle of preservation in the Hindu trinity. Mynah birds, known to pick up and reproduce human speech, were often taught to say the name of Hari. Here, the woman secluded in the inner quarters so that they are not 'seen' by men other than their close relatives, are compared to a bird in a cage. Just as the bird will not learn to say the holy name of Hari if no one cares to come to the cage and repeat it, so the woman in seclusion will not be able to gain education unless efforts are made.

9

CHARUSHILA MITRA

Charushila Mitra (1882-1979) was a social worker. After completing her studies from Bethune College, she joined Eden High School in Dhaka as a teacher. In 1928, as instructed by her maternal uncle, Swami Paramananda Maharaj, she went to America to work for Ananda Ashram, returning after three years to work for it from India. She established Ananda Ashram Home for the refugee women on the request of Dr. B. C. Roy, the Chief Minister of West Bengal, in 1951. She had already accommodated refugee women in a rented house in Dum Dum, where gradually she established Sarada Vidyapith, Sarada Shilpapith and a boarding house for female students. In 1962, with the financial help of the Government of West Bengal's Rehabilitation Department, she transferred her schools and boarding to Bonhooghly permanently. The aim of teaching was to empower women in the family and society.

Our Society (1914)

These days much is heard about social reform, but in reality nobody comes forward to dedicate his or her life for the development of society. Perhaps that is the reason why Bengalis continue to be notorious talkers who hardly ever execute what they profess. Currently, we are engaged in political rhetoric, striving eagerly for autonomous rule. Alas! The oppressions and problems which exist within our society and which call for urgent eradication are often neglected. 'Disunity among Bengalis is thought to be their chief defect.'

Our duty is to put an immediate end to the various undesirable customs which exist in our society such as child marriage, dowry and so on, since such practices jeopardize the progress of the nation. There are innumerable cases of householders who feel burdened with the girl child. Such instances would never have surfaced if only Bengalis had more fellow feeling and sympathy for one another. Everyone has to bear the burden of a daughter's marriage, but all seem to forget this while extracting huge amounts with proper interest as dowry from the bride's family. This is done to recover the dowry lost through the marriage of a daughter. Is this not an indication of absolute cruelty? ...

The father of the girl child is harassed with the task of arranging for a dowry without which the daughter cannot be married. Despite this, the groom's father is often dissatisfied with the amount and as a result the bride's father is left with no other option but to sell his house and land to gratify him. One can easily gauge the misery that such poverty inflicts on the father of the girl child in Bengal. Despite such calamity, nobody is willing to discard material greed. In this respect, the exemplary conduct of Radhakrishna Dutt, the district court lawyer of Darbhanga, is well worth recording. He did not accept any dowry from the girl's family on the marriage of his worthy son Manmohan Dutt. This generous precedent should be emulated by all of us.

Marriage is one of the chief sacraments. However, it has now become a commodity acquired through monetary exchange. The person with a deeper wallet fetches a groom of commensurate goodness. Is it not more shameful that guardians of sons, who have supposedly received a creditable modern education also make extravagant dowry demands from the girl's family? Is the sole aim of a son's education and his university degree to make him a better commodity in the marriage market?

But what far outstrips this surprising fact is that the groom's family while engaged in a similar transaction is more apt to consider it as a matter of pride rather than shame. Yet again, our society never ceases to consider a girl as open to insult if she remains unmarried till a relatively late age. Continuous scorn makes it difficult for the girl's parents and her relatives to mix freely in their social circle. This kind of social injustice has led to many suicides of the parents of the bride, who are ground between the two sharp blades of monetary demands from the groom's family on the one hand and social censure on the other. Hence, the birth of a girl child is always looked upon as an inauspicious event in the Bengali household.

Does not our duty lie in the eradication of such oppressions? Careful study of our ancient texts like the *Puranas* and of history would enable us to judge that child marriage was never a part of our tradition. If ordinary people were more observant, they would surely understand that the many princesses who used to choose their own bridegrooms had already reached a mature age. A ten or eleven-year-old girl child cannot be said to have reached that mature age. Is it possible indeed for a ten or eleven-year-old girl to select her own partner? Therefore, it is clearly evident that child marriage is not sanctified by the Hindu *Shastras*, otherwise ancient Aryan kings would not have given their grown up daughters in marriage, thereby risking the weight of sin. ... Comparatively recently child marriage is being enforced as a custom combined with higher dowry rates which are ruining many families.

Can these oppressions against the girl's family be justified as religious by any means especially when the same wife is accorded the status of companion and religious partner conjoined in life and after death by the Hindu religion? Are not the violent sacrifices of girls like Snehalata[1] and Nibhanani[2] enough reasons for us to wake up from our social slumber? Who shall take the responsibility for their deaths? Is there not a single pious selfless person in our society who would be willing to take a girl for his son's bride because of her own worth, without succumbing to the base greed for material wealth? If not, indeed it is a most shameful affair. ... Let us fervently hope that these incidents of woman slaughter do not recur in our society. ... Let humanity rule in us so that such brutal customs can be given up. ...

Women are not mere creatures of neglect and disregard. Given an opportunity, they can work miracles. Therefore, Sisters! Come forward in an effort to end these pernicious customs. Let us vow never to take dowry from the girl's family for a son's marriage. Success will attend us if we work united. If innocent girl children could establish a precedence of greatness, sacrificing their youth and life, then could we not be more humane and forbear our greed? Alas! The misery that our cruel social customs inflict on us by depriving many people of their daughters is beyond description! Therefore, one should lead from the front to prevent the recurrence of such tragic incidents and ensure the well-being for all. Let the world discover, that a woman's physical weakness is not to be mistaken as her incapacity. Also let our efforts in removing such disgrace manifest Aryan womanhood before the world. Who will understand a woman's suffering better than a woman? Let the blood of Snehalata and Nibhanani remove this stigma of our society forever.

Translated by Sohini Sengupta
School of Women's Studies, Jadavpur University

'Amader Samaj', *Bamabodhini Patrika,* May 1914/Baisakh 1321 BS, kalpa 10, barsha 51 (year 51), bhag 3 (part 3), sankhya 609 (no.609), pp.20–23.

Notes

1 A sixteen-year-old girl from a poor brahmin family in north Calcutta, burnt herself to death on 30 January 1914, because she feared her family would be ruined by the excessive dowry the groom's family had demanded. The Snehalata case remains one of the earliest and most widely discussed cases of dowry related suicides in colonial India. Rochona Majumdar, 'Snehalata's Death: Dowry and Women's Agency in Colonial Bengal', *The Indian Economic and Social History Review*, 41: 4, (October-December 2004), pp. 433-64.

2 Nibhanani, a young brahmin girl from Dinajpur, committed suicide in February 1914 to save her family from the dowry demanded by the grooms side. Pradip Kumar Dutta discusses the report in *Amrita Bazar Patrika*, 7 February 1914 in *Rabindranath Tagore's* The Home and World: *Modern Essays in Criticism*. Anthem South Asian Studies (London: Anthem Press, 2005).

10

BANGANARI

In this essay, Banganari (a Bengali woman) was the pseudonym of Anindita Devi (1871–1941), an eminent writer of essays and articles. The daughter of Upendranath Moitra, she was the wife of Dwijendra Nath (Dwijesh Chandra?) Chakravarty, the diwan of the Gauripur estate and the mother of the eminent Bengali poet, literary critic and academic Amiya Chakravarty. She published her writings in well-known periodicals and journals of her time, such as *Bharati, Prabasi, Sabujpatra, Bijali, Jayasree, Uttara* and so on. Some of her writings were compiled in an anthology *Agamani* (Alochani). Her essays have been published in *Anindita Devir Rachana Samkalan* (Calcutta: School of Women's Studies, Jadavpur University, 1997). During the period covered by this anthology, Anindita Devi was only a budding writer. It is in subsequent years that she wrote her major pieces.

The Spritualism of Hindu Marriage (1921)

We are in the habit of forever proclaiming the virtue of spiritualism inherent in the Hindu marriage ceremony. Even if one were to admit that it is superior to the rituals of other nations, how ideal it is as a nuptial ceremony can be debated from an objective point of view. In fact, nowhere in the world has the ideal marriage ceremony evolved successfully; or even if the custom were beneficent, most people have not acquired happiness through it because of human frailties. Therefore, it is not right to condemn a ritual merely by observing its demonstration without expending careful thought upon it. Until human nature undergoes specific change it is impossible for or a ritual to yield results that may be deemed as unmitigatedly beneficial.

However, in order to evaluate whether a tradition or law is beneficial, it is necessary to observe if it is abusive of good and innocent beings or if the tradition itself forms an obstacle to expressions of goodwill and attainment of the ideal state in the case of those individuals. Before applauding the marriage custom of our country, it is essential to take a deeper look at these issues.

In the West, if a couple is unhappy in marriage, one easily gets to hear about it. Due to the prevalence of practices like Divorce,[1] such dissatisfactions become easily evident to the casual observer. But here, we never hear anything about couples who are happily married. It is because of this that we hasten to the firm conclusion that no one is unhappily married in our country.

Perhaps it would not be so easy to laud the customs of our own country if comprehending the real situation were as easy as is possible in the West. A marriage involves both man and woman. Therefore, it is necessary to observe whether both parties are living happily without experiencing any hindrance in achieving the ideal conditions. Is it possible for anyone to assert that the reasons for which divorce takes place in the western world do not occur in our country as well? Does anyone bother to write about what the woman has to undergo if even a trace of such circumstances becomes apparent in her case? Indeed, why is there no furore at all over such matters? It is not difficult to explain the reason behind this silence, and an attempt to do so would throw light on the exact areas wherein the much-vaunted spiritualism of our marriage system lies.

One need not ponder much over where this spiritualism lies. It is obviously vested in that convenient scapegoat, the woman—for whom males, from the revered sage Manu to pre-pubescent schoolboys, have fancied themselves as worthy counsellors and guides. Matters of truth and falsity cannot be judged upon one-sided testimony. Therefore, since one of the parties is rendered voiceless and well-nigh inanimate under this ancient law-giving eminence, how can the real facts about marriage in our country come to light... how spiritualism in marriage might be attainable when the entire burden of control and governance has been placed only upon one of these parties. Just as it is extremely lowly to demand forcibly from an individual the gift of self-sacrifice, so is it dishonourable to enforce compulsory or unfelt, law-bound giving. It is indeed wonderful how the Hindu man fails to realize how low he falls when he sings praises of the ideal Hindu woman, and takes great pride in such activity.

True marriage is not about self-sacrifice. The relationship of giving and receiving within it cannot be one-sided. Marriage is essential for both men and women. It fulfils the need for self-expression, perfection of human existence and lifelong companionship, as it helps to balance the shortcomings of each partner with virtues of the other, realizing, in the process, the powerful human instinct for the propagation of the species. Therefore, the success of marriage depends upon the ability of both the individuals to live complete lives together. That each will be more fulfilled and replete by the other's presence is the ultimate aim of marriage. But how far has this condition been satisfied by our marriage customs? Our custom has been to exclude one of the partners from the beginning. There is no place for this partner's own happiness and sorrow, needs and expectations in this arrangement. ...

So infallible are the laws of nature that if they are suppressed in one place, they will be expressed elsewhere in some other guise. Thus, in the marriages of our country too, by denying the needs of one, both the partners have been left unfulfilled. If an individual has to keep on providing without any arrangement of receiving anything in return, then how can she acquire the wherewithal appropriate to the amount given? Indeed, what might be the value of the amount conferred when the giver herself is so destitute?

Again, we might have had cause for some pride if the reasons that lead to those exceptions among marriages in the West that are so very remarkable for us, would at least be absent in our own society! However, since nobody can deny the existence [of such exceptions], let us see what solution our society has provided; and it should also not be out of place to analyse whether that solution has been beneficial to human society in its entirety. Marriages are broken in the West due to betrayal and the abandonment that is concomitant to it, due to cruelty, and other similar causes. What does the society of our country do in such circumstances? ... The femininity and humanity of the women of our country are trampled upon when it comes to matters regarding the depravity of a husband and other related vile issues. However indescribable and unspeakable the humiliation and pain these women might suffer, there is not even a single loophole through which they can seek relief. Even when the law should be able to give succour, the venerable heads of society have left women unprotected, without rights and opportunities. Do they mean to call even this deprivation 'self-sacrifice?' If they do, then it will indeed be more worthwhile to remove the word from the dictionary.

On the other hand, what happens should even an iota of suspicion fall upon the wife? The husband can desert her and get married as many times as he desires without incurring the ire of the courts. If there is even a shadow of just such a cause, even if she were to be in danger of being disgraced, he would not hesitate a moment to shove her on to the path of damnation! If this is spiritualism, then it is necessary to know where the word 'barbarism' should be applied.[2] It is the misfortune of the West that it has not learnt to solve these complex questions with such ease. But then, it has already been noted above that the western way of marriage too is not ideal and our own custom of marriage is far superior to it in many ways. But since its praises are always being sung, it is my purpose to show a little of the other side as well.

Moreover, nowadays, whatever be the husband's age and notwithstanding the number of times he might have been married previously, girls of eleven, twelve, thirteen to fifteen, sixteen years of age are widely available in our marriage market. When such a maiden is tied in marriage to a forty-or fifty-year-old widower (and let us not even speak of grooms even more advanced in age), then may I ask where spiritualism lies in that marriage? ... The greatest demand of a man and a woman is upon each other. Therein lies the exaltation of wifely chastity! But the Almighty has sown in the heart of every woman the right and innate instinct to make exactly the same demands upon her husband in absolutely equal ways. This instinct merely slumbers, a trifle occluded by social rules, the government and even a lack of training in self-realization. But a flaw is such a strong instinct that it cannot be completely buried even under discipline. Therefore, what could be more cruel than to disallow from the start the space for even so small a demand? In a way, this is far more unfortunate than the villainy of a husband after a normal marriage. For, however hateful and humiliating that might be, it does not take away from the rights and claims a wife has upon her husband. But in this case, he belongs to someone else from the beginning; and the rights of the earlier spouses are greater than those of the later one in every way. Even if the previous wife is deceased, the husband, children, and everything else in the household are hers. The new bride merely effects an unauthorized entry; therefore even if we do not take into account the abominable abnormalities that rise from the difference in age, marrying a virgin to a widower achieves nothing but the humiliation of the young girl.

Upon deliberation it seems that although according to the true ideal of marriage polygamy should not be countenanced in either men or women, nevertheless in light of the current state of human nature, the spread of the practice of widow remarriage in society is proper and to be advocated. Such practice would enable the retention of equality and normalcy[3] to some extent. Indeed, if the lofty ideal of marriage has to be diminished, following the adage *pravrittire sa bhutanam*,[4] then it might be somewhat more reasonable to marry an elderly widower to a widow past her prime. As companions too, the two people experienced in domesticity would be able to understand each other well. Therefore, although as an ideal this form of marriage might be of an inferior class, such a marriage is not an abomination and does not abuse the order of nature.

Translated by Debapriya Bose
Department of English, Jadavpur University

'Hindu Bibaher Adhyatmikata', Bharati, mid-June to mid-July 1921/ Asarh 1328 BS, barsha 45 (year 45), sankhya 3 (no. 3), pp. 217–20.

NOTES

1 This, and the subsequent use of the word is in English and capitalized in the original.

2 The original is *paisacikata*, meaning nefariousness or fiend-like conduct. Much of the effect of this chiastic sentence and its sting would have been lost if the two opposing terms did not rhyme, as they do in the original. Therefore the meaning rather than the linguistic effect has been compromised here by rendering 'fiendishness' as 'barbarism'.

3 The original prints *silata*, which signifies natural disposition, conduct, manners, behaviour or character.

4 'These are the natural instincts of all existent beings'—Sanskrit phrase from the fifth chapter of the *Manusmriti*.

11

SRI USHAPRABHA SEN

No biographical details about the author could be found.

The Plight of Women (1923)

Men have vociferously claimed, 'You are born to enjoy equal rights as men do, not just to serve as their object of desire.' Let's see how far men keep their words.

The *shastrakar* who composed the scriptures is male, not female. So according to the *Shastras*, a woman does not have any religion, work, action, thought, her achievement lies only in attending to men. So Bankim babu[1] has written that even after attaining special powers and with a specific *dharma*, Prafulla[2] understood that all these would not enhance her status, hence she came back to family life. The training of Bhabani Thakur turned out to be futile. I am quite surprised how, after practicing *gyanyoga* or the discipline of knowledge, under the tutelage of a *sadhak*[3] like Bhabani Thakur,[4] undergoing training in self-control and penance and acquiring confidence in her own activities, *sanyasini* Prafulla could come back to family life again. The Bhagavad Gita[5] always says '*Ka taba kanta, Kaste putra*' (Who is your wife? Who is your son?) Mirabai could not remain within the family, embracing the feet of her husband. If the husband is the Lord then Mira's leaving the husband in quest of another Lord is improper and blasphemous. One may immediately answer that Mira attained the Lord by His grace, she attained true *gyan*, knowledge. She was designed by the Lord, but Prafulla was a householder, sensual, subordinate to a man and an object of his desire. The altar of Mirabai was established on the rights of human being and truth, and Prafulla's on the self-interest of men. From time immemorial, men have been doing this; Bankim babu has shown nothing new . . . The benefit of comforts and the advantages of position that a man enjoys are predicated on this. If women understand their rights and maintain their distinctive identity, if they understand the power of truth as the basis of human rights, then the edifice of male supremacy, the male claim to divinity would collapse. Man is the lord for woman. Otherwise, what quality do men possess, where do they excel in comparison to women that make them lords? . . .

If every other direction is blocked and a horse with blinkers is directed towards a single alley, it will blindly follow the route to which it has been directed, because it cannot look either right or left. Similarly, all paths were blocked and women had been directed towards only one path by men. Today, the blinkers have come off; women have realized that there are several other options available in life. Following a single path blindly can be detrimental to the well-being of women; in fact, it is impossible to understand this without knowledge. It is knowledge which has made the human species superior to other creations of God. And women have been deprived of that knowledge. He, whom woman has allocated the pedestal of the divine, whom she loves devotedly and worships with great faith (let's forget blind faith), for whom woman has sacrificed her self-interest, soul and life; he who constitutes her world and beyond, her driving force, salvation, happiness, dharma, that great husband-preceptor of woman, what has she received as reward from him? The *Udbhat slokas*[6] from scriptures have also pronounced the meanness of women:

> What does the man not say under the influence of alcohol?
> What do the women not do on this earth?

> Which activity of a woman, what evidence against her, is responsible for this inherent distrust and aversion that man feels about her?

Just as the naïve child is beguiled during initiation into formal learning by being introduced to various charming things, similarly women have been misled by the promises of a heavenly after-life, and have thus been deprived of all comforts in this life. For future happiness human beings put up with hardship, but there is no comfort in store for women in this world. Then for what reason should women tolerate her situation? She should receive something at the end of it. The comfort of this life is transient, but the comfort of life after death is beyond limits, permanent, hence, gallant; religious men have preserved this life for themselves leaving the after-life for women. What sacrifice! What nobility! Whatever be the level of oppression, be it for or by men, seats in heaven have been reserved for women. ... Not only after the demise of the wife, even while she is alive, let the man marry a thousand times—marriage is good indeed! Without marriage men drag women into sin, it is not a sin for them as they are men. It is women who are responsible for this sin! Has the Lord divided sin in two different parts—for men and women? Does the school impart such moral education where the lies spoken by a boy child or an act of theft committed by him are not counted as sin whereas the same acts committed by a girl child are? If this is not the case, and the boy and girl are equally in the wrong when it comes to such trivialities, then in considering adultery, the most heinous sin in society, why do women alone have to bear the brunt? Why is it not an act of sin for men? If it is considered as sin why does society overlook it and not give it much importance? ... Why has society preserved terrible consequences for the woman as punishment for a sin for which man and woman share equal responsibility? ...

The tyranny of the mighty towards the powerless is neither fantasy nor untruth. Let us not talk about the native losing his life for a crime he has been held responsible for in contrast to what happens to an English subject who has been accused of committing a similar crime in similar circumstances. In antiquity, the brahmins would go scot-free despite indulging in an activity which was punishable if others did it; at that time, that was considered natural. But now, since the brahmins and sudras are being governed and ruled by rulers of a different faith, we have realized how unjust and parochial our ancient rules were! Similarly, in the eyes of the creator of man and woman, is not his entire creation equal as far as dharma and adharma, society and humanity are considered? If this is true then on what grounds, by what right do men dominate women?

The foremost duty of the human is to survive and thus it food is essential. ... According to the *Shastras*, women should not satiate their hunger! Let gluttony be the watchword for a male centenarian, but the young widow must observe penance and chastity! Happiness, peace, in this world are for men. In such terrible circumstances, lest the widow's leaving the house is delayed, or lest she is susceptible to the desire to get married, men have kindly advised that she should be thrown into the holy pyre of her husband and burnt alive! . . . Let the man enjoy all sorts of privileges, there is no need to extend all these towards the woman; because she has life after death to enjoy all that! Men do not have to wait for that.

I shall refrain from citing examples from the lives of the uncivilized or the non-Aryans, since the Aryans have severe aversion for the non-Aryans! So let us consider the civilized Aryans and their ancient society. Remarriage of widows and women who have been abandoned by their husbands is a common practice amongst the Muslim and Christian community. It is not present among the Hindus as the Hindu religion is liberal! And they have special regard for women! . . . Men forget that the reason why men marry again and again might be applicable to women also.

In *Manasi o Marmabani*,[7] (mid-March to mid-April 1922/Chaitra 1328 BS) issue, Jatindramohan Sinha[8] in his article '*Satitva banam Manushvatta*' (Chastity *versus* Humanity) has extensively discussed the character of Abhaya in Saratchandra Chattopadhyay's *Srikanta*.[9] He has tried his best to show how the actions of Abhaya invoke severe criticism and shame. Had remarriage been a common practice in those times, Abhaya would not have had to take the path of sin to fulfil her instinct for motherhood. . . . Abhaya's question is 'What is the status of such children?' the only answer to such a question is—nothing and that is as it ought to be. But the rules prescribed by society should change. Christian and the Muslim women could have lived in the house with due respect in the family in such a case, and those societies would have also accepted her ... When there is no such provision, when the women are not separately provided for within the law, then the laws governing men should have been stringent. There should have been laws which could prevent the man, who had abandoned his wife, or was notorious as a tormentor, from getting employment with the state. . . . Since there is no law, no restriction, no fear of any retribution, men can afford to be lecherous. Had there been certain laws, an Abhaya would not have been created. Abhaya is the product of her husband—a creation of man. Had Abhaya's husband treated her well, she could have also been as dedicated a wife as Savitri or Sakuntala. Though Sakuntala was abandoned by her husband without any valid reason, there exists a huge difference, between Abhaya and Sakuntala as is the distance between hell and heaven. Dushyanta could not recognize Sakuntala and refused to accept the woman who belonged to another man, but he was not abominable and lecherous like Abhaya's husband. On recognizing what he had done, conquered by grief and sorrow, and lamenting his misdeed, Dushyanta took the initiative to find Sakuntala and accepted her like *rajlakshmi*, the goddess who protects the royal assets.[10] One regretfully notes that people who compare Sakuntala and Abhaya overlook this fact.

If you have people like Abhaya's husband, you can expect a character like Abhaya. Everyone cannot be Sita or Sakuntala. Can every man be Rama or Yudhishtira? ... Are not the men responsible for the plight of Abhaya? ... Does her desire for a family life fade away? ... Being rejected by her husband, Sakuntala, by the divine intervention of her *apsara* mother found refuge in the hermit's cottage in the forest; who knows, had she been offered refuge in a hermitage, even Abhaya could have been like Sakuntala? But within the framework of this world built on desire, it is difficult to be Sakuntala.

Let us consider the case of the widow. The reason for penance and the life of chastity is that one remains in this world the partner of a single person, whether dead or alive, so that one can unite with him in the next world as well. ... what is life after death? ... If there is something called life after death then very specific spaces are allotted for individuals depending on their deeds of this world. Hence it is impossible to reunite there. No one knows where the deeds of the past life lead us. Then there is rebirth. And the *Shastras* do not assure that in every rebirth the couple will remain with each other. People are reborn depending on their deeds, so even if they are man and wife in this life, in their next life they might well take birth in distant places. None would recognize the other! I was reading a Bengali novel where the husband is born as the younger brother of the wife! She nurtured the husband of her yesteryears like a little boy. Now the question is if the widow does not find her husband in life after death, how will she get him as her husband? Her *brahmacharya* becomes futile. And in life after death the husband and wife do not share physical intimacy! Men do not observe penance and brahmacharya with such dedication in this life so as to be reunited with the dead wife! This sort of dedication and devotion has devolved on the woman. ...

Love, affection, faith cannot be established in a void; even the greatest of the sadhaks needs an idol. It is not possible for everyone to invoke the formless. Hence, Hinduism believes in idol worship and Budhhism could not retain its stronghold here. Babu Jatindramohan and others should consider how far is it justified for such a religion to give directions to the widow about how she should preserve her love for the dead husband. Everyone is not capable of loving the intangible or worshiping the formless. Reciprocity is the essence of conjugal love. ... Coercing a soft tender young girl is barbaric, ruthless and cannot be justified. The woman should be able to choose between the life of a widow and remarriage the way men do. Many lament that the English have eradicated sati by passing a law. When a woman loses her husband, she seems to have lost everything. ... Men believe, if women are given freedom, they will question this subordinate status. Hence a woman has no right to choose her religion, cannot participate in the activities of the state, and even has no control over her own body.

The widow is given the status of *brahmachari;* does being a widow qualify her to be a brahmachari? ... much of this is regulated by social impositions which have become binding forces ... The character of the widow Manorama in the novel *Viparjay,* published by *Bharatbarsha* is worth mentioning. Manorama is pious and devoted, yet she takes part in 'music and merriment', wears petticoats, engages in 'various discussions', in hearty tête-a-têtes with female friends ... hence they do not mourn the absence of their husbands. But Manorama gradually regretted her way of life. According to the author, the widow should not do anything but sit and lament over the fact that her husband is dead; otherwise she is being disloyal ... Time is the best healer; one even transcends the grief of losing a son or husband. This is the will of God, otherwise human beings would not have survived, and might have also gone mad. The ideal might exist in the world of fiction, but the quest for an ideal character within the mass is absurd. ...

People who are scared of widow remarriage can look at the Muslim and Christian societies. Don't these societies have *patibratas* or loyal wives devoted to their husbands? Or have only the Hindus inherited this ideal? Since these religions are not as liberal as Hinduism, instead of subjugating the woman, these religions have given up the equal status. The Muslims do not easily give anyone the status of God like the Hindus do. Muhammad is the holy Prophet, he is not God. But for us everyone is God—Buddha, Chaitanya, from Vivekananda to Mahatma everyone! The Hindu woman encounters God every now and then, so for her '*Punarjanm na Vidyate*', there is no need for rebirth.

Single-mindedness is praiseworthy and hence not easily attainable. Though the social reformist men talk about widow marriage, they cannot accept it. Their writings bear testimony to such claims. In his novel *Ratnadweep* Prabhat Kumar Roy has shown how the widowed heroine had mistaken another person to be her husband and loved him, but the moment she realized the truth, her feelings changed. In the story '*Khokar Kando*', the author speaks through the character of the hero, 'No, the widow should not marry, etc,' when the dying hero realized that his wife will be someone else's after his death, he could not take it. His desire was that his wife should remain his even after death. But what would he have done on the death of his wife? Would, she have liked her husband to acquire another spouse? ...

On getting a glossy new plaything, a child is elated—the worth of the object never comes to his mind. Now, how can you mislead someone without giving anything? She is deprived of education to ensure that she does not have access to knowledge; she is kept in fetters so that she cannot have access to the world outside and claim her rights, yet are bestowed with material gifts to mislead her.... 'Satiate them with clothes and jewels'—men have taken great pains to toe the line of Manu. The women should not be given access to the *Shastras*, education and freedom! If they understand their worth and realize that they are not born just to attend to others, that even they have the right to enjoyment, then what if they refuse to accept male supremacy? So do not grant the woman access to knowledge! We all know what access she has to clothes and wealth! Sri Sourindramohan Mukhopadhyay[11] has highlighted the lapse in his lyrics:

> 'Lessons are not for me lest I have access to everything,
> Lest their happy dreams are broken by our clamour,
> Cooking-serving and lamenting for honour is our world!
> We live for their cause, for what else do we live, oh—
> If they are hurt, the best way is to pass silently—'

Do men feel ashamed of this lampoon? Just notice how pertinent and justified is the statement of Mr. Sinha—'The married woman [in the West] can prove the guilt of the husband and come out of wedlock to be united with another man with ease and composure.' It is not true that women in the West unite easily with men who are not the husbands. 'The society does not criticize this act', is again a misconception. They have a distinct decorum governing the mingling of men and women in public. ... If someone claims that they have no restrictions, he does not know how to esteem truth.

... if Mr. Sinha does not accept the second marriage, then what about Hindu men getting united with other women after the death of their first wives? 'First put your own room in order'. Have not our *Puranas* made provisions for accepting a second husband? I suppose Mr. Sinha is not aware of the *vachana*[12] of Manu *'naste mritey'*, that is, if the husband is not here, he may be considered as not alive—how could he be surprised at the independent acts of members of an independent society. But people who do not forget that even women are human beings are not surprised. According to Mr. Sinha, only a man is entitled to take the other path because he has ordained hell for the woman who gets married for the second time. His entire essay is crammed with such fanaticism. His Anupama is a product of this unidirectional vision. He has presented the testimony of a widow against widow marriage. But the Hindu widow refuses to remarry because of age-old custom, her lack of knowledge and unease regarding society's response. Since she has no way out, she accepts all forms of despotism. ... If being intimate with many men was considered a sin, then Draupadi and Kunti would not have been glorified. Rules and regulations are predicated on the general consensus of a particular moment in the history of a society. Hence, society and its norms should keep pace with the changing sentiments of human beings ... though the love of men and the chastity of women have been glorified, in reality they do not deserve that status because when the question of actual practice arises, these do not hold. There is no loss in not glorifying them.

The widow will not become Devi if attempts are made to deify her with extravagant talk. Human dharma is natural in man and woman; we are suffering the effects of preventing that natural flow. To create the Devi we need the Dev. ...

Mr. Sinha has asked what will happen to the woman who because of her own weakness or coercion by her despotic husband has to leave home. Where and how can she achieve fulfilment in life? As answer he has this to offer: 'sorrow is in store for the woman who fails to worship such a husband and be loyal to him ... and hence attain fulfilment in the next life.'

This is a question for men: what would the man have done in this case? Would he have accepted it as something preordained and succumb to fate? Do men bear all this? One has to worship a lecherous, despotic husband! One has to love him! Why?

... There is an end to the sin committed by men, they rise, expiate, but the women have nothing. If the woman commits sin under the spell of illusion, she cannot undo her deed. Does the sinner remain an eternal sinner? Extreme repentance, unbearable agony and remorse, can nothing reduce her sin? The sin of women is beyond redemption! Do women have to accept the despotism of men as their fate? Is not redemption justified? One should not be astonished to learn that the fatalistic Hindu might accept this as fate. Then why are the Hindus creating this furore about the outbreak of malaria in the country? Why do they visit the court of the king as suppliants, seeking financial assistance? Why do they not accept all this as fate also? ... Hindu women will not dedicate their entire lives for men; instead they will find their own salvation.

Women are vulnerable, and at times, they seek help. Taking advantage, men have manipulated to take away all power, all rights from women. They have robbed women of all happiness, peace, independence and even the faculty to think. Men have not been satisfied with being responsible for all the wretchedness and hardship and prescribing the various forms of starvation for women; they have gone to the extent of burning them alive.

Alas! Women, you have worshipped self-seeking, voluptuous and deceitful men on the altar preserved for God. Unveil the hypocrisy of those who have robbed your homage, and you shall find mere baseness. Women have perceived the truth at long last and thus men are now terrified. Since they have understood what bondage is, women shall break through the chains.[13]

Translated by Dheeman Bhattacharya
Department of Comparative Literature, Jadavpur University

'Narir Abastha', Bharati, mid-April to mid-May 1923/Baisakh (1330 BS), barsha 47 (year 47), sankhya 1 (no. 1), pp. 43-49.

Notes

[1] Bankimchandra Chattopadhyay (1838–94) was a famous Bengali writer, poet and journalist. He composed India's national song '*Vande Mataram*' as a Bengali and Sanskrit *stotra* personifying India as the Mother Goddess, which inspired activists during the Indian freedom movement. He was born to an orthodox brahmin family at Kanthalpara, North 24-Parganas, educated at Hooghly College and Presidency College, Calcutta, and was

one of the first graduates of the University of Calcutta. He served as deputy magistrate and deputy collector.

2 Prafulla is the chief protagonist of Bankimchandra Chattopadhyay's novel *Devi Chaudhurani* (1884), which was banned by the British as it portrayed the oppression of the British empire and suggested that by cohesion to the cause of freedom, the masses could struggle against the empire. The novelist re-enforced his belief here that armed struggle was the only way to win independence. The ban on this book was lifted after India gained her freedom.

3 Refers to a worshipper.

4 A character from *Devi Chaudhurani*. In the novel, Bhabani Thakur, who was a worshipper of Goddess Kali and had dedicated himself to end British rule, tutored Prafulla (later known as Devi Chaudhurani), trained her in self-control and penance to gain confidence.

5 Refers to the Bhagavad Gita, now considered one of the principal Hindu scriptures.

6 The *Udbhat slokas* are attributed to Bhatta Udbhat. His slokas have even found a place in the Charvaka philosophy, 600 BC.

7 The first issue was published in March 1908, edited by Phakir Chandra Chattopadhyay and Shibratan Mitra. In 1914, Jagadindranath Ray became editor. From 1915, he also started editing another weekly magazine named *Marmabani*. In 1915, the two magazines were merged together and was published as *Manasi o Marmabani*. The joint editors of the magazine were Jagadindranath Ray and Prabhat Kumar Mukhopadhyay.

8 Born in Faridpur, in East Bengal (Bangladesh), Jatindramohan Sinha (1858–1937) was a well-known novelist and essayist. Among his eminent books are *Urishyar Chitra, Shakar-o-Nirakar Tattvabichar, Anupama, Tapasya, Galpa Malya, Tora, Sahityer Shastharakhya* and *Sandhi*. He was also a well-known short-story writer. *Urishyar Chitra* was praised by Rabindranath Tagore. His literary criticism covered Bankimchandra Chattopadhyay, Rabindranath Tagore and Saratchandra Chattopadhyay.

9 *Srikanta* is a very popular novel by Saratchandra Chattopadhyay (1876-1938) in four parts, published in 1917, 1918, 1927 and 1933. The character of Abhaya, one of the women in Srikanta's life, has tremendous influence on him. She lives on her own terms. In the Burma episode of *Srikanta*, Abhaya travels to Burma to live with her husband. But on learning that she has to share him with a co-wife and tired of his abusive behaviour, she leaves him to set up home with another man. Abhaya's act of remarriage is considered as sinful, given that leaving one's husband who was also supposed to be the *pati-paramguru*, was not only rare but almost

unthinkable then. In this essay, the writer points out Abhaya's dilemma, the circumstances she had to face as a character set in the nineteenth century.

[10] Sinha Mahashay has tried to poke fun at this situation by asking what would have happened had Sakuntala filed a maintenance suit? But this was not common in the ancient world. Did not Devyani curse Yayati for not showing interest? Those were the days when people had faith in the power of spoken words and hence there was no court. Now that is not possible in this hapless *Kali Yuga*.

[11] Born in a family of lawyers in Ichapur, Sourindramohan Mukhopadhyay (1884–1966), received the Kuntaleen Award more than once for his short stories. He was the editor of *Bharati* magazine for many years with Manilal Gangopadhyay. He wrote prose, poetry, novels, plays and undertook translation. His writings for children include *Lalkuthi*, *Pathan Muluke*, *Chaliat Chandar*, and so on. Among his novels and short stories, *Alo Chaaya* (1936), *Agrabartini* (1937), *Aranya* (1945) are quite famous as are his plays *Daria* (1912) and *Harano Ratan* (1929).

[12] Means sermon.

[13] The author of this essay had written another one with the same title in *Bharati*, mid-April to mid-May 1923/Baisakh 1330 BS, 47, 1st ed., pp. 25-28. Each has been translated by two different translators, each making a different decision regarding the word 'abastha', which can refer to both condition and bad condition, i.e., plight, in Bengali.

12

SRI USHAPRABHA SEN

No biographical details about the author could be found.

The Position of Women (1924)

'Women are goddesses', did men say that just to console women or do they really believe in women's venerability? In Sri Prabhat Kumar Mukhopadhyay's short story '*Devi*' (Goddess), we find that after repeatedly being worshipped as a 'goddess' by her father-in-law as well as others, the heroine Daya started to believe that she was really a goddess. Similarly, women have come to believe in their status as goddesses. But are women really above all human frailties? Are we—Hindu women—unmoved by the natural emotions of anger, lust and infatuation? Or, are we, like men, under the spell of these? If the mere fact of being a woman could place her above such weaknesses—which are quite common and natural as well as intricately related to normal human existence—then it would not have been an exaggeration to refer to her as a goddess.

A frog in a well can only measure the water in that well, and will not have an idea about the waters of lakes, rivers, ponds, seas and oceans in the world. It is wrong to take it for granted that the forever imprisoned and sad condition of Hindu women is the normal situation in the life of women in general. No other women in the world—civilized, uncivilized, independent or dependent of any other race apart from Hindu women—have to live in such unredeemed inertness. In Hindu society, the affairs of the outside world do not reach the women, no wave can arouse their emotions. In the ever-changing world Hindu women live in their own limited unchanging circle which no other women of this vast universe do. When we observe this strange difference, don't we feel like asking why God should exercise such discrimination in creating Bengali women? Is it like placing a sick person beside a healthy man who takes the risk of infecting himself in order to illustrate his superiority of being healthy? But in this case who is sick? Hindu women (here 'Hindu' women implies Bengali women) or the entire sorority of women in the whole world?

No other society has imposed such codes and norms on women as has Hindu society. Let alone the western world, Europe or America, in India itself, in the Parsi community, in Maharashtra and Rajputana provinces, women enjoy equal status with men. The Parsi, Maratha and Rajput do not belong to foreign nations. It is heard that even in barbaric and lawless Arabia, men think that women are physically and mentally weak. Whereas men are punished severely for certain offences (such as immorality, and so on), for the same offences women are exempted as they are considered to be weaker. But in this country? Some offences do not entail punishment and some are not even considered as an offence or cause for guilt in the case of men, but for those very offences—however mild they may be—the strictest punishment is meted out to women by the society.[1] Men will tolerate and forgive their own weaknesses; but will never be able to forgive women's weaknesses: is this an instance of the honour fit for goddesses?

We must understand what it means to be a 'goddess'. The man or woman, who can survive every criticism–veneration, torture–adoration, and neglect–importance and remain balanced in any situation whether good or bad, can be put on the pedestal of god/goddess. ... If only men had been able to be sure of Hindu women's chastity and without any qualms allowed them complete independence; then it would have been justified for men to boast that women are indeed goddesses. Those very Hindus who have kept their women hidden in the dark as if they are dolls made of glass and would break any moment, who themselves dare not look properly at their women, let alone allow others to do so, who are afraid to venture deep inside their women's hearts lest whatever is hidden inside their minds should come across—how can they boast that their women are goddesses? ...

Men believe that women have unflinching devotion to men, that their place in the heart of women is reserved forever. But that is only because women are forced to remain devoted to men. ... On analysing the nature of women throughout the world, it becomes clear that women are naturally more affectionate towards their children than towards their husbands and women can sacrifice their lives for their children. Hence, this characteristic quality is real and natural to women. But the way chastity or devotion to one man is depicted as an inherent characteristic of all Hindu women does not hold true for the entire world's womankind. Also, the belief that single-minded devotion is akin to chastity might not be true. Hence, this is false. 'Zainab'[2] of the Muslim scriptures had married twice, but is a chaste woman like Zainab not venerable to the Hindus? Ann of 'Enoch Arden'[3] had also remarried but does anybody dare call Ann unchaste? In one of the stories by Sri Jaladhar Sen, a Muslim widow had taken a second husband but the writer has treated her with the respect of a chaste woman.[4] Thus it is not difficult to understand that single-minded devotion is not chastity. Is the single-minded devotion for which Hindu women are so much respected in the world an intrinsic characteristic among them? In that case, there wouldn't have been a single prostitute or a woman who had remarried.... Since prostitutes and women marrying for the second time are not creatures of fantasy but do exist in society, it must be understood that single-minded devotion or rather godliness is not intrinsic to Hindu women. ... This is the norm of the world. Nothing is completely pure.

All this is not meant to infer that if men are committing sins, then why can't we? 'Men take nautch-girls out in the gardens; we shall take fops out into the streets.' It isn't like that; it is not like fighting over what share of sin and impropriety we can commit. Any human being is susceptible to mistakes and errors; women too are not free from these. No matter how many norms are created, how much Manu-Parashar[5] is cited, human beings will remain human beings forever. If men's sins can be forgiven, their mistakes rectified, then correction of women's mistakes and forgiving their sins will not lead to the doom of creation. Those who have forgiven women have not become extinct. We do not claim to be allowed to become wayward just because men are wayward. ... Our intention is that just as men want women to be restrained, honest and obedient, women too desire the same of men....

Guilty women should be given a chance to reform themselves. Helping hands should be extended to them to give them support. It is not proper to leave a woman in a troublesome situation by saying that she has chosen her own path. Even the greatest of sinners hopes to become pure one day. There is so much hatred for the 'nautch-girl' or 'prostitute', but who created them? ... These helpless women had no other way out, thus they were left with no choice but to tread this path.

When hidden truth is suddenly revealed before one's eyes, it feels untrue; since we are not used to it, we do not find it acceptable. But even if we do not like it and even if it is concealed, truth always remains the truth. Whatever happens naturally to all women of the world except those confined to specific communities, does not happen to Bengali women just because their paths have been blocked. ... Women are not consciously devoted to men; devotion is extracted from them through allurement.

For a long time women have sacrificed their lives on the funeral pyres of their husbands, endured their tortures silently, and lived by eating the remains of their meals. But have men ever looked at these tortured women with affection? Women have prayed for men's happiness and long life, but have men ever taken notice of the well-being of women's bodies or minds? ... Since the days of our great grandmothers, have women achieved any improvement in either knowledge or courage or education? ... Since time immemorial women have remained the same in matters regarding eating, cooking, dressing, ornamentation, household work and conversation. Rivers, mountains, the sun, the moon and the earth change, but women remain unchanged. Change in women is a terrible sin. ...

We have heard, due to the bandying about of the scriptures, Hindus do not see any difference between women and beauty. ... The household that does not honour women is not blessed by God. ... Because they have so much respect and honour in society, Hindu women are subjected to such torture everywhere, even forced to commit suicide to free themselves from this torture. At present, the value of women in society is so great that they cannot get married without dowry. This must surely be because only women need to get married, men do not!

Men are too considerate towards women. 'We will die and you will remain alive, that can't be! When God kills us, and not you, then we will kill you and take you to heaven because you do not have the wherewithal to go to heaven on your own. You must be gagged and burnt alive, for who knows what you will be upto if left alive! Then you would have to go to hell, hence we are burning you to death for your welfare, otherwise what do we gain out of this?' ... What a pity that such a noble custom got abolished by the law of the foreigner king!

Jatindra babu[6] in his book *Tapasya* and Srimati Anurupa Devi[7] in *Bharatbarsha* have sung praises of the custom of child marriage. The far-sighted leaders of the society have introduced the custom of child marriage after much consideration. Conjugal bonding becomes very strong in cases of child marriage which is quite beautiful. It is beautiful too when the child-wife loses her health forever by giving birth to a child even before she herself has attained full physical and psychological development! And it is even more beautiful when she dies due to premature birthing. It is greatly fortunate indeed to die leaving behind husband and son, very few women are lucky enough to die like this! Or else if the wife becomes bedridden due to her health and is unfit to perform the household chores, it allows aged men to use that as a pretext and remarry. And, old men will invariably get married to pre-pubescent girl children, because marriage to adolescent women is considered a great sin. When after two–three years it is time for the aged husbands to die then the girl children are turned into widows; it's really a very nice practice indeed! For the rest of her life whether she survives by eating once daily, performing *ekadashi*[8] and sacrificing herself at the altar of men's greed, or chooses the path of immorality, the example is unparalleled in the history of world civilization and justice!

Had widow remarriage been in vogue, widowers would have been able to take wives of their own ages or young widows would have been able to remarry after the death of their aged husbands. A fifty-sixty-year-old widower had no other option but to marry a girl child of thirteen or fourteen. When he died at the age of sixty or seventy, it cannot be termed as premature death. But the wife would be at the most twenty-six or twenty-eight at the time of his death . . . the age to extinguish all desires and renounce family life. Have Jatindra babu and Anurupa Devi taken this into consideration? Certainly not! Had they considered this they would have spoken against child marriage. . . .

Taking the role of an advisor in his novel *Anupama*, Jatindra babu has said, 'It is man's weakness to re-marry after the death of his wife.' For this very reason, we are in support of widow remarriage. Why won't the hapless widows be given the right to marry again? Are women devoid of weakness? And why does he shiver at the thought of a 'widow's love'? That means widowed women do not have the right to love but widowed men do. It is the norm of the world that when what is natural is thwarted, it tries to come out through crooked ways. Everybody will admit that those who are widows or those women, who have to spend the rest of their lives as widows in their parental homes in spite of being married, are usually sour-tongued and quarrelsome. Since their hearts have been deprived of love they turn sour. Love is the softer, beautiful side of human life, it is something that gives utmost pleasure. The other softer sides of human nature can blossom only if love blossoms. . . .

In *Tapasya*, Jatindra babu has said, 'Western society has given so much freedom to love that it has grown wings, now it is no longer desirous of wasting itself by remaining confined to daily household activities . . . the husband gets care and affection from the wife but not that strange mysterious thing called love.'

If there is inherent hatred for something, then it cannot be judged in an unbiased manner. Jatindra babu's is a similar case. There is so much hatred for western society ingrained in him that the truth is not visible to him. It is very difficult to determine the truth without universal opinion. Neither blind emotion nor blind faith is good. On the basis of what evidence does he voice this opinion? Probably on seeing western women marry after the death of their husbands. But had he been able to transcend the limitations of his fixed ideas, he would have realized how wrong his notions were. In the event of the wife's death a Hindu man marries again, but does that mean that he does not love his 'someone else's' wife?[9] In western society, women are as independent as men. Long ago, our society was like that too. It is unnecessary to say much on this issue . . .

'A married or widowed woman has eloped with some neighbour'—in such a case Jatindra babu has severe condemnation for the 'woman' only. He says nothing to the 'neighbour' . . . He is dead against modern women but cannot find any fault with men.

Anurupa Devi cannot think of a blushing bride who is in her youth. But our exemplars, Sita, Savitri, Uma, did not get married while still in the laps of their mothers . . .[10] They had married in the prime of their youth. After them, Padmini, Karmadevi, Sanjukta[11] too got married in their youth. Probably they had become so 'shameless' after seeing the Europeans! Otherwise how could one of them accompany her husband to the forest in front of her parents-in-laws? How could they reject proudly the potential grooms? Savitri defeated everyone in shamelessness. She declared the name of her chosen husband in the open court . . . And all of them I presume were educated in their marital households.

Kanyapyebang palaniya shikshaniyati yatnatah,
Deya baray bidushe dhan-ratna-samanwita.

This means that daughters must be educated with care before handing them over to their husbands. Then was Manu a European who came from across the sea? Otherwise why would he say that it is the duty of the father to give lessons on how to honour and take care of the husband, and that the father should give away the daughter in marriage after giving her lessons in these matters? Manu has not given this responsibility to the parents-in-laws. No, instead of playing with dolls the little girl has to be dragged into lessons concerning the honour and care of her husband, while she is in her father's house.

By specifically saying 'Hindu', does Anurupa Devi forbid us to look at other communities apart from the Bengalis? Does she not know that people living in 'Banga, Bihar, Utkal, Madras, Maratha, Gujjar, Punjab, Rajputana' are all Hindus. It is not necessary to talk much about this. It is quite surprising, though, that in spite of learning the *Shastras* she makes such remarks.

Anurupa Devi has reasons for supporting child marriage. Bhudev Mukhopadhyay,[12] her grandfather, was in favour of child marriage. Her reverence for her grandfather is praiseworthy, but is there any reason for everybody else to support this view?

She has relegated Bankim-Vidyasagar[13] and placed Bhudev babu on a higher pedestal. She has cited Bhudev babu's opinion every now and then ... a lot of his ideas or advice are impeccable and beneficial to society, but are all his ideas infallible and irrefutable? In one place Bhudev babu has mentioned, 'Even if the mother is weak, the child will not be harmed, it will be strong if its father is strong. Because, the offspring of a weak cow and a strong bull is always strong.' But if both cow and bull are strong, then the offspring is bound to be healthy and strong. This is evident in the cattle of Europe and America. This same rule applies to human beings too. If both the parents are healthy the child will be healthy and well-formed; the people of Europe and America are evidence of this fact.

However learned Anurupa Devi might have been, she could not have supported child marriage if she had at least some knowledge of medical science. Of course she can say, what is the need for women to learn medical science? There are so many male doctors in the country, must they starve?

In the essay on child marriage, Anurupa Devi, discarding the restrictions imposed by freedom, has let her pen flow freely to discuss such issues which are permissible in feminine conversations only ... inappropriate for publication in a monthly magazine. Further discussion on this matter will end up transgressing the boundaries of good taste.

It is even more amusing to note that 'a girl should get married in her childhood, but if a desirable groom is not available then it is better to allow her to remain a spinster forever, but not to hand her over to an unsuitable groom.' The logic is sound indeed. For how many years does this childhood last? Twelve? ... if the groom is found one-two years later, then there is no point in giving her in marriage to him because by then the daughter will be in her youth. If she gets married then, how can that be counted as child marriage? ...

Even in ancient times, marriages used to take place in our country at the prime of youth. When mature young women expressed their opinions freely in the royal courts about their choices and willingly chose their own husbands, only then were such men born who were as powerful as Bhima-Arjuna,[14] as restrained as Bhisma,[15] as truthful as Rama, and as affectionate towards his wife as Aja. When the physical development of women was complete, they would get married in order to conceive children. The children of mature mothers were able-bodied, powerful and intelligent. After the introduction of child marriage and the harem,[16] men have become weaker day by day. It is easily understood that the child of an undeveloped mother can never be a proportionately structured human being. This is evident even in the plant kingdom. It does not take long to realize this fact if we look at the present generation of short, underweight men. Looking at the western world we find both men and women to be well structured. They are healthy, powerful and well developed. What is the reason behind this? They are not born of physically weak, imprisoned mothers; their mothers do not survive on the food thrown away by men.

By torturing women, men lose their strength, intellect, longevity, independence, everything. Yet they are not conscious of the fact. Has the western world faced any degradation because of the equality of men and women in their society? Day by day Europe has been surprising the world through its numerous new discoveries and inventions. However lavishly they might lead their lives, it would have been impossible without their great inherent strength. But how has our country benefited from putting the child widow on a pedestal, taking away all rights from her and keeping her confined in darkness forever? When there were women like Draupadi, Kunti, Satyabati—was our country developed then or is it developed now in this era of 'goddesses'? Complete independence for men and women can never harm a country or a race. Mental qualities like affection, love and charity, and physical strength blossom only in independence. Nothing can develop if it is curbed.

Men have made women extravagant to satisfy their own desires; and for the sake of their family life and for their own advantage they have kept women as servants. Women have not been granted equal status in terms of knowledge and education. That's why women lament that since they have not been given the opportunity, they have not been able to develop. But expecting help from men would lead to nothing; women shall have to take care of themselves.

If men had a little bit of respect, honour and faith in women, then their position would not have been like this today. 'Women can't keep things to themselves', 'what can a woman understand of this?' 'Women have disastrous ideas'—do these words mark a great respect towards women? ... Those who consider women as insufferable leeches sucking strength, virility, blood, flesh, wealth, happiness—how can they honour women as goddesses? Those who consider women as gateways to hell, how do they call her goddess?

Those who utter contradictory words from the same mouth—which one of their statements should be considered true? Again—

Na danena, na manena narjonena na sevaya
Na shashtrena na shashtrena sarvada vishamastriyah.

(Neither sacrificial offering nor honour nor oblation/neither the scriptures nor weapons, women are deemed for none of these)

When the ear, used to hearing 'goddess', hears these words it becomes clear that the term 'goddess' is nothing but an elaborate joke! By observing the norms made for women by men, by analysing the position and rights of women in society, it is clear that men do not at all believe in women's venerability. ... Just to serve certain purposes they have diverted women's attention and called them goddesses. Men know very well that women are not goddesses.

Today we are declaring in unison that we are indeed not 'goddesses'. You have never placed us on that pedestal, you have never treated us with that respect either; you have just given us the name of goddess. And we have been stupid enough to remain satisfied with that. Human beings commit errors, but those errors do not remain forever. Our mistake, too, has been rectified. We are human beings, not goddesses, and we can never become goddesses in your hands.

Translated by Swagata Bhattacharya
Department of Comparative Literature, Jadavpur University

'*Narir Abastha*', *Bharati*, mid-February to mid-March 1924/Falgun 1330 BS, barsha 47 (year 47), sankhya 11 (no. 11), pp. 1046-53.

Notes

1 In the Ashvin edition of *Bharati*, Anurupa Devi has said, 'Why are the upper-caste women worried about women like Abhaya? She has chosen her own destiny. Will our beloved writer-friend be able to accept her as her own daughter-in-law?' ... We may not be ready to accept Abhaya as our daughter-in-law, but if one of our unfortunate daughters went the wrong way... shall we, as women, not try to save her? Will the mother ... not long for the daughter to come out and lead a normal life once again? A mother wants nothing short of good for a bad boy. Jatindra babu and Anurupa Devi need to place Abhaya in the position of their daughters and think whether they have any duty towards her. (*Note*: This footnote is provided by the writer and translated here. For details on Abhaya, see Essay 11, n9.)

2 Zainab bint Jahsh was a wife of Prophet Muhammad, and therefore, also called the Mother of the Believers. Before her marriage to the Prophet, she was briefly married to Zayd ibn Harithah, his adopted son.

3 'Enoch Arden' is a poem by Alfred Tennyson published in 1864. The hero of the poem, Enoch Arden leaves his wife, Annie, and three children to go to sea with his old captain. Enoch, who had turned into a sailor from being a fisherman, as he needed the job to provide for his family. However, during his voyage his ship is wrecked and he remains lost and missing for ten years. After his long absence, when he finally returns home he finds that his wife, who believed he was dead, is married happily to his childhood friend Philip and also has a child with him. Annie had known both men since her childhood, and this had made the friendship between Enoch and Philip, not a very comfortable one. Extremely heartbroken, not only because he had lost his family, but also because he had lost his family to

someone he had always thought of as his competitor, he never tells his wife and children that he is alive and dies a tragic death.

4 Jaladahar Sen was one of the editors of the Bengali monthly *Bharatbarsha*, which was published from 1913. Also see n 7.

5 *Manusmriti* is one of the earliest *Dharmasastras* in India.The *Dharmashastra* is presented in the form of a discourse from Manu or the father of all mankind to a group of rishis who want to know the laws that all must follow. The stance of the *Manusmriti* about women has also been debated. While certain verses such as (III - 55, 56, 57, 59, 62) glorify the position of women, other verses (IX - 3, 17) seem to attack the position and freedom of women. The education of women is also discussed in the text. Certain interpretations of Verse (IX - 18) claim that it discourages women from reading Vedic scriptures. Verse (II-240), however, allows women to read Vedic scriptures. Similar contradictory phrases are encountered in relation to child marriage in verses (IX-94 and IX-90). Following are certain excerpts from Chapter 9 where Manu deems women as unfit for independence in their lives. Parashar's *Brihat Parashara Hora Shastra* is considered to be a seminal work on Indian astrology. Parashar does not have views on women as such but in his lengthy exposition on astrology he writes about the planetary positions in the natal charts of a woman that must be considered when a man is forming an alliance. In the chapter called the '*Yuvati Bhava*', Parashar talks at length about the astrological alignments that a man must keep in mind for a happy marriage; also see Essay 30).

6 See Essay 11, n8.

7 *Bharatbarsha* was a popular Bengali monthly magazine. It was first published in August 1913 and edited by Jaladhar Sen and Amulya Charan Vidyabhusan.

8 *Ekadashi* literally means eleven, *ek+ dus*, i.e., one+ ten. There are two ekadashis a month, ekadashi of the *shukla* (bright) *paksha*—when the moon is the farthest from the earth, and ekadashi of the *krishna* (dark) *paksha*—when the moon is the closest to the earth, in the lunar month of the hindu calendar. Fasting bimonthly on the ekadashis was one of the many ways in which the widows could purge their sins, sins that had also supposedly led to their widowhood.

9 It is a term used by Jatindra babu himself. He says that when a woman marries for the second time, her husband is akin to 'someone else's husband'. Accordingly, the wife by a second marriage should be considered as someone else's wife. (*Note*: This footnote is provided by the writer herself.)

[10] In order to show that just like women who did not choose to remarry, there were even men who did not remarry when their wives died. Rama's story is found in Valmiki's *Ramayana*; Satyaban's in the *Mahabharata*. Aja is Rama's grandfather, and his wife is the celestial being Indumati; their story is told in Kalidasa's *Raghuvamsa*.Rama did not remarry when Sita entered the womb of mother earth; Aja wanted to immolate himself on his wife's funeral pyre. Uma, the wife of Shiva, who did penance in order to become his consort, forcing him to accept her. Sita had a *swayamvara* when she was 12 years old. But one has to notice that the marriage of Rama and Sita happens in the 'Balla Kanda' of the *Ramayana*.

[11] Rani Padmini (Padmavati) was the queen of Chittor and the wife of king Rawal Ratan Singh who had another queen, but went to Singhal for Padmini's swayamvar, defeated Malkhan Singh, and married Padmini. Sultan Alauddin Khilji attacked Chittor to obtain Rani Padmini by force. Ratan Singh was forced to allow the Sultan to see her, a shameful act in those times. Rani Padmini consented, provided the Sultan saw only her reflection in a mirror. The Sultan got Ratan Singh arrested, which led to a great battle between Alauddin Khilji and the Rajputs. Realizing that the Rajputs would lose, the women led by Padmini, committed *jauhar* to avoid being dishonoured by the enemy. A huge pyre was lit and led by their queen all the women of Chittor jumped into the flames.

Sanjukta, daughter of Raja Jaichand of Kanauj, loved Prithviraj Chauhan, the Rajput king of Delhi and Ajmer and a rival of Raja Jaichand. To insult Prithviraj, Raja Jaichand announced a swayamvara for Sanjukta where he invited all kings except Prithviraj and made a clay statue of the latter at the door, resembling a doorman to his court, and Prithviraj hid behind the statue. Sanjukta ignored the rest in the swayamvara and proceeding towards the door to put the garland around the statue of her beloved. At that moment, Prithviraj appeared from behind the statue and whisked her away on his horse and they eloped to Delhi. Owing to the consequent rift between Kanauj and Delhi, when Mohammad Ghori attacked Delhi and Prithviraj asked Kanauj to join in to confront the foreign aggression, Jaichand refused. Delhi was conquered bringing an end to the last Hindu kingdom in Delhi. Maharani Sanjukta committed jauhar. Also see Essay 35, n 5.

[12] Bhudev Mukhopadhyaya (1827–94) was a writer and intellectual in nineteenth-century Bengal. His works were considered ardent displays of nationalism and philosophy in the period of the Bengal Renaissance. In one of his essays, the *Parivarik Prabandha* written in 1882, Bhudev writes that when two young people are united by their parents, they

grow like creepers intertwined into one another. The kind of permanent affection that grows between them can never be the same between adults. He feels that among the young, the senses are irresistible, the imagination is powerful and the attraction is intense. The intelligence and patience that is required to test each other's characters is not usually exhibited by the young ones. One arch look, one peculiarity of movement and a sweet smile is enough to win a young heart. At a young age, one does not reflect too much on matters like the strength of character, taste or disposition.

[13] For details on Bankimchandra Chattopadhyay, see Essay 11, n1. Ishwar Chandra Vidyasagar, 1820–1891 was a polymath and a key figure of the Bengal Renaissance. Philosopher, academic, educator, writer, publisher, entrepreneur and philanthropist, he is best known as a social reformer who tried to ameliorate the status of the high caste Hindu widow, being instrumental in the passing of the Widow Remarriage Act, 1856.

[14] Bhima and Arjuna are the two Pandava brothers who were chosen by Draupadi, during her swayamvara, along with Krishna, as being legitimate to string the bow and lift it. However, Bhima did not attempt doing so and Arjuna won Draupadi who became the wife of the five Pandavas.

[15] Bhisma practiced celibacy and remained a brahmachari, in order to keep his Father's sons by the second marriage to Satyavati free from rival claims to the throne.

[16] The secluded part usually of a Muslim household allotted for women.

13

KAMINI ROY

Kamini Roy (October 1864–November 1933), was born into a Brahmo family, where social reform and education for women were favoured. In 1886, she passed her B.A. with honours in Sanskrit from Bethune College; later becoming a teacher in the same department of the College. She was one of the first women graduates of India. In 1889, at the age of twenty-five, her first book of poetry, *Alo o Chhaya* was published with an introduction by Hemchandra Bandyopadhyay. She was awarded the Jagattarini award by the University of Calcutta. She was also the *Saha-Sabhapati* of the Bangiya Sahitya Parishad between 1932-33. She came from a world which was quite open to westernization. Her father Chandicharan Sen was a sub-judge and her husband Kedarnath Roy was a civil servant. She was one of the first investigators of the Women Labourers Commission (1922–23). Among her many collections of poetry are *Mahashwata o Pundarik, Malya o Nirmalya*.

Dowry (1926)

What is dowry? The money paid by a Bengali father to buy a groom for his daughter is dowry. According to the Hindu religion, marriage is a religious ritual, essential for all and is not contractual. The marital vows cannot be broken. The wife is a true partner in the material as well as religious and spiritual domains. At present, unfortunately, marriage includes a contract in monetary terms, namely, the buying and selling of grooms. In a slave market, slaves are bought and sold while in the marriage market it is the master who is bought. Poor fathers, who do not posses much wealth but have many daughters, are impoverished by the practice of giving dowry. They borrow heavily to marry off their daughters and fall into the debt trap as a result of which their property and home are mortgaged to the moneylender. The poor, who cannot pay dowry or borrow from moneylenders, have to resort to begging from door to door to arrange for their daughters' marriage. The other option is to let the daughters remain unmarried. Both situations are shameful. Many sensitive girls commit suicide to save their parents the burden and the shame of having unmarried daughters.

Yet the evil practice of dowry, which debases both the giver and receiver, cannot be eradicated by society. We demand *swaraj* or self-rule and freedom from foreign rule; we take pride in proclaiming India to be the pinnacle of moral and spiritual wealth. Yet we feel no shame in being slaves to our greed, and disrespect Indian women by continuing the heinous practice of dowry.

Under Indian customs and laws, daughters had no share in the father's property. Those who support the practice of dowry try to justify it by saying that it was the only way for the father to settle a part of his wealth on his daughter. Since the financial responsibility of supporting the wife rested on the husband he had the right to demand some small amount of money from the father of the bride in the form of dowry. If this truly was the motive behind paying dowry then its amount should be according to the capability of the father of the bride. Also, the dowry should remain in the hands of the bride instead of being paid to the greedy husband and father-in-law.

The origins of the evil practice of dowry might be greed or necessity. Whatever be the reason, time has come to eradicate it. It is also necessary to amend the law of inheritance: so the son and daughter should be treated equally and cared for by the parents. Scriptures point out that it is the duty of parents to care for their children, be it son or daughter.

A householder must support his wife, educate his sons and protect his kin and friends. He should care for his daughter in the same way, educate her and marry her to a suitable groom with some wealth.

The scriptures mention of giving wealth to the daughter at her marriage but the amount is not fixed. It would seem plausible that the scriptures do not ask the father of the bride to pay more than his means. Dowry is paid by the father of the bride voluntarily out of love for his daughter and not because he is forced by others.

Child marriage and the joint family system are linked to the practice of dowry. The joint family is disappearing and child marriage has been proved to be harmful. We have also come to realize the importance of women's education for the creation of a healthy social order.

Young girls should remain in the realm of education till the time they reach maturity which is the right time for marriage and motherhood. Then they will surely understand that it is insulting to marry a person bought by their father's money, given in the form of dowry. Nowadays, the amount of dowry varies according to the educational qualifications of the groom. A graduate would demand higher dowry than a matriculate or someone who has passed the intermediate. Educated young women would find such conditions intolerable. They would surely feel insulted and dishonoured at the idea of being bartered like dumb animals or inanimate things. They would find it less undignified to work for their living. In today's world, it is difficult to sustain a household without the women of the family earning a wage. Do women not labour in their parents' or husbands' homes? Many women of poorer households work to sustain their families, sisters work to pay for their brother's education.

If self-respect and financial independence are the results of a proper education, then surely, the young men would not try to marry out of greed before they are financially capable of supporting a family. I argue that there are many young men who believe that the practice of dowry is a crime and wish to root out this evil from our society. I sincerely request all like-minded youths to devote their time and energy to eradicate such customs.

We Indians, especially Bengalis, are emotional. Often we talk a lot about the need for certain actions but do not take active steps to resolve the situation. Simply delivering speeches or shedding tears at the death of a Snehalata[1] or composing poems at her unfortunate death will not end the practice. Passing resolutions against the practice of dowry or organizing discussions, forums would be of no use if we cannot ensure that the practice of dowry is banned. We need to vow never to accept dowry and prevent our friends from taking it as well. We should boycott socially all those who accept dowry. In our country, people are ostracized for trivial reasons. Straying from the rigid rules and customs of society inevitably results in the ostracization of those deemed guilty, as well as the family concerned. All those social reformers who are against the practice of dowry should take steps for socially ostracizing all grooms who agree to take dowry and those people who encourage and tempt them to do so. The practice could be rooted out in this manner. Amendment of inheritance laws, eradication of child marriage and emphasis on women's education would also help in eradicating the custom of taking dowry.

Translated by Prakriti Mitra
School of Women's Studies, Jadavpur University

'Barpan', *Bangalakshmi*, mid-April to mid-May 1926/Baisakh 1333 BS.

Also available in *Kamini Rayer Agranthita Gadya Rachana*, compiled by Abhijit Sen and Anindita Bhaduri (Kolkata: Dey's Publishing and the School of Women's Studies, Jadavpur University), April 2005/Baisakh 1412 (BS), pp. 37–39.

Note

[1] See Essay 9, note 1.

14

FAZILATUNNESA

Fazilatunnesa (1905–75) was the first Muslim student at Bethune College, receiving her B.A. in 1923. She was also the first Muslim boarder in the college hostel. She was not only the first among the Bengali Muslim women to study for an M.A., but also the first Muslim female student at the University of Dhaka where she completed her M.A. degree. In 1928, she went abroad to study further. She taught mathematics in Bethune College and was also the vice-principal of the same institution. After Partition, she migrated to East Pakistan and became the principal of Eden College in Dhaka.

Freedom for Muslim Women (1929)

All those who have tried to open their eyes just a little must have clearly seen the extraordinary challenges that the Muslim community has had to face in this country. The only solution to all those problems is one's own discernment and conscience. So, I am expressing here whatever little I could think of, given my knowledge and common sense. If my words hurt the sentiments of some, please forgive me, for I mean no offence.

'Freedom for Muslim women'—here 'freedom' stands for the freedom of the soul, and freedom of the soul means the independence of thought and expression that can be useful for society and the world at large, which can stimulate one's own reasoning and intellectual growth. The scriptures, sayings of holy men, and so on, are also ways of developing one's powers of reasoning. The very purpose of these is lost, however, if the mind is numbed into irrational fanaticism.

The world is ever changing. Strong gusts of the nineteenth century have shaken the age-old dormant spirit of Muslim woman. This movement has forced them to look outside, to look at other women; and having realized the magnitude of their physical and mental degradation, and their lack of rights, they are thoroughly ashamed. The woman shall no longer remain an object of another's sensuous gratification, she will not forget her womanhood and selfhood. Enfolded in the veil of illusion, the woman has, for too long, kept herself away from enjoying the beauteous world. But today, the repentant woman wants to snap the noose of fragility and luxury, and establish contact with the world outside. Every woman's mind has rebelled today. But she lacks the very weapons of this battle, that is, education and knowledge. All she has in abundance is apathy towards the self, heart-wrenching remorse, and above all, an insurmountable desire for freedom. Just like a sinner's deep remorse burns his sin and purges him, the woman's self-reproach transforms her into a proper human being. However, the prerequisite for this is education. When I say education, I don't mean being stamped with a certain number of degrees; education is that which trains and nurtures the mind, directs and polishes the ability for reason: that is education; it is that which gives strength to the personality and dignity to a being. That is education! The education of Muslim women generally means having a couple of Bengali books, writing a few letters, and learning the Arabic that is taught by heart like a parrot without understanding anything. I am not against the learning of Arabic—all I mean to say is that learning the language of religion[1] without even understanding it, is as good as learning a foreign language.

The number of Muslim girls in primary schools is much higher than non-Muslim girls, but by the time one reaches the university, these Muslim girls disappear. Many may think, why should girls study all that much? But, I think, at least from what I have seen that sometimes this partial education becomes dangerous and leads to a dramatic fanatical turmoil. The pride that they are a little educated often stays with many of these women. So, I want to re-affirm that primary education is not all, that sometimes incompleted learning invites only more trouble. Of course, I also agree that with the systematic spread of education, this pride will fade into an eagerness to learn more. These women can bask in self-glory and throw their weight around only because there are just about one or two educated girls every now and then. When every girl gets educated, there will be no one to throw these tantrums.

If Muslim women are not nurtured to become capable, will this society ever develop? Men who bestow every worth upon us do not help us. Women have to take upon themselves the responsibility of their own education. It is they who have to redefine themselves as able human beings of this society. Instead of begging like paupers, throwing themselves at men's feet, suffering their slights and insults, women have to fight like brave warriors to reclaim their rights and dignity, freeing their entire species from suffocating shackles. Where there is no education, there is no courage; but this education has to be earned.

The shackles that have been forced around the feet of Muslim women, the shackles that have portrayed them as poor, lowly and distressed woman before civilized society, must be broken into fragments, the feet may bleed and the wounds could be deep, but freedom from insult, and the freedom from shame shall be their glorious victory. The shackles have not just fettered women, barring them from the rights they deserve; they have also steadily drawn the entire Muslim community towards doom.

Probably many understand that the development of any society depends largely on its women, yet, those who pretend not to know the extent of their involvement, those who fail to respect and acknowledge their indebtedness to their contribution—women must refrain from accepting their pretentious gratitude, for it is not heart-felt, only a mockery.

I think it will not be a bad idea to treat the men in the same way that a woman is treated: always caged inside; held back from breathing, feeling and seeing the beauty around her, left suffocated, preventing the rays of knowledge from reaching her mind. I think, no one will ever say that women alone are responsible for all the sins in the world. Then why shall a woman remain imprisoned? And if she is, even men should be; because, every living being has equal rights and demands of living freely on this earth.

Satitva or chastity has been held as one of the most important virtues of a woman, unanimously across the ages. But when the woman, who lives caged behind bolted doors and windows, where even the rays of the sun do not touch her is called a *sati*,[2] what value does her satitva hold? The real sati is the woman who lives actively in the world, overcomes all obstacles, and protects herself from its temptations. The scriptures of Islam have never declared that women shall be imprisoned in cages; instead, Islam talks about giving women the rights they deserve; it is even mentioned that they will be judged for their actions. If this be so, then a woman too has every right to educate herself and independently choose the way she wants to live.

The kind of education that is imparted in schools is definitely not the ideal education. But this form of education is at least better than sitting at home and accepting whatever is said, like a blind fool. The issue of education is, indeed, a complex one! Everyone has his own opinion on the ideal form of education. Leaving all of that aside, I have in mind some ideas about a form of education for Muslim girls that has resulted from my gross intelligence, which I shall now outline.

We are far behind other women. The ones who take the first steps would probably have to forget about achieving the paradise of our imagination. Since we have been sent to this earth, it is but desirable that we develop some understanding and learn to walk hand-in-hand with others, instead of stumbling around one place like the fixed, immobile root. Women's education is the most important building block of any civilized or successful society. I think translating books over many many days and making speeches that stretch across several pages is not going to help. One has to put in real effort. The Muslim girl has to be educated. Higher education may not be possible for many, especially for the poor. If the women whose fathers can afford to educate them, choose to try and help their kind, only then can we think of progressing. If a small group of such women can be formed now, something really large can be achieved later. Eden School[3] or Bethune College[4] were not built in one day. What had started with a handful of young students has over a period developed into large centres of education. If Muslim girls did something similar over a period of time, even they could establish two or four schools and colleges and educate other Muslim girls in accordance with the Muslim philosophy of life. Not just that, they may have something like Bethune School, where if they want even they can, at least to avenge themselves, say, 'This school will not permit non-Muslim girls.'[5] Only in this way, with immense hard work, can the Muslim woman achieve freedom in the future, or else, we shall remain deluged in darkness and ignorance till eternity.

It is my ardent request to all my young Muslim brothers that they should let their sisters rise: only then can we hope for freedom. Or else, not only will the sisters be doomed, but the humanity of the brothers will also be extinguished for ever. Hence, I make an appeal to them and pray that they should try to be instrumental in the freedom of the Muslim women.

Translated by Anindita Roy
Department of Comparative Literature, Jadavpur University

'*Muslim Narir Mukti*', *Saogat*, mid-August to mid-September 1929/ Bhadra 1336 BS.

Also available in *Zenana Mehfil: Bangali Musalman Lekhikader Nirbachita Rachana 1904- 1938*, edited by Shaheen Akhtar and Moushumi Bhowmik (Kolkata: Stree, 1998), pp. 167–70.

Notes

1 *Dharmabhasha* is the word used, meaning the language of religion.

2 Refers to Shiva's wife who entered the sacrificial fire, distressed by an insult to her husband; a chaste woman.

3 Nabakanta and Brajasundar Mitra, Members of the Brahmo Samaj in Dhaka, responded to the government's encouragement of education for girls by converting a female adult school into a girls' school in 1878. The management was handed over to the government and the school renamed as Eden School in honour of Sir Ashley Eden, the Lieutenant Governor, who supported female education. In 1880, according to *Bamabodhini Patrika*, out of 153 students, one was a Muslim. By 1911, there were twenty-five Muslim girls, two hundred and nine Hindus, eight Christians, one Parsee and one Eurasian. See also, S. Amin, *The World of Muslim Women in Colonial Bengal 1876-1939* (The Hague: Brill, 1996).

4 The first women's college in India, founded as a school in 1849 with the active participation of John Drinkwater Bethune, Law Member, Governor General's Council, who donated his house and funds to the school. In 1879 a college was founded so that women could study for university degrees. In 1883 Kadambini Bose and Chandramukhi Basu qualified in the degree examinations of the University of Calcutta; in 1888 Bethune College received affiliation to the University of Calcutta up to the B.A. level.

5 The author suggests that the new college, which was essentially built for the education of Muslim girls, could also practice similar discriminations against Hindus to avenge themselves.

15

SANTISUDHA GHOSH

Santisudha Ghosh (1907-92) completed her M.A. from Presidency College. In Barisal, she formed a students and youth committee called the Santibahini. She was also the President of the Barisal Zilla Congress Committee. She wrote several stories to inspire the nationalist movement. During the 1930s she was a teacher at the Sadar Balika Vidyalaya, Barisal, a school for girls, inspiring her students to fight for freedom. While pursuing her M.A. degree, she got involved in the Chatri Sangha founded by Kalyani Bhattacharya. This was the time when she wrote *Golokdhandha*, a novel, which was published in *Jayasree* serially. During 1930, another novel named *1930 Sal* was published. This novel was based on the Chittagong Armoury Raid by the militant freedom fighters in East Bengal (today's Bangladesh).

Shell Bangles–Vermillion–Veil (1938)

It is not as if this arrangement is made in our society alone; it is present in many civilized and uncivilized societies of the world, as we know. When the new bride covers her head with a *ghomta*, an end of the sari, adorns her forehead and the parting of her hair with vermillion and stands before us shyly, she looks quite beautiful. The white shell bangles on her hand are not immediately visible, the bride knows that the bangles are so necessary; they are indispensable for her. These three ornaments together bring about an unprecedented beauty on her form and mind, which she herself considers beyond expression, and prompts everyone else to say so as well. Perhaps because of this reason, modern women, who have discarded many social customs, have not yet been able to reject these three signs. Covering the head (with a ghomta) has become less common now; the removal of the practice of the purdah has caused the steady decrease of the length of the ghomta which has now been limited to the top of the coiffure, but no one has yet had the courage to discard the covering altogether. The white shell bangles or *sankha* still add to the beauty of the womanly form along with other ornaments, but many do not consider them as indispensable as before. But the vermillion, *sindur,* remains triumphant and is above all; I have yet to see anyone who has freed herself of its alluring spell. Even the women of the Brahmo Samaj, the Brahmikas, who have rebelled against many negative customs of Hindu society and become part of the emancipated group, still sport the sindur, associated with Hindu norms, upon their foreheads proudly. More surprisingly, I have seen even Bengali Christian women and Muslim women, wearing vermillion.

There is something wrong with my own nature. I am unable to satisfy myself with a partial understanding of anything, and curiosity prompts me to get to the root of the matter. Hence, I often think many things about the custom of sankha-sindur; perhaps these thoughts are redundant. But can anyone actually explain women's attraction towards and society's strict requirement of the customs of sankha-sindur and ghomta as being indispensable to married life? I admit that these look beautiful, and perhaps that is why the Brahmo and Christian women are desirous of accepting them despite there being no compulsion. But is this beauty an attribute of the vision or an attribute of the mind? I do not understand how by covering her head with the end of her sari and adorning the parting of her hair with a streak of vermillion the visible beauty of a young maiden with a hitherto uncovered head would suddenly increase manifold. If, for the purposes of debate, one does accept that this is so, then what is the sin in adopting this method of beautification even when a woman is unmarried? As there is a tradition of wearing a vermillion dot upon the forehead even for unmarried women, and Brahmo, Christian and Muslim women, even if unmarried, begin to cover their heads on reaching a certain age, it is meaningless to think that these adornments take on some kind of inexpressible allure and impart some novel dimension to the womanly form only after a woman is married and not otherwise. That we consider these as indispensable additions to the beauty of the bride, which cannot be otherwise attained, is the result of our entrenched belief. Seeing these customs being followed everywhere since birth and reading descriptions of them in literature and scripture, we have become so used to this picture that anything different from this strikes us as lacking in beauty. We seem to associate these symbolic representations with the woman's love for her husband and the auspiciousness that she represents. So, Hindu women cannot do without them. . . . the absence of any one of them, especially the vermillion, automatically disturbs the mind, signalling some sort of a bad omen . . .

I am neither for nor against the discarding of the sankha-sindur-ghomta. Because these are merely external ornaments, added to the many embellishments of women, there is no harm in their being or not being adopted. But we must consider why it was decreed that some visible signs must mark out the woman's body as soon as she acquires a husband. This arrangement is not exclusive to our society alone; as we are aware, many civilized and uncivilized societies of the world have such customs. But Hindu society's extra effort to impose artificial differences between men and women and make their inequality an inherent part of the social organization causes them to overdo it. There is a specific difference between married and unmarried life, and there can be no objection if specific practices and customs or external signs in dress and so on are fabricated in order to demarcate this difference. In fact, in certain cases, it is beneficial for married couples to preserve such a difference. Just as a man and a woman go through the rites of matrimony to obtain social sanction for their desire to live together as husband and wife, so also, as long as the relationship remains, accepting some form of external sign in behaviour or dress in order to convey its continuing stability does not seem to be a bad idea.

The question arises: why does this matter have to be one-sided? What are we to make of the fact that the woman announces her acquisition of a husband with much fanfare, but there is no such compulsion on the part of a man to mark his married status? The wife wears vermillion, the husband too may adorn himself with a *tilak*. Just as covering her head is imperative for a woman, similarly, the use of a shawl might be made compulsory for a man (I am not going so far as to suggest that he must cover himself with it). As unmarried women do not wear white shell bangles or, in some areas iron bangles until they are married, when it becomes mandatory, a similar mandate may be proclaimed for men that unless they are married they are to refrain from wearing rings on their fingers; or at the very least, let something of this nature occur. In other words, if the organizers of society had so desired, they should have made similar provisions for men too. But they have not. . . . In the absence of any such arrangement, we cannot but conclude that the love towards her husband may be recognized as the woman's greatest vocation, her dharma, but the husband's love for his wife may not be considered as his duty or even a necessity by society. . . .

This leads to a single conclusion that the main aim of our social organizers was to circumscribe the meaning of women's lives completely by matrimony. Simultaneously, though men avail of the advantages of married life in equal measure, they have no social compulsion to acknowledge it as an important part of their existence, let alone allow their lives to be totally regulated by it. The lives of men have been shaped to a great extent by their human identity, but the lives of women, instead of being conceived of as human, have been fragmented, separated from the broad spectrum of humanity and confined within the bounds of matrimony. (In this context, it will not be redundant to note that in our society, there is no place for the woman as a woman. She is not to be accepted as a virgin, but as a married woman or a widow, in other words, an identity derived from matrimony, which means the stages and the organization of her life are regulated by the institution of marriage). . . . It is futile to deny that these symbols of marriage for women are alluring webs of *maya* within which the woman's mind is entrapped so as to indelibly imprint upon her consciousness that her life follows that of her husband. The virgin unmarried woman sees that as soon as she accepts her husband unto herself, the appearances and practice of her outer as well as inner self are completely changed; the agonized gaze of the widow sees exactly the same thing. The same woman—as a virgin, as a woman blessed with a husband and as a woman who has lost her husband—ends up becoming three different persons in clothing, food and behaviour, in ritual and custom and practice. What amazing power the husband has! But a man, from childhood till old age, cannot be pinned down from any quarter to make it obvious for others to gauge whether he is married or unmarried, a widower or possessed of a wife. This means that he is not bothered at all by his marital status. It is mainly because the woman's mind must be shielded from all thoughts of independent identity that the shell bangles, vermillion and so on have been decreed and implemented with such force.

But there is another reason at the root of all this. As soon as she gets married, the Hindu woman becomes the property of her swami (notice, in this case, the etymology of the word 'swami', which means master). Prior to her marriage, even if she has her father and brothers, she is not considered to be their responsibility. This means that while she is unmarried, any man may desire her to the extent that even if they are unable to control their lust and actually acquire her, such acts are still accepted by the Hindu *Shastras*. But there is no such allowance granted the moment she becomes married. No one can touch even a strand of her hair because she is the property of someone else. The Hindu *Shastras* have no stringent norms about the Hindu girl child, but there is no dearth of stricture to police the wife of another man (otherwise men themselves will be put in a tight spot). Hence, unless a virgin is made to appear different from a married woman with clear and visible markers, men are liable to be misled into error. In other words, it is difficult for them to decide whether they have the right to freely lust for her or not. Hence, shell bangles and vermillion are indispensable signs to prevent mistakes. Men have never required similar trademarks because the married man has never been seen as his wife's property. If an unmarried girl is attracted towards a man, it is not necessary for her to know whether he is married or not. This is because Hindu society allows polygamy generously and freely, so all you need in such a case is an exchange of garlands. The question of a married woman being attracted to another man does not arise because she does not even have the right to glance upon 'another' man, so feelings of attraction–repulsion are quite beyond her.

Let me say a few words about the covering of the head. Though only married women do so in Hindu society, among the Brahmo, Christian and Muslim communities, women start this practice around the time they reach puberty, which I have already referred earlier. This indicates that this practice is not a declaration of the married state as much as that of nobility and an attempt to shield the beautiful virgin body from the gaze of men. Everyone knows that this is the root of the purdah practice. But these days, one does not see women covering their faces in such a manner (I leave out of reckoning the Muslim women who use the burqa). It is now just a formal mark of earlier practices. So its relevance is more symbolic than functional. And even if we think of this as a symbol, it is hardly indicative of any deep respect shown to womankind; rather it may be construed as quite insulting to the masculine nature. The attempt to conceal oneself from the gaze of men, which underlies the practice of veiling, makes it clear that the more debauched the nature of men in a particular society, the more pronounced becomes the need for concealing the woman behind a veil. And, the practice of covering one's head and face is a residue of such uncivilized societies, whose memory we have kept alive in modern times as well.

Using simple shell bangles, vermillion and the ghomta as the fulcrum, I have commented many things. These signs may be trivial but the concatenation of causes behind them is so deeply entrenched and influence our society in such grave yet subtle ways that every educated man and woman must give some thought to their continued existence and effect. How far it is useful to preserve those trivial practices rooted in uncivilized barbaric times, clearly fostering inequality and partiality towards a certain group only because they are part of tradition and hence bind us in nostalgia, is a matter for serious contemplation.

Translated by Ipshita Chanda
Department of Comparative Literature, Jadavpur University

'Sankha-Sindur-Ghomta', Mandira, mid-May to mid-June 1938/ Jaishtha 1345 BS, pp. 66-69.

Also available in *Santisudha Ghosh: Nirbachita Rachana Samkalan,* edited by Sarmistha Dutta Gupta (Kolkata: Dey's Publishing and School of Women's Studies, Jadavpur University, June 2008), Asarh 1415 BS, pp. 45–48.

PART II

THE EMERGING 'NEW' WOMAN

16

ANONYMOUS

An Attempt To Save the Orphaned and Fallen Women (1882)

Almost fourteen or fifteen years ago, a woman from a good American family came to Calcutta. There are many Christian missionaries in this country who bring teachers from England and America and send them to families of the bhadralok to teach the scriptures. The woman, mentioned earlier, came to this country to work as a teacher under the aegis of such missionaries. She had already decided to be a nun so that she could spread Christianity, which she adored and followed, to every household.

She began her work when she came to Calcutta, simultaneously taking up another venture. Readers might know that many ailing people came to the Calcutta Medical College Hospital[1] for treatment and did not get the kind of care they received at home or from their close relatives. There was no one even to speak a few comforting words to them. When they felt low because of their painful illnesses, there would be no one at hand to turn their minds to religious thoughts. This kind woman decided that each Sunday, when she did not have any work, she would go to the hospital. She would nurse the patients and read the Bible to them. Days passed in this manner. She was so caring, loving, kind and gentle that many patients earnestly waited for her every Sunday. She helped many patients who missed their mothers and sisters.

At that time a few European prostitutes were being treated at that hospital. These unfortunate women had come to Calcutta to earn their living, but had strayed into evil, and faced great sufferings. The devout woman felt unhappy when she learnt about these women. She sat beside them like a sister and interpreted the meaning of religion to them, read religious books to them and showed them the horrible nature of evil. Once, one of these unfortunate women told her with tear-filled eyes, 'Sister! Why do you talk about religion? We have no way to return to the honest path in life. No relatives will take us back. No friend cares for us. Society also bars its door against us. It leaves us in this hellish condition to live in this way until our deaths. Could you give us shelter and rescue us from this ignominious life? If not, then please do not raise hopes of our repentance through religion.'

These words pierced the kind devout heart of that noble woman. When she had decided to read religious books to the patients every Sunday, she had not even imagined that she would have to take the responsibility. She returned home, thinking of what she could do to help them. God helps those who helps themselves. When a friend and his wife came to know about her distress, they agreed to provide shelter for the women in their house, and the woman, Sister Phi—[2] happily accepted their offer. She continued to work on Sundays at the hospital, and gradually two or three other women in similar straits begged for shelter. Then it became necessary to rent a house. Sister Phi—rented a house to which she brought them and became their supervisor. She took donations to meet the expenses as her main duty was to educate and protect them.

The number of women gradually increased, and it became difficult to bear the expenses with donations. The problem deepened. One day, there was no money to cover the expenses of even a single day. The large-hearted woman felt very low. She did not know where the money would come from. On the one hand, she was so indebted that it did not seem right to take more loans. On the other hand, there were so many helpless women depending upon her. In this painful condition, she shut herself in her room and succumbed to tears. She cried out, 'O God! Do I have to abandon them at last when I have brought them away from their earlier paths of evil?' She wept and prayed to God, 'O God! I am the daughter of a poor man and a helpless woman. Do I have the power to take care of these women? If you rescued them from evil, give me the power to look after them.'

The next morning, something surprising happened: a friend donated a large amount. She was free of the worry of debt, her work proceeded smoothly and she did not have to keep asking for money. Eventually the government came to know about her noble mission and gave her a large piece of land, where she built a huge house for such women with an expenditure of Rs 75,000. At least twenty to twenty-five women were sheltered and educated in that home. Every year many women from this home found work outside. Some got married and lived happily. Some were well educated and became teachers. This great woman is still alive, still working with enthusiasm, sincerity and unshakable belief in God. Hence, we are not disclosing her name here.

Who would not be moved knowing about this kind woman? This is only one example. There are several women who became nuns to sacrifice their bodies and minds to serve God's great design. In our unfortunate country, women have no life of their own apart from being confined to their marital homes. Even the innumerable child widows in Hindu society have no other way of living than to depend upon others' mercy. Certainly, there are many widows in the darkness of the inner quarters, who can do much for this world by serving God's purpose. But the goodness of their hearts is diminished. The real development of society will be possible when the women of this country will lead their lives by following a holy and religious path; depending upon God's blessing and mercy; and taking steps to eradicate the agony of the country, wiping out the pain of people, obliterating the poverty of the poor and rescuing the fallen.

Translated by Sanchayita Paul
Department of English, North Bengal University

'Anatha o Patita Ramaniganer Uddhar Cheshta', Bamabodhini Patrika, September 1882/Bhadra 1289 BS, kalpa 2, bhag 4 (part 4), sankhya 212 (no. 212)2, pp. 138–41.

Notes

[1] Established in 1835 in Kolkata, it was the first college of European medicine in Asia. The main objective was to train the natives about the medical practices prevalent in Europe.

[2] This is how she is addressed in the original article.

17

SWARNAKUMARI DEVI

Swarnakumari Devi (1855-1932) was the daughter of Debendranath Tagore and Sarada Devi and an elder sister of Rabindranath Tagore. Educated at home, she was married to Janakinath Ghoshal, a deputy magistrate, at the age of twelve. She played a key role in the cultural and literary activities of her natal family, the Tagores of Jorasanko. She was a poet, a novelist, a literary editor and a committed social worker. From 1885 to 1894 and 1908 to 1914, she edited *Bharati*, a distinguished literary journal. In 1886, she established the Sakhi Samiti for orphans and widows. In 1888, the first Mahila Shilpa Mela or women's crafts fair was organized by the Sakhi Samiti on the grounds of Bethune School (founded in 1849). In 1905, the national handicrafts fair had become an integral part of the protest against the Partition of Bengal 1905. For her contributions to literature, she was awarded the Jagattarini Gold Medal by Calcutta University in 1927. In 1929, she became the president of the Bangiya Sahitya Sammelan, the Bengali literary conference. She was one of the few women who attended the Indian National Congress Conference at Bombay in 1889. Among her novels are *Deepnirban (1870), Chinna Mukul* (translated as *A Broken Bud), Snehalata ba Palita* (translated as *Snehalata or the Adopted), Kahake* (1892–93), considered as her best work, was translated as *The Unfinished Song* in 1898. She wrote two plays, *Bibaha Utsav* and *Pakchakra Gatha*. A collection of her poems came out as *Kabita o Gaan,* and one of her songs as *Geetiguccha*. She wrote twenty-five books in Bengali.

Another Proposal (1886)

In the last Baisakh number of *Bharati* (mid-April to mid-May 1885), this writer had discussed to what extent the progress of the country depended upon the proper education of women, and proposed that a *samiti* or society be formed to allow the women confined to the antahpur, the inner house, to meet educated women. Some successful, learned women have enthusiastically taken up this proposal, and, accordingly, set up a society known as Sakhi Samiti, a society of female friends. This samiti now brings 'Another Proposal' to the public.

Everyone is concerned about Hindu widows. Some hearts have softened at their plight, and people have begun to make whole-hearted efforts for their remarriages. Many of the widows are considered as millstones hanging around the necks of their less endowed householders, who provide the widow food and clothes with much difficulty. The widow too accepts this charity with tears; this is enough to cause friction between them. The householder thinks, I have put my heart and soul into providing food and clothing for her, yet she is not satisfied; the widow thinks, alas! how cruel is destiny that I have to bear such insults for a handful of rice.

Now the samiti proposes that younger Hindu widows must be educated in the ordinary way and become teachers of the women of the inner house and of their children thereby getting involved in some work beneficial to the country. If the unprotected widows are able to earn a living from such good works, they would be spared many insulting situations and harsh words and their relatives too could be at peace. We do not wish to prevent those widows who desire to get married from doing so. Our request is directed at those who wish to follow the customs of widowhood outlined in the Hindu *Shastras*. Hindu customs and beliefs will not be changed a whit if this is done. Charity and a life in accordance with dharma are approved in the *Shastras* as befitting work for a widow. There is no gift greater than that of education. Doing well for others is the greatest dharma. If Hindu widows take upon themselves the responsibility for educating the women in the inner house, much good would come of it. Now women of the Christian faith fulfil this task. Many families do not let these women enter their inner houses for fear of losing their dharma. These women also do not know Bengali well. In many other matters, too, the way they impart education is not satisfactory. Moreover, the kind of education that must be given to women in these times is beyond their capacity. The education that will preserve the Hindu faith in their hearts and simultaneously enliven deep love for the country is today most important and necessary. Whether men or women, all humans have their first steps in learning guided by women. Education during childhood is the basis of all education. If women's hearts are aflame with love for their country, their love will spread fast throughout the land. This education can never be imparted by women from abroad. So we make repeated pleas to Hindu widows that they should come forward in this sphere, putting their hearts and minds to the task. After acquiring the necessary training, let them come forth like embodiments of love for the country and enter the inner houses, and suffuse those rooms with their deepest feelings and examples. Thus they will be fulfilling the dharma of widowhood for the benefit of selves, relatives and the entire country.

If a young widow, without the means of livelihood, takes a firm decision to devote herself to work for the country and wishes to be educated to this end, then this samiti will take it as one of its main aims to help her. The samiti accepts donations to this end, and the money that has been thus collected is enough to finance the education of some widows at Bethune School. Education at Bethune School is comparatively cheap, and the members of the samiti will be at hand to help and guide them if they are admitted.[1] If the widows do not live on the school premises and go there only to study, then one expects that this will not detract them from their dharma in any way. When they finish their own education and start teaching in the antahpur, they will be given a salary by the samiti.

We are very eager to hear the responses to this proposal from the widows themselves, as well as their friends and relatives.

Translated by Ipshita Chanda
Department of Comparative Literature, Jadavpur University

'Ar Ekti Prastab', Bharati o Balak, mid-April to mid-May 1886/Baisakh 1293 BS.

Also available in *Swarnakumari Devir Rachana Samkalan*, edited by Abhijit Sen and Anindita Bhaduri (Kolkata: Deys Publishing and School of Women's Studies, Jadavpur University, mid-September to mid-October/Ashvin 1407), pp. 267-69.

Note

[1] John Elliot Drinkwater Bethune (1801–51) was a barrister and in 1849 founded an institution for women's education in Calcutta. With the support of Dakshinaranjan Mukherjee, Ramgopal Ghosh, Iswar Chandra Vidyasagar, and Madan Mohan Tarkalankar, John Drinkwater Bethune, law member of the Governor General's Council and a pioneer in promoting women's education, set up the secular Native Female School in 1849 and donated all his movable and immovable property to the school. It was the first such effort in Kolkata and had a major impact on society. The government took it over in 1856 and renamed it Bethune School in 1862–63. Iswar Chandra Vidyasagar, Dwarkanath Vidyabhusan and other liberals supported the school for twenty years but the institution did not receive wide public support because orthodox Hindus reacted against the education of women. The school went through a rough time until it was amalagated with Banga Mahila Vidyalaya, initially established as Hindu Mahila Vidyalaya by Annette Akroyd, and some Brahmo gentlemen, including Dwarkanath Ganguly. A number of bright students joined the institution: Kadambini Bose, Sarala Das, Abala Das and Subarnaprabha Basu, all of whom became prominent figures later. Bethune School was an eye-opener for the Bengali bhadralok.

18

ANONYMOUS

Women and Art (1886)

It is universally acknowledged that men are able to devote themselves to the perusal of a particular subject in order to become successful. If women have such aspirations, they have to pursue these with equal devotion and be properly educated to acquire a social status for themselves. Whatever be the roles that women are asked to play—wife, mother, homemaker, social worker, dresser, cook, pupil, artist—they have to be expert in each that they enact. A woman has to nurture her talents seriously else all her attempts would be in vain and there would remain no possibility of doing anything noble and good. It is believed that women are restless by nature and lack concentration. The extent to which a woman shifts her focus from one occupation to the other, at times undertaking creative work while at other times reading and writing, proves her restlessness.[1] In addition, women keep themselves busy with various domestic chores and responsibilities. Hence, a woman's 'work' is of varied nature. There remains a gap between what a woman does or practises and what she discusses or believes. This results in a complete waste of hard work and labour. These women fail to do something useful for the family. Hence, the common belief is that any responsibility given to a woman results in fruitless toil. Like Gargi, Lilavati and Khana, every woman must devote herself to the task of pursuing a goal religiously.[2]

Art is believed to be something naturally given to women; it is innate and inherent. Then why is it that a woman is not allowed to cultivate it? The only possible answer to this could be that women are devoid of absolute dedication and are unable to undergo rigorous practice. Those who have succeeded have seriously rehearsed it too. Rosa Bonheur,[3] Elizabeth Butler,[4] Elizabeth Strong[5] are such famous examples.

It is commonly believed that marriage is an obstruction in women's emancipation. All her creativity is expressed when she is unmarried. Once she steps into holy matrimony, such creative energy ends forever. At times the married woman has to compromise and work according to her husband's will. But people who think that women always live such distressed lives are totally mistaken. Their ideas are false and outdated. Indeed, there are examples where the husband has shown enough courage to risk his life in order to inspire and support his wife and allow her to flourish. George Eliot is a remarkable example.[6] But there are also instances where the wife is dominated by the husband to such a degree that she accepts the man's ideas and discusses what he likes, showing complete obedience to her spouse. This reveals how a woman has to sacrifice her likes and dislikes, her tastes and opinions and engage in discussions, sometimes unpleasant, despite being reluctant. To show absolute allegiance to the husband, even in a case of personal choice, might result in a peaceful family. But for the sake of individual improvement, catering to the husband's will is useless; the wife has to ignore it. A devoted wife might not rail against such ignorance. But why would those women agree who do not really help but merely follow their husbands? The creativity in youth and the study of scriptures in married life advances the maintenance of the house in the early stages of middle age and these shifting tendencies never allow women to do anything properly. Hence nothing works out in a well-organized and orderly fashion as it is supposed to.

Translated by Debolina Guha Thakurta
Women's College, Kolkata

'Streejati o Shilpakarja', Bamabodhini Patrika, August 1886/Sravan 1293 BS, kalpa 3, bhag 3 (part 3), sankhya 259 (no. 259), pp.120-21.

Notes

1 The author refers to the ability of women in multitasking. Perhaps this would have earned them much criticism—being frivolous, not docile

enough to remain within the set norms of the household, and restless and daring, always keen to explore.

2 Gargi, as mentioned in the Brahmanas of the Brihadaranyaka Upanishad, questioned sage Yajnavalkya about the nature of the atman. She is supposed to have lived around 800-500 BCE, and belonged to the court of King Janaka of Mithila. The *Yajnavalkya Samhita* is a dialogue between her and Yajnavalkya. For details on Lilavati and Khana, see Essay 1, n3 and n4, respectively.

3 Rosa Bonheur, daughter of Marie-Rosalie Bonheur, (16 March 1822-25 May 1899) was a French animalière, realist artist and sculptor. As a painter she became famous primarily for two chief works: *Ploughing in the Nivernais* and *The Horse Fair.* Bonheur is widely considered to have been the most famous female painter of the nineteenth century. Seen as a proto-feminist, she is perhaps most famous today because she was known for wearing men's clothing and living together with fellow artist Anna Klumpke.

4 Elizabeth Thompson (1846-1933) was born in Lausanne. At an early age she was encouraged to paint and draw. Inspired by the Franco-Prussian War, she began to paint military subjects. Interested in recording the pain and suffering of ordinary soldiers, in 1874 she submitted a painting entitled the *Roll Call* to the Royal Academy in London, portraying a group of British soldiers during the Crimean War. She helped to change peoples' attitudes towards women artists. However, her popularity diminished owing to her sympathies for the Catholics in Ireland. In the 1880s, at the time of the first Boer War, the British became very patriotic, wanting pictures that glorified British victories and not those that emphasized the pain and suffering of soldiers as they were unlikely to encourage men to join the British army.

5 There are two women by that name in late nineteenth-century America, both living up to the first decade of the twentieth century. Elizabeth Strong Worthington (died 1908) was a popular American writer during the latter part of the nineteenth century. Her first books *When Peggy Smiled: A Love Story* and *The Biddy Club* were published in 1888. *The Little Brown Dog* and *How to Cook Husbands* (arguably her most popular work), came along in 1898, and her final book was *The Gentle Art of Cooking Wives* in 1900. She sometimes wrote under the pen name Griffith A. Nicholas.

Elizabeth 'Bessie' Rockefeller Strong (23 August 1866–14 November 1906) was the eldest child of oil tycoon John D. Rockefeller(1839–1937) and his wife Laura Spelman Rockefeller ('Cettie') (1839–1915). Bessie

Rockefeller was a special student at Vassar College 1886–1888; Strong Hall, the school's first dormitory, was named in honour of Bessie in 1893 by her father who contributed $35,000 toward the expense of the construction.

6 However, contrary to the author's views, Eliot was not married to George Henry Lewes with whom she had lived for 25 years. She married John Cross after Lewes' death, and died within two years of her marriage.

19

ANONYMOUS

What Means of Livelihood Might There Be for the Poor Widows of India? (1898)

There are many views on the means of livelihood for the orphans and the widows of India. Some are of the opinion that widow remarriage is the solution to their problems, others believe that making them self-reliant by allowing them to earn their livelihood will help. In our opinion, we should discuss the various means through which they could obtain it. Earlier, brahmin widows would roll the holy thread (into strands),[1] other orphans would thresh paddy, sell (cotton) thread spun on the charkha,[2] or earn their living by doing other kinds of work.

These days education has led to a lot of change in outlook and social mores. Keeping in view the present outlook of society, we should devise such ways and means which are acceptable to it. Education paves the path towards a proper livelihood which is not achieved in any other way. Education is not only the means of livelihood; it builds character and helps in achieving physical and mental well-being, both in the present life and in the life hereafter. Who would want to part with the world of happiness derived from education? Oh, why would I lament otherwise? ... Would it help to discuss women's education with those heartless Indians who have no understanding of the pleasures or pains of women, particularly those of widows? However, at present there has been some improvement in the education of the girl child. We feel assured that society will not be antagonized by the means which we shall propose to provide a livelihood to poor Indian widows and orphan girls.

People hold divergent opinions about women's liberation. We

should try and follow the prevalent opinion of society on this issue. There are various views on making women self-reliant. We too do not suggest that they work as clerks, but they could educate themselves to be teachers in girls' schools, newspaper editors, librarians, midwives, gynaecologists, by means of which they could easily earn their livelihood and would not cause any harm to society.

Manufacturing provide the means of livelihood to a majority of women which is not expected in other areas. Income in this area is quite amazing! There is a famous winter garment known as erendi, produced by women in Assam priced at rupees ten, fifteen, twenty or more. Various kinds of muga silk are also produced by them, yielding high profits. There is a certain tribe called Vyadh or Dom who are wanderers. They travel with their families and make cane artifacts. There is a saying that if they are not able to earn at least Rs. 5 from a certain place, then they move on. Due to this, the profits that they reap from producing wicker baskets, platters, conical flower baskets and other cane artifacts are substantial, or else this saying could never have come into use. If our orphans and widows imitate the Assamese women and the Vyadh tribes, they wouldn't have to face the ordeal that they do. Women could find their means of livelihood from the above-mentioned examples and also the following: cloth weaving, knitting woollen garments like socks, mufflers, caps, and so on, drawing, making paper streamers in the shape of creepers or vines, pottery or clay toys, jute items and artifacts made from bamboo cane.

Translated by Soma Mukherjee
Delhi Public School

'Bharater Dukhini Bidhaba Streelokdiger Jibika Labher Kato Prakar Upay Haite Pare', *Bamabodhini Patrika*, March 1898/Falgun 1304 BS, barsha 35 (year 35), kalpa 6, bhag 2 (part 2), sankhya 398 (no. 398), pp. 418-20.

Notes

1 The holy thread worn by a brahmin male from the time of his upanayan ceremony when he is initiated into becoming a brahmin.

2 A small, portable, hand-cranked wheel ideal for spinning cotton and other fine, short-staple fibres. Mahatma Gandhi popularized its use and it became a symbol of self-reliance and independence.

20

SUKHADA GUPTA

No biographical details about the author could be found.

Bengali Women in Hindu Society (1904)

At an age when the physical and emotional faculties of girls are about to blossom, when they step into adolescence leaving behind their childhood, Hindu social norms expect them to forsake their carefree life and play, and get married and enter domestic life. Their intellectual growth and development remain confined within marriage and domesticity. Like robots, they learn to live within the prescribed limits. From the list of daily duties that they need to fulfil, it is apparent that there is little else that they are able to think of apart from cooking, serving people, and so on. They are bound to derive satisfaction from performing these household chores, irrespective of the circumstances being favourable towards them or not. An unprecedented desire or an urge to undertake greater responsibility does not occur in their minds; this makes it clear that they seldom feel a deep-rooted pain for lacking knowledge. It is this ignorance which keeps them unperturbed and carefree.

If a lack or loss is felt, the human mind can never rest in peace until efforts have been made to remove that inadequacy. It is not possible to quench such fervent thirst by merely performing certain responsibilities. Since the root cause of our present distress lies in the fact that this has not been experienced, it is of utmost necessity to evoke this feeling of deficiency through whatever is being taught or done. Everything in our lives as women, whether big or small, is dependent on others. Self-reliance and independent thoughts seem almost non-existent.

As a matter of fact, the individual potentials for intellectual development do not get the chance to attain fruition in such conditions. Unless both men and women are given the opportunity for the proper growth and development of knowledge, their existence as human beings cannot be justified because they have been chosen by the Creator as being the supreme and best example of creation over His other creations such as animals and birds.

Education might have many advantages, but women have not derived any benefits from it in its current form. The most important reason for this is the presence of various evil social practices and norms. We are afraid that we have to acknowledge that the main obstacle to the overall improvement of Bengali women lies in their subservience to these social norms. Realizing their position and deficiency completely, they should strive to improve their physical and intellectual conditions with determination. But even the strength for that is limp within their distressed hearts. Isn't it a matter of great distress and cause for grievance that despite the gratuitous affection of the Creator they have to spend their precious human lives in darkness, unworthy of being called human, remaining as mere puppets in the hands of men? But do we have the strength to acknowledge this? Had that been the case, would we have been dying to make our lives fruitful by decking up in finery and beaming with pride and wealth within our households?

These days almost all Hindu bhadralok households encourage some education for women. Doubtless even some education would have been effective had it been directed properly. But it is regrettable that in spite of acquiring knowledge, several of our sisters fail to uphold the glory of education. As soon as they begin to learn, they start reading things devoid of good taste, such as novels and plays. Reading such books leads to the destruction of wise thoughts and ideas, makes them too capricious and acquisitive, and eventually, leads to the loss of the finer senses. Situated at the opposite pole from this educated state, the illiterate women of earlier times had proved to be much more efficient and able in household activities. These days, our sisters of the educated class are incapable of performing household duties and do not even consider such things worth doing. Hence, household chores are not performed efficiently and smoothly. On the other hand, such incompetence gives those people who are against the spread of female education and higher education in society the chance to strengthen their argument.

In fact, if every woman had the ability and enthusiasm to maintain her dignity and self-respect and take care of her own health and well-being at the same time, it would have been easy for them to overcome all obstacles. But where is such power?

The health of Bengali women fails quite early, the reason being the practice of early marriage. 'Old at 20' is a common idiom; that it is true is evident in every Bengali household. I do not know whether the practice of marriage at such an early age is prevalent among any other civilized race. Girls get married at twelve, thirteen or fourteen, and within a year give birth to a child. These girls are incapable of looking after the child as well as taking care of their own health. In such a situation, it is fantasy to expect that they would try to develop their intellectual faculties in addition to looking after their children's improvement and struggling to keep their own strength intact.

It is true that nowadays schools have been organized for the spread of female education. These efforts have caught the attention of many broad-minded people and several of them have realized the efficacy of female education. But where is the real education, which leads to the triumph over evil practices and strengthens the mind by making it pure and capable of overcoming its own shortcomings?

The only obstacle to the improvement of our race is the lack of female education. Where does the root of improvement lie if the seed from which the human race springs remains ineffective? Women are the pillars upon which society's improvement could rest ... What children learn and how their characters develop depend a lot on their own mothers. Keen observation will reveal that these mothers, uneducated and weak (deficient in both physical and mental strength), can in no way help in imparting strength of character to their children or encourage greatness within them. So many children in Bengali households have fun by lying and using abusive words amongst themselves in front of their mothers. The mother does not scold them because she herself is unable to realize that such a practice is actually causing great harm to her children's future. ... Owing to their ignorance they are unable to realize the ignominy of their actions. Just as the growth and development of a child depends on the nourishment obtained from the mother's milk, similarly the development of its personality is attained by emulating the mother. ... if the mother is not educated, how can one hope for a superior child? And isn't it obvious that a country like this where the mothers are in such distress would be destined to doom?

There is a great hue and cry in modern Hindu society over the dowry given for a girl's marriage. The birth of a daughter has become a major offence; when a girl is born, let alone the pain of her parents, even relatives and neighbours show signs of distress and annoyance. Must we explain what feelings such incidents evoke within us? Are we not creatures of flesh and blood? This indicates how women in this country lead their lives. I feel women themselves have a lot to do in earning respect for themselves and the lack of action on their part has led to them being considered as huge burdens by everybody. This evil custom is steadily gaining ground. None will disagree that this is detrimental to every member of the society.

Everybody has sons and daughters, people share the joys and sorrows of their children. If proud mothers who had borne sons looked at the dowry system with contempt and considered it a great humiliation for women of their own race, would every household today lament the birth of a daughter? If they had such noble thoughts in their minds and inner strength, their sons would not have dared to waste their precious lives in conforming to such horrible customs. Every mother prays for her son's well-being; but it is needless to say how unjust it is for a mother to sympathize with her son who participates in such a humiliating, distasteful and disgraceful act.

Careful observation reveals that society has imposed various rigid rules and norms upon women at every step. If women lose their husbands, their lives are considered to be useless; they have to observe severe penance and lose all rights of participation in any form of entertainment or joyous occasions celebrated by the household. As long as they live, they are forced to remain in a state of neglect and are dependent on the mercy of their relatives. When young women are widowed, their condition is especially distressful. Their tender hearts have to bear tremendous social torture and everyone is aware of the poison this custom is generating in every household. Even stones melt at their heart-wrenching condition, but the rigidity of society does not slacken.

A mere betel leaf used in the household is [for making paan] more valuable than the life of a woman. If each one of us tries to understand our distressful condition and we discuss amongst ourselves ways of overcoming the present situation, then we could hope for some improvement. We could definitely not live in peace and happiness given our present state of non-existence.

It has been said earlier that there has been no improvement in the field of female education in Hindu society. Even before the body is ready, the mind and the heart enter into a state of cohabitation; women get married, the result being that they are unable to bear the responsibilities of their married lives. Failing to realize conjugal love, they find satisfaction and fulfilment in exploring their basic instincts. In a society where the husband is educated and the wife isn't, and there is great difference in their tastes, the couple cannot realize the power and sanctity of love, nor can such a society where this is prevalent hope for any kind of improvement.

All becomes clear if one looks carefully at the aim of a woman's life in Hindu society. A woman is to depend on a man for bearing children and looking after the household; there can be nothing else in her life beyond this. It is unnecessary to say how much freedom she is granted in household affairs and matters of procreation. The main reason for every type of humiliation that Bengali women are subjected to is lack of proper education. Their tremendous agony shall not subside till this inadequacy is dispelled.

In every household in Hindu society, Bengali women are forced to suffer. It remains, then, the responsibility of every educated person to judge whether such women can bring prosperity to society. The principal aim of society is to help both men and women in directing all their physical and mental abilities voluntarily towards activities of social welfare. Alas, it is unnecessary to describe the extent to which women have been assisted in the development of their independence and mental strength in this hapless Hindu society.

Society generally refers to a cluster of men and women. Any society, whether Hindu, Muslim or Christian, is not composed of only women or only men. Just as by body we mean a coordinated cluster of hands, feet and all the organs, similarly, men make for one half of society, the other half comprising women. When an organ of the human body does not function properly, one cannot say that the body is healthy. Similarly, improvement of society is impossible when one half of it, the women, are barred from improvement. It is absolutely certain and clear that no matter how much progress is achieved by men, without the improvement of women, society can never prosper.

My dear respected sisters! Today at this auspicious hour we have assembled in this house; none of us is unaware of the other's condition.

If we do not take steps for our own improvement, our distress will never be allayed. Come, let us make this our sphere of activity and try to dispel the shortcomings of our lives with the blessings of the Creator. May God help us!

Translated by Anindita Roy
Department of Comparative Literature, Jadavpur University

'Hindu Samaje Banganari', *Antahpur*, April 1904/Chaitra 1310 BS, barsha 6 (year 6), vol. 6, sankhya 12 (no. 12), pp. 269-74.

21

NIRUPAMA DEVI

Nirupama Devi (*c.* 1883–1951) was born in Behrampur, Murshidabad. She was the daughter of Nafarchandra Bhatta and she spent her childhood in Bhagalpur. She was married to Nabagopal Bhatta. She became a widow at an early age. She was inspired by her elder brother Bibhutibhushan Bhatta and the writer Saratchandra Chattopadhyay to turn to literature. In a handwritten magazine under the direction of Bibhutibhushan and Saratchandra she wrote her first piece. Her first novel *Ussrinkhala* and many of her songs and poems which were written during the Swadeshi movement brought her fame. Her novel is about the clash between love and conjugal life. *Didi*, published in 1913–14, is considered her best novel. In 1938 she was awarded the Bhubanmohini Swarna Padak and in 1943 she received the Jagattarini Swarna Padak, both from the University of Calcutta. In 1943 she was also felicitated by the Burdwan Sahitya Parishad. She became a Vaishanava during the last years of her life. Her other novels are: *Annapurnar Mandir, Amar Diary, Devatra* and *Anukarsha*. Many of her novels were made into films or produced as plays.

Obstacles to the Education of Girl Children in Contemporary Times and Ways of Overcoming Them (1904)

In our country a girl child is considered a great misfortune for the parents. Though sons and daughters are equally adorable to their parents, they are often not treated in the same manner because of the prevalent evil practices to which parents succumb. That is precisely why the idea develops that a son is worthy of greater affection and a daughter is born to be neglected. These ideas have somewhat changed due to the spread of education; still, there are several reasons as to why such ideas have not yet been eradicated completely. After completing his education, the son begins to earn money and the responsibility of the aged parents automatically shifts to him. But the daughter cannot serve her parents or be responsible for them. That is why parents and relations are more inclined towards educating the son well. ... As long as such misconceptions are not removed from our minds, there is little hope for the betterment of our race and country. Women make up households; joy, sorrow, good and evil whatever occurs within the household depends on the conduct of women. How can their inadequacies ever be addressed if parents fail to provide their daughters with good education? Only recently has education of women commenced in our country. ... Nobody finds it necessary to observe whether the intellectual faculties of women are being enriched through proper education. Many people tend to think that if a woman goes through a few pages of some book and learns how to keep household accounts, she is educated adequately. Parents feel that it is enough if the daughter is able to communicate with them through letters written from her husband's house after she gets married.

A few years back, that is, in the old days, norms were such that getting a daughter married off by the age of nine or ten, that is, performing a *gouridan* (ceremoney during which on eight-year-old Hindu girl is given in marriage), earned the girl's parents great piety. As soon as the daughter was past twelve and still unmarried, not only her parents but also her ancestors up to fourteen generations were in grave danger of being doomed to perdition. The parents felt helpless and had to endure the tremendous mental trauma of constant censure from people because of their inability to marry off an ageing daughter. Women in those days were made to enter the unknown and unaffectionate households of their in-laws at a very tender age and were forced to attain maturity. ... They knew very well that for even the slightest mistake they would be treated with contempt and malevolence. ... Being completely uneducated they could be led down a path and convinced that this alone should be their responsibility and the goal of life, and they would accept this unconditionally. ...

The young girls resent their compulsory and unconditional submission to the domination of so many authorities in their household, and they develop the desire to live independently. Thus, it is the responsibility of the parents to see that their daughters receive proper education which ... should be imparted to them in such a way that it leads to the fullest development of their lively, tender souls which are meant to adorn our houses, and prevent arousing any negative feeling, such as selfishness, in their sensitive, zestful hearts. The bond of marriage is one of the most wonderful things made by the Creator. It is an absolute necessity to maintain His creation; but being unable to realize His good intentions, we end up doing things against His wishes. Recently, there were hundreds of parents keen to get their daughters married off, losing their heads over men with a B.A. or M.A. degree from the university. ... Getting the daughter somehow married off to a well-established, suitable man makes them feel that their lives are justified. ... But parents fail to realize that the huge burden they seem to shake off from their shoulders eventually rests on those of their dearest, innocent daughters.

Often the girl child brings trouble upon herself at her in-laws' place because of her inability or immaturity. She begins to consider her own parents, whom she once worshipped, as her enemies and ends up cursing them. At an age when her mind and body are still undeveloped, when she could have played happily in her mother's lap, when her mother is supposed to teach her the purpose of life and through her own speech and actions set examples for her to emulate, in such a phase of life, precisely, all efforts are directed towards finding her a suitable husband and dumping her on him. As a result, the girls' tender hearts do not have any opportunity to bloom, adolescence dies a premature death in the rigours of domestic life. When a trembling kid approaches the sacrificial altar, the poor, mute creature considers the entire world to be the epitome of cruelty. Similarly, young Bengali girls consider themselves helpless and without shelter as they leave their mothers' bosoms and head for their in-laws' place in tears. The pain they feel in their tiny hearts at that moment is indescribable; their tears become their sole life-long companions. ... but it is observed that once a girl gains maturity, she realize, that no other place in the world is as comfortable and dear as the house of her husband. ...

Some people think, what is the harm in getting the daughter married off early? The son-in-law might as well take responsibility for her education and make her worthy. But I must say this is a very misguided belief. After marriage, the husband invariably goes off to another place either for higher studies or to earn money, leaving behind the child-wife. The opportunity to educate her never arises. Once girls get entangled in domestic affairs, they, too, lose all interest in studies. Naturally, they tend to think it is enough for them to manage domestic affairs and run the household smoothly. Then, as soon as one or two children are born, all their time is taken up by them. Hence, for all these reasons, most Bengali girls do not get the opportunity to become educated. At the time of marriage romantic fantasies reign in the minds of the young men as they marry their child-wives. But unacquainted with the realities of life, such fantasies soon tend to bring sorrow and pain into their domestic lives. How can the immature wife fathom the depth of the husband's love for her? ...

Early maturity should not be seen as a good quality in girls. Just as a fruit does not taste good if it ripens prematurely, similarly, it seems quite unnatural and devoid of sweetness if instead of childish innocence, girls exhibit excessive maturity. Instead of considering the life of a daughter completely useless and unnecessary, if parents sowed the seeds of education in the minds of their daughters with care and affection, then their lives could advance greatly towards development. Good education could lead to the betterment of their households and domestic lives eventually. It is not that this significant task depends only on the efforts of the parents, the girls themselves need to show interest. If the aim of their lives is to be good wives and daughters-in-law and to look after their households, well, then it is not impossible to translate such thoughts into action. Women take pride in decking themselves up with jewellery gifted to them by their parents or in-laws and become conceited, thinking that they have reached the summit of joy in acquiring the material pleasures that they had yearned for eternally. This is the result of their ignorance and one of the prime effects of poor education. They are blind to pride resulting from excess wealth; what can be more deplorable than this blindness that eclipses the true aims of life completely?

... It is very sad that in spite of being born as members of the most intelligent species in this creation, we spend our lives in such an ineffective and inactive manner. Virtuous discussions and conversations remedy the shallowness of the mind. Many good deeds can be done even while remaining within the confines of domesticity if one is willing and efforts are made in that direction. After taking care of domestic needs, if Bengali women engage themselves in discussions about the improvement of religion, domestic life and art instead of wasting their time in idle talk and gossip, a lot of progress can occur in these areas. It is not at all logical to spend our lives in comfort, enhancing our physical beauty and engaging in the pursuit of physical pleasures instead of using men's hard-earned money in socially useful activities.

Translated by Sharmistha Chatterjee (Sriwastav)
Rishi Bankim Chandra College for Women, Naihati

'Bartaman Samaye Balikader Sikshar Antaray ebongTaddurikaraner Upay Ki?' Antahpur, mid October to mid-November 1904/Kartik 1311 BS, barsha 7 (year 7), vol. 7, sankhya 7 (no. 7).

22

BIBI KHAIRUNNESA KHATUN

Bibi Khairunnesa is one of the many Muslim female writers whose details seem to have been lost in the ravages of time. However, in a piece by Saiyyad Abdul Maqsood (a writer, reporter and researcher from Dhaka), on the essays by Khairunnesa, one finds that she was closely associated with the Hossainpur Balika Vidyalaya at Sirajganj. In the essay, '*Amader Shiksha*' that appeared in *Nabanoor* (vol. 8, no. 2, 1904), Khairunnesa mentions that she is extremely worried about the financial crisis at the above-mentioned school where she was also the headmistress. According to Maqsood, Khairunnesa must have died between 1908–11. He notes that *Satir Patibhakti* by Khairunnesa first appeared in 1908, but when it was published again in 1911, she was described as the 'late Khairunnesa'. In the original essay she used the prefix 'Bibi' before her name.

The Hindrances to Our Education (1904)

Recently we have noticed society's eagerness regarding our [women's] education. Many accomplished and generous individuals are actively engaged in this mission. The country's newspapers too are not silent about it. It is unanimously accepted that if we are not properly educated there is hardly any possibility of the overall development of society. There is no doubt that this is a rational view. A life without education is comparable to a world without the sun. An uneducated person can be compared to animals. Is there any reason why the education which makes men elegant and virtuous should not enhance the accomplishments of women who are naturally graceful? When virtuous women are also provided with education it seems to be like adding rare jewels to an already brilliant crown. She makes society more pleasant like a breeze which when cool refreshes us even more. In the *Hadis Sharif* it is written that education is absolutely necessary for both men and women[1]—'*talebi elme farijatan ala kulle moslemin o moslemat*'.[2] There are enough treatises even in the Hindu scriptures supporting the necessity of women's education—'*kanyapyevang palaniya shikshaniyatiyatnatah*'.[3] Therefore, whichever way you choose to look at the matter, our education is not only necessary but also our responsibility; there is no room for doubt here.

Men now understand about the need to spread education among all sections of women—the rich, the poor, the *bhadra* and the *abhadra*.[4] Now many of our sisters have understood that too. But if this is the situation, why has education not spread among us? Has anyone ever thought about the factors hindering our education and the necessary steps that must be taken to eradicate them? I do not remember seeing or hearing anything of the kind! Do I have to say in so many words that even hundreds and thousands of lectures and hundreds of essays would not help in spreading education if the fundamental problems and hindrances in acquiring it are not solved? In the following lines we shall discuss the obstacles to women's education and the ways in which these problems might be solved.

We are Muslims and, therefore, we have to live according to the rules and regulations of Islam. We cannot transgress the boundaries within which Our Lord has created us: that would be improper. We do not have unrestricted rights to travel from one village to another like the Hindus. After growing up, a woman is not allowed to visit someone's house without respecting the tradition of the purdah. Therefore, the unavailability of proper educational institutions at places where we need them is one of the major obstacles. The second reason is that in Bengal, Muslims are very poor. Most cannot earn enough to run a family properly. They cannot even pay for the male children's education; supporting the education of the girl child in this case seems out of the question! There is a dearth of schools and of money. Money might be the root of all evil, but getting an education without it is not possible. In addition to the monthly school fees one needs to have books, slates, pen and paper. There are many good traditional values within the Muslim community, but we still lack a few basic ones. Much good could have been done if we could generate goodwill in the same way in which Hindus help and encourage each other. The desire for education among the Muslim children dies out at the very outset if they lack the basic means of survival. Therefore, it is not surprising that poor children remain uneducated. When someone generous starts a school and is not able to bear all the expenses (if he too is not a rich man), it cannot be run as a 'free school'. Moreover, there remains much doubt regarding the permanence of the endeavour without proper community support to back it up. Many would donate large sums for sterile titles but seem to be smitten with pangs of extreme poverty whenever asked to donate for purposes which are significant socially. Donations for education have become extremely rare.[5] One can hardly expect that someone in his personal capacity would go on begging to support a school of this nature. That education has not spread among us generally, despite a desire for it, may be understood from the point just mentioned. I would like to write a few words on how the all-illuminating brilliance of education could enlighten us.

First, according to our educational needs, schools will have to be set up in every city, village and small locality. In the city schools we have to recruit women teachers of good moral character; and those schools should be set up where the girl students will not have to compromise with the rules of the purdah and no man gets a chance to enter the school premises. The girl students who live in their own houses or in rented ones near the school should be able to go to school accompanied by their maids, or if that is not possible, form a group of four/five girls who could go to school together. It is not proper for older girls to walk in public, therefore, a proper system of transport has to be made available for them.[6] There is no need to recruit female teachers for village schools immediately; old, sincere and religious male teachers could teach them. Parents of older girls might not agree to send them to schools but they should not have any major cause for disagreement with regard to the younger ones. I think that society does not need to be too eager in educating the older girls immediately. Their guardians (husbands or fathers, brothers or whoever it might be) would decide for them. The future of our society and its development depends on the younger girls. Therefore, educating them would be the best thing for our society.

We need to decide who could bear the cost of establishing and running such schools. There are several rich men in the cities. Hence, there should be no reason for paucity of funds. If anyone wishes, he can fund such a school, otherwise, it could be run by public donations. But the real difficulty is in running schools in villages. In most villages, the condition is such that it is almost impossible to find even ten economically stable families. A few prosperous families can be found among the uneducated lower class but they are against women's education. One can hardly expect an eagerness to spread women's education among those who have had no relation with education for the last fourteen generations. The main point is that if there is no other source of income, a village school cannot be supported by the village economy. I do not know if the attention of the Regional Muslim Education Society has been drawn to this.[7] I wish to know more about the way it really works. Without the benevolence of the rich, it will not be possible to educate poor women enshrouded in the darkness of illiteracy. Would the rich come forward to do good for their own community by educating the downtrodden women? Can they be made to understand that to get good children we need good mothers? Mothers of those Muslims who once rose to the peaks of profound scholarly knowledge are today wallowing in the deepest dungeons of ignorance—could they go on being indifferent to this plight? This is quite unbelievable!

Translated by Jayeeta Bagchi
School of Women's Studies, Jadavpur University

'Amader Sikshar Antaray', *Nabanoor*, 1904, barsha 2, (year 2), sankhya 8 (no. 8).

Also available in *Zenana Mehfil: Bangali Musalman Lekhikader Nirbachit Rachana 1904-38*, edited by Shaheen Akhtar and Moushumi Bhowmik (Kolkata: Stree, 1998), pp 39-42.

Notes

1 The scripture which provides the norms of right/proper behaviour for the believers of Islam, modelled on the accounts of the life of Prophet Muhammad.

2 Learning the *ilm*, i.e., knowledge of the Qur'an and other essential scriptures, is the duty of Muslim men and women.

3 In the bringing up of daughters also, care should be taken to provide education.

4 Literally 'civilized' and 'uncivilized', but in Bengali, referring also to the middle class, who are *bhadra*, educated and genteel, and those who are of a lower class, *abhadra*, uneducated.

5 That donation towards a good cause is nowadays a rare phenomenon, may be well understood if the case of the Shirajgunj Hossainpur Girls

School is cited. This school was established by Munshi Muhammad Meherullah Sahib some eight or nine years back, though in dire straits, he has been bearing most of the expenses of running the school himself. No tuition fee is taken from the girl students of this school; moreover, they are often supplied with pens and paper. Most of the residents of this village are extremely poor. There is no chance of getting any help from them. There is a need for furniture like benches and tables. Many letters have been sent to the rajas, nawabs and other rich people of this land asking for donations so that some of the needs could be taken care of, but upto now not a paisa has been received from any of them. The readers should understand from this the character of our people is like. (*Note:* This is a footnote provided by the author herself).

6 See Essay 32, 'Trouble on the Train' for another account of women being unaccompanied and how women dealt with such occasions when, compelled by circumstances, they travelled alone.

7 The all-male Muslim Educational Congress was formed in 1886. In its second meeting, it established local Muslim educational councils, and in 1896 first brought up the topic of women's education. In 1896, the annual last executive session of Muslim Educational Conference in Sir Syed Ahmad Khan's lifetime, made a proposal to start a women's education section. The proposal was accepted and Justice Karamat Hussain was appointed as its founding secretary. Nawab Mohsinul Mulk, Sahabzada Aftab Ahmad Khan, Janab Sultan Ahmad and Haji Ismail Khan were asked to assist Justice Karamat Hussain. In the annual session of the Muslim Educational Conference of 1898 in Lahore, a separate department of women's education was established and Sahabzada Aftab Ahmad Khan was elected its secretary. This resulted in angry reactions from the traditional Muslims of India but a dedicated team of Janab Ummid Ali, Ghulam-us-Saqlain and Haji Ismail Khan wrote several letters and articles in Aligarh Institute Gazette and other reputed journals to defend the decision of the Muslim Educational Conference to start a women's educational movement. Justice Amir Ali presided over the annual session of AIMEC in 1899 at Calcutta. The idea to start a girl's schools in the state capital was accepted. It was also agreed that the ulema would be consulted to develop the curriculum of the schools and modern subjects like science and humanities would also be included in the syllabus. In the session of December 1902 in Delhi under the leadership of H.H. Sir Agha Khan, young Shaikh Abdullah was appointed as secretary to look into the women's educational project and was asked to start the activities very aggressively.

23

ROKEYA SAKHAWAT HOSSAIN

Rokeya Sakhawat Hossain (1880-1932) was born at Payrabandh, Rangpur district East Bengal (today's Bangladesh). She was a prolific writer and a social reformer with thoughts far ahead of her time. She was taught at home. She learned English from her elder brother. At the age of eighteen she was married to Sakhawat Hossain of Bhagalpur. He was also a supporter of women's education. Ten years later, after the death of her husband, she came to Calcutta and immersed herself in the work of social reformation within the Muslim community. Amongst her major contributions to the cause of women is the establishment of the Sakhawat Memorial Girl's School on 15 March 1911. Though the school started with only eight girls, the strength soon grew in number. She was also the founder of a women's committee called the Anjuman-e-Khawatin Islam and a fighter of social justice and reform. Even today we can see the relevance of her writings such as *Abarodhbasini* (1931), which was translated into English as *Those Dwelling in Seclusion*. She wrote *Sultana's Dream* (1905) in English, a utopia where women are the rulers and men are forced to live a secluded life. She also wrote a novel named *Padmarag* (1924).

The Frog in the Well Visits the Himalayas (1904)

We are in the Himalayas now. My yearning has been fulfilled. I have finally got the chance to see the mountains. Women readers may not find anything new in this, but to me it is a completely novel feeling. Reading about oceans, mountains, waterfalls, and so on, had always aroused in me a strong desire to see them but such feelings would often be dampened in a deep sigh of silence. I used to think that I would never have such an experience. I felt sadder thinking that even Europeans have travelled such a distance to see the Himalayas, while we, within our own country, have not. But by the grace of the Almighty, I did get to see the Himalayas!

We reached Siliguri on time. A railway runs from Siliguri to the Himalayas. Eastern Bengal Railway coaches are smaller than the East India coaches. The Himalayan Railways are even smaller, with tiny carriages like toy cars, which look really nice. And the coaches are very low, so the travellers can easily get on or off them.

Meandering through the plains, the train which we board from Siliguri starts moving uphill slowly, making a clattering sound like *'katatta'*, swaying sometimes to the south and then north, and zigzagging up through the magnificent surroundings; at times along tall peaks, at other times through thick dense forests.

At regular intervals, the train stops at stations where there are refreshment rooms. Almost every station has a ladies' waiting room. The rooms are well furnished, and our co-travellers, the European sisters, rest at least once at almost all stations. There are many wash basins in the waiting rooms—four people can easily use them at the same time. The sisters, without fail, carry with them a comb, brush and powder. Bengali girls would never be able to dress their hair this frequently. The energy of these European sisters is praiseworthy. The waiting rooms have shadowy attendants.[1] Gradually, we reach a height of 3,000 feet above sea level; though we are moving through the clouds, I do not feel the cold. The dense white fog covering the low-lying valley can easily be mistaken for a river. Trees, creepers, grass, the terraced hillsides—everything looks so spectacular! I have never seen such tall grass! The green tea gardens augment the magnificence of the natural bounty even further. Mountain ranges, running one after another, look so awesome! And amidst this natural beauty, the narrow road tracks laid down by humans on the earth's surface appear merely as marks drawn on the earth. The dense green forests look like tresses of Mother Earth, and the tracks, like the winding parting of her hair!

There are so many waterfalls on the way; their beauty remains inexplicable. Their sources are unknown; none can forecast their path; they flow down incessantly ripping apart the stone-hearted snow-clad Himadri.[2] Can one even believe that the mighty Jahnavi springs from one of these?[3] The train stops before a huge waterfall, and we think that perhaps it is deliberate so that we can enjoy the sight to our heart's content; actually, the train stops for another reason: to re-fill water.[4] Whatever the reason, our wish has come true.

We are now 4,000 feet above sea level. Yet I do not feel the chill; in fact, it is a respite from the torturous heat.[5] The wind blows mildly. The Mahanadi Station is at 4,120 feet. I cannot read the name very clearly, but from whatever little I can make out, it is most probably named Mahanadi. If I make a mistake in reading the name, the fault is not mine, as my coach stands at a distance from the station.

Finally, we arrive at our destination: Kurseong Station, which lies 4,864 feet from sea level. Finding the station overcrowded, I decide to sit in the ladies' waiting room. I watch the European sisters wash their faces and comb their hair. There is a little boy with one of them, and she orders me to wash her son's face, while preparing to climb on to the train. Why should I wash her son's face? She then wipes the boy's face with the towel she has discarded, and then about ten seconds later runs back towards the train. This is what happens when one depends too much on servants. The crowd thins out as the train charges away; we leave the waiting room thereafter.

Our lodging is not far from the station, so we reach quite quickly. Some of our trunks are booked to the Darjeeling address. Hence, certain essential belongings are missing, owing to which despite reaching the quarters (much before evening), I do not feel at home. Our trunks have come back by the evening mail. Even before we could reach Darjeeling, our trunks have returned after having breathed the fresh air there. From the following day, we begin to feel at home completely. That is why I say that a mere roof above never makes a comfortable home, one also needs the necessary furniture and fittings.

It is neither too cold nor warm like summer. Will it be apt to call it the alpine spring? The rays of the sun are scorching. It has rained only once since we have arrived. The air is supposed to be extremely good for health, but the water, as I hear, is not pure. We strain it through a filter before use though it appears crystal clear. There are neither wells nor rivers, the only source of water being the waterfalls. The clear cool waterfall is such a treat to the eyes, that one automatically puts one's palms together with a wondrous gasp of appreciation occasioned by the mild salubrious breeze and the dense fog that engulf the soul.

The air is light and clean. The interplay of winds and clouds, as if playing hide and seek, is simply wonderful! In one moment a mass of clouds is brushed aside by a gust of wind whistling past. Every day the setting sun creates a kingdom of magic with the winds and clouds. It appears as if molten gold is poured on the mountains in the western skies while small clusters of clouds hop, skip and frisk along the even golden slopes of the mountains. I spend all my time following the clouds, enraptured and lost in the surroundings.

I remember having read about the dhenkir shak in an issue of *Mahila*.[6] I had only read in geography books that there were tall dhenki trees in the carboniferous age. Now, I am seeing them with my own eyes, I feel elated. I snap a branch and measure it; it is 11 feet long. The tree itself must be almost 20–25 feet tall.

Some areas are covered with thick forests. Luckily, there are no tigers; we stroll about the forest fearlessly and love travelling through the desolate paths. The forest is infested with snakes and leeches. Though we do not see snakes, there are leeches, who have had a taste of our blood two or three times.

The women in these parts do not fear leeches. Our Bhutiya house-servant 'Bhalu' says, what damage can a leech do?[7] Once it sucks enough blood, it goes away on its own. The Bhutiya women wrap up yards of cloth around their waists, falling beyond their knees like the long skirt of a *ghagra*, and wear jackets with shawls around their shoulders. Saddled with a load of one or two maunds on their backs,[8] they stream up through the narrow winding paths to the mountain tops effortlessly. They walk downwards in the same way. They travel on the paths with such carefree dexterity that in comparison we appear timid before them.

The editor of *Mahila* had once written about women: 'The women-species is called *abala* because they are weak.'[9] Let me then ask, are these Bhutiya women not a part of this weak species of abalas? To quench their hunger, they do not rely on their men folk; they contribute equally to the gathering of food. In fact, it is mostly women who carry boulders—men do not carry much load at all. The abalas carry the rocks, lay stones on the paths, and young boys and girls help them in doing so. It seems that the abalas here are nothing but a mere extension of this group of young boys and girls.

The Bhutiya women introduce themselves as the *paharani*, women of the mountains, and call us '*niche ka admi*', implying the uncivilized. These women are inherently hardworking, courageous and honest. However, owing to their association with the 'niche ka admi', they have lost their innocence to some extent. Thus, instances of pinching away some amount from the money given to them to purchase provisions,diluting milk with water, and so on have become frequent—fruits of their intermingling with other communities.

Many may not understand that it is quite possible to travel the country and abroad as a *purdahnashin*,[10] keeping with the decrees of Islam. Hence, such individuals consider stepping over the domestic threshold as a huge problem. The dictums on purdah to be observed in the theatre are rigid, but the popular norms of purdah as practised in our society are even more stringent. In comparison, living according to the *Shastras* may not be as difficult as is assumed. In my opinion, the best purdahnashin would be one who considers others as her brothers and sisters.

About a mile from our quarters is a huge waterfall; the surge of frothy water is visible from a distance. Every day and night, sweet songs of the gurgling water double and triple my fervor of devotion to the Almighty. I ask Him, why does the soul not flow like this waterfall and then merge into the Supreme Being, touching His holy feet?

I am extremely happy for being able to come to the mountains, and am so thankful to God! I had seen a small extent of the vast expanse of the Bay of Bengal earlier, some familiarity with the mountains was left unfulfilled. Now, even that desire has been met.

No, actually the more I see, the more is the desire fuelled—the thirst to see multiplies. But I have only two eyes to behold, how much can seep into these two eyes? The more I see, the more I think, the more inexpressible it becomes. Every high range, every waterfall seems to call out to me, 'Look at me first. Look at me!' And, when I stare at them wonderstruck, their warm smile teasingly questions, 'Why do you stare at me? Think of my Creator.' This is so very true! The painting stands for the brilliance of its painter. Or else who would know the other just by its name? How big, how vast, how great is this land at the foot of the Himalayas! And the Himalayas are so tiny in the vastness of the great Artist's creation. They are not specks of sand!

What ingratitude on our part, if we do not thank the Creator for all the beauty that seeps into our eyes, ears and mind! Only in meditating with the body, mind and soul can one find contentment. Repeating only a few words (at least that is what I think) like a parrot is not meditation. In such a form of meditation, where is the involvement of the soul? When basking in sylvan splendour, the mind and the soul should sing harmoniously, 'God be praised. He is great!' and then, one need not utter even a word.

Translated by Anindita Roy
Department of Comparative Literature, Jadavpur University

'Kupamanduker Himalaya Darshan', Mahila, November 1904/Kartik 1311 BS, bhag 10 (part 10), sankhya 4 (no. 4), pp. 108-12.

Notes

1 Siliguri was a small station in those days. Attendants were rarely visible.

2 Referring to the snow-clad Himalayas.

3 Referring to Ganga, who was brought down by Bhagiratha from the Himalyas, the abode of Lord Shiva, where she was locked in his hair. When she reached the plains, her torrential flow devastated the field of Rishi Jahnu, who consumed all the waters of the Ganga to teach her a lesson. However, at the request of the gods he released her through his ears. So Ganga is also known as Jahnavi, the daughter of Jahnu.

4 Trains in those days were run by steam engines. Steam engines require water which when heated generated steam.

5 The author lived in the plains where the temperature was higher.

6 The leaves of a tall mountain tree.

7 A term used by the local inhabitants to refer to the migrants from the neighbouring princely state of Bhutan.

8 Before the metric system this unit of measurement was used; 1 maund= 37.3242 kg.

9 Refers to one who is weak, without strength.

10 A woman who observes purdah, i.e., veiling, as prevalent in Muslim society.

24

CHARUMATI DEVI

No biographical details about the author could be found.

The Premature Death of Children and the Duties of a Mother (1912)

Recently, the mortality rate of children in our country has increased. Concurrent with the development of science, the child mortality rate has decreased in Europe, but unfortunately in India, things remain as before. Newspapers report that in 1910, 219 children out of a thousand have died in Lahore. In Punjab the number is 335. In the whole of India it is 445. In England and Wales the number of children dying per thousand is 117. The number of children dying in the year of 1909 is 368 in Calcutta, 300 in Bombay but it is 170 in London. Last year the number was 223 in Russia. Hence, it is clear that in India the child mortality rate is almost double than that of England. Therefore, in order to bring the figures down, men and women should maintain certain rules for health. The Lahore municipality has formed an enquiry committee to probe the matter. The committee has prescribed certain strictures in this regard: first, an overall improvement of health of the local people; second, encourage maintenance of health rules at the domestic level; third, appointment of a nurse; fourth, establishment of a committee to build up awareness about health rules within each and every family.

In many cases, babies die owing to the absence of a proper midwife. Today, we need not depend entirely on fate as we used to; an effort ought to be made everywhere to improve health. But as long as a proper system of education for women is not developed, advice regarding health shall not be followed. Unfortunately, even a few people who are educated keep the mother and the new born baby in such conditions that it becomes difficult for them to stay healthy; indeed, their lives are often greatly endangered. We should pay attention to this particular point. The major reasons for the great number of children dying untimely in Bengal are the lack of favourable climate, clean and healthy environment and awareness amongst the young mothers in rearing a child.

Motherhood is not an easy task. The duty of a mother is really a difficult one. Bengali girls are initiated into motherhood at a very tender age. They have to shoulder this responsibility before the completion of any sort of education. They do not have any experience in this matter either (it is difficult to have any at this age). The mother does not know how to take care of her own health ... at an age when she is supposed to play with dolls she has to play with a living doll. This is one of the major reasons for the untimely death of so many children in Bengal. Though 50 per cent of them can manage to remain alive, their lives drag on, ... without merit and physical and mental strength. They do not have a long life span. ... As early motherhood is one of the major reasons for child mortality, so is early marriage of men. Just as male bodily organs do not properly develop before the age of twenty-five, female bodily organs cannot develop before the age of eighteen. Is it surprising then that children born to parents who have not yet attained that age will live a shorter life? Further, the moment she, who is merely a very young girl, achieves motherhood, a new life of self-sacrifice and responsibilities begins. Sacrificing her own happiness, her own interests, she must now devote all her energy and attention to her baby. Even if the mother is an empress and surrounded by maids and servants, looking after the child's interests is her sole duty.

Now we must find out why so many children in our society die untimely deaths. First, the lying-in room should be in the best place of the house; instead, it is always in the worst place, often with moist earth as the floor. The lying-in room is often so small that fresh air cannot enter it. There is smoke from unseasoned wood. Moreover, there is dearth of trained nurses.

Though the girl becomes the mother of a child by overcoming all her physical pain, she is inexperienced in all matters connected to motherhood. Many mature women, despite mothering three or four children cannot save their children from dying due to dependence on others and because of their own ignorance. Mothers in our country do not have any strength of their own and cannot take as much care of the child as required. They are not provided with appropriate, healthy and nutritious food and clean clothes that are necessary for the hygiene of the mother. In many cases, such things take place at the orders of a superstitious mistress of the household. Weak mothers, without proper care and food cannot generate sufficient breast milk; they start feeding their children with the milk that the milkman often dilutes with water (it is not possible for everyone to keep cows) from the lying-in room itself, without knowing how harmful it is to their babies.

Every mother should know that the baby should be nourished with breast milk until eight or nine teeth are cut. This is why she should take sufficient milk, soup and nutritious food; it helps to generate a good supply of breast milk. It would not be an exaggeration if the milkman's milk is labelled as 'poison' for children since most diseases are borne of it. If children are to be given milk at all, then light goat's milk is best for a new born baby. A quarter portion of cow's milk and a three-quarter portion of water (however the quantity of water would decrease as the child grows up) should be mixed and boiled and then should be given with a small quantity of sugar candy or plain sugar. But one has to be careful about using a feeding bottle. The feeding bottle is meant for those who can clean it properly (by the mother, giving up laziness) and for those who can apprehend the dangerous consequences resulting from an unclean feeding bottle. It is better to feed children with a clean shining traditional *jhinuk,* a cockle-shaped spoon.

Appointing a nurse in the lying-in room means a huge expense; many well-off families have this job done by an untrained maid from a lower caste in order to avoid such a huge expense. But it is really a matter of regret that they do not understand that as it involves two lives, expenditure should not be the most significant concern in such circumstances. Every mother alone cannot ensure the smooth delivery of the baby. Old housewives often keep saying, 'Didn't we give birth to children? Didn't we survive?' maybe this is true, but in this world of flux, everything could change, and they do not accept the fact that weather ,climate, health, constitution and so forth have really changed since their time. What took place in their time cannot be compared with the present. The custom of early marriage of girls was almost non-existent in those days; the young bride was not allowed cohabitation with her husband till she reached the proper age. An interesting custom, in this connection, was in practice in the south-west part of Bengal. The custom may seem savage, but it is equally practised in civilized society. First of all, as far as educated families are concerned they do not marry off their children at an early age; even if they do, the ceremony of *gouna*, that is, going to the marital home, is postponed till the bride is seventeen or eighteen years old. Newly wed couples are not allowed to meet before this ceremony. Everybody knows that in ancient days, Sita, Savitri, Damayanti, all these legendary women, got married at a mature age. Now people in our days, reverse this tradition to get the benefit of marrying off their daughters at an early age, without even thinking what damage they are causing to the country.

Translated by Sandip Mondal
Department of English, University of Kalyani

'Shishuganer Akal Mrityu o Jananir Kartavya', Bamabodhini Patrika, mid-October to mid-November 1912/Kartik 1319 BS, barsha 50 (year 50), kalpa 10, bhag 1 (part 1), sankhya (591), no. 591, pp. 217-20. In this essay, only the first part of the article that was published in *Bamabodhini Patrika* has been referred.

25

SRI SONAMAKHA DEVI

No biographical details about the author could be found.

Concerning Women (1922)

A few days ago some women came from Nari Karma Mandir[1] and when they requested that they should become members of the Congress I could not honour their request. Ignorant creatures like us who live in the dark, leading mundane lives, unaware of our responsibilities, would become members just on the strength of four annas, and thereafter, would bloat up with pride. Being disrespected is far better than earning respect for being fashionable because rights asserted without understanding responsibilities are like suppressing truth which is unavoidable. If the people whose movements against particular aspects of custom in society, obstructed since time memorial, are suddenly asked to spread their wings in the space provided by the state and avail the freedom and rights that the citizen-members are granted, they would become only a butt of new jokes. At present, the main method of the work of the Congress is the promulgation of non-cooperation and the policy of abandonment of foreign goods. My soul does not find any resonance at all in these activities. The reason is that the intense pressure of a century-old policy of abandonment has caused the souls of the women of Bengal, if not those of all Indian women, to become so sick that at present they have reached a point when they are beyond the capacity to feel the pain of such abandonment.

It cannot be denied by anyone today that the prolonged display of neglect, non-cooperation by patriarchy have made mothers weaker, more inert and narrower, gradually leading them to succumb towards destruction. Despite a thousand attempts, one-half of humanity cannot construct a national life without the participation and cooperation of the other half. The reason is that the blood of this other half bears the effects of the ignorance, inability and narrowness of the mothers who have remained inactive. However much they progress on the one hand, there is regression to an even greater degree on the other hand. The complaint that the mentality and the knowledge acquired by the Bengalis within the last few years, over a period not more than half the life span of an average man, has been exhausted by inertness and by the practice of giving up easily, has been a common one.

This is generally felt, despite the fact that many of those who are erudite are attempting to transform this callous and disrespectful mindset into useful work. The mindset has come into being because of the contradictions between formal education and general living practices, between confinement to the inner apartments and an entry into the drawing rooms, symbolizing the outer world, of the Bengalis. When a section of its society spends most of its lives in the inner quarters, in seclusion, ever deprived of the sun's rays, and is confined to passive silence due to a custom dating back to the sixteenth century then, even if the other half, with its wings spread, attempts to constantly fly up higher, towards the illuminated sky of the twentieth century, all its endeavours become futile and end in a mere fluttering of wings. At the time when there was cohesion between the internal and the external lives of Bengalis how splendid was contemporary Bengali society in the fields of ritual, religion, righteousness and handicrafts, which were well suited to that period. At that time, the main ideal of the simple Bengali life was sociability. This sociability could easily blossom, through acts of offering worship, ceremonies performed in the households and religious and social practices. This was possible because it depended upon the simple cooperative participation of both men and women.

Many claim: 'the women, of that time were proficient housewives.' However, those people who blatantly express this opinion in spoken verses and in compositions in newspapers, and castigate the educated women of today as inefficient and powerless, do not even once ponder the fact that the masters of the households of those days were nothing but proficient male householders. Hence, their minds were confined within the boundaries of the ceremonial functions of their households.

That is why, women of that era, having been given the opportunity to become participants in the ritualistic performances and practices, used to consider that being a proficient housewive itself was the chief ideal of their lives.

However, the difference between the *kartas* or the householders of that time and the *babus* or the gentlemen of present time is vast enough to be apparent even to the eyes of a child. And, that the households of those times are not the same as today can be proved through the very way in which households are run in this era. At the place of the Chandi mandap, where worship and community gatherings used to be held, there is a garage, and instead of sitting on the floor, there are tables and chairs in the sitting room in the style of western offices. In the place of *paandans* or boxes for the betel leaves, and various hookahs or traditional pipes, now tea cups and cigar cases have been brought in. No longer is the same Rama there, nor does the same Ayodhya exist; nevertheless, Sita has to remain the same.[2] Starting from being selected as the wife by the present-day Rama, who is dressed in a short-coat, wearing his hair fashionably plastered with the traditional tuft on the crown trimmed to being almost extinct, prompted by his selfish needs or of someone else's views. But Sita must accept it all without protest. If this is the situation in the land then can anything be a greater mockery than summoning the country's women to participate in working for the uplift and freedom of the country!

Following this consideration is the subject of the education of women of Bengal. Although everyone in modern educated society has verbally admitted that education of women is necessary, in reality, does he or she approve of the independent education of women? Even today some people in this country argue that the ability to keep an account of their daily household expenses and the ability to write a standard letter are the limits of women's accomplishments with regard to their attainment of knowledge, although in the opinion of this group more than a meagre amount of knowledge possessed by women is terrifying for the people in general.[3] There is another group of people, comprising a very small number, who, probably because of the fact that they themselves are very fashionably educated, quite like their wives' reaching the fame of Khana and Lilavati,[4] through their ability to recite books. However, try to discuss any subject related to the national or social rights of women with them and you will see that they have covered their ears well in advance. Therefore, it is perceived very clearly that people of both these groups, want to see in their own wives the preferred image of the housewife and do not consider them as companions who could walk with them down the various roads of life.

This is why even after hundreds of meetings and associations, the so-called education of women has still remained only a part of several different sophisticated social arts and graces. It has not become a support or the means to earn a livelihood independently or to drive one's life on the path of fulfilment. Therefore, whether in the field of education or religion, everywhere it can be seen that the women of this country are just like machines designed to fulfil thousands of social necessities. Nowhere do they have an opportunity to unite the sources of the country's thought, its mind, with its soul. In fact, such a thing rarely occurs. In their enthusiasm to make the country's welfare and economy work, a new burden is thrust on the shoulders of women, and, against such a backdrop, if the patriots today cannot claim to know the opinions and minds of women themselves, then there is nothing to be surprised about. That is why we propose to them that without specifically ending the non-cooperation, now made stagnant due to internal conflict in the Congress, success in this effort which is alien to half of the society is almost impossible despite chanting the newly coined mantras enthusiastically.

Translated by Mrittika Ghosh
Department of Comparative Literature, Jadavpur University

'Narir Katha', Bharati, mid-September to mid-October 1922/Ashvin 1329 BS, barsha 46 (year 46), sankhya 6 (no. 6), pp. 614–16.

Notes

1 Between 1905 and 1946, as part of the women's movement at the national level, the women's movement in West Bengal became very strong This situation led to the formation of a huge number of groups like the Nari Karma Mandir in Bengal.

2 Rama is the mythical ruler of Ayodhya, the hero of the epic *Ramayana,* represented by Valmiki's text of the same name. Rama is held as a model

of conduct for the ideal king: and under his reign Ayodhya was the ideal kingdom. 'No longer is the same Rama there nor does the same Ayodhya exist', is a saying common in Bengali, referring to the difference between this ideal situation and contemporary reality.

[3] A proverb in Bengali, literally translated as 'Partial knowledge is a dangerous thing' where little or partial knowledge is rendered feminine in gender, *bhayankari*.

[4] For details on Kana and Lilavati see Essay 1, n3 and n4, respectively.

26

SANTA DEVI

Santa Devi (1893–1984) received her B.A. from the University of Calcutta and was awarded the Padmavati God Medal. She spent her earlier years in Allahabad where her father, Ramananda Chattopadhyay, was the editor of two influential journals, *Prabasi* (founded in 1901) and *Modern Review* (founded 1907), which he ran with the active support of her mother, Manorama. Santa Devi's husband, Kalidas Nag was a teacher and one of the well-known leaders of the Brahmo Samaj. Santa Devi was fluent in Bengali, Hindi, English and Sanskrit, and particularly interested in economics and mathematics. She spent two years in Santiniketan, studying painting from Nandalal Bose. She was a prolific writer of novels, short stories, travelogues, children books and a translator.[1] Later, she took over the editorship of *Prabasi*. In 1952-53, she gave a series of lectures at Macalester College, USA.

Women's Arts and Crafts Education (1927)

Those who are acquainted with the schools of our country need not be told that it is essential to change our education system. Education in this country does not prepare men for life's struggle or make them normal human beings. The same method of education is also applicable to women in most cases. So it goes without saying that it does not enlighten their future paths either to any great extent. The present system of women's education needs change, extension and reform of various types. I will only discuss one aspect of it.

First, why do we want education? Education enhances the mind and mental beauty, induces knowledge of right and wrong, empowers one to sustain life by earning and other means. These are more or less the few reasons for which we want education. Like men we also want women to be educated so that they learn to differentiate between the good and the bad, the propitious and the unpropitious, the beautiful and the ugly; so that their minds are embellished with beauty and their vision is extended beyond the confinements of their homes. We also want them to establish goodness, virtue and grace through their education by eradicating from their minds the poverty of thought, wickedness and ugliness. We want education to help them in finding solutions to all their troubles at home, where poverty is one of the main problems. So I am sure not everyone will be shocked when I voice the desire to educate women which can make them employable. I am not saying that they cannot achieve it through the education they receive. But it is not done the way it should be. There are many fields of knowledge and aesthetics where we women have no rights. After spending sixteen or seventeen years in school and college with this mutilated education, women enter the domestic sphere; and we are not even talking about all those girls whose education ends when they are seven or eight years old.

I will not bring in music, drama, nursing, home science, child rearing, body and health care. I will limit myself only to saying a few words about painting, sculpture, various kinds of decorative arts and cottage industries, and so on.

Literature, history, and so on, are taught to men from their childhood because the human mind gets acquainted with the world and can relate to it through good literature and the study of the history of various races; this enhances one's vision, enables one to understand human joys and sorrows and extend affection in many directions. Not everybody will believe that arts and painting can also assist in that education. It can be understood if one thinks about it.

One or two examples will prove how a painter has an eye for detail. While we see trees every day, probably we could never say how, in what rhythm, the tree emerges from the lap of the earth, how its branches grow, how its leaves, flowers and fruits blossom from its body of branches, in what direction the veins of leaves appear, what is the difference in colour of the upper and lower part of the leaves or how the roots of the tree are fashioned. People see each other every moment but they never notice any minute detail, so when you ask any ordinary man about the shape of his nearest relative's forehead or eyes or lips or throat, what will he say? He may say that she has a broad forehead but if you ask how the forehead inclines, which side is elevated and where exactly does the parting of her hair begins, you will never get an answer . . .

This is true not only for uneducated people; ask well-educated people and you will get the same answer. So it is evident how people's visions remain idle despite basic ordinary education . . .

But a painter is one whose eyes have opened up. She knows what a blade of grass looks like, what the colour of the grass-flower is, how a wave undulates, what natural laws a tree leaf follows, how colours of the feathers merge consecutively in the wings of a bird . . . Only a painter could see the many facets of the world, her relationship with the world becomes closer . . .

Those who learn to see nature through poetry can see just as much as the poet has been able to express, as deeply as the words have been able to touch the reader's mind; it is always a borrowed vision. But one who has studied art befriends every detail of the area in which she enters otherwise her own creation becomes meaningless. We can see a student who has passed in poetry without an iota of imagination whereas the most academically deficient fine arts student is always an artist. Every step in her education is an examination. Arts education proceeds only through creation of art, therefore, however immature that creation is, it always opens up one's vision. Hence, her diligence and patience are more than those of an ordinary student.

Little wonder then that one whose subject of study is the beauty of the world will have an enhanced mental beauty, however meagre it be. We call women, *sree*.[2] If they do not learn to see the magnificence of Viswalakshmi, the beauty of creation, with their own eyes how are they going to embellish their homes? The world in our country has become office and court and the home, godown and inn. We have driven out sree from home and the world only because men in our country have no leisure, they have to earn by writing[3] in the office, factory and court with eyes closed to the larger world; and women, having no education, cling on to ugliness because they think beauty is luxury.

Because there is no money, a Bengali girl does not have hangers in her house and hangs her clothes only on a line. She does not know how to make hangers from joists. She keeps her knick-knacks in an ugly painted cigarette box for she has forgotten how to paint an ordinary wooden box attractively. She lets her son sleep on tattered sheets only because she is not acquainted with needlework. Where will she get a *cowrie* basket.[4] She puts all her money and needles, and so on, in a soap paper wrapper. Her house is cluttered with cheap hideous enamel and aluminum utensils; she does not understand the significance of bell metal, brass, terracotta or stone things. She buys badly cut expensive dresses for her children as she has not learnt to make dresses with little effort and even less expenditure. Her aptitude and eye have not been trained to make her aware about putting things in appropriate places in home ... Yet in the name of art education she has probably spent two useless hours every day during her eight years of school life ... Since they have never learnt to perceive colour or beauty, whatever they make are rarely attractive ... The painting that they were asked to copy down was probably a French or German painting which made no sense to them at all.

Art which will not be of any use to the women in our country and yet will cost money should not be given too much importance in education. If little girls in school were first taught to stitch a *kantha*, a quilt fashioned out of old pieces of cloth, instead of a comforter, then that would not only be economical but also useful. Before attempting fashionable foreign arts without understanding their necessity and worth, useful local arts should be revived through the education of women in these arts. It is only then that sree will return to our homes.

The problem of poverty has engulfed almost all middle-class families in our country. Yet when the husband has no work for two months or financial problems arise, the wife can do nothing. She will only blame her fate. She will bang her head and cry moaning about her own ill fate that has caused this to happen, and will chastize herself and try to make amends by depriving herself of food. But if she knew some kind of craft, could she not earn some money even while sitting at home?

... It is difficult for women to go out to work. Had she learnt any useful art or craft form for even half an hour every day at school, she would have earned something staying at home. Nothing like this is taught in the schools. In the name of arts they are taught to make a handbag one day or lace the other day or to spin on the tenth day. If every school taught girls one or two kinds of craft from the first class to the tenth class and made them experts in those fields then it would probably have less diversity but every girl would get the opportunity to learn one pleasant functional art which she may use in future. These arts should be such that they would need modest raw materials and little time to make but would fetch some money ... It is practical to teach tailoring, embroidery, toy making, book binding, ornament making, making of cane goods, minor carpentry and so on. I have seen women earning thirty to thirty-five rupees by making toys at home or earning sixty to seventy rupees from tailoring at home. Handloom also fetches good money but Bengalis have but one room in the house, so where will they keep the loom and where will they place cumbersome equipment that comes with it? So there is no need to teach handloom weaving in a general school . . .

I will finish by saying one last thing in this regard. There is no need to say that women are more helpless than men. They have to confine themselves in a limited space given their physical power and the obligation of child rearing. Apart from this, a woman's relationship with her children is an intimate one, and further complicates her life. So every girl must have education such that she can earn her bread when she is in trouble. The girl sent to school must learn Bengali and English but with it she must also gain some expertise in arts and crafts. We have to accept that schools which do not teach even one marketable craft are unqualified to be called girls' schools.

For this reason it is important for us to know about the local crafts and cottage industries of our country. We need to keep track of crafts that are being practised by people in various districts and villages by going from village to village and from district to district. Then we must find which can be learnt and practised by women who stay at home without spending much money or without needing too much space. At least two of these should be taught in schools. It also needs to be seen that girls should earn at least between ten and fifty to sixty rupees per month from these crafts during their leisure months. If such a list is made then we can proceed towards campaigning for the implementation of this plan.

Translated by Jayeeta Bagchi
School of Women's Studies, Jadavpur University

'Narider Charu o Karu Shilpasiksha', Prabasi, January 1927/Magh, 1333 BS, bhag 26 (vol. 26), khanda 2 (part 2), sankhya 4 (no. 4), pp. 525-28.

NOTES

1 In 1912, Santa Devi translated *Folk Tales of Hindustan* by Srish Chandra Basu as *Hindustani Upakatha*, which was illustrated by Upendrakishor Roychoudhury, the grandfather of Satyajit Ray. Her first novel, *Uddayan Lata*, was published under the pen name of Sanjukta in 1918, and later translated as *The Garden Creeper*. In 1919, a collection of her short stores were translated and published as *Tales from Bengal* .Among her short stories are *Ushashi, Sinthir Sindur. Badhubaran, Sat Rajan Dhan* and *Hukkahua*. She wrote two travelogues: *Mohenjodaror Katha* and *Japaner Diary*.

2 Beauty borne of the harmonious balance of many elements; charm. This is also another name for Lakshmi, the Goddess of Wealth and Prosperity.

3 The word 'writing' implies the jobs of petty clerks that English-educated Bengalis found in colonial administration; they laid the foundation of the growing class of bourgeoisie who formed the social and economic strata of Bengali bhadralok.

4 Tropical mollusk with bright shell; used as currency in some parts of Asia.

27

RADHARANI DEVI

Radharani Devi (1903-89) was primarily self-taught. She studied with a scholarship at the Cooch Behar Chabirunnesa Balika Vidyalaya. She first wrote for her brother's magazine when she was twelve. For some of her writings she has used the pen name of Aparajita. In 1929 her first collection of poems, *Lilakamal,* was published under the name of Radharani Dutta (her name after her first marriage). *Kavya Dipali*, another collection, was published in 1927 and was edited by Narendra Dev. Radharani Devi was a young widow and she married Narendra Dev as her second husband in 1931. Apart from poetry, she wrote several fairy tales for young children and a number of notable essays, for example, '*Antahpure Rabindranath*', where the *antahpurikas* were her protagonists who rate Rabindranath and his contribution to society. She received the Kuntaleen Puraskar for *Alo Kothaye Ore Alo*, and was awarded the Bhuvanmohini Swarna Padak by the University of Calcutta, and also receved the Lila Puraskar. In 1986, she won the Rabindra Puraskar for *Aparajita.*[1]

A Brief History of the Magazines Edited by Women in Bengal (1931)

The very first magazine edited by a woman was published in the land Bengal almost half a century ago. Women's education had just about started then; it was yet to spread. In those times, having overcome innumerable obstacles and many social and familial obstructions, the ever-timid and faint-hearted dweller of the inner house, the antahpurika, set out upon a literary pilgrimage and not only associated herself with diverse literary pursuits but also accepted the responsibility of organizing them. It is undoubtedly something that brings joy and wonder because it is extremely tough to imagine the vast difference between the times we live in and the situation about half a century back.

Fuelled by the desire for the betterment of education and an instinctive urge to grow in life, the success that the daughters of Bengal have achieved in literature remains unparalleled in any other field. In spite of this success, with sorrow and shame I have to admit that our country does not yet have one woman poet or author, whose name can be taken in the same breath as the literary giants of the world. However, seeing the progress of women in literature today, it looks as if this hope will not transform itself into hopelessness in the near future.

The first ever woman-edited magazine appeared in 1875 (1282 BS): *Binodini*, edited by Srimati Bhuvanmohini Devi. Bhuvanmohini Devi was also the first female editor of any monthly magazine. Unfortunately, after a few editions, the magazine was out of circulation.

Then, in 1885 (1291 BS), Srimati Swarnakumari Devi dawned upon the literary scene as the second female editor of a Bengali monthly.[2] However, in the truest sense of the term, it was she who was the first female editor of any Bengali magazine because, the late Bhuvanmohini Devi's *Binodini* did not garner much acclaim, and neither did it live long. But in 1885, when the late Dwijendranath Tagore eased himself out of the editorship of *Bharati*,[3] Swarnakumari Devi set such an example, that her skills as an able editor remain crystallized in every page of the magazine even today. She was no less than any competent male editor of her times, and she proved this by taking charge of the *Bharati* a number of times.

In 1886, Srimati Jnanadanandini Devi[4] edited a monthly magazine called *Balak*, which was adorned with many writings from the adolescence of the world's renowned poet Rabindranth. It was in *Balak* that we saw for the first time, articles by Balendranath Thakur[5] and Sarala Devi, both young. Years later, young Balendranath Thakur became one of the most prolific writers of Bengali literature. It is a great misfortune for Bengal that he died young.

After two years of publication, *Bharati* and *Balak* merged. Then, in 1896, the very able daughters of Swarnakumari Devi, the duo, Hiranmoyee Devi and Sarala Devi,[6] took upon themselves the responsibility of the extremely popular magazine, *Bharati*.

The year 1898 saw the birth of another monthly magazine *Punya* edited by Prajnasundari Devi, which ran for five years, until 1902.[7]

Another contemporary female magazine, the famous *Antahpur*, arrived in 1898. Run by a woman, *Antahpur* appeared regularly, enriched with beautiful articles contributed by many women. The first female editor of *Antahpur* was Banalata Devi and she edited *Antahpur* meticulously for four years. After her death, the editorship was accepted by Hemantakumari Chaudhurani.[8] She remained the editor-in-chief between the years 1901–04, after which it was taken up by Lilavati Mitra and *Antahpur* was published in 1905 under her editorship. Due to the lack of resources, however, she could not keep the journal going.

In 1902, the famous monthly *Paricharika*'s editor was Mohini Devi. *Bharat Mahila*, a monthly, exclusively dedicated to women, was published in 1906. The editor of *Bharat Mahila* was Sarajubala Dutta. This magazine ran commendably well through nine years, until 1914.

A wonderful magazine called *Suprabhat* emerged in 1910, under the editorship of Kumudini Mitra (Basu)[9] and ran for five years.

In 1912, a monthly magazine called the *Mahishya Mahila* was published especially for a certain community.[10] This magazine was edited by Krishnabhamini Biswas. Till 1916, for about five years, *Mahishya Mahila* stayed alive. It was around this time that the poet, the late Girindramohini Dasi,[11] started editing the monthly magazine *Jahnavi*, which was published for two years under her editorship.[12]

The extinct *Paricharika* was revived in 1917 by the poet Nirupama Devi[13] from 1917–24 who published *Navaparjay Paricharika* efficiently.

In 1922, the famous *Navyabharat* was edited by Fullanalini Devi, while in 1331, Sarala Devi took up the editorship of *Bharati* once again.

From 1926–32, we see Surabala Dutta as one of the joint editors of *Matrimandir*. Sushila Nandi succeeded her as the editor of *Matrimandir* in 1932.

Kumudini Basu had been editing the *Bangalakshmi*, a monthly dedicated to women's education and their development, between 1926 and 1928. In 1929 , Latika Basu took up it is reins. Since 1929 today, this magazine, committed towards the uplift of women, has been wonderfully taken care of with precious inputs from Srimati Hemlata Devi.[13]

Translated by Prakriti Mitra
School of Women's Studies, Jadavpur University

'Bangladeshe Mahila-Sampadita Patrikar Sankshipta Itihas', *Jayasree*, mid-April to mid-May, 1931/Baisakh 1338.

Also available in *'Radharani Devir Rachana Sankalan 1*, Compiled by Abhijit Sen (Kolkata: Dey's Publishing and School of Women's Studies), Jadavpur University, November 1999/Agrahayan 1406, pp. 71–73.

NOTES

1 In 1930, a collection of thirteen poems were written under the pen name of Aparajita and published as *Buker Bina*. After her marriage to Dev, the second edition of *Kavya Dipali* was published jointly in 1931. She wrote several fairy tales and a number of short stories: *Bimata* (1925); *Patano Ma* (1929); *Masi* (1927); *Param Trisha* (1929); *Je Nadi Marupathe Haralo Dhara* (1929); *Nishitha Rater Badal Dhara* (1928). Among her essays are *'Purush'* (1925); *'Satitwa Manushatwer Sankachak na Pracharak'* (1925); *'Narir Bhalobasha'* (1926); *'Sahitya Bichare Purus-Nari Bhed'* (1931); and *'Shib o Shakti'* (1942).

2 See Eassy 17.

3 The eldest son of Debendranath Tagore and grandson of Dwarkanath Tagore of the Jorasanko branch of the Tagore family, Dwijendranath Tagore was an Indian poet, song composer, philosopher, mathematician and a pioneer in Bengali shorthand and musical notations. After Dwijendranath (1876-1890), *Bharati* was edited by Swarnakumari Devi (1883-93)Hiranmoyee Devi and Sarala Devi jointly took charge as editors for the years 1894-96, and Rabindranath was its editor for a year (1897). Sarala Devi single-handedly carried on as editor from 1898-1906, and Swarnakumari Devi again took over from 1907-13. Manilal Gangopadhyay and Sourindramohan Mukhopadhyay were joint editors from 1914-22. Sarala Devi took charge again from 1923-25, when the journal folded. Thus, in its fifty-year history, the journal had the rare privilege of being edited by women for over thirty years.

4 Jnanadanandini Devi was the wife of Satyendranath Tagore, an older brother of Rabindranath Tagore. He was the first Indian to join the Indian Civil Service. She was very accomplished, editor of *Balak* (which later merged with the other Tagore journal *Bharati)*, a modernizer who designed the way the sari could be draped so that women could move

easily in public spaces. She went about in western drawing rooms with ease, conducting herself in public with dignity. She was, indeed, at home in the western milieu since she had spent many years in England.

5 Balendranath (1870-99) was the only son of Birendranath, the fourth son of Debendranath Tagore. He was a particular favourite of his uncle Rabindranath who dedicated his book *Nadi* to him. He was active in the national movement, marketing goods that were manufactured locally. He wrote for *Bharati o Balak, Bharati, Sadhana* and *Pradip*. He published essays, *Chitra o Kabya* and *Madhabika o Shrabani* in 1907. He died young of tuberculosis. Rabindranath published his unfinished writings in *Pradip* as *'Balendranather Asampata Rachana'*.

6 Hiranmoyee Devi (1870–1925) was the eldest daughter of Swarnakumari Devi and Janakinath Ghosal and granddaughter of Debendranath Tagore. She started writing poetry as a child; her first published poem possibly appeared in *Sakha* in December 1883. She married Phanibhushan Mukherjee, professor of chemistry and biology, at fifteen. Her prose and poetry were mainly published in *Bharati o Balak*. For some time she edited *Bharati* herself, later co-editing it with her younger sister Sarala Devi. When Swarnakumari Devi started Sakhi Samiti for educating women, Hiranmoyee became its head and was responsible for running it. She started a women's handicrafts association for poor widows at her residence. For details on Sarala Devi Chaudhurani (1872–1945), see Essay 52, 'Communion'.

7 Prajnasundari Devi was the daughter of Hemendranath Tagore, third son of Debendranath and the elder brother of Rabindranath. She married the famous author Lakshminath Bezbarua of Assam. Her cookbook *Aamish o Niramish Ahar* (1900, reprinted 1995) was a standard gift given to every Bengali bride with her trousseau, and earning her the appellation of 'India's Mrs Beeton'. *Punya*, started as the in-house publication of *Thakurbari* and she was its editor 1897-1902. Containing fiction, poetry and domestic science and cooking, it was later edited by Hitendranath and Ritendranath Tagore.

8 Hemantakumari Chaudhurani (1868–1953) was born in Lahore and sent to Bethune School, Calcutta, when she was twelve. Sivanath Sastri, the famous Brahmo scholar, was her guardian. Married at seventeen to Rajchandra Chaudhuri, she accompanied him to Shillong and Sylhet. Deeply committed to women's emancipation, before her marriage, with the encouragement of her father, she had set up a women's society or group at Lahore. A mother to eleven children, she continued to work for

women and the underprivileged. While at Shillong she helped to establish a hospital for women. At Sylhet, she organized a meeting where women discussed the plight of the tea garden coolies and submitted a petition to the district commissioner. She went to Patiala as an elderly women, and at the government's request started the Victoria Memorial School for Girls. She later moved to Dehradun and served as the municipal commissioner.

9 Daughter of a leading member of the Brahmo Samaj Krishnakumar Mitra and of Lilavati, the daughter of Rajnarayan Basu, a famous Brahmo scholar and nationalist, Kumudini Mitra (1882–1943) was an early graduate of the University of Calcutta. She married Sachindraprasad Bose. She was deeply involved in nationalist politics especially the opposition to the Partition of Bengal (1905) and the ensuing Swadeshi movement. She wrote many patriotic books like *Sikher Balidan*, a biography, *Jehangirer Atmajibani*, and a life of Mary Carpenter, the English social reformer. She edited *Suprabhat* (1907–14) and *Bangalakshmi* (1925–27).

10 Communities of people engaged in the same trade or caste formed guilds. Also, religious communities had their own periodicals and newspapers for expressing and sharing issues specific to their community concerns, exhibiting the community's position on issues of national and/or general importance.

11 Born in Calcutta and educated in a school run at her home, Girindramohini Dasi (1858–1924) at ten was married to Naresh Chandra Dutta of the eminent Bowbazar family. Akshay Kumar Dutta the eminent scholar and editor of *Tattwabodhini Patrika* was a relative. Her husband's family was known for educating girls and housed the famous Savitri Library. Her first book was *Janaik Hindu Mahilar Patrabali*. She also wrote poetry published as *Kabitahar* (1873) and *Asrukana*, which appeared after her husband's death (1874). She translated Kalidasa's *Kumarsambhavam* to Bengali. Closely associated with Swarnakumari Devi, she was a contributor to *Bharati, Sahitya, Narayan* among other journals and she herself edited *Jahnavi* for three years. She also wrote a verse drama on Mirabai. Her works have been collected and published in *Girindramohini Dasir Gadya Sangraha* (Kolkata: School of Women's Studies, Jadavpur University, 2001).

12 For details on *Jahnavi*, see Essay 23 n3.

13 See Essay 21, 'Obstacles to the Education of Girl Children'.

14 Hemlata Devi (Sarkar), daughter of Pandit Sivanath Sastri, a distinguished leader of the Brahmo Samaj. Born in 1868 as Hemlata Bhattacharya, she was aware of the neglect of education for girl children. After her marriage

to Dr Bepin Behari Sarkar, she accompanied him to Darjeeling and established the Maharani Balika Vidyalaya on 1 September 1908, one year before the establishment of the Rokeya Sakhawat Memorial School for girls. This school was one of the first to be managed by Indians and offered in the district, modern education in Bengali medium. It was raised to the status of high school.

28

JYOTIRMOYEE DEVI

Jyotirmoyee Devi (1894–1988) was the granddaughter of Sansar Chandra Sen, dewan of the Maharaja of Jaipur. Though she was born in the last decade of the nineteenth century, it was not easy for her to break all the barriers of an orthodox Hindu household and come forward. At an early age of ten, she was married and came to Hooghly to live with her parents-in-law. At the age of twenty-five, widowed, she returned to her father's place with six children. At this stage, self-analysis led to her journey towards the free expression of thought. She used writing as a weapon to fight against social orthodoxy. Her essay '*Narir Katha*' and another poem were first published in *Bharatbarsha*, around May–June 1921 and around this time, her essays began appearing regularly in various journals that were published in Bengal. In her early days as a writer she used the pseudonym 'Sumitra Devi'. She was a supporter of Gandhi, and her own views on Gandhian thoughts can be found in her book, *Harijan Unnayan Katha*. In 1965, the Calcutta University awarded her the Bhuvanmohini award. She also won the Rabindra Puraskar from the government of West Bengal for her collection of short stories *Sona Rupa Noy*. Her novels include: *Baisakher Niruddesh Megh* and *Moner Agochore*. Her short stories include *Aravallir Arale* and *Aravallir Kahini.*

Abandoned Women and Separation in Marriage (1931)

Human beings are always prejudiced. Prejudice and [men who are] the guardians of [our] past and future are the true masters in matters of marriage, separation, polygamy, widow remarriage and child marriage. It is customary to 'do' what prejudice proclaims, that is, what the masters proclaim.

For a long time, from time immemorial (in fact), the entity known as woman is subjected to tests and trials. When they hear this, the foolish get angry, but the clever ones say, 'We have always cheated you? Didn't you yourselves let go of the ruler's sceptre for the sake of your own comfort, luxury and contentment?' The women, in their gold and iron bangles [the markers of marriage] and holding containers of Kajal, their arms, satiated in comfort and palms plump with regular daily ration, sit perplexed, without an answer. They are not even aware that an answer exists. Wealth, motor cars, gold and silver—what do they not have? What more do they want? It is like throwing smoked mustard seeds at your head.[1] You become dumb, as a result, unable to speak a single word.

There is a great loophole in the government's work, but for the moment we will let it go. According to the census report, there are hundreds of thousands of widows in Bengal, aged between one and ninety. Some say that it is good, some say bad, and some do not even say anything. We will let it go. We are not trying to find fault with that government's report; it is flawless.

But apart from these widows, there are millions of married women whose husbands are alive—and there is always a discrepancy in their numbers. One just wishes the flaw is mended next time. That is, perhaps the government will condescend to write a separate report of how many among the married women are abandoned.

If a separate report is published about the women—those who are not widows, not married with husbands, not unmarried and dependent on fathers and relatives, wear vermillion and iron bangles, with children or without—it will be seen that there are hundreds of thousands of such entities who are 'no one'. Entities whose husbands have married, once or several times, differently or indifferently—I do not see the need to explain everything. Like others, such husbands have their professions. Food and clothes are not scarce in their homes. But the fact that they have broken their ties with those beings who had one day been handed over to them with much fanfare and celebratory proclamations, remains unremarked upon, although it may be well known in their locality and even in society at large. But then, no one knows it as a fact. That is, no one knows it as a shameful fact to be condemned because there is no such thing as separation in marriage in our society. We inform the world and everyone with pride that there is holy matrimony in our society but not its dissolution; we preserve it through life, until death. There is no dearth of applause for this within our country and abroad.

And only those vermillion-adorned, conch-bangle-wearing entities[2] silently wipe away their tears with the surface of their palms that bear broken veins and stains of ashes used to wash utensils. Whoever shall smite you on your right cheek, turn to him the other also. Of course there is an ideal; this life is not all you get! They curse their fate silently.

And the thing that has escaped, that always escapes everyone's eyes, is that separation in marriage does exist, and, after separation, with moral practice, desire, selection and convenience afforded to them by patriarchy, men continue to enjoy their sensual existence.

Well, let them do whatever they want or not, I do not have anything to say. My point is that separation in marriage exists. Women are simply abandoned without any reason, for no fault of their own. They are abandoned when they are beaten or abducted. They are abandoned when branded with slander and disgraced by people or by their own family. And they are abandoned for disobedience or ugliness or because of their fathers' poverty or vanity; abandoned most of the time with children, or when they are merely girls. Neither the husband, nor his family shows any responsibility towards the children; and if the woman happens to be childless, she is left alone all the more; then it is no one's headache.

So, if separation exists why are there so many arguments and altercations? Men argue for and against it; women almost always against it, and perhaps their argument is coloured by love for the men who strike them. And they always have to tolerate being struck.

For one of the parties involved in [the institution of] marriage, there is nothing that prevents the person from engaging in it a number of times after abandoning the first wife, or after her death. And such a marriage, of course, does not humiliate her, or insult her memory if she is dead.

But whenever, for the sake of argument, there are talks of separation from the abandoned or the humiliated party, the whole world is struck dumb by the pinnacles and summits of idealism characterizing the explanatory rejoinders. This is not all that there is to life, and so on. You will act badly only because others are bad: what sort of ideal is that? And, other similar issues arise.

We are not talking about those who abide by ideals and are very happy about it. We only notice the enslaved, immoral lives of the abandoned; and more often than not they are simply starved into such moral wretchedness. It would not have happened if they had supportive husbands and children, if they did not have to worry about food and comfort. There are times when the abandoned woman is helpless, sometimes she is tempted, and at other times she falls into moral depravity because of her own nature.

Many argue that on an average everyone enjoys a happy and comfortable family life. If two are wicked, then twenty are found to be virtuous. Therefore, 'if separation in marriage becomes customary here, then, as it happens in Europe and America, it will be continuously resorted to for the most trifling reasons.' And that would destroy the idyllic nest that is called a home.

The same thing can be said in counter argument. Women are generally virtuous. Of twenty, five men can be wicked, that is, 20 per cent of them can be wicked; but it is quite doubtful that even one amongst the women can be considered such. Filial affection, love for home and husband and traditional devotion are more deeply and firmly rooted in women than in men. Also, the desire and propensity for a family life is greater among them. And, in those cases, when for trifling reasons or without any reason at all, for a new object of 'inseparable' matrimonial bonding, a new life, to satisfy a new love or as a hobby, men abandon women too frequently, when with reason or without any reason, as described earlier, they abandon women at whim, and for the abandoned, meanwhile, even food and drink become scarce, let alone the domestic idyll, then, surely it can be said that if such separation is allowed, it will be resorted to for the most trifling of reasons. And, it is usually customary to 'abandon' one's wife rather than 'separating' [a mare's nest!] for trifling reasons.

But, in any case, we have our consolation that it cannot be equated with the foreign notion of a divorce!

The authorities dislike the use of law regarding such things. They believe the hallowed institution of marriage will lose its sacredness, solemnity and charm. Perhaps these qualities are retained when the wives are secretly abandoned.

Let us now look at the outcome and consequences. The abandoned woman occupies the lowest position among her relatives, and there is no end to her affliction, privacy and misery. It is the same for women with children, though they hope that god willing they would be able to rebuild their home. Most childless women are tempted and harassed in many ways; perhaps they are forced to lead corrupt lives because of social pressure, for it is a fate not infrequent among women with children. It is they who are often pitched out of the frying pan into the fire because of their kinsmen's torment and their own weakness. They are also extremely helpless in their economic condition: only some paltry pieces of jewellery or a pitiable amount of money remains in their possession. But kindly kinsmen often try to relieve them of even those paltry possessions. And they have no power to earn money, nor do they have the right to.

According to law, abandoned women who are honest can ask for subsistence. And that makes me wonder: why is she abandoned at all, if she is honest and innocent? I admit the utility of food and clothes in life, I know that these are extremely necessary, but if the husband has the power to fulfil every such need, why at all is the woman abandoned? A woman with no beauty is, and should be, understandably desirous of living a life with husband and children. There is no normal answer to this because the Master dictates the deed. And even if she is legally entitled to subsistence, it is an entirely different matter whether she actually gets it. A greatly convenient thing is that there is no need to explain the abandoned woman's crime. Nothing can come above the master's desires and dislikes. We only see that most men are dreadfully intent on spiritual meditation for salvation in afterlife while they preside comfortably over the plight of tormented women, of girls and women unable to procure bribes for marriage (in the form of dowry), of women abducted and of fallen women. Only a handful of men, with true masculine propriety, try hard for daily absolution.

There is no law, no civility, no help to redress the plight of these women. Learned sociologists say, 'It is so distasteful to haul everything within the ambit of law.' Indeed it is. But you do not quote the law regarding a feud between brothers, do you? In that case, not an inch is given without a fight. One requires law in times of distress and to redress oppression one does not think of it in times of prosperous well-being. We are not talking about happy, well-loved women; we are talking about unfortunate women deprived of their husbands' love, women who, abandoned silently, eke out a terrible existence, women who are often unable to keep even their dignity and the entire society does not even bother to inquire about their misfortune. The perpetrator of this misfortune, prompted by his father and mother or by himself, marries again. The great advantage is that in this country polygamy is perfectly legal.[3] There is of course no such advantage in occidental countries. And then, in times of need, you can even call back the abandoned for service, and reclaim that jewellery after her death. But of course she was given in marriage to the husband along with the jewellery! His claim therefore is a rightful one!

Perhaps there are no laws for women. Most people say that given the small number of abandoned and distressed women, there is no need for much discussion. Perhaps that is so, but our view is this: the small numbers of such husbands (who have abandoned their wives) should strictly observe celibacy – and this should be made into a law. If separation within marriage did not exist, there would have been nothing for us to say – the married couple would have kept their vows until death. But one-sided separation does exist in this country and it is achieved quite easily, more easily, as a matter of fact, than occidental countries where the husbands and wives need to show reasons in court for separation. But there is no such compulsion in this country. It is sufficient to say that I do not approve of her, or my father, mother, father's sister, mother's sister do not wish that I live with her because she is dark-skinned, or educated, or uneducated. Most of the time, though, there is no need for any reason, argument or explanation; the women are just packed and sent away to their fathers' homes and forgotten, thus separation is achieved. In due time, the father's family is 'cordially invited' to witness and bless another ceremony of holy matrimony.

But then, we do have our consolation that this phenomenon is genuinely indigenous to our country. Like jaundiced liver, malaria, *kala-azar*,[4] drought and flood, it is quite native and there is nothing imported about it. This would not have been the case if it was 'divorce', or a foreign sort of separation, or Muslim *talaq*.[5]

The proposal for separation in marriage has been rejected in the Women's Congress held at Calcutta, though the executive council in the state of Baroda has passed it.[6] They are investigating it, and we too should enquire into it. The number of such women in each locality and their fault, the reasons their husbands show, their means of livelihood and whether they have any guardian, or are educated enough to be self-sufficient, or are in a condition to keep their moral dignity—should all be inquired.

And there should be a stringent injunction that one who has left his wife for no reason must never be allowed to marry again. Otherwise, separation in marriage will be socially dignified as a 'mare's nest'. The masters of society know very well how the ritual of such 'easy abandonment' helps to foster debauchery.

A few people of questionable character may support prostitution or the mass desertion of women on the basis of their own whims—if sentimental indulgence for such exploitation is not rooted out, there will come a time in this unfortunate country when the fate of he who insults and he who is insulted will become the same. Those who support their abusive clan often forget that they shall have to pay for their injustices.

Translated by Somesh Roy
Department of English, Alipurduar College

'Parityakta o Bibaha-Bichhed', Swadesha, mid-October to mid-November/Kartik 1338 BS.

Notes

1 A traditional practice of witch doctors in rural Bengal during which smoked or burnt mustard seeds are thrown at a person possessed by evil spirits as part of the exorcism process.

2 Further marks of the married state

3 Polygamy was made illegal for Hindus by the Hindu Code Bill passed in independent India in 1954-55.

4 A slow-progressing indigenous disease caused the Hindu Code Bill protozoan parasite, and noticed in India since 1824-25. Initially mistaken for malaria, in 1903 it was identified as a separate disease.

5 Divorce.

6 Prior to the session of the Indian National Congress scheduled to be held in Calcutta in May 1931, Congresswomen decided to demand a separate Congress for women. Santi Das, acting as convenor of this Congress, asked each district to send delegates to Calcutta. In preparation, they had held meetings in the districts and discussed social reform. When the delegates gathered in Calcutta, the session was first addressed by Sarala Devi Chaudhurani, who began by pointing out how women are discriminated against since childhood and went on to demand that women who had participated in the political struggle be recognized as law makers. The meeting made a charter of ten fundamental rights for women.

29

JYOTIRMOYEE GANGOPADHYAY

Jyotirmoyee Gangopadhyay (1889-1945) was the daughter of Dwarkanath and Kadambini Gangopadhyay, the first woman doctor to practise in India. Jyotirmoyee received her B.A. degree from Bethune College and her M.A. from the University of Calcutta. She was an ardent nationalist, supporting the early Swadeshi movement and the Non-Cooperation movement in 1920. She was the founder of the Nari Svecha Sevika Vahini in 1920 and left her job at the Calcutta Corporation's Primary Education Department in 1930 to work full time as a nationalist. She was elected as a municipal councillor. She was arrested in 1930 for her participation in the Civil Disobedience movement in 1930 and again in 1942 during the Quit India movement. Jyotirmoyee encouraged the participation of students in the nationalist movement and in 1946 during the INA trials, a procession of students was fired on and Rameshwar Bandyopadhyay was killed. At the head of a march for justice where the corpse was also carried along, she died when a lorry hit her car.

Grandmother's Letter (1931)

Bhai Jnanadadidi,[1]

You have written that today it seems women have heralded a movement for their emancipation, raising the blood-red flag of revolution in the sky. You say that it seems that the woman today has recognized, known and understood herself; no longer will she allow herself to be bound by men's selfish web of convention; and she will demand freedom. Very good! But may I ask a few questions?

Accha Bhai,[2] . . . Is it today that the woman has recognized herself for the first time? If that is not the case, then surely there was a time before when she did know herself? Then what occurred suddenly that caused her to forget who she was? . . .

Selfish men, for their own happiness and well-being, their own domestic peace and comfort, kept women in the inner chambers, such that the sun remained invisible to them; they crippled women by trussing them up in the bonds of economic dependence. I understand and accept all that. But why did the woman approve of this? What allurement possessed her? When did the woman give the man permission to fragment the sovereignty of her mind and body?

When man made his home with his beloved, or rather, what seems even more natural and truthful to me, when the beloved woman forced her loved companion to enter into a marital relation and build a home, assuring that this only could ensure that he reigned in her heart, did this same woman not immerse herself totally in the household on her own free will? Did the woman herself not push away all that was external to her to minister to the needs and comforts of the man, whose touch had awakened her maternal feelings that lodged dormant within her consciousness? Woman enters an impermanent temporal stage when she has to push the outer world away and claim the inner space for her own. But that impermanent stage did not permanently engulf her, did it? I seem to feel that this is what had happened. Comfort-loving man, taking advantage of woman's temporarily eclipsed self-consciousness, imprisoned her within that inner space. In the joy of having the beloved totally dependent upon him, and rendered oblivious to society's welfare due to the masculine pride of winning the heart of the beloved, man devised means and methods, fabricated laws and customs, to keep her in his sole possession. 'Love is the essence of feminine life', so in loving with her whole heart, she wanted to forget everything . . . she loses herself in the joy of service, remains entranced with the fulfilment of loving; did she not realize what trap she had walked into?

Lest some other man, entralled by his beloved's beauty and qualities tries to win her over, man carefully tried to shield her from the eyes of other men; the custom of purdah, veiling or covering the face, was propagated within the human community. Woman did not try to understand the inherent meaning of this custom. She did not try to gauge the ill effects that this custom may generate in the long run. She was only joyfully enraptured by the fact that . . . he considered her attractive to other men and hence expended effort and vigilance to keep her exclusively as his own. She accepted the purdah and the veil as praiseworthy marks of glory.

As soon as man said, 'You are *tilottama*,[3] perfect in every respect, if any man sees you, I fear that he will be as entranced as I am', why did the woman immediately believe him considering herself to be beautiful enough to conquer the cosmos? The flower-bedecked arrows of love may nest in the eyes, lips may shower elixir, but who said that every man will be attracted by only one and the same woman? Helen, Cleopatra, Mohini, whomsoever you name, any woman who according to history or poetry is known to have won many hearts, as evident from their biographies, even they too had to expend immense effort to make themselves impressive. You will say, 'Even today we may see that the lure of beauty is no small thing, many women have had to give up their lives for their beauty. They have had to bear immense pain.' But, may I ask you, who actually prodded the lure of beauty to such mammoth proportions? Did this not happen because purdah and the veil were made such indispensable parts of life? Women have been weakened, made fearful and hesitant by nature and men have become lustful, greedy for beauty. Taking woman as the object of fulfilling their desire for indulgence, treating them as handmaidens and playthings, has become the characteristic masculine habit. Woman too, mistaking what is in truth an insult to her womanhood and above all to her humanity, as a tribute to her beauty and as an acknowledge-ment of her ability to enthral, chews betel leaves calmly and admires herself in the mirror. If man wants to enthrone the woman as tilottama, the perfect one, then it is the woman who needs to reassure him with a smile and say, 'Do not fear. I am beautiful in your eyes and I want to remain so. But I shall not appear to be so in the eyes of another. For, how can the love for you that drenches my heart and makes me so tender, so gentle in your eyes, be felt by anyone else? This love is for you alone, not for anyone else.'

But has the woman thought from such a perspective? Have all those who have renounced the purdah had such confidence in their own feelings? Are you looking unhesitatingly upon men as human beings? Do you experience their gaze as undefiled and pure? You may well reply 'Yes,' but it seems to me from time to time that not everyone has reached that state even today. Let me tell you what happened one day. At a gathering, the mother-in-law of a very beautiful woman said, 'Let it be, she need not remove the covering from her face.' But the woman herself whispered, 'Those men stare at me open-mouthed, you know.' Monididi said, 'Forget that they are staring at you, do not remember that you are exceptionally beautiful.' I said, 'We too were staring at you open-mouthed.' The woman laughed and said, 'But that is different.' We said, 'That is not different at all, everyone looks at someone beautiful. If the beautiful accepts this gaze easily and naturally, if the beautiful understands the unstained adoration inherent in such a gaze, then the gaze does not remain defiled. It is rather, purified.' Someone said, 'Those who are bad have the fire of lust in their hearts.' We said, 'This becomes possible only because we behave out of petty conceptions, and thus encourage them to demean themselves.' In fact, the place where our society has reached today, it is easy enough for fires of lust to rage in people's hearts. Perhaps instead of respect for beauty, it is a thirst for beauty that is rampant, but that is not the natural state of the human mind. We must turn the tide of this condition. And to do that we must renounce the path that we have walked upon in the past as that path is not one that will douse the fires of lust, rather it will intensify it. To defeat the evil gaze, woman must look within herself for armour. Her own speech, behaviour, courage and strength will protect her. Burqas, veils, shawls and purdahs will not be able to help. We may quote the daily reports of harassment of women by anti-social elements that we read about in the newspapers as proof. Hence, prepare yourselves as you change strategy. Try to understand [yourselves] as humans.

It makes me happy to see that now you have demanded property rights, in specific cases, even condoned divorce. But why have you not demanded the right to sit in the jury in law courts? Do you not think that in legal cases involving women to have women jurors is imperative? Have you not noticed that whenever there is a case, of abduction, harassment or disrespect of women, the other party always tries to prove that the female complainant is 'of bad character'? Whenever I see this I burn with rage. Does the woman herself not have any right over her own body? If a woman does not behave according to the dictates of contemporary society, assuming that she might be a widow or an abandoned woman, who due to social strictures cannot marry the man whom she might have been interested in, does that mean that any Ram, Shyam, Jadu or Hari automatically gain rights over her body? What is the meaning of this? Then the law will state, 'In such circumstances, the perpetrator is not actually at fault, he must not be punished too strictly.' Can a woman who lives by selling her body as commodity not refuse a customer if she so desires? What is the special fault of such a woman that she is meted out such heartless punishment? Why is woman still allowing man to flex his muscles in such a manner, even today?

Because we thought we would be defiled by the touch of another man, because we thought that we would never be free from the stigma of this defilement, we are in this state of endless misery today. She who did not have a shred of sin within her, she who had a pure, chaste heart, such an unfortunate one also had to sacrifice this life as soon as she returned home. The stain of sin upon her was not cleansed, even in the eyes of women themselves. So many women who know that they are blameless still lead a life of hopeless remorse marked by the stigma of sinfulness due to the torture of debauched men. Will you turn your clear sparkling, intelligent gaze upon their faces?

You are setting out on a mission to emancipate women—that's very good. You wish to raise a war cry against man-made discipline—do so by all means. But simultaneously, do not forget to announce a revolution against yourselves as well. Because those who desire true emancipation cannot afford to forget their own weaknesses and avert their discerning gaze from their own shortcomings.

I am curious; these are questions that have come to my mind, so I have said this much. Don't be angry; rather, if you can, explain all this to an old woman.

With blessings,

Your Grandmother.

Translated by Ipshita Chanda
Department of Comparative Literature, Jadavpur University

'Didimar Patra', Jayasree, mid-August to mid-Setember 1931/Bhadra 1338 BS, in *Jyotirmoyee Gangopadhyayer Rachana Samkalan,* Compiled by Abhijit Sen and Anindita Bhaduri (Kolkata: Dey's Publishing and School of Women's Studies), Jadavpur University, April 2007/Baisakh 1414, pp. 65–68.

Notes

1 Bhai literally means brother; here it is used as a term of endearment to indicate the special friendship between the grandmother and granddaughter. It is to be noted that though bhai is masculine, it is easily used by women to address each other in circumstances of friendship.

Didi refers to the elder sister; another affectionate form of address used by the didima (maternal grandmother) for her granddaughter.

2 Literally 'Tell me'. The original has been preserved to indicate the tone, affectionate and conversational, between the letter writer and her addressee.

3 Viswakarma, the God of Creation under the instruction of Lord Brahma created a beautiful woman named Tilottama to kill the demon brothers Sunda and Upasunda, sons of the demon-king Nikumbha. He collected all the best items from the three worlds and created Tilottama who was an exquisite beauty.

PART III

REFIGURING THE FAMILY AND RELATIONSHIPS

30

SHYAMASUNDARI DEVI

There is a certain degree of ambiguity in the identity of the author.[1]

On Whether Or Not the Hindu Widow Should Marry Again (1885)

If we are to decide in this essay whether the Hindu widow should remarry, we must clarify many things at the outset.[2] Whether something is right or not may be decided by dharma,[3] so we must first see how Hindus look at dharma; then we must understand what they mean by *bibaha,*[4] marriage. All events in this world can be seen in two ways, from two different perspectives . . . a human may be described as a combination of chemicals and fluids, flesh and blood, breath and air; or as a unique amalgamation of flesh and blood, bones and systems, cells and vessels; or as a form where the heart, head, stomach, thigh, hands, feet are bound together in a particular manner. We may also say that the human being is a storehouse of great knowledge, the playground of intelligence, the space where beauty and its feats are displayed, and the receptacle of unmatched devotion. Similarly, a little flowering plant may be seen as an outcome of the union of its roots, stems, branches, twigs, leaves, flowers; a state of beguiling beauty; a mine of the most alluring fragrance; a picture of gentleness that lifts the heart; the origin of an emerging brilliance. Again, the vast expanse of Bharat (India) can either be seen as the home of more than twenty crore slaves, or the land where eighteen languages coexist within an area of four lakh square *krosh*[5] of space, or a place through which the Ganga, Yamuna, Sindhu, Kaveri flow, where the Vindhyas-Himalayas stand, where trees like shal-tal-tamal flourish, and which is bounded by the Indian Ocean, Southern Sea, Arabian Sea, where the three oceans meet and lash against one another. We may also see it as the meeting ground of all aspects of dharma—the Vedic, the philosophical, the Buddhist, the atheist, the Vaishnav, the Islamic, the Christian—flowing from an infinite origin towards the centre of the extensive and all-embracing expanse of world history; a place where dharma is tested by its ability to confront adharma; an ideal sphere where tolerance is practised; an arena where the ways of this world whirl like a giant wheel; a huge pendulum which regulates the progress of time in history; and a temple of union where the courageous and the valiant of past times meet the delicate and the immensely tender and gentle future in devout welcome. Everything can thus be seen from two angles, in two ways; so every human event has two sides. One aspect may be self-centred, material, this-worldly, related to rupees-annas-paise, hence physical; the other may be of dharma, other-worldly, idealist, seen from the psychological perspective of benefit-goodness-love.

For those who know English, there is a beautiful example, which explains these two aspects, as shown by the famous historian Henry Buckle.[6] Adam Smith wrote two books. One is called *The Wealth of Nations*, dealing with the ways in which different nations acquire material wealth; the other is *The Theory of Moral Sentiments*, on different views on the principles of morality. The first is a text on economics; it talks about the accumulation of wealth; there is not a whiff of mercy, dharma, and so on, in it. Like a true shopkeeper, characteristic of his nationality, Adam Smith weighs the means and methods of wealth acquisition, and outlines the pros and cons of the different methods for this purpose like an experienced accountant. He does not cast a glance towards dharma or adharma, or right or wrong; there is no sympathetic evocation of the beating of something called a heart, no desire to conceal the more crafty means of wealth acquisition and no surrender to humane feelings. Yet when he himself considers the theory and principles of morality, he appears in another form. There the deepest human emotions, the most subtle human capabilities are being discussed; his sole capital then is the vibrating human instrument called the heart, that is what he analyses, that is what he lends out on loan, supplies and augments.

... These days there is a terrible wind sweeping across the land. Many people are intent upon seeing things only from the scientific perspective; concerns of right and wrong, devotion and love, mercy and charity and considerations for the benefit of all are now being scientifically dissected. Many great scholars dare to say that everything in the Hindu scriptures is scientific. This is a frightening move. We wish to accumulate our limited energies to protest against such views.

The science of any theory can see just a single facet of the matter, which constitutes only an insignificant part of the Hindu beliefs, ... comprehending a larger expanse of dharma and adharma more deeply, ought to be one's primary and ultimate duty. If we are to understand what is appropriate and what is not, the touchstone of dharma alone will give us the true answer. If we are to comprehend this, we need to consider many other things too.

Let me give one or two examples. Is it proper for humans to eat flesh? This has always been a disputed issue. Scientist Komuth says that it is fitting for us to eat what is nutritious; to eat only that which tickles some nerve in the tongue is not correct. But such an argument is limited to looking only at the scientific aspect of the matter.

The great sage Manu is famous among the exponents of *Dharmashastras* or the science of dharma;[7] he casts his keen eye upon dharma, yet he does not neglect that which was seen in his time as science. Taking the help of both he has given instructions about what ought to be eaten and what to be rejected. He has mentioned that certain things are legitimate and certain things are not. But then, listen to his final verdict—he who kills the non-violent beast for his own pleasure will not be happy in this world or the next. But he who does not wish to entrap the living being in the snare of death and wishes good for all, will be able to experience immense joy. Now we may argue: does this statement have some logic behind it? Certainly, science follows logic. But is there a reason behind dharma too? There certainly is. There is no way of getting meat without showing violence to animals, but the killing of animals is not a good act, so it is best to avoid meat as food.

At this point, the argumentative person may ask, what kind of an argument is this? What is meant by killing animals is not right? In order to answer such questions Manu continues: We must understand that the flesh is born in the body of the animal, and that trapping any living being in the bonds of death is wrong. So to free oneself from the inclination to taste meat is the most desired outcome: the *mahaphal.* Today, science says that food with high gluten content is beneficial. Based on dharma laws that are founded on science and history, some say the flesh of pigs is a taboo, others say it is the flesh of dogs, but the pronouncement of dharma is '*nivrittastu mahaphala*',[8] that is, freedom from the inclination to eat flesh is the most desirable outcome which again is common to all religions....

I shall give another example. A man has fallen in the river and is drowning. You are standing near a learned man on the bank; the question of whether you should rescue the man arises in your mind. See what science advises. First, it says, 'See what possibility of rescuing him exists, compare the strength of your body with the force of the current.' You reply that it is not possible now. Science says, 'Then calculate the force that is required to rescue him, by subtracting your body weight from the force of the current, and then decide whether you have that much force, and consider the extent of the possibility of losing your life in the effort. If there is even a remote possibility, then I cannot ask you to go forth to do this job, because you are four times as capable as that man who is nearing death.' Thus it is impossible for you to go to his rescue, in the opinion of science. ... So you turn to dharma, and dharma says to you, 'What calculations are you wasting time on? If you help, the man might be saved, so why are you standing here without making any effort?' The words strike a chord in your heart. Just as the feet move faster to mount the vehicle when the departure bell rings, similarly, the sound in your heart causes you to jump into the river all of a sudden; your strength increases fourfold; you rescue the man.

It is clear from this that it is often impossible to act according to the dictates of science. The dictates of dharma are simple yet clear; but following them is not so easy, not '*practical*'.[9] Since they are not '*practical*', dharma is not to be followed—such is the kind of common belief these days.

This matter has come to the fore a long while ago, but last year, when it was uttered by the ruler himself,[10] it became a cause of great shame. Now everyone is inclined towards practicality.... Now anything that does not reek of the clanging of coins or decrease the pangs of colonial rebuke seems to appear impractical. Hence, to get a salaried job appears to be the only practical option. ... Now we hear from the ruler that if dharma is not practical, it is not dharma.[11] The practitioners say that there are theories which have never been attempted seriously because they are considered impractical.[12] ...

The essence of this is that which is not easily done is not dharma. Such a horribly diabolical view, such a distorted explanation of dharma cannot be true. Dharma is the name of the system that organizes and regulates human character. Because it is an ideal, it is impossible to adhere to it completely. And as complete adherence to it is impossible, it remains as an ideal.

... As would occur in the case of an angular crooked line that tends to move along towards the centre of a hyperbola, a man of good character can come closer and closer to dharma, but will not finally reach it. But at the same time, dharma is not illusive, nor is it something like a mirage that tempts the onlooker and draws him towards it or recedes from him, arousing false hopes and then suddenly throws him into the stark darkness of despair. Dharma is a real substance; it remains eternally bright, calm, unmoving and radiant. The closer you move towards dharma the more you are becalmed, hopeful and restful; he who has moved even an inch towards dharma will never be deprived of hope or cast away; instead, the noble person, from one birth to the next will come closer and closer to dharma, though he will not be able to touch it ...

This strange, living mystery is the beauty of dharma, its glory, its idealism and its utility. He who does not understand the inherent mystery of dharma will attempt to make dharma *'practical'* or exercise complete control. *'Practical'* dharma is as untrue as a horse laying eggs. Replacing that which is *'unpractical'* today, and making tomorrow *'practical'* is the aim of scientific endeavour. And dharma is that which we will *'practice'* despite knowing that it is *'unpractical'* today, and will remain so tomorrow and forever.

... We will try to renounce ourselves within us, without which we have no identity of our own, and which is impossible for us to forget. Forgetting ourselves, we will try to serve others; even if we cannot gather enough food for ourselves, we will provide two handfuls of rice for others; though we ourselves may get perturbed by our illness and sorrow, we will console others when such things occur in their lives. Many a time, speaking the truth leads to unpleasantness, and the pleasant is not true, yet we will try to speak both the pleasant and the truth, as often as we can. Though we are aware that continuous devotion, contemplation and meditation of the One who is boundless, infinite, beyond imagination is not always possible, we will make these our goals, desires and work, as does the *dharmik*, who follows the path of dharma. Making what is impossible in the present possible in the future is called science and striving for the impossible ceaselessly is named dharma. Hence, the words 'scientific dharma' sounds as comical as *'practical'* dharma.

We need to remember this element of mystery that exists in dharma. There is no dictum stating that the performance of a certain solemn rite should be modified so that its related religious ceremonies can be conducted in entirety; if the ritual is virtuous, then it is our duty to see how we may best carry it out. Should the Hindu widow remarry? This question may also be rephrased as: should the Hindu widow observe brahmacharya[13] or chastity? If the widows' conforming to brahmacharya is a solemn ritual, then it is certainly desirable; even if difficult, it needs to be carried out.... Yet, to understand whether brahmacharya is desirable or undesirable for the Hindu widow, we must first understand what is understood by Hindu marriage.

As all matters can be analysed from two perspectives, Hindu marriage can be considered from two aspects. From one angle, we might say that the purpose of marriage is to fulfil sensual desire. If seen from the insensate material point of view, this is certainly the truth. If this is the sole objective of marriage, then why are there so many bonds and vows? Just some sort of a loose tie would have been enough. The answer to this has been that it is necessary to marry in order to beget sons. Well, so what is the need for sons? Sons are necessary to conduct *pindo daan*, the sacrament of food offering to the bereaved soul, enabling it to cross over from this world into the next.[14] Since this ritual relates to the satisfaction of the soul, the question of 'why' does not arise. Nurturing of the self, contentment of the self and preservation of its interests—all function in one or the other way as some sort of a final indisputable logic for such cases.

That the sole necessity of marriage is to beget children is a justification used to downplay the importance of marriage as being minor and negligible. But the Hindu marriage has a much higher, purer and a wholly spiritual aim; the Hindu way of life is acutely concerned with the spiritual. In the matter of marriage too, spiritualism is expressly evident.

The universe traverses its set path—from the large to the larger, from the larger to the largest, and then merges into the void—and in this lies its inherent beauty. The culmination of the tiny human life into a larger and then the largest entity is the ultimate reality. According to the Hindu *Shastras*, there is a regular course, a proper progression of this journey to the final culmination. First begins your physical and mental development, then the development of the family or householder's life, then social development, and, finally, the development of the spiritual. The four stages of life give rise to the four *ashramas*.[15] In the second stage, the householder's life is bound mainly by the mistress of the house; the home is organized around her. The stage of household life is impossible without the wife. But progression into the subsequent stage of *sanyas*—renunciation of household life—is not achievable without living through the stage of the householder. The stage of sanyas signifies the movement from the larger social life to the largest community of all, becoming one with the universe. Hence the learned have said, 'The aim of Hindu marriage is emancipation. Marriage is the best and the most laudable path to salvation, *moksha*.' ... 'An incomplete man when united with his wife achieves completeness.' The union which occurs between the husband and wife in the Hindu marriage 'such commingling, such oneness has not been imagined by any other race on earth'. 'When the process of such marriage gets under way we see two different individuals, but when it is complete, we see only a single individual.' 'Just as water mixes with water, just as wind mixes with wind, just as flames mingle with flames, so does the man mingle with the woman and the woman with the man.' 'The self-born one had divided himself into two in order to create humans, now these two parts have merged together again to return to their original form.'[16] 'The complete union of man and woman results in humanity.' The aim of Hindu marriage is 'such union, such oneness'.

It is true that the union of a man and a woman is called marriage, but that man is not one who appears out of the blue or from a nowhere land; he belongs to a specific *gotra* or clan, a specific community, a specific lineage and is thus a part of all these collectives.[17] So, as held by Hindu traditions, if the woman has to become a part of the man she is married to, becoming his other half, so to say, then she must change her gotra and adopt that of her husband's. The Hindu does not consider marriage as the coming together of two individuals, each having distinct qualities (physical and mental) and beauty as is common in English marriages, neither is marriage seen as some arbitrary and temporary arrangement between two distinct isolated individuals.... Hence, the union of one and one is not marriage; the coming together and mingling of a woman into a family to complete the half and make it whole is called marriage. Marriage establishes the auspicious Lakshmi, the guardian Goddess of Fortune, in the household; heralding the appearance of the mistress of the house into the household. In the West, the young man and woman, after marriage, spend a month alone, on honeymoon and away from their families, clan and society.[18] But in our culture the new bride, after returning from *diragaman*,[19] appears as an empress, serving the vast empire, her whole household. With her face covered in half-a-hand-long veil, she absorbs herself in household chores[20] in the kitchen. The Hindu marriage, thus, is a family ritual.

We must understand that a Hindu virgin gets married into a family, not to an individual. This is evident from our customary conversations and conduct. 'Where did you get your daughter married, sir?' 'In the North, in Sripur's Chaudhuri family.' 'That is very good; there will be no want of food or clothing.'[21] Then the next question, 'And how is the groom?' 'He is studying in college.' So the main issue remains how established is the family, because according to Hindu understanding marriage means an association with a family; the man is a mere *patra*.[22]

In the marriage mantra, the groom says,

'Om dhruba dau, dhruba prithivi,
Dhrubang bishvamidat jagat,
Dhrubasah parbataimey,
Dhruba stree patikuley iyam.'

(The sky, the stars and the world are constant,/this universe is constant,/the mountains are constant,/and this woman too is constant in her husband's family.)

The bride says,

'Dhrubang asi dhrubahang,
Patikuley bhuyasam.'

(O constant *dhruba nakshatra*, O Pole Star,/Just as you are constant, so may I be constant in my marital family.)

The groom says to the bride,

'Om samragyi sasurey bhav,
Samragyi swsrang bhav,

Nanadarich samragyi bhav,
Samragyi adhidebrishu.'

(May you be as blessed as an empress in the company of your parents-in-law, sisters-in-law and brothers-in-law.)

Hence, the wife is not only the 'empress of my heart' but 'the slave empress of a whole family'. The wife has a specific relationship with each member of the family. The Hindu is careful 'to keep the wedded wife eternally constant in her husband and in his family', like the constant Pole Star.[23] During the Hindu marriage, two stars are to be seen: one is Arundhati, the other the Pole Star. Taking Arundhati as the witness, as the ideal, the bride says, 'May I be bound to my husband, as you are.' Arundhati is the wife of Sage Vashistha, she is his companion in the sky as well which means that she desires to be bound to him in this life as well as the next. And taking the Pole Star as witness she says, 'May I be constant in my marital family as you are constant in the sky.'

So far we have not said a single word about the remarriage of widows, now we may hesitantly and with great humility ask, does not remarriage sound a little strange in the context of Hindu marriage? If we look at it from the point of view of dharma, the marriage of a Hindu woman is a kind of event whose repetition seems impossible.

Once the Hindu woman is taken into, connected to and married into a particular family, she cannot abandon that family in any way. In the Hindu's dictionary, she who abandons the family, she who is a disgrace to the family and she who is promiscuous carry the same meaning. ...

Besides this, we must notice that marriage is an event where the most intense spiritual communion occurs—the union between hearts, minds and souls. The Hindu firmly believes that when the body is reunited with the five elements,[24] the soul is not destroyed; it is the dharma of the species to believe in after-life. Now can you tell me, how can the Hindu woman remarry after her husband's death? If remarriage is acceptable in such cases, then she should also be permitted to marry when her husband stays in another place. I feel embarrassed that during a meeting held at this library, which is named after the pristine Savitri, I have to make such observations. We seem to be forgetting Savitri's performance of the fourteenth day ritual; the *Shastras* tell us that the chaste woman who was a 'sati' did not even fear Yama, the God of

Death, who failed to separate her from her dead husband. We do believe that the sati can never become a widow, whether her husband is in the country or elsewhere, whether he is in this world or in another, if they are separated for a day, ten days, an era, several eras, she remains her husband's and he hers'. So how can the chaste sati ever become a widow? This is the deeper wisdom revealed by the story of Savitri's fourteenth-day ritual performed for the good of her dead husband. The woman who is able to take this wisdom to heart will never have to tolerate the agonies of widowhood. What an amazing dharma! What stupendous wisdom!

It appears that the two stars that the Hindu woman calls as witness of her marriage are against her remarriage. Arundhati says, 'But you had said you would remain your husband's companion in this life and the next, where are the promises you have made?' The Pole Star says, 'You had said you would remain constant and unmoving in your husband's family, where have those words gone?' So it is not possible for the Hindu widow to remarry. If that is the case then what will happen to the *sloka* about the indestructibility of the soul that every five-year-old boy knows by heart. Amongst the twelve kinds of sons,[25] Paunarbha[26] is also a legitimate son, what is to be done about him?

If I have been able to clarify my points in the first part of my long explanation, it must have become obvious to you that in order to offer a resolution to the debate I have used Manu's logic on the eating of flesh.

We have rules about when the deer and the goat may be eaten. However, *'Prabrittiresha bhutanag nibrittistu mahaphala'*, that is, if you are able to free yourself from the inclination for eating flesh then you are able to follow the path of dharma. There are exceptions, when one is travelling. Again, *'Prabrittiresha narinang nibrittistu mahaphala'*, that is, if women abstain from their natural cravings, they will attain salvation.

We may gather courage enough to say that Debal, Narad, Parashar, Manu—all the contributors to the *Shastras* have the same opinion; the entire Hindu *Shastras* have the same view too. If we read the sloka after the one cited above, then we may understand this. Just as Manu has counted the *paunarbha* as son, similarly, he also included the *kanin*, a child born to an unwed mother, and the *gurhautpanna*, the child whose birth is a secret.[27] If the remarriage of the widow is justified by the fact that Manu has himself counted the child born to such a mother, then the Penal Code[28] should also take within its scope the sons born out of wedlock as well as those whose births are concealed, and provide shastric legitimization for laws that will do so. No, it is not proper to 'interpret' the *Shastras*. The *Shastras* are not about the ideal rules and laws of a society. Their primary objective is to present the ideals of dharma and along with the attempt to preserve the ideals enunciated, also to reform society. In a country where forest-dwellers of Vindhyachal as well as the Veda-conversant brahmins have always coexisted, eighteen types of marriage, twelve kinds of sons and a hundred forms of organizational laws for a hundred types of work are bound to exist, or at least are naturaly to prevail.[29] So while meat-eating is common, it is also forbidden; while sacrifice of animals is prescribed, *ahimsa* is also advised; though widow remarriage is forbidden, it is also accepted—all this is bound to be present, but does that mean all of this is in accordance with dharma? None of the authors of the *Shastras* ever mention this. They have differentiated all kinds of work into major and minor, but what ought to be done are the injunctions that are taken to be major, though they may not in practice be completely followed. We have mentioned earlier that this is dharma. So the main injunctions of the *Shastras* constitute dharma. Why should we be concerned about which minor instances to include in our analysis of dharma and which to exclude? What ought to be done, and what ought not to be, can be determined through the application to dharma itself; what ought to be done is determined by dharma; '*nashtey-mritey*'[30] and similar such minor injunctions cannot be the means of determining what is 'ought' and what is 'ought not' about dharma.

When we consider the method that Raja Rammohan Roy employed to legislate the event of the wife accompanying the husband on the funeral pyre, we may get a glimpse of an understanding of the essence of Hinduism. The path of brahmacharya for widows and the practice of accompanying the husband on his death are legislated by the *Shastras*. Mahatma Rammohan says that though these two are mentioned in the *Shastras*, the widow needs only to maintain chastity.[31] There was a great debate upon this matter in those times. Let us see what arguments Rammohan used:

It is true that in some *Shastras* it is said that 'the woman who accompanies her husband in death or accepts death after him is awarded heaven'. Yet see and follow what Manu and the others have said. 'The widow will follow the rules regarding food and will practice the rules of brahmacharya, thus living with the sole desire of following dharma.' When the wife accompanies the husband in death it is the result of desire but brahmacharya negates desire. 'Bhagwan Manu is the most knowledgeable about the Veda, so he has understood both these as injunctions of *Sruti*[32] and identified the one that is without desire as the appropriate one and has directed the wife to follow the rules of brahmacharya after the husband's death.' As 'an act performed to yield any temporal or spiritual gain is considered to be a manifestation of a desire, such an act should be forbidden.' And those who take the opposite view have written, 'Nowhere is it said that an act performed from desire is wrong, so this is not within the *Shastras*; to legislate the acts performed due to desire into both *Sruti* and *Smriti*[33] will result in another whole book.'[34] It is true that the raja did not write a whole book, but if we analyse what he has written, we can understand that 'to do what dispassion dictates is prescribed in the Hindu *Shastras:* in *Sruti* and *Smriti*, Upanishads and Gita, the act done out of desire is forbidden'.

Now, following the argument of the Mahatma regarding the desireless act, think once which path would be right for the Hindu widow to follow—the widow can remarry, she can give up her life along with her husband, or she can follow the rules of brahmacharya for the rest of her life. Consider that the *Shastras* mention that all the three ways do exist; but would you think that all three of them are right? That could not be possible. A Hindu should have no difficulty in identifying which one is to be followed and which to be shunned.

A woman, who marries after her husband's death, brings embarrassment to her own self, showing her keenness to satisfy only her lowly instincts. So her act is one of those prompted by intense desire. Such customs exist in lower societies, and always have been prevalent. The snake-princess Ulupi,[35] the demon-queen Mandodari,[36] the monkey queen Tara[37] have remarried as some communities had this custom. The *Shastras* have designated them as acts of desire, but the *Shastras* are also full of injunctions forbidding such acts. Accompanying the husband in death is also an act of desire, but as the urge to seek spiritual happiness is connected with the absolution of her husband's lineage dating back to thirty million generations, such self-sacrifice is yet considered as the most prestigious among all desirable acts. Nevertheless, it was born out of desire, so for the Hindu widow, brahmacharya is the only apt way to follow.

Those women, who after the loss of their husbands spend the rest of their lives with the memory of their departed husbands and keep their passion under control, are respected in all civilized nations more than the *punarbhu*.[38] Those who follow brahmacharya until death and spend their lives in doing good for others, such women exist in almost all civilized countries and people of all religions of the civilized races show great reverence towards such brahmacharyas, as do Christian Europe, Muslim Arabia, Persia, Turkey and Buddhist China and Japan. But among the Hindus, brahmacharya is not to be followed only by a small community. Brahmacharya is supposed to form the foundation stone and the protecting roof of every home. Before the present decadence, there were times when people used to take up brahmacharya in adolescence, then become householders in adulthood, and return to sanyas in old age. But this is nothing unusual for a race that thinks that the whole life is to be spent following one endless, unchanging form of discipline.[39]

The ideal of chastity among the Hindus clearly entails that according to the spiritual principles applied for the construction of the Hindu society which underlie the laws of the Hindu household—set up in accordance with the rituals and the Vedas—the Hindu widow remains a *brahmacharini* for ever.[40] Devotion to the husband, love for the husband, staunch belief in an after-life, immense and heartfelt respect towards social norms, ability to serve the family without desire—all such pure and holy emotions ensure that the Hindu widow remains a brahmacharini for ever. Though we may, generally, applaud those who speak of the tortures of brahmacharya inflicted upon the childhood widow *('enforced widowhood')*, despite sympathizing with them, we are yet not prepared to accept that they have understood a Hindu woman's heart's ability to remain limpid, pure and diligently constant.

Owing to the spiritual aura of the Aryan dharma, the excellent social structure devised by the great Manu and others in keeping with dharma; the attraction of the splendid creations of beauty by Valmiki and other great poets;[41] the unique advice imparted by the great sages through the many tales of the *Puranas*; the education imparted through generations; and the living examples in society[42]—the Hindu woman's devotion to her husband has become her practised dharma, the natural dharma, the dharma of her character.

Yet the Hindu woman's unflinching devotion to her husband is a very rare thing. A utensil used by everyone or a rope that is used for binding things cannot belong to whosoever happens to own it for the moment. The root of Hindu spirituality is *soham*.[43] The Hindu woman's chastity is also rooted in soham. In dharma, everything for the Hindu stems from the indivisible one,[44] and that is also the root of the Hindu woman's chastity. Those who are prepared to destroy such emotions of chastity of the Hindu women, ... let us not for a moment say that they understand the dynamic force of Hindu society. The Hindu woman is intimate with one man alone; she is devoted to her husband and when that husband becomes one with *Brahm*, she becomes brahmacharini, the one who is devoted to Brahm.[45]

In that image of hers, she remains glorious, calm, active yet without desire, gentle but strong within, like a shadow of the other world. There is nothing luxuriant in that beauty, there is no passion in that gentleness, that pleasing *bhairava raga*[46] does not need displays of virtuosity to make it beautiful; it is *behaag*;[47] it does not imitate the clinging dependence of a woman who needs support. That image knows how to depend on itself, and does so. It knows how to serve the world without valuation. For the widow, service is not a coin of exchange; her work is truly an action without desire, her dharma is the true Hindu dharma, her life is the true example of dedication, she is the one who has taken the vow of service to the divine; though a mortal woman, she is a goddess.

In Hindu society, the married woman's image is that of the nurturer of her children, the image of Durga nurturing her elephant-headed son Ganesh. ... it is true that the mother has forgotten herself, but only for herself, for her children. The poets of Europe have put this image in their hearts, their scriptures have accepted this image of the goddess and worshipped it; for them Mary with the child Jesus in her arms is akin to Durga, mother of Ganesh. But neither the European poets nor the European theologians have been able to understand the Hindu widow's world-nurturing image, that of a chaste brahmacharini. Europe does not understand the respect that widowhood brings. By attempting to replicate brahmacharya in the nunnery, they have debased it. The chaste brahmacharini who lives in society but is not embroiled in it, she who serves the family yet remains its principal support and actor; a servant manifested as a goddess; Europe is not aware of nor can it appreciate such uniqueness, such mystery. It is not there in Europe's poetry, its literature, its dharma or its society. This woman, ... the principal actor to offer service and the director of all, a dedicated brahmacharini, is the one who is protecting Bengali society.[48] You, I, we all are in one way or the other busy pandering to our stomachs on the one hand, and being crushed by the blows of fate upon our backs on the other. The woman of the house is agitated about the well-being of the children.[49] Only the Hindu widow protects the dharma of the Hindu. She safeguards the Hindu way of life. Or else, by now our daily rituals would have become defunct, the *puja*-room would have turned into a *'drawing room'*, crotons would have replaced the holy tulsi, and the shalgram[50] turned into a billiard ball, ... instead of daily service to guests we would *'subscribe'* to the *'poor fund'*, and chase away the mendicant asking for alms. That this has not yet happened, ... is due to the widow's dedication to service. Because almost every household has a burning example of such service which is provided without any expectation of reward, we are able to see glimmers of light in the midst of this deep darkness ...

In all humility I pray, do not with your wiles, strength, strategies, laws, rebellions, civilization and sympathy dethrone this sole preceptress of Hindu society from her pure and high pedestal. Due to the lack of true teachers, we are faced with a crisis in education. Teachers in schools and colleges do not educate; they push students from class to class, prepare them for examinations, and make arrangements for an ensuing battle. The guru[51] who shows the light utters some dead chants in one's ear; that mantra has no life, why should it appeal to the heart? The priest can hardly educate as he is more busy calculating the cost of the offerings to be provided to seek blessings for the worshipper, he is not interested in imparting education, rather he is the beggar incarnate. So who will impart education?[52] Will history do what is necessary? ... To educate in dedication and commitment, to explain the great vow of life, to teach the meaning of humanity to the inhabitants of Bengal, there remains only the Hindu widow who can teach, explain and demonstrate. I pray she should not be removed from her glorious role of service, from her high pedestal.

Hindu society is intimately bound with the Hindu widow's education, belief, joy, sorrow. Just as taking care of guests and Gods, daily ritual worship, performance of the last rites, and so on, make up the Hindu social fabric, none of which can be sacrificed, so also the practice of brahmacharya by Hindu widows is an integral part of this society, and so must be adhered to.... If the high-caste Hindu widow is married off, the Hindu way of life is not preserved.... The Hindu woman's devotion to her husband pacifies the heart. In such circumstances where the heart needs to be mollified, how can the warmth of widow remarriage serve the purpose? ... In the lower classes,[53] this is in practice, and will remain thus. So, to try to propagate widow remarriage in the higher classes of Hindu society is to attempt in a way to make the impossible come true. If we consider the history of the Hindus we will see this. The state of the thirty-year-old law[54] proves that this argument can be historically substantiated. Why only this? The entire *Kaliyuga* stands witness against widow remarriage.[55] Parashar was the propagator of scriptures in the Kaliyug; there is prevalence of widow remarriage in Kaliyuga; so why do we not see widow remarriage in these times? Did the Muslims stop it? But no one seems to say that. So we must say that the law of widow remarriage exists across Kaliyuga, but it operates where appropriate.

We do not wish to go into the details of the pros and cons of widow remarriage. In the course of the argument, I may have reiterated all the points used to substantiate the position against widow marriage, but let me summarize these in sequence. I shall not refer, for many reasons, to the difficulties of observing brahmacharya, the misuse and profligacy, resulting from it the obstruction to extending the generation, the ease with which the problem of unmarried men may be solved.[56] To those who wish to accuse me of such an oversight, I say that I accept this accusation.

There are some facts besides this: there is a position which is rooted in western socialism. If the widower can marry again, why should the widow not be allowed to? But modern socialism itself can answer this question: then let the widower's remarriage also be banned. But the Hindu will not say that. The Hindu does not accept socialism, he understands relativism. ... As the relation between A and B are, so should they be treated, their relative worth should thus be judged. The Hindu is such a type of relativist. The Hindu does not believe in the equality of man and woman, so cannot imagine that they can be treated equally. Socialism is not for the Hindu. Those who believe in socialism will say that socialism does not dictate the remarriage of widows; rather it would dictate banning the remarriage of widowers.

Another argument is that the practices of widowhood are difficult to maintain; hence impractical; they cannot be carried out to completion, so brahmacharya is not dharma. In our long discussion we have come to realize that that which cannot be carried out to completion, but must be observed nevertheless, becomes easier in practice: the more you perform the observance, the more it enters within you, becomes easier, becomes the dharma. So the widow's observance of brahmacharya is *mahadharma*.

The last point concerns *'Individual Liberty'* or following the self.

The Hindu says, sociability is dharma, to be humane is dharma, but acting in accordance with one's own wishes is not dharma. It is the greatest, deepest adharma. He who has recently started arguing in favour of widow remarriage in Bengali society has himself agreed with this; he too has clearly said that acting in accordance with self is not dharma. Without mentioning names, we quote the portion relevant to the learned one's arguments, in English:

> 'I advocate it (widow remarriage) on the broad ground of the individual liberty of choice.
>
> 'I have no daughter. If I had the misfortune to have a young widowed one in my house, I would have certainly tried my utmost to get her remarried; but in that case I would have thought of her and her only, and never cast a glance about the effect of her marriage on the community at large. In other words I would have claimed my individual liberty, the liberty of choice of my daughter and *not the claims of Morality*.'[57]

The writer here is clearly saying that when he displays a desire to get a widow remarried, he only tries to fulfil his desires, he does not glance at society, nor keeps an eye on dharma. This is nothing other than adharma.

Now I shall present two excerpts from the essays written by women who responded to the proposal of the leaders of Savitri Library[58] to write an essay on this matter, because I am of the opinion that these are worthy of your attention and discussion.

Srimati Pateswari Adhikari of Taki Sripur was widowed at the age of eight. She says, 'Child marriage is the cause of widowhood.' We say this is true. Marriage in childhood is against the *Shastras* and customary law. Why don't we all come together and protest effectively against the marriage of children? If we do so, we shall also be stopping child widowhood ...

If Hindu society condones the marriage of the boy child with the under-age girl, then I do not know how it will reply to the argument posed by Srimati Shibdas Devi of Baharampura from Muzaffarpur, how it will protest against her proposal. She writes:

> Unless the first and second stages of marriage are completed, the marriage cannot be said to have taken place. In the first stage, the father gives away his daughter according to the *Shastras*, but the

> father has no right to give anyone the right to enjoy his daughter's body. That no one other than one's own self can have. Hence, after that particular act is completed, the wife's surrender of self is called the second marriage.
>
> So unless the second marriage is completed, the marriage itself is not complete. If the husband dies before the second marriage, then the wife is free, for the person to whom her father had given her no longer exists. Then, of course, she has the right to surrender herself to another person. When the marriage itself had not been whole, then why should she not marry again?

We don't know the proper answer to this question; I have asked Tarkachudamani and others, but have not received a reply. What is relevant to the point is that if the Hindu has some objection to consenting to the marriage of this widow only in name, then it is our collective duty to protest effectively against child marriage.

Here I wish to quote the final part of the essay by Shyamasundari Devi of Dhaka.[59] ...

> There is no doubt that if widow remarriage is popularized in Hindu society, there will be more harm than good. Every man and woman must be careful to make efforts such that the Hindu widow is enabled to carry out the duties associated with chastity; he who helps even one widow to stay on the path of good will earn a thousand accolades from Hindu society as a whole.

Hindu widows, my humble request to you is that whether you have been widowed in your childhood, youth or old age, take up and carry out the duty of chastity with sincerity; whether the husband whom you married was sinful, unsympathetic, remain true to his memory and spend your life in remembrance of him. Will forgetting the married husband and transferring your love to another man make you happy? Certainly not!

You will wear better clothes, eat good food and be blessed with capable children, but is that the substance of human happiness? Just as men get some form of benefit through remarrying when their wives die, you too will get certain benefits, but does that indicate your own greatness? When you can remain true to the practices of dharma without the presence of a husband, then I fail to understand the joy of accepting the slavery of a man. If one spends one's life in the contemplation of the dead husband, then one proceeds a long way on the path of dharma.

... How beautiful is the picture of the widow lost in contemplation of her dead husband. What great respect she commands! The very sight of her fulfils one's life. The concept of dharma marks the superiority of human life; birds and animals are also capable of sensual pleasure but human life is complete only with the ideal of dharma. Consider all other pleasures minor and immerse yourselves in the ideal of dharma. Do not be disturbed by what people say, open the true way to happiness for yourself and purify the whole of Hindu society. Let the world once more be entranced by the glory of the women of Bharat, this is our only wish.

Translated by Ipshita Chanda
Department of Comparative Literature, Jadavpur University

'Hindu Bidhabar Abar Bibaha Howa Uchit Ki Na', Nabajiban, mid-May to mid-June 1885/Jaishtha 1292 BS, bhag 1 (part 1), sankhya 11 (no. 11), pp. 689–711.

This essay was read in the Savitri Library Calcutta on 11 May 1885/ 28 Baisakh 1292.

Notes

1 For details, see Introduction 1, n 7.

2 The word used is *uchit*, an amalgam of what is proper, apt and morally defensible.

3 Dharma is translated throughout this essay as an amalgam of many things: the right action to be taken in particular circumstances in keeping with the duties of the station in life that the actor occupies. Thus the dharma of people placed in different situations will depend upon their location in the linked spheres of the social, political and religious.

4 All Bengali and English words/phrases that have been italicized here are not translations but are as they appear in the original article in Bengali.

5 One krosh equals to 3–4 km.

6 Henry Thomas Buckle (24 November 1821–29 May 1862), a renowned English historian, started writing the *History of Civilization* but died before its completion.

7 According to mythology, Manu evolved from the body of Brahma. The

human race is believed to have started from Manu's children. Fourteen Manus were born within four thousand years. All Manus were supposed to have written religious texts. According to Hindu mythology, the collection of scriptures ascribed to the first Manu whose name was Swayambhuva is known as *Manu Samhita*.

[8] The rules about eating meat are mentioned in *Manu Samhita*, Chapter 5, 26–56—on what is not considered sinful to eat (30, 33 and 37); about sacrifices (31, 35 and 39); about analogy, the number of animal's hairs and so on (38); list of seven slayers of an animal (51); and regulations on meat eating (56).

[9] This English word is used by the author in the original Bengali text.

[10] Possibly a reference to the note written by Behramji M. Malabari to the colonial government on 'Enforced Widowhood' in 1884, which is later referred to in this essay.

[11] The ruler here refers to the British government. Apparently, the context is Malabari's note and the debate following it. The law permitting widow remarriage had been passed in 1856. But Malabari lamented the fact that despite the long life of this legislation, it had had no effect in improving the condition of widows.

[12] 'There are theories which are never serious because they are not practical. We all hold theories which might be called dangerous if we ever thought of carrying them out; we all hold the theory, for instance, that we ought to love our neighbour exactly as ourselves, but no one seems afraid that we shall ever do so.' This note appears as a footnote in the original article.

[13] Brahmacharya connotes to sexual abstinence.

[14] The *Manu Samhita* (Chapter 5, 137) mentions that through a son, the father conquers the worlds, through a son's son he obtains immortality, but through his son's grandson he gains the world of the sun. Because a son delivers (*trayate*) his father from the hell which is called *put*, he is called *put-tra* (a deliverer from *put*) by the self-existent (Swayambhu) himself.

[15] Refers to the four stages of life as mentioned in the *Dharmashastras*—*brahmacharya, grihasthya, vanaprastha* and *sanyas*. Special duties and responsibilities are prescribed for each stage. Ashrama also means hermitage.

[16] Swayambhu means 'one which is created by its own accord'. Based on details in the *Bhagavata Purana* and *Matsya Purana*, Narayana or Krishna is said to be the self-manifested Swayambhu form of Brahma, the first cause of creation.

[17] Gotras are named after different sages, namely, Bharadwaj, Gautam, Parashar, and so on. In Hindu marriage, a woman has to change her gotra and take up her husband's gotra to become a member of her husband's family.

[18] Women of bhadralok families were being influenced by the West. Learning about the position of women in western society, and with the influence of education, certain Bengali elite men wanted to educate their wives, or teach them western norms. Satyendranath Tagore's wife Jnanadanandini Devi, deeply influenced by the women of the West, introduced a new way of wearing the sari. For details see, Essay 37, n 3.

[19] Diragaman is a ceremony conducted when the newly weds visit the bride's house for the first time after the marriage. The purohit ties a thread around the wrist of the bride at the time of marriage, which is cut during this ceremony.

[20] The original article mentions cutting vegetables, an important ritual in the kitchen in which the newly wed bride partakes.

[21] Food and clothes are offered by the groom to the bride as a part of the domestic rituals that are performed on the day after the bride enters her husband's house. The implication is that he will take care of these needs during her lifetime.

[22] *Patra* means a vessel; here it refers to the groom who is the vessel through which the marriage occurs; the bride in this case is called *patri*.

[23] The quotations regarding marriage are all taken from Babu Chandranath Basu's essay read at an earlier annual session at the Savitri Library: 'The Aim and Proper Age of Hindu Marriage'. This essay was published in the last part of *Bangadarshan*, vol. 7. Those who have taken the trouble to read this essay thus far are requested to read the one cited above. There is no clearer explanation of Hindu marriage. (This footnote has been inserted by the author.)

[24] Five elements or the *panch bhoot* which constitute the material body. These include: air, fire, earth, water and space.

[25] The *Arthashastra* and *Manu Samhita* provide a classification of the twelve kinds of sons. Kautiliya emphasized on biological sons and Manu on social sons, on the inviolability of marriage and Paunarbha. *Manu Samhita* mentions about eight kinds of marriage (Chapter 3, 20-44); eight outcomes of marriage—four were good and four bad (Chapter 9, 158-81); and twelve types of sons—six kinsmen and heirs, six kinsmen only (not heirs).

[26] Sons of women who remarried, mostly virgin widows, who left their husbands or those who left their husbands' families because there were no brothers-in-law who could father their children.

[27] *Manu Samhita* (Chapter 9, 158) enumerates that among the twelve sons of men who sprang from the self-existent (Swayambhu), six were kinsmen and heirs, and six not heirs (but) kinsmen (see n 25). However, Chapter 9 (159) explains that the six kinsmen and heirs include the legitimate son of the body, the son begotten on a wife, the son adopted, the son made, the son secretly born and the son cast off. Chapter 9 (160) mentions that the son of an unmarried damsel, the son received with the wife, the son bought, the son begotten on a re-married woman, the son self-given and the son of a sudra female comprise the six kinsmen (not heirs).

[28] It refers to the Criminal Law Amendment Act 1885 'to make further provision for the protection of women and girls, the suppression of brothels, and other purposes'. It was the last in the twenty-five-year series of legislation in the United Kingdom of Great Britain and Ireland, beginning with the Offences against the Person Act 1861 that raised the age of consent and delineated the penalties for sexual offences against women and minors. It also strengthened existing legislation against prostitution and recriminalized male homosexuality. This Act was also notable for the circumstances of its passage in Parliament. Under the Offences against the Person Act 1861, the age of consent was twelve (reflecting the common law). It was a felony to have unlawful carnal knowledge of a girl under the age of ten, and it was a misdemeanour to have unlawful carnal knowledge of a girl between the ages ten and twelve. In addition, the 1861 Act declared a penalty of two years' imprisonment for indecent assault or attempted rape of a girl below the consensual age. Although the age of consent was subsequently raised to thirteen upon amendments made to the 1861 Act in 1875, these pieces of legislation were enacted to protect mainly the very young and the very wealthy. This was the state of affairs in England. The Penal Code that may have come within the purview of this legislation is the Indian Penal Code of 1860.

[29] Indicative of two different worlds coexisting in the world of the brahmins and the world of forest dwellers, each having its own 'civilization', with specific rules and customs, languages and cultures. The Brahminization of this diverse society was a project taken up by the Sena ruler in Bengal (for details on kulins and brahmins, see Essay 3, n 1 and 2). This established the caste system firmly and attempted to iron out the diversity, trying to increase the reach and social power of the brahmins. In this article, the author supports purity of caste and agrees that the burden of maintaining this purity falls upon the woman who must remain monogamous at all

cost in all circumstances. The few references to the 'other' castes and communities are offset by this point where she insists that despite cultural differences a 'human' society will always attempt to maintain the ideal of dharma, which must be the same for everyone. In this article, we have seen that this ideal is legislated by the *Dharmashastras*, and in practice, interpreted by the orthodox brahmins.

[30] When the person is destroyed (*nashta*) or dead (*mrita*): implying that when the husband is not alive, i.e., his physical body is destroyed or dead (*Manu Samhita*, Chapter 5: 57-109).

[31] He was called the Mahatma because of the reforms he introduced into superstition-ridden Hindu society ameliorating the condition of women (for details about the work which projects Rammohan Roy's views, see n 28).

[32] The Vedas, literally referring to that which is revealed.

[33] Meaning recollection; refers to legal texts.

[34] The cited sentences are taken from the essay on the wife's accompanying her husband in death, 'News of the Activists and the Resistance', collected in the *Granthavali of the Mahatma*, published by Srijukta Anandachandra Vedantabagish and Srijukta Rajnarayan Basu. This information was provided by the author as an annotation in the original article. The 'mahatma' referred to here is Rammohan Roy.

[35] Ulupi, a widowed princess, who was drugged and abducted by Arjuna. She became his wife and bore him a son.

[36] Mandodari was the wife of the demon-king Ravana.

[37] Wife of monkey king Vali of Kishkindha.

[38] Punarbhu is a married woman or widow who has married for the second time (see n 26). Paunarbha is the son born to such a woman.

[39] The ashramas, the different stages of life, with rules for each as laid down in the Dharmashastras, are referred here.

[40] A woman who follows the path of brahmacharya.

[41] Valmiki, who wrote the *mahakavya* or epic called the *Ramayana*, and Veda Vyas who is supposed to have dictated the *Mahabharata* to Ganesha, the elephant-headed god.

[42] The widows lived a life of austerity. Manu's prescriptions do not include sati but do rule against widow remarriage and enumerate the austerities (*Manu Samhita*, Chapter 5, 156–66).

[43] Means 'I am the supreme being'.

[44] Brahma, the Adwitya, the one and the only entity who cannot be divided.

[45] The creator of the universe.

[46] An early morning raga denoting the purity of dawn.

[47] An evening raga denoting love. The woman is no longer under the illusion of love, making her dependent for support.

[48] This is a belief of caste Hindus which attempts to preserve what they thought of as an ideal social structure; the position of women, when mentioned, was constructed to fit within this ideal structure, with little thought to the suffering and deprivation resulting both from the patriarchal ideal and its corruption in the actual working of society.

[49] Except the widow, none seem to have time for spirituality or the following of dharma. They remain busy with the travails of worldly life.

[50] The stone representing Vishnu, worshipped at the beginning of most rituals.

[51] Author refers to the diksha guru, the spiritual teacher who guides the disciple on the path of dharma.

[52] By education is meant here imparting a sense of the correctness of customs and the methods of following custom, in other words, educate for a life according to dharma, which is for women, not a formal education like it was supposed to be for men.

[53] By the lower classes, it primarily referred to Muslims, but also those who were not brahmins or kshatriyas.

[54] Referring to the Widow Remarriage Act of 26 July 1856.

[55] Yuga is age or era, an astronomical cycle. Kaliyuga is the last of the four yugas named after 'Kali' by whom it was established. The span of Kaliyuga is 4,32,000 years. It started from 3, 101 BC.

[56] The author explains how the lineage may be preserved. As there were not enough kulin women each kulin man married several women. This was a possible solution practiced to enhance their number, but polygamy itself was a subject of reform. Also see Essay 3.

[57] This extract is presented as it appears in the original article.

[58] See Introduction, n 7.

[59] Ibid.

31

SRIMATI SATYABATI DEVI

An essay written by Satyavati Devi is also found in *Bharatbarsha* the issue dated mid-March to mid-April 1919 (Chaitra 1326 BS). Unfortunately, nothing more is known about her. It is possible that she also used to write in other journals like *Narayan*.

Mothers-in-Law and Daughters-in-Law in These Times (1898)

In our society, girls get married at the age of eleven or twelve. In most cases, marriage puts an end to their formal education. Some people give their girls in marriage at the age of fifteen or sixteen and so they receive some education before they marry. These girls could make ideal wives when they went to live in their marital households. But the convention of letting the girl be a bit older at the time of marriage is not widely followed in Bengali society.

Girls of a tender age leave their natal homes within one or two days after their marriages. The girl becomes a wife thereafter. She is a newcomer in her husband's family. Everyone in this new family introduces her as a relative. But how many of them are really close to her?

The first task of the neighbours and the family members is to criticize the new bride. Following a long-standing convention, the mother-in-law herself welcomes the girl into the house. A chaotic situation develops as soon as the newly wedded couple comes and everyone gets busy seeing and blessing the girl. Everyone, though close to the groom and his family, forgets the fact that the bride also has a place in the family. They unthinkingly start criticizing the girl and her relatives, which develops into slander. On a particular occasion, a guest is heard making the following remark while welcoming the new bride: 'Does this girl at all match our sweet boy?' Someone else might say something jeeringly to the girl's mother, that is, the mother-in-law of the groom, which surely goes against the ethics of such relationships. Someone says: 'The match is not good. They have given clothes of inferior quality. A good silk cloth could have been bought if they spent a few more rupees.' Some say, 'My goodness! See the ornaments; it seems that a puff of wind will make them fly away, so light, and made of such little gold.' Someone else comments: 'Have you seen the articles given as gifts? How could they display those in front of everyone? Didn't they feel ashamed?' This sort of conversation goes on and on in the presence of the new bride. Many words are spent on the impeccable beauty of another new bride and the large amount of money provided by the father of another newly married girl and other similar topics. Nobody takes into consideration whether the new bride can do anything to repair the defects of beauty or the paucity of money that has come with her.

The girl's state of mind at that moment is indescribable. She has just arrived at the father-in-law's house. She still remembers the tearful faces of her sister and affectionate parents. When she has to listen to criticism about her parents, she feels so sad that she cannot endure it any longer and starts crying. Then everyone comes to console her saying unanimously: 'What a shame! It is so unusual for a grown up girl to cry. Keep quiet, do not cry any more' and similar things. Few among those assembled say something in defence of the new bride, but their voices may well fade out in the noise of collective opinion. So they seem to remain silent.

The bride spends seven or eight days at her father-in-law's house and during those days she endures this sort of a tense situation that surrounds her. After a week, she goes to her father's house. Usually, after the passing of a year, she returns to her father-in-law's place to lead the life of a housewife.[1] Now she finds that nobody treats her with the kind of affection as her mother would have. On the contrary, if she does not know how to do some work, or fails to do it, if some minor mistake is done by her, everyone in the family rebukes her without any restraint or forgiveness. Perhaps in these moments, her tender heart questions: 'My mother never treated me in this way, why do these people rebuke me so much?' The new wives receive only the love of their husbands in that phase of their lives and so they consider their husbands as beings closest to them in the family. Therefore, they find it impossible to obliterate the suffering of their hearts until and unless they reveal these to their husbands. As a result, the son becomes extremely displeased with his own mother.

The mother-in-law thinks that since the coming of the wife to the house, her son's behaviour has changed towards her. Then she assumes that such a change is owing to the influence of the wife, as it is difficult for a mother to recognize the shortcomings or faults of her son.

Before marriage the son would come to me, he wanted so many things, and he would talk a great deal to me, but now he seems to have changed. This unfounded belief and thinking, leads the mother-in-law to become dissatisfied with the new bride. She assumes that the son's wife would take all the responsibilities of the household, perform them correctly after coming back to the marital home from her father's house and show more respect to her mother-in-law than she does to her own mother. But her expectations remain unfulfilled. Perhaps the new wife cannot do the tasks well as her mother has not properly trained her. Instead the mother has only taught her how to study, to crochet and to remain neat and clean. So the mother-in-law does not get the daughter-in-law she expects. She begins vilifying the mother of the girl and finds avid listeners in her neighbours.

This is how the dispute begins in most cases. The wife does not love or respect her mother-in-law, as was common in earlier times. The mother-in-law of today too no longer treats her daughter-in-law with affection. The seed of discontent about one grows in the other's mind because of trivial family matters. Under these circumstances, the mother-in-law angrily scolds the daughter-in-law mercilessly without considering whether the latter has made the minor mistake deliberately or not. In such a situation, it is impossible to expect the daughter-in-law to respect the mother-in-law. After being scolded by the old lady, the daughter-in-law unjustly beats her children to vent her own anger which in turn gives a heavy blow to the heart of the mother-in-law. The mother-in-law seems to regard the unjust punishment of the grandchildren as her own punishment. After observing such unjustified torture, the mother-in-law finds her anger doubled and in that excited state she does not hesitate to strike the daughter-in-law with sharp and piercing words. Having failed to win the verbal battle with the mother-in-law, the daughter-in-law ultimately drives her husband mad with requests to leave the household and live separately. The couple continues their quarrel for some days and the wife firmly refuses to stay under the control of the mother-in-law. She takes a firm oath to move into a separate house. The husband finds himself in a severe crisis. On the one hand, the husband faces the request of the wife and, on the other hand, he feels that he would then be abandoning the woman who has given him birth. He thus is caught up in an intricate dilemma. In many cases of this sort, it has been seen that the embarrassed husband disagrees with his wife on a few points, but his voice of dissent is simply washed away in the flow of her words. Struggling desperately to escape, the husband prefers comfort more than happiness. Therefore, in the long run, the wife succeeds in maintaining her position. Even after moving to a separate establishment, the wife fails to develop proper respect and devotion for the mother-in-law. Her malice remains deep-rooted. She does not want to take any initiative in serving the mother-in-law when she is ill or when she is old and infirm. Nor does she think it necessary to help her with a penny.

In those days, many wives did not get the love of their mothers-in-law. What is more some wives received such brutal treatment from them that these stories when told seem to thrill the listeners with horror. So, as the suffering gradually became unbearable, the wives made efforts to be free. Overwhelmed by anger and jealousy, some of them went to the length of torturing their mothers-in-law and some, under the heavy burden of grief, committed suicide.[2]

Today, most of the wives do not want to be overpowered by their mothers-in-law. It may be a consequence of their imitation of the western convention or their failure to endure the inhuman and terrifying torture of the mother-in-law. Wives, in our times, being proud of their education (it is doubtful whether they are educated or not),[3] no longer pay heed to the old ladies. They think it disgraceful to accept the dictates of the ladies of the older generation or to act according to their will, which is why many daughters-in-law and mothers-in-law fail to treat each other courteously.

Many wives are unaware of the modes of behaviour that can prevent psychological conflicts. It is not possible to quarrel with anyone if people spend their lives with a consideration of their own well-being. When the child bride for the first time comes to her father-in-law's house, leaving parents, brother, sister and other relatives behind, it is the mother-in-law's duty to provide her with motherly care and affection. Even blood-thirsty animals like tigers and lions can be controlled by humans if they are treated with care. Then, why doesn't a child bride remain submissive to the mother-in-law? There is no doubt that any remark against her parents would disturb the new bride. It should not also be forgotten that affection invites affection. Girls who become new brides initially are unable to show any sense of responsibility and take time to develop tender feelings for others. When the new bride gradually realizes that everyone in the house views her as close to his/her heart and accordingly treats her with affection, she would naturally have fond feelings for them too. Strangely enough, many women who have suffered to a greater or lesser degree at the hands of their own mothers-in-law, when they come to that role, they forget what happened to them in the past. There is no denying the fact that they could have been regarded as ideal mothers-in-law if they behaved kindly and lovingly with the daughters-in-law instead of repeating the ill treatment which they themselves have received as daughters-in-law.

Let no one among the readers think that every mother-in-law gives trouble to the daughters-in-law and quarrels with them. It is not also true that all the daughters-in-law quarrel with their mothers-in-law and end up establishing separate households. There are many mothers-in-law who treat their daughters-in-law in the same manner in which they bring up their own daughters. They know well that if they make no discrimination in the treatment of their daughter and daughter-in-law, the possibilities of strife in the family would cease to exist. Moreover, they think that the son alone is not capable of providing love and care. For this reason, the wife is appointed as his representative, and therefore, the mother-in-law should love her like her own daughter. Impressed by the qualities and the caring spirit of the sensible mother-in-law, the daughter-in-law spontaneously feels drawn to her and adds to the delight of the family members by acting in a gentle and docile manner, like an angel in the house. Seeing the qualities of a mother in the mother-in-law, the daughter-in-law, too, loves her as if she were her mother. In such a situation, respect and devotion are automatically generated. The qualities of the daughter-in-law, reminiscent of Goddess Lakshmi, have pacified many unmanageable mothers-in-law. Such good wives turn their household into happy and prosperous families.

Translated by Chirantan Sarkar
Department of English, Nagar College

'Ekaler Sasuri-Bou', Bamabodhini Patrika, mid-November to mid-December 1898/Agrahayan 1305 BS, barsha 36 (year 36), kalpa 6, bhag 3 (part 3) sankhya 407 (no 407), pp. 274-78.

Notes

1 Girls married at eleven or twelve years were sent back to their natal homes after spending the first week of marriage in the husband's home, returning when they were old enough for the marriage to be consummated. The age for consummation of marriage was raised to twelve by the Age of Consent Bill in 1891. However, the incident of Phulmani, an eleven-year-old girl who died after her husband raped her, occurred in 1893.

2 Being unkind to the mother-in law or committing suicide are means used by the daughter in-law to attain freedom from her sufferings.

3 The author is sceptical about the quality of education that is being imparted.

32

SRI KAMALEKAMINI GUPTA

Sri Kamalekamini Gupta was a daughter-in-law of a Hindu family who were the zamindar of Autshahi village, Vikarampur (now in Bangladesh). She was a spirited and powerful woman and a pioneer in the nationalist movement and was much influenced by Gandhian ideas. She was the mother-in-law of Priyabala Gupta, a leader of the Vikrampur Mahila Samiti, also a nationalist.

Trouble on the Train (1902)
(True Story)

This happened almost five years ago. I was going to Calcutta from Allahabad in a mail train accompanied by a male relative. After crossing Bankipur Station, I found that I had a terrible headache. I had boarded the ladies compartment while my relative was in the adjacent one. Among my fellow passengers, I discovered that many were from my district. Amongst them was a young girl of around sixteen or seventeen, travelling with her seven-month-old daughter to Calcutta. As the rest of the passengers would get off ahead at other stations, I made a request to the young girl, 'Please look after my luggage. I have a terrible headache and I think a short nap will cure it.' I then went off to sleep. Suddenly the young girl shook me awake at Baidyanath Station, saying, 'Look! Three sahibs are pointing at our station and saying something!'

I woke up at once and saw that the other women passengers had already left. Three sahibs were sanding on the platform, speaking among themselves and pointing to our compartment. I said to the young woman, ' Oh, that's nothing.' When we reached Deogarh, the guard pulled everyone out from the next compartment, saying that it was reserved. My relative came to me and told me not to worry, that he would be close by. I asked him for my ticket and tied it to the loose end of my sari, my anchal. The young girl's husband who had also come to see her went away without mentioning anything to her.

We were deeply engrossed in conversation when the train stopped a little before Madhupur Station. Suddenly we heard a loud cry, which made us stand up. We could see the railway storekeeper standing on the footboard of our compartment shouting at us, 'Get down quicky!' I asked, astonished, 'Why should we get down here? He replied, 'Because the compartment has been cut off!' I have been travelling in trains and steamers since childhood but had never faced this danger of being cut off. I told the storekeeper, 'If you could put me in the mail train, that is, the one that will be going to Calcutta, then I will give you a ten-rupee tip!' 'That train has gone, Ma.[1] Now get down fast, this one is going to Giridih.'

I then called out loudly to my relative. Two coolies standing nearby said, 'Ma, that babu has left on the mail train.' Aghast, I clutched my forehead and dropped back on the bench. It was dark now and there we were two women, unescorted, in the middle of a field. I hope readers will understand our predicament. Instead of referring to the young girl as my young companion, I shall address her as 'Bou' or daughter-in-law hereafter.[2] Bou, terrified, started wailing loudly, saying, 'O what will happen to me now? I have lost my caste, my respect!'[3] Her wails certainly made things worse. While the storekeeper kept ordering us to get off the train, I reassured Bou, 'Don't worry. If I can find a way, you will too. I won't leave you alone. But if you howl like this then we will surely fall into the hands of evil men on the train. In that case I will certainly leave you and go away.' This scolding made her fall at my feet, pleading, 'You are my mother, my sister.'

Putting aside my fears, I first removed all her ornaments, tied them into a bundle and tucked them into the folds of her sari at her waist. I asked her to carry her daughter and held her hand. Seeing a faint light in a distance we [and the two coolies] slowly proceeded towards it and reached the platform. The faint light was from the oil lamp hanging on the station wall. Since by then the mail train had left, there was neither any other light nor any coolie at the station. It was totally deserted.

I made Bou sit at one end of the platform and repeatedly admonished her against crying. With the help of the two coolies, I managed to call another seven or eight coolies and went back to the train. I got the luggage loaded on to the coolies' heads and we returned to the station. There I found Bou rolling on the floor, lamenting loudly. I tied to calm her down, explaining the circumstances, but it did not work and then I had to threaten her to stop her crying.

I lured a coolie with two rupees, promising him the amount if he did my work, and he agreed immediately to do so. I usually carried extra money with me while travelling. I asked Bou if she had any money but she said she did not have a paisa (maybe she was afraid of spending any).

First I asked the coolie when and which train would come, but did not receive any satisfactory answer. Then I asked him if the deputy magistrate was available. He said, 'No'. All offices and personnel were based at Deoghar and not in Madhupur. I was disheartened. I had hoped that I would be able to tell the deputy magistrate about a close relative who was also a deputy magistrate so that I could seek his assistance. Being so worried, I suddenly thought of sending a telegram. I asked the coolie, 'Is there a telegraph office nearby?' He said, 'Yes.' I asked him to take me there and to explain our situation to whoever was on duty, also telling him that we had an acquaintance who was a telegraph superintendent. About ten to fifteen minutes later, a Bengali officer arrived with the coolie. The first thing he asked was whether I had summoned him and when I said yes, he started asking me where I was coming from, where I was going, who else was with me, and so on, and kept glancing at Bou. I pulled her nearer me and answered the questions. Suddently the officer, said, 'Oh, pardon me. Come inside, I will give a room to sit in.' I knew all about the character of railway telegraph officers but I concealed my thoughts and politely explained that the platform was a better place in summer. The officer went away, saying he would come back soon, and about seven or eight minutes later he came back with a mat, two lanterns and two peons. The two peons sat on either side of us and the officer continued expressing his concerns. 'Now tell me what I have to do,' he repeated and kept asking about Bou. 'Who is she and where will she go?' 'Who is she to you?' My stern answer every time was 'I will not go anywhere leaving a helpless woman alone.'

Then I asked him to send two wires one to a certain telegraph superintendent in Allahabad and another to a deputy magistrate in Calcutta explaining the trouble we have landed in. He said, 'It is useless to telegraph them since they will not be able to come and help you now. Whatever has to be done would have to be done by us.' I gave him a rupee and said, 'Please call the station master at Asansol to say that the person I was travelling with has left by this mail train and that he should be detained.' He went away to telegraph. After a few minutes two fellows came (they were probably also personnel in the office) and asked me, 'We have sent the two telegraph messages but let us ask you something. How are you related to the telegraph superintendent?' I replied, 'I belong to his family. But this is not the situation to discuss my relationship with him.'

The three officers paced up and down a little away from us. Sometime later, the first officer went to the office to see if any answer to the telegraph had arrived. A little later he said, 'No answer to your telegraph has arrived. Now tell me what is to be done?' I retorted, 'Telephone the station, if you still don't get an answer then take me to this certain place in Calcutta.' One of the officers went to get some news and came back soon to say, 'We have called and got news that your companion is waiting at Asansol. Pardon us for wasting the rupee in useless telegraphs. We think it is better for you not to take the 3 a.m. train tonight. What is your wish?' I thought it was safer to be in a train than on a deserted platform. So I said, 'I will take the passenger train tonight.' The three officers protested saying, 'It will be difficult for you.' I did not pay heed to any protest and started to get ready. Soon, it was time for the train to arrive. The officers asked, 'Do you have tickets?' I said, 'I do but my friend here doesn't.' One of the officers tried to say that a ticket has to be *bought* at which I protested, 'Why should we? The trouble started due to the railway company's mistake. Her husband is carrying the ticket. Who should take the responsibility now?'

Then the train arrived. The officers and the peons took us to a compartment and put our luggage in and dusted the benches for us to sit. I held Bou's hand and boarded the train. The three officers asked, 'What do we have to do now?' I said, 'Please tell the guard and the driver that my companion here has no ticket for which she should not be penalized when getting off at Howrah Station. They should also enquire about our requirements at every station before the train reaches Asansol.' Having heard this, the first officer went away and came back after some time. He said, 'I have organized things according to your orders. Don't worry.'

As long as the train was in the station, the three officers and the two peons were with us. I thanked the officers and paid the peons four rupees. The peons were very happy; they said, 'Ma whenever you come this way, do remember us.' I thought, Almighty, may I never have to face this again! At three o'clock the train started moving and we were relieved to leave the station.

Till now I had not talked to Bou. Now, she said, 'We got news of your companion but none about my husband. What will happen to me?' I said, 'Since your husband was in the same compartment with my relative he is probably also in Asansol.' Bou said, 'What if he has gone without stopping at Asansol?' I said, 'Then he is indeed an idiot. And even if he did not get down, he would definitely wait in Howrah.' I consoled Bou by saying, 'Since we have escaped such danger, don't worry now. Even if your husband is not around we will take you to your home if you know the way.' Early in the morning the train reached Asansol. I looked around in the station and spotted my companion and called him. He jumped into the next compartment. When I scolded him he said, 'I did not know anything about cutting off train compartments. When the train reached Asansol Station a few gentlemen entered our compartment. I told them to go elsewhere since there was no space at which they said, "Don't you know some of the compartments have been cut off at Madhupur?" On hearing this I got down with my umbrella and cane and went straight to the telegraph office. I reached my pocket and realized that I had no money with me. I did not think about it but the people at the telegraph office said it was closed and nothing could be done. I saw that my insistence was useless so I narrated the trouble to them. At this they telegraphed the station master at Madhupur without asking for any money.' I said, 'Neither your telegraph nor your station master helped us.' ...

On the way back I bought food for Bou and her daughter. The train reached Howrah Station at two in the afternoon. I told Bou, 'Now, dear, you take a look around and see if you can see your husband. I don't know him.' A coolie standing near the compartment heard my words and shouted, 'Hey, Mister, your lost wife has been found.' At their commotion I looked out and saw a man rolling about on the platform crying. Seeing him a little boy of about three/four years was also crying. When he heard the coolie's yell he came near the compartment and started screaming at his wife, 'I had to spend two rupees for you and telegraph to the Bankipur Station saying I have lost my wife.' I was dumbfounded.

We got off at the station with our luggage. We had telegraphed saying we would reach early in the morning so no one from our house was at the station to receive us. Bou's husband and I hired two carriages, one for each group. When we were getting into the horse carriage Bou said to her husband, 'I have taken fifteen paisa from her. Please give it to her.' The husband took out a *siki* from his pocket. Initially I refused but when he insisted I told my companion to take it but to return a paisa.[4] When my companion tried to return the change he said, 'After all that you have done for us let that paisa be.'

Translated by Jayeeta Bagchi
School of Women's Studies, Jadavpur University

'Raile Bipad', Antahpur, August 1902/Sravan 1309 BS, barsha 5 (volume 5), sankhya 4 (no. 4), pp.65-70.

Notes

1 Literally Mother; here a form of addressing an unknown woman with respect.
2 Married women are often addressed as Bou.
3 Travelling in a train meant associating with different people, whose caste was often not known. Being left alone, i.e., without a male escort in an unknown place is an unusual circumstance. She is afraid that finding her in such a situation people may doubt her character.
4 A *siki* is 16 paise; these monetary measures were all fractions of a rupee. Most of them are no longer in use.

33

SRIMATI PRAMILABALA MITRA

No biographical details about the author could be found.

The Responsibilities of Women (1915)

These days it is often heard that even if a groom's father refuses dowry, the women of his household say in sweet soft voices, 'We want a pretty bride and a set of ornaments, or else there will be no wedding. And they must be able to send proper gifts to the in-laws' house, or else the ladies in the neighbourhood will say, "They have brought a pauper's daughter into the family." Take such things into consideration before you start negotiating on the matter, or else we shall hang ourselves.'

Alas, how unfortunate it is! Does not the self-respect and pride of all women drown in such words? Every woman must take it as her duty to ascertain that such things should not happen. If all mothers are keen to fetch pretty daughters-in-law, bringing in a huge dowry with them, then we would like to ask, should the ugly and poor girls remain eternal spinsters?

These days the happy auspicious occasion of marriage very often casts a shadow of great dejection upon the house of the bride. It even ends in suicide sometimes; yet we have not learnt our lesson. When daughters and sons are sent by the same Creator and are born of the same womb, then why should they be seen differently in the functional world? Why are they valued separately? Once, hearing that a daughter had been born to one of my relatives, I went to see the child and asked her, 'Bakul, what is your daughter like?' She sat up a little straighter, hesitantly, and said, 'What can a daughter be like, *bhai*[1]? Even if they are beautiful, they are still ugly. The moment Khuki[2] came to this earth, I was as if struck by lightning, and the light went out of the faces of everyone at home.' The new mother's pathetic voice still rings in my ears. Then I saw the small child, illuminating her mother's lap as she lay there like a little rosebud. She seemed like a dazzling ray of light, escaped from heaven. How beautiful the baby was! And then I looked at her mother's tense, frightened, pathetic face. . . .

Hindu society these days counts the birth of a girl child as a rather inauspicious event. Are not the people in society themselves the reason for this? If one exchanges his or her daughters and sons in marriage without any dowry, then perhaps, no one will consider the girl child as a bad omen. The son can earn money on his own, but money alone does not run the world created by God. If every woman desires to be the mother of a son, then the world will at one stage come to a standstill. Everyone desires a son so that the family lineage . . . is continued. But we have seen even parents of the rhythmic cycle of the six or seven sons losing their peace of mind on the birth of a daughter.

The refusal to love daughters is increasingly evident in society to such an extent that parents of an adolescent daughter at times even wish for her death. . . . Because marriage is such an expensive affair, girls are shunned and deprived of love in this society. So every woman's duty is to make an effort to eradicate this disrespect for her kind from society. Perhaps she, whose parents cannot stop worrying about her marriage, for which they are perhaps driven to mortgage their home and property so that they can somehow manage to tack her on to an eighty-year-old widower and cottage-dweller, will tomorrow, on becoming the mother of a son, demand, 'Fifty thousand golden coins, a diamond ring and a *jadowa*[3] ornament set for the bride. The bride's father must arrange to send gifts to the marital home thirteen times in twelve months. Where will they get a boy like my dear child? Is it easy to get a boy who has failed to pass his exams twice? Those who have good fortune written in their fate will become his parents-in-law.' Does she not remember her own wedding? Does she not remember her father weeping with anxiety and her mother's helpless face?

And I have often heard the men of the house say, 'They are womenfolk, what brains do they have? If you act according to their advice everything will go awry.' So I ask if they think everything that women say ought to be ignored, why do they listen to them when it comes to weddings? Why do they say in all seriousness, everywhere, 'My wife has said, "The bride should be beautiful. She must bring with her such jewellery that the Rai Sahib's elder wife cannot come and boast before me about her own finery. And, obviously, my son's father-in-law must bear the cost of our youngest daughter Nalini's wedding, he will also pay for my son's education. And, I must be able to distribute the gifts sent by my son's in-laws in the neighbourhood and still have enough left for our own household. Such is the kind of relative-by-marriage that you must look for." I wanted very much to take your little daughter into my own home, but what can I do, my wife's throwing this tantrum.' May the man who says this without batting an eyelid be shamed a thousand-fold! Are not these the people who demonstrate their concerns about society? Alas! Are these not the same men who write in their novels, 'It is a vile thing for a man to demand dowry for the benefit of society. Our Haranathbabu was a great and good man; he did not take a paisa when each of his four sons got married.' Are they not the ones who stand on the high dais at meetings and gatherings and proclaim, 'There is no greater sin than taking dowry, so it is our duty to unite and act such that our society is freed of this evil' so loudly that the sky resounds with their screams and our ears start buzzing? And when they hear the audience clap aloud and voice its approval, they sit down wearily, relaxing in the cool breeze of the electric fan and consuming bottle after bottle of iced lemonade. And then, they return home and following the advice of their wives, demand twenty thousand rupees as dowry for their own dandified good-for-nothing sons. Let them be shamed a thousand-fold!

These men project themselves as the regulators of society. With leaders like these, our society will very soon lose all its credibility. If writing novels and giving speeches cost money, then there would certainly not be a surfeit of such people. It appears that none in our society can commit his actions according to the words he utters. So, Hindu society has lost its inner coherence. There is no one who is capable of bringing back its former beauty. Yet, there is an attempt to revive it through empty words in lecture rooms. Instead, if they sat in their own rooms and tried to practise self-control, there would be some visible result that would benefit society . . .

Sisters! Is it not our duty to act in a way so that society does not say anything against our kind, or does not destroy us the moment we are born by calling us inauspicious? If we are all united in our firm resolve to eradicate the dowry system from our society, then certainly this custom will be wiped out. Weddings will once more become auspicious, happy occasions, and these gloomy ominous weddings will be a thing of the past. Come let us make a concerted effort such that the woman of the household renounces her greed for gifts from her son's in-laws and inspires her son and husband to reject the dowry system. If women do not work for women, if women do not feel for their own fellows, who will? Their sons and husbands? Those days have long gone. Now the men have no hesitation in spreading canards about their wives even while claiming that they are under their wives' thumbs. The son shows smiling indifference to his mother's wishes as he does exactly as he wishes. The husband thinks that he has kept his image intact in society by saying that he acted in deference to the wishes of his wife, and shown respect for her in the process. The wife who easily accepts such respect from her husband is unworthy of being called a woman. We do not wish for such respect . . .

We do not hesitate to torture the poor man's daughter who becomes the bride of our son because her father does not give us gifts regularly. So many brides are giving up their lives due to our lack of sympathy and our callousness. Alas! Hindu society is ill-fated indeed. Why does it not dissipate into nothingness? The mothers-in-law of these daughters-in-law were once young brides themselves. I have heard that the punishments meted out to daughters-in-law in those days were very harsh. So when those daughters-in-law became elevated to the status of mothers-in-law, how could they behave in a manner that had oppressed them in their youth? We have seen the insulting oppressive behaviour of the mother-in-law who is supposed to take the place of the affectionate mother, such behaviour which some people may not even believe is true. When will the daughters-in-law of Hindu society find motherly affection from their mothers-in-law?

Alas! Mother, you are considered the flowering vine of love! Pity, the simple innocent young virgin! Did you think that by sacrificing yourself in the holy fire of marriage the clouds of inauspiciousness marking a woman's birth will clear? The menace of the dowry system darkens the sky. Is there any way of dispelling this darkness, emerging free of this hopelessness? Your deaths had opened the eyes of society for a brief period, but the eyes of knowledge have once more been shut, perhaps this is the slumber of death from which none ever wakes up. It does not seem likely that society and the parents, who are willing to sacrifice their virgin daughters to maintain the dowry system in Bengal, can ever divest themselves of the greed for wealth.

Do ugly women not have hearts? . . . once the dowry system is eradicated, the exchange between the ugly and the beautiful will be easily possible. We have seen beautiful women bear dark daughters.

Many Europeans turn up their noses at 'black Bengalis', but some having acquired a slightly lighter skin than these 'black Bengalis' behave in a similar way. Then we should submit petitions to the Creator, saying that we do not like dark girls. Among our Hindu gods and goddesses, Krishna, the son of Devaki, and [Kali] the great powerful emancipating female force who is the mother of the world, are dark-skinned. Then should we not live in a world created by them? How can we experience joy and sorrow in situations created by them? The devotees of yore alone know by what quality they came to see a world-illuminating light within these very dark forms, and described it as such.

I hope I am not taken as being dark-skinned just because I am being partial to dark beauty, everyone says that I have a complexion as bright as gold.

... Sisters, if you yourself make the effort to preserve your own dignity, then try to protect your son and husband from the fire of greed for wealth and allurement towards beauty. Only then will woman once more become like Lakshmi, the Goddess of Wealth and Auspiciousness in our society. The girl child will once more be the object of everyone's affections, heaven will reign on earth. If even one of my sisters comes to an understanding and accept even a portion of my overwhelming concerns caused by the needs of times, and to use even a speck of it for the correct purpose, then I shall gratefully count my labours have borne fruit.

Translated by Ipshita Chanda
Department of Comparative Literature, Jadavpur University

'Narir Kartavya', Bamabodhini Patrika, May 1915/Baisakh 1322 BS, barsha 52 (year 52), kalpa 10, bhag 4 (part 4), sankhya 621 (no. 621), pp. 25-29. The essay carries 'Gaya, 23-5-15' as the place and date of writing.

Notes

1 The word 'bhai' literally means brother, but is used by all as a term of endearment for friends or even youngsters including females too. See Essay 29 'Grandmother's Letter'.

2 Means 'little girl', a nickname often given to girls.

3 Jewellery set with precious stones.

34

BANGANARI

Essay 10 offers offers a note on the author.

Man and Woman (1921)

For long, man has been moulding woman according to his will. That is why her nature has gradually been deprived and stripped of general human attributes. She has become only a woman. She has been allowed nothing more than recognizing those rights, capabilities and opportunities which are essential for performing the duties of a woman. As a result, men feel threatened of her prospective loss of womanhood if she displays any qualities that may be ascribed to general human nature. Perhaps women do have the capability of being different from the way men mould them. The apprehension that men feel in this case would have been baseless if a woman's social identity like her biological structure, had been unchangeable.

The roles and identities shaped by men for women are artificial for the most part. This may be the realistic rationale behind the apprehension on the part of men. Women are not merely 'womanly beings', they are human too. This part of a woman's identity being completely denied, her behaviour and presence have, consequentially, become unnatural. It would be interesting to contemplate the condition of men had they been limited and confined only to their manly qualities and duties of a husband, father, and so on. Since men have a monopoly on every aspect of 'human' nature, whenever a woman undertakes anything beyond the boundaries set for her, she is said to be doing a man's job. But these activities are not anyone's sole property—every human being has equal right to them. Since men retain their masculinity in spite of possessing and displaying those common human qualities, there is no reason why the fear (of becoming unwomanly) should arise with women. A woman will remain one even if she were to become human.

In this context, one is immediately reminded of the damage done by the disparity practised between men and women with regard to education, opportunities and rights granted to them. Men and women have perpetuated this disparity in practice. For a woman, this practice has given ample scope only to womanly and motherly qualities. However, since intelligence, reason, education, and so on, have been completely denied to women, even the womanly and motherly qualities have not blossomed completely.

Men, on the other hand, have sought to practice humanism without considering the demands and rights of women. As a result, despite making great forays into intellectualism, men too have been denied the privilege of growing into complete human beings. Considering woman as a bond to tie him down to material affairs, sometimes man has tried to free himself from these bonds and pursue religion. But as this is against nature and rather difficult, men have generally failed in this. They have created a self-advantageous ethical principle instead. According to this principle, they have trivialized their relationship with women and carried on their intellectual pursuits in various other areas. What has happened as a result of this is that though his intellectual quest has led him to touch the stars in the firmament, it has ignored one of the primary aspects of nature. A lack of suitable education has not allowed them to progress much further than the dark ages of the savages. In reality, they have run into trouble because of their denial of women. Their condition is, as Marcus Aurelius said, 'Either uneasy without them or intemperate with them.'

Men are chained by women because of their denial of women. If both men and women get equal opportunities to become human, if each accepts the demands and rights of the other; it is women who can help men to be free human beings. A woman is a man's primary source of self-control. If a man denies a woman, can anyone save him from anarchy and destruction? Women provide life, the primary energy of existence, and that is why, in spite of the chains, men have continued to protect women. Women have caused destruction only when they have been insulted. This is only the inevitable revenge of nature.

If one considers the condition of society now, men's indiscriminately self-serving behaviours have become very apparent. The real story behind those who belong to the uppermost echelons of society generationally or in terms of intellect, wealth, and so on, is known to everyone. Society is regulated by men. Women have hardly any space here (whatever space they do possess is far from being enviable), and therefore, men remain content to measure and draw up parameters of work, intellect, behaviour only amongst themselves. Reforms in women's condition do not affect them much and enquiry into this area is considered irrelevant. At the most, the condition of women may become a topic of comic interest among them and few men may even feel gratified to think of the dismal condition of women. But nature has not forgotten. Whatever might be the position of such men in a patriarchal society, the condition of the women in their lives clearly reflects on the extent of their humane feelings. Society has not only kept these women confined to the mire, but even the men associated with them have been compelled to step into this mire. This is the irony of the effort to create different worlds for men and women!

Many say that it is bad if women are of loose moral character. But the same is not true in the case of men. If a woman veers away from the path of virtue even minimally, she is pushed into the world of sin. Let alone education or honour, such a woman is not even spared the means to earn her livelihood. It becomes difficult to imagine what she would do other than take some wrong measures for survival in such a situation. What is surprising is that men, who enjoy the privileged position in society in terms of education, honour and lineage, continue to enjoy their privilege even if they display such lapses!

In the process of creating this biased ethical principle, men have ruined themselves as well as women. This is because however fierce men's control of women may become, men cannot practise their vices without women. So women are required to fuel these evil desires of men. Realistically, man's demand from woman is strange. As a wife she is required to be chaste and pure. On the other hand, she has to be the vile woman who would be the medium for his vices. It is a perfect scheme to keep men's self-interests intact and given priority whatever be the situation!

Earlier it was said that woman is extremely vile and sensual. So she should be kept under special control. That men possess this trait to a greater degree is unheard of. So such laws and rules cannot be applied to them. If the result of such a position were not so grave, it would have been comic. But if men really have lost their self-control, it is their own doing. By denying women, they have given up their chance to reform and control their sensual desires.

Man has reached the pinnacle of the sciences, poetry, arts by virtue of his education, intelligence and talent. It is difficult to believe that such a man would find it hard to fulfil the primary human duty of keeping his mind and body pure and virtuous if he tried to. In this respect, man has been singularly negligent. This manifests itself as an unnatural attribute, as a result of which he has been defeated in his own life in spite of his artistic and aesthetic pursuits. Keeping aside the ideas of religion and morality, if art is denied even in everyday life, where else would it accommodate itself? In this context, a little examination would reveal the unnaturalness of the taste for popular literature. The realist novelists who try to portray their heroines in a positive light hesitate to make them commit any sin or mistake at all. This infringes upon their aesthetic sense. But in the case of the hero, however virtuous he may be, he sins and falls. One gets the impression that his life would not be complete without committing these vices. The biased novelist fails to realize that such a portrayal of the hero might again infringe upon the aesthetic sense. Descending purposefully into the mire of sin cannot become the sole path to virtue just because certain unique people have become virtuous by atoning for the sins they had committed and thereby transcended their fallen state. ... This proves that their virtuous nature did not grow holistically and completely in all respects. In fact, they have never been able to remove completely from their mind and body the sinful stains of their earlier lives. Moreover, if each individual had to examine every idea with one's body and mind and if this were to become the sole means to attaining completeness; knowledge, science, religion, morals would cease to have any utility. The knowledge possessed by the seers of the bygone era has been recorded as it was accumulated through experience. Future men and women inherit this knowledge and utilize it to smooth the trials and tribulations which they face in their lives so that they can progress towards a greater completeness. In reality, the same time or the same situation cannot appear twice in the lives of men or women. However great a poet or litterateur one may be, one's third or fourth love can never be like the first one. Like the theories of mathematics, this principle is true in every aspect of life.

One cannot help remembering these issues whenever one contemplates the possibility of women as complete human beings. This is so because men have dishonoured woman's primary demands and rights borne of her marriage. She must acquire these rights at the very outset. On the other hand, those women who have been assigned the task of catering to the sensual desires of men should also be rescued. Both are interdependent, one cannot occur without the other. If women are recognized as humans they have to be given rights equal to their husbands and their demands have to be met. Again, they cannot be confined as slaves to serve the sensual pleasures of men. That is, if any incident occurs which might question her moral status in society, instead of dealing with the situation in the same old rigid and conservative manner, she must be given an opportunity to live and earn her livelihood in a manner befitting human nature and ability. The very roots of the commodification of women which is occurring in contemporary society must be destroyed, since it places the entire onus of blame and sin on the shoulders of women who have already been sinned against. Otherwise there is no meaning or rationale for women's education or freedom.

Translated by Sukanya Pal
School of Women's Studies, Jadavpur University

'Purush o Nari', Bharati, mid-August to mid September 1921/ Bhadra 1328 BS, barsha 45 (year 45) sankhya 5 (no. 5), pp. 416–20.

35

PRASANNAMOYEE DEVI

Prasannamoyee Devi (1857 [1854]–1939) was an eminent Bengali poet and writer and one of the first women to write her memoirs. She was the mother of the renowned Bengali poet Priyambada Devi (1871–1935). Her father, Durgadas Chaudhuri, and her brothers, Asutosh Chaudhuri and Pramatha Chaudhuri, were litterateurs and involved in the freedom movement. Aged ten, she was married to a wealthy kulin zamindar Krishna Kumar Bagchi of Pabna (now in Bangladesh). However, Prasannamoyee refused to live with her lunatic husband and after her daughter was born she lived mostly with her father and brothers. Prasannamoyee started her education at home and published her first book of poems *Adho Adho Bhashini* at the age of twelve. She wrote regularly in prestigious periodicals and journals of her time such as *Bharatbarsha*, *Manasi o Marmabani*, *Matrimandir*, and so on. After the death of her brother Asutosh, she started publishing his biography in *Matrimandir*. She published *Banalata*, *Niharika* (volumes 1 and 2), both collections of poems, *Ashok*, a novel set during the time of Indian Rebellion or Mutiny of 1857, *Aryabarta*, a travelogue,[1] and a memoir *Purbakatha*, published in *Suprabhat*.

Recollections from a Time Past (1924)

Childhood Memories

We belonged to the 'older branch'[2] and my middle Jethamashai to the 'younger' one.[3] We lived in the same house; the separation marked only by a locked door in between. In the past we ate together [the main marker of a joint family] and spent much time together too. Later, however, because of our aunts' intrigues, we formed separate households. Today neither Rama exists nor does his kingdom Ayodhya. Everything is empty. The house is deserted and at nightfall, it is difficult to move around alone. There are foxes and boars in the jungle and wolves reign nearby.

When we were small, each household had five or six sisters, four or five brothers, and other children from the village. There was no dearth of playmates. Days passed happily in play and pandemonium. My elder Jethima was the mistress of the house.[4] The discipline that she had installed was followed by everyone. Any exception created trouble. The leader of our group was Haripriyadidi (chhoto Khuki[5]), the younger daughter of the elder Pishima[6] of the junior side. She was a amiable girl, proficient in quarrelling. She was dark with big bright eyes and a head full of thick curly hair.

First game

At that time, games were very different from those played today. Pishima, Jethima and others used to play chess, dice and draughts. We never saw them playing bridge and similar games with men. . . . It was a land without the Ganga. Close at hand, was the Padma, a swift turbulent river which destroyed villages and towns below Kushtia. People could not forget their misfortune of not being able to take a dip in the holy Ganga. Moreover, many Ganga-bound people would come to our guest rooms during the *yajnas.*[7] It is for this reason that in the end, imitating them became one of our minor games. We and our playmates, used to move towards the open grounds with a bowl, an ewer and some puffed rice wrapped in a towel. Chhotodidi led us in this game. We, the younger children, would follow her fearfully. We would go near a pond, bring water in the ewer and eat the puffed rice sitting on the bathing steps. Everyone took turns in washing and carrying Chhotodidi's bowl and towel.

Second game

The second game involved the jatra song.[8] All our pishimas, except one or two, were child widows and had no children. There were a few *ghar jamais.*[9] The women were given land, from which the income would amount to four or five hundred rupees, some rent money as deposit, and a house as dowry during their weddings. Those with children lived in their father's house for eight or nine months and left before the Durga Puja. After spending *Chaitali*,[10] they would return to the house of their brothers and fathers. Childless widows were lifelong residents in their fathers' houses and were the mistresses of the house. They were ardent supporters of their brothers. After their deaths, their property reverted to their brothers and nephews. Their property deeds were prepared that way. Since the aunts lived with the 'older side' or the 'younger side' most of the time, their empty houses were our play areas. After lunch in the afternoon, we gathered in Chhotodidi's mother's house with our singing troupe. She marked my forehead with white lines of sandalwood paste, combed my locks around my cheeks and dressed me up as Radhika while our niece Gangamoyee (Nagendranath's sister) was dressed up as Sri Krishna with headgear and other necessities. The other sisters were made to be Radha's friends: Lalita, Bishakha and Chandrabali, and she herself became the messenger of Vrindavana.

At that time, the jatra songs of Loka Dhepo and Gobindo Adhikari were very popular in that area. We would begin to sing. The ghar jamais played the clowns. Playing *Gostholila* meant a miserable day.[11] The other sisters dressed up as shepherd boys—Sridam, Sudam and Balarama,[12] with topknot and chewing stick in hand. Chhotodidi herself became Kanhaiya and came to the cowshed. In order to clear the weeds of the inner courtyard the little girls had to act as the cows: Shyamali and Dhabali.[13] They had to eat grass, that is, they had to pick up grass and it was a very difficult task. They had to pick up grass with both their hands and simultaneously imitate the sound of cows eating grass. Chhotodidi also wandered around tending her flock with her chewing stick, making noises like a shepherd. Within a short time, the courtyard would be clean. After that the tired girls would go back home crying and cursing. Having received the prize of fasting, they would lock themselves in their houses for the next four- five days. The aim was to clean the garden and having achieved that the troupe owner—Kanhaiya—was not at all humbled. She would proudly roam around in front of the mothers and aunts.

Third game

This was a strange game. All our pishimas were child widows. Right from the time we were born, we saw them wearing white. They reigned in the house with their rigorous code of conduct, hard rules of ritual and fasting, and praying like daughters of the sages. We heard that the Kashyap clan women were fated to be widows.[14] So Chhotodidi turned that into a game and made us play 'widow-widow'. Once in a while, at any time of the day, she would get us to remove our beautiful dresses and ornaments and make us take dips in the pond. Then covering our faces with a veil, we were forced to sit in a corner wailing loudly. Those who could not participate in this sorrowful game had to sacrifice the majority of their sweetmeats and puffed rice snacks, and were thrown out of the group. If by chance my elder cousin[15] Kaliprasanna-dada[16] went that way to hunt and heard this artificial howling, he would jump at us like a tiger in the flock and rescue the poor girls. At that point, our leader, Chhotodidi, used to vanish from the scene. Kaliprasannada smacked the frightened girls who would disperse in different directions, crying.

Last game: robbery in broad daylight

Near our house lived Baikunthanath and Jadavchandra Chaudhuri, both of whom my father addressed as Uncle, since they were elders who belonged to the same village. Generally, all well-to-do households in a village have gardens full of fruits, flowers and vegetables. Their gardens were abundant too and they consumed what they could and distributed the rest among their neighbours. Even if we picked something up 'without permission', it was not considered as 'stealing'. Every morning, children could pluck beautiful scented flowers for prayers. Those who damaged things without reason were justly punished.

They were babus.[17] They spent their time in the luxury of music and dance, chess and draughts. They were not professional slaves. They remained at home and the gentlemen of the village gathered at their place in the evening to make merry. They tended their garden and pond with care. From time to time they would call the children and gift them martyaman banana,[18] papaya, lime and vegetables in large quantities. There was nothing to prevent people from gathering fruits and flowers when required. The garden was surrounded by a high wall and thickly knit bamboo fence for protection against cows and cattle. People could not enter from the sides, they had to walk in from the front or walk around it.

One day, the idea of stealing sweet shaddock from their garden struck Chhotodidi's mind. Objections or difficulties could not deter her. If she wanted something then that was to be got at any cost. She called the group of girls and ordered them, 'Today when the owners close their doors and go for their siesta, we will go in to steal. Everyone get ready. Come immediately after lunch and run behind the garden'. One by one, two by two, the girls gathered beside the garden and tacked tightly the loose end of their sarees around their waist. The leader of the gang forcefully broke the fence, then hoisted the little girls on her back and pushed them inside, ordering them to steal the shaddocks. She herself waited outside guarding the area. Evil activity can never be hidden. To top it all, the robbery was done in broad daylight. There was no dearth of people moving in the streets. Our maids who went to the pond to wash their daily utensils saw us entering the garden to steal the shaddocks. They ran home to call Jethima and showed her everything. She became furious and started shouting at which chhoto Khuki vanished from sight with one leap. The poor little girls were caught.

Translated by Jayeeta Bagchi
School of Women's Studies, Jadavpur University

'Purbakatha (Balyasmriti)', *Matrimandir*, mid-March to mid-April 1924/Chaitra 1330 BS, pp. 355–56.

Notes

1 Prasannamoyee Devi, *'Aryavarta'* in *Pather Katha*, edited by Abhijit Sen and Ujjal Ray (Kolkata: Stree, 1999).

2 Refers to the elaborate extended joint family system, where several brothers, their wives and the children lived together. In many cases, the children of the elder brother or the first wife was referred to as the 'older' branch, whereas those of the younger brother or second wife as the 'younger' branch.

3 Jethamashai: elder paternal uncle, regarded as the head of the family.

4 Jethima: elder paternal uncle's wife.

5 Didi: elder sister; Probably pet name. Chhoto means younger.

[6] Pishima: father's sister.

[7] Yajnas involved elaborated religious ceremonies entailing sacrifices.

[8] Jatra: theatre performed by a group of artists moving from one place to another.

[9] Sons-in-law residing in the house of their fathers-in-law.

[10] Chaitali during the Bengali Chaitra month mid-March to mid-April, i.e., the end of the Bengali year.

[11] Gostholila: musical composition with the pastoral theme of Krishna and his friends.

[12] Balarama is Krishna's brother, and Sridam and Sudam his friends.

[13] Shyamali: black cow, Dhabali: white cow. These were the names of Krishna's cows.

[14] Kashyap was one of the Saptarshi Brahmins, one of the 10 *manasaputras* of Lord Brahma, the creator of this world.

[15] Here the son of elder paternal uncle.

[16] Dada: elder brother.

[17] Babu: decadent class of landed gentry in nineteenth-century Bengal.

[18] Martyaman: a species of high quality yellow banana.

36

SARAJUBALA BASU

No biographical details about this author could be found.

Life as a Daughter-in-Law (1924)

In most Bengali families, women lead unhappy lives as daughters-in-law. As girls grow up, mothers express their horror and transmit similar feelings to the girls' minds: 'You shall see what fun it is to be in the marital home! You will forget the taste of hot rice, where will you get food if you feel like eating at the end of the night? Your mother in-law might throw you a piece of sweetmeat at twelve noon.'

With the expression of such fears, mothers catalyse a feeling of hatred in the girls' hearts towards life as a married woman. From their very childhood, they have an eerie intuitive fear about the marital home and as the time for them to leave for the husband's place draws near, the girls begin to drown in a pool of sorrow. For some this depression results in some kind of disease too.

How long will it take to quench this sacrificial fire that consumes women from Bengali families? Why does a mother-in-law forget her past life as a bride? Instead of showing sympathy, she passes sarcastic remarks to the bride, 'Bouma, you are leading a luxurious life, I had to go through several ordeals as a bride.[1] I had to digest all the taunts of my sister-in-law and mother-in-law. I had to massage their feet late into the night.'

Just see the irony at this juncture! What has the bride been taught by giving a distorted description of the care she had offered to her in-laws and the lack of self-restrain that she depicted? Thus, the lesson that the bride learns is that like her mother-in-law she should also consider her present condition sorrowful and the task of looking after her mother-in-law and sister-in-law as a very burdensome and difficult task.

If somebody cannot afford to have servants then who will run the household errands other than the women of the house? Nowadays servants are expensive; hence, everybody cannot afford one. Doing household tasks should not be a painful task for women. If required, it is sometimes also necessary for the housewife to look after her sister-in-law and mother-in-law. On such occasions, the members of the household should be sympathetic towards the housewife; she should be won over by their cordial behaviour.

It is necessary to distinguish between the just and the unjust properly. As a mother, you hold a responsible and respectable position in the family. To show respect to motherhood, you should occupy the place of a mother in the heart of the newly wed bride providing all your love and affection for her: that would make you truly maternal! This will result in a peaceful family life for Bengali women and will put an end to their tears.

First of all, you have compelled the bride's father to sell his ancestral home thereby lighting a bush fire in the bride's family and then brought the bride into your own through the sacred ritual of marriage.[2] Thereafter at each step you started pointing out hundreds and thousands of faults, 'You, daughter of a low-caste person! Daughter of a chamar! Does my B.A. pass son deserve such low-grade gifts? Such a tacky watch and chain? Such an ugly wife?'

Thus you continue criticism of everything, finding loopholes in whatever the new daughter-in-law does. Given such a situation what kind of dedication do you expect from the bride? You can compel her to work, you can even get her verbal but that is superficial dedication and obedience. Is that going to last forever? These are merely temporary the future is doomed.

That is why the chained women of Bengal are crying today! Where lies the ray of hope for those families in which wives and sisters who emulate the goddess Lakshmi are continuously in tears? The women are depressed, causing many men to lose their way in the dark allies of life; they get drunk and loss their moral values.

As a newly married bride, she weeps in private after being taunted by the in-laws and never forgets to inform her husband about her pain and sorrow at the very first chance. Many husbands with educated minds express sympathy for the chained wife, many do not even care to do so. When the wife becomes the mother of a son or a daughter, then many a heartless husband becomes sympathetic towards her as she is the mother of his children. From this time onwards begins the sorrow of the in-laws. The new mother now starts avenging all the tortures she has faced.

At the age of ten or twelve, a young bride marries into the family to illuminate it with a soul as pure as the breaking dawn, but with the flow of time the stark difficulty of family life turns the flower-like softness of her heart into the hardness of stone, and fills it with vengeance! But she will forget her past ordeals, sorrows and painful experiences or will keep them suppressed until she becomes a mother-in-law herself. As soon as the son's newly married bride arrives such women start to practice all the tortures they have faced in the past with renewed enthusiasm. They feel that it is necessary to keep the daughter-in-law under strict vigilance, so that the bride fails to get the sympathy of her husband and she is enslaved just as the mother-in-law had been as a bride in the past.

All this is the result of inadequate education and lack of freedom. Women remain shackled throughout their lives and thus they do not give up any chance to display their dominance over others inside the house. If today women get a good education and freedom, then such a situation will not remain. A daughter-in-law will never feel that her life as a daughter-in-law is sorrowful; mothers will no more picture the marital home as a place to be afraid of, there will be peace in every house. Even men will no longer be subjected to daily family squabbles. They will be able to accomplish their responsibilities towards their mother, sister and brother, as well as towards their wives.

When will this take place? When will we open our eyes? Today, even respectable men get furious on hearing women's mute appeals; men's responses to these appeals are sometimes appalling and sarcastic!

Times are changing. Today enslaved women are rising in protest; their sorrows and sufferings have crossed all limits—they have cried alone in the corners of their houses for a long time, and they cannot do this any more. O great men, why are you still showing such cruelty? Why do you want to remain submerged in the mire of selfishness? Why do not you try to understand the sufferings of women?

... Why do you have this misconception that freedom will make women unchaste? Maybe you are scared to imagine women treading the same path that you walk on? Think of your wives, mothers and sisters who face tortures, day after day, without saying a word? You cannot imagine it.

Will you only keep on pursuing your own happiness and your own quest for autocratic authority? Will you always keep women in chains, drain them of all their strength and still move on with great pride and comfort? . . . Unable to bear the pain and suffering any longer, Bengali women want to break the shackles that bind them; that is why they are appealing to you, to apprise you of their problems, but this is making you furious. Is this what is expected of you?

Why do tears flow in Bengali households on the birth of a female child? Why are a son and a daughter not equal for parents? Isn't it because of you? Alas, the mother sobs with the girl child on her lap thinking that the ancestral home will be sold; loans and abuses from the moneylenders will have to be swallowed in order to provide you men with a dowry for marrying her daughter. . . .

Little girls who become widows at a young age are turned into servants or cooks; alas! does nobody feel for them? Their illness is considered as an act; if they are hungry they are dubbed demonesses; and if they feel sleepy they are cursed for being ill omens! Their beauty is a sin, long beautiful hair is also a sin, all their talk and laughter, everything is considered an aberration; is this not torture? How can she sacrifice her youth, her beauty, her feelings of love and hope at the feet of society? . . .

Just because you are men, you get married five or ten times; there is nothing sinful in it. It does not occasion any comment. Being unable to bear the pains inflicted by society, so many women are destroying their lives. Does that set a healthy and commendable example for society? . . . In a monthly magazine, two or three women have expressed their sufferings, making intelligent men furious as a result.

There are many caring husbands, who provide their wives with food and clothing. By taking care of all the problems of their wives, they make those women happy, but such examples are few. In most families, women are tortured, abused and insulted; nobody cares to look after them. In Hindu society, the parents of the bride have to silently watch the tortures perpetrated on their daughter by her husband and in-laws, without being able to offer any solution to the problem. They have to tolerate everything, afraid that if they don't, the son-in-law will abandon their daughter and marry again; people will abuse them; and their daughter will again return to them for shelter. It is not a happy business for the parents. But why does such a custom exist? The reason is the lack of freedom for women! Given such a situation, the inner instinct says that it is better to kill a girl child as soon as she sees the light of this world.

A young man beats his wife with his shoe while the wife cries, which makes him say, 'Shut up, shut up, do not make a noise!' At that time this young fellow was drunk. But what about these men who in their proper senses torture women and threaten them continuously: 'Shut up, your cries should not be heard, keep quiet!'

Translated by Mukulika Dattagupta
Department of Comparative Literature, Jadavpur University

'Badhujiban', Manasi o Marmabani, mid-November to mid-December 1924/Agrahayan 1331 BS, barsha 16 (year 16), khanda 2, sankhya 4 (no. 4), pp. 395-98.

Notes

1. Bouma literally means daughter-in-law–mother; parents-in-law often use this form of address for their sons' wives, calling them both daughter-in-law and mother.
2. In order to pay the dowry, which was often a very large amount; a bride's father could even be selling the ancestral house.

37

SRI INDIRA DEVI CHAUDHURANI

Indira Devi Chaudhurani (1873–1960) was the daughter of Rabindranath Tagore's elder brother Satyendranath and his wife, Jnanadanandini Devi. At a very young age, her translation entitled *'Bastille'* first appeared in the monthly magazine *Balak* which was run by Rabindranath Tagore and edited by Jnanadanandini Devi. She was awarded the Padmavati Gold Medal after having come first amongst the female candidates in the B.A. examination.[1] Her many translations of French pieces into Bengali have been extensively published across several magazines like *Sadhana, Sabujpatra, Parichay*, and so on. Her essays on the empowerment of women have been collected in a book called *Narir Ukti*. In 1944, she was awarded the Bhuvanmohini medal by the University of Calcutta. In 1956, she became the *Upacharya* of the Visva Bharati. In 1957, Visva Bharati bestowed upon her the title of the 'Deshikottom', and in 1959, she was given the Rabindra Puraskar by the Rabindra Bharati Samiti. She was married to Pramatha Chaudhuri, the brother of Prasannamoyee Devi (see Essay 35, 'Recollections from a Time Past').

What Is the Ideal for Women's Education? (1931)

In an essay written decades earlier, I had tried to sift through evidence that though over the last fifty years women have lost some of their former skills and assets because of the spread of education among them, those skills were either replaced or replenished by new skills or been modified. Hence, education has already proved to be anything but disadvantageous to women.

Today, again, I have undertaken the responsibility of studying and highlighting the new possibilities emerging in women's education. But my stance is entirely neutral and hence must be excused for any errors. While on the previous occasion women's education was analysed and compared with relation to its historical development, now it is being compared to men's education. Thus, what has changed is not the idea but the orientation. Having already stated my opinion on women's education at various places and on various occasions, I would humbly apologize for any kind of repetition on my part.

I never had the honour or disgrace of actually being a student, nor does such an opportunity present itself before me any more. So if anyone harbours the slightest doubt about my ability in thus expressing my opinions about women's education, it would neither surprise me nor pain me. I have heard a person saying on one occasion that after one is past fifty years of age, he or she acquires the authority of expressing his or her opinion. Though I cannot wholly agree, I would nevertheless like to accept such a premise for my thesis.

The same subject can be viewed from different perspectives, and this is particularly true of a subject as vast and complex as education, which goes on to mark the impossibility of restricting it or doing justice to it within the scope of a small essay. So it is absolutely necessary to draw a broad outline to make such a discussion easy and possible. It is undoubtedly criminal to be a Bengali and be counted among those who oppress women into silence. But then my readers too fall in this same category and hence I wish to quickly and briefly express my opinions so as to provide them with some opportunity to protest as well.

Within my proposed scope the first argument is that it is necessary to differentiate between the education of men and that of women, since to indicate such a difference is the main purpose of this essay. I believe that most people nowadays feel that the time for making such a differentiation has arrived. One instance readily presents itself in this case. The All India Women's Education Society,[2] which held its convention in Lahore of late, agreed upon the following:

It is necessary for schools and universities to take up a fresh perspective about women's education. Hyderabad and Cochin have explicitly suggested the setting up of different and independent branches of study for men and women.

As in the absence of an appropriate traditional dress in their own culture, women had adopted Muslim or Christian modes of dressing to make themselves presentable in the social world, similarly devoid of a tradition of education for women, liberal men offered women the education they themselves acquired and practised.[3] Thus educated women must now think of opportunities to expand the advantages of such an education, and it is generally assumed that men would join them in such an endeavour. Unfortunately, however, it is difficult to find an easy way to do this. To abandon the conventional way requires not only intelligent application but also an alert mind, conscious of what is available and what is required.

The first question which arises then is why do we think that there should be different avenues of education for men and women? There can be two possible answers: the first is by discussing the very root of the problem; and the second is through learning by experience. It can be assumed that quite a few among us have undergone such an experience or have been dissatisfied in our attempts, or else why would the question of modifying the system of education arise at all? So let us concentrate on the root of the problem.

Had not the advocates of equality opposed it, one could easily have said in public that just like their anatomical differences, the minds of men and women also differ in their basic structure and nature. That every girl is born to be a mother, and that most girls want to be wives and mothers is a simple truth that can be safely stated without inviting many opinions to the contrary. On such a ground it can be said that just as men receive general education up to a point and then go on to acquire specialized education based on the differences of their natures, women also should be given special education. . . . Why should the same measures not be taken for women as well? If their natures are different, their education must respect such differences.

I could have accepted that such differences exist naturally and different women should be given the freedom to pursue their respective choices justly. But this would restrict me within my defined territory. It may not be possible for most men to become doctors and engineers (though that is largely the case at present); however, it is necessary to raise women with a similar ideal in life so that they accept motherhood as something that comes naturally to them, as most women will be mothers. The young boy is more intimately related to his mother than to his father, and to make the best use of such an intimate association for the child's future, mothers of such children must be given the education appropriate to this end, otherwise it would prove detrimental not only to the mother and son but also to society at large. The education that contributes in making a knowledgeable adult man or a fitting head of a household, capable of earning to support a family can never be the same as that which will fulfil the purpose of making a good wife and a good mother. This is because the two have their own respective functions, purposes, different bodies and minds as well. In our country, at least, such differences are clearly evident and are likely to remain so in the ages to come.

So I shall consider the mission of identifying education suitable to the needs of our country as the third sphere of my discussion, and I believe this will be universally accepted as well. The resources a person might have or the skills that he might possess are without doubt considered as the fruits of good education dedicated to the service of the nation, though there may be exceptions to this rule. The criticism that men's education in our country is largely inspired and modelled on western liberal education is not applicable in case of women's education in our country.

The fourth aspect of my discussion would focus on the fact that there is much to say on the advancement of education which resonates with the progress of society. Taking up measures suitable to the occasion and acquiring the ability to assert one's personality, naturally falls within this category. The new schools we intend to establish must not be narrow in their scope but must easily make available a variety of opportunities so that all classes and groups of women can gain access to them.

Outlining the structure fulfils my commitment. To give shape to such a structure remains the task of specialists. However, I believe my task would remain incomplete till I have established in clear terms the boundaries within which the project should be restricted.

The first requirement that I would like to impose is that women's education in the final analysis must be different from men's education. The second requirement is that as all women must eventually become wives and mothers and there exists an intricate relationship between the two, it is imperative that related issues be discussed at the same time. A number of subjects that would suit women's education can be deduced from such a discussion like health, food and nutrition, nursing and first aid, cooking, stitching, book-keeping, home management, child care, and so on.

The third requirement that I would like to impose is that once our education is so modelled to fulfil the needs of serving our national interests, it should influence learning and training in other related areas like religion, customs, rituals, festivals, languages, literature, history, legends and folklore, geography, the arts and aesthetics.

The fourth would be to stress the need for a parallel system of vocational education for all women along side the general education they receive. As with the changing times women require to be financially independent, such education could yield good results. If women can contribute to the family income many families can be saved from starving. And especially, for a widow living in a joint family, such attempts to earn can help her and her children live with some dignity rather than being dependent on others. If girls' schools take this initiative at a rudimentary stage then the shelters for the aged in our country would be spared the burden of reflecting the sad plight of dependent women. Apart from such vocational training women nowadays are also inclined to other forms of education like learning to read and write languages other than their mother tongue, understand Sanskrit and adopt the manners and customs of foreign countries as well as acquaint themselves with literature as a subject.

When all the needs and demands that influence the national interest have been taken care of, a little space must be left over so that I can establish a few reasons why women often do not participate in the field of education. First, they are considered physically incapable of bearing such a load, and second, they are often denied such an opportunity though they desire it. The third reason may be some sort of a mental resolve or inclination that tends to make everyday life lose its regular appeal, such as overwhelming religiosity or some form of artistic inclination.

To conclude, I have arrived at the very conviction from where I had started. Hence, I reiterate the same proposition, that is, initially children of both sexes, say between the ages six and eleven, must be given the same education; girls between eleven and sixteen, should be given special education in the manner discussed earlier, together with a form of vocational education. Girls who drop out of school should appear for matriculation or some equivalent examination. Among those who choose to study further, the ones who look forward to an early family life can choose a few subjects for specialization from among the subjects they have already studied. However, the rest, who either seek or are forced to undertake life's journey alone, can receive the same education as given to men, be it in the general or vocational area.

It is impossible to gain a complete education if schools and colleges are made to shoulder the entire responsibility. The home should complement the school in educating an individual. There are certain values which cannot be inculcated outside the home, like maintenance of the honour of family name, socialization and acquaintance with societal rules, regulations, manners and customs. There are many good habits like a basic sense of cleanliness, tidiness, punctuality, discipline which are impossible to inculcate only in school. Most importantly, an individual comes to believe in and practice his or her religion only in the family, though the influence of the religious guru and religious community are inevitable in later life. However, women seem to be more driven by necessity in pursuing religious beliefs and practices, for life is a long journey and is not always a bed of roses, and women are usually more tender and soft-hearted than men. It is most often the woman who shoulders the responsibility of running a household smoothly; it is she who is more affected by its ups and downs; and it is she who shelters the dependents of the family. Given this situation, she needs to fall back upon and rely on some source of strength so that she can be strong while executing such a role in the family. Religion as the source of such strength was something our ancestors believed in, and if their devotion and sacrifice can be coupled with today's education and work ethic, only then can we deserve to be called well educated.

Translated by Priyanka Saha
School of Women's Studies, Jadavpur University

'Stree Sikshar Adarsha Ki?', *Bangalakshmi*, mid-June to mid-July 1931/ Asarh 1338 BS, barsha 6 (year 6), sankhya 8 (no. 8) , pp. 606–09.

Notes

[1] She uses the male form, Sri, before her name, and adds her qualification B.A. Though Sri is not frequently used to prefix women's names, its use is not incorrect.

2 There is no record of the meeting in Lahore, though the Asian Women's Conference was held at Lahore in 1931. The promotion of women's education and the establishment of a fund for the same began with the second sitting of the AIWC in Delhi in 1928, where the following resolution was passed: 'That an All India Fund for the promotion of Women's Education be established and a sub-committee be appointed to collect funds and submit a scheme for its administration to the Standing Committee'. Between 1929–32, a movement for social and educational advancement of women originated in the country and a number of women leaders like Sarojini Naidu, the Margaret Cousins, Rajkumari Amrit Kaur, Rani Laxmibai Rajwade, Rustomji Faridoonji and others championed the cause of their unfortunate sisters and struggled hard through the forum of the All India Women's Conference (AIWC). In 1930, the Pachmari session of the AIWEFA declared that the education of women had thus far incorrectly been identical to that of men. Women's needs and roles were multi-faceted, it was agreed, so they needed a special curriculum. This, envisaged in 1930, was to consist of everything for a woman's all-round development and for her many and varied roles: the physical, biological and social sciences, humanities and arts, the domestic sciences: needlework and tailoring, laundry and textiles, dietetics and cookery and child development. There were to be extra-curricular activities and sports and community out-reach programmes.

3 The dress of women in the inner houses in Bengal was not considered 'civilized', a fact changed by the new way of wearing a sari introduced by the women of the Tagore family, especially Jnanadanandini Devi. She was influenced by the *Parsi garas* or garos—saris with Chinese embroidery in white or variegated silk threads, which she saw in Bombay. The style of wearing the sari with a blouse, often modelled on the western dress, with a fine muslin *sudreh* (undershirt), was soon adapted by those involved in the social reform movement in Bengal and in other parts of the country. The introduction of the sari blouse (*jama*) and petticoat (*shaya*) was essential before upper- and middle-class Bengali women could come out in public.

38

MAHMUDA KHATUN SIDDIQUA

Mahmuda Khatun Siddiqua (1906/7–1977/79) has carved an indelible niche for herself as a Muslim female poet in Bengali literature. The rebel in her was so strong, that even at the age of twelve her grandmother had failed to force the purdah on her. Her first poem was published in the *Al-Islam* magazine, when she was around twelve or thirteen years of age. Her first anthology of poems is called *Pasarini* (1931). She was awarded the Bangla Academy Award in 1967 in Dhaka and the *Ekusher Padak* in 1977.

Drinking Tea for the First Time (1933)

It was a backward and remote village. Seated on a stool in one corner of the verandah that was like a thatched room with eight roofs and not partitioned by walls, the mistress of the house tended the stove with a smile. A large pan of water was boiling on it. Seated afar on a wicker stool, narrating stories, was the lady's aged husband who had just returned from Calcutta. He was waiting for the water to boil for tea. He had never been to Calcutta before and having tasted tea there for the first time in his life, he was now teaching his wife the wonderful preparation. The man of the house was restless to share with his wife the spectacular taste of this beverage called tea. The lady, having lit the stove, from time to time, stared wonderstruck at her husband, not merely listening to all that he was saying about Calcutta but literally gulping it all down. The daughter-in-law hovered around, some of the young girls were making chapatis, some were kneading the dough, while some others gazed at the master of the house, leaving whatever they were doing to listen to the stories of Calcutta. In one corner, rolled out neatly in a heap were balls of rice on a wooden plate. And the children had their eyes fixed upon them. Every now and then, each person eagerly turned to the pan checking to see if the water had boiled, impatiently waiting to taste the extraordinary drink. The master came forward, drew the lid and declared, 'Won't take much longer.' When the master thus turned happily, his wrist brushed against his wife's ears, and the ear ornament she wore swung in ecstasy. The dangling jhumkas that the other girls and women wore swung in bliss too.

The mistress noticed that it was actually getting late, her daughter-in-law's sari was already shining as the rays of the sun fell on its borders. Strangely, the girls and the daughters-in-law had not noticed that their precious jamdani saris were gathering dust on the ground—what a day it had been today. Even the master looked at the sun and said, 'It is getting late.' And then, with great pride declared, 'Wife, how majestically the lion roared in the zoo! I was frightened at first. And you will never believe how large the hippo in the water was unless you see it with your own eyes! What colourful birds, uncountable! I wish I could show all these to you.' Overwhelmed with an unimaginable happiness, she turned her face and replied, 'Oh, no no! I would be scared.' And her nose pin jolted with the rhythm of her refusal. The water boiled just after this. The master had noticed it before anyone else could. He almost screamed aloud, 'Wife, bring the pan down, bring it down. The water has boiled.' Shocked by the scream, the wife plunged into action and brought the pan down with the border of her *sari*, though, lying close by was another piece of cloth meant for this purpose. Valiantly he marched forward and strewed the tea leaves in the pan. There was amazement in every gaze. All were eager to know what may happen.

After some time, the master filtered the tea and added some milk and sugar. The children immediately broke out in a frenzy, 'Me first, me first,' peals of laughter, incoherent babbling, shrieks and screams, such utter commotion! With great difficulty, the master was able to pour the tea in the cups and pass it on. Girls–boys, mistresses–maids, all began to express their happiness and the joy of anticipation. The youngest daughter-in-law shyly stood at the corner of the doorstep; as soon as the mistress saw her, she called out, 'O *dear*! What are you waiting there for, come here quickly.' To make the youngest daughter-in-law happier, she even poured a little extra tea in her cup. Today, there was a subtle pride in her ways. After all, only *her* husband had been to Calcutta in the entire village, and it was at *her* home that everyone tasted, for the first time, an extraordinary new beverage—tea. This joy and pride was reflected in everything that she had been doing. So when the cowherd boy had asked her for tea, she had filled his bowl to the brim. Finally, the master and the mistress exchanged glances as they sipped their cups of tea. When their tea tasting sessions had ended, he looked at his wife sharply and said, 'Tomorrow is Id. When our new son-in-law comes, he must surely be invited to have a cup of tea.'

On both sides were gold strewn mustard fields. The bearers with the new son-in-law in the palanquin were on the narrow track which ran through the fields. A chilly breeze had brushed the mustard fields into a restless wave. There was a low murmur in the great forests afar. Though the flowers of spring had not bloomed yet, the new bridegroom's mind had bloomed with red, pink, yellow and many a colourful flower, and even the palanquin bearers had sung, 'The storks dig dig dig for grain on the river banks.' And when the palanquin reached the doorstep, the new bridegroom covered his face with a handkerchief in order to hide his broad grin. His maternal grandmother-in-law walked up to him and asked, 'What do you say, new bridegroom! Were you thinking about me on the way or your bride?' Immediately came a grinning reply, 'You.' 'Oh, sure,' said the grandma and walked towards the bride's room. Earlier, brothers-in-law, sisters-in-law, all had gathered around the bride. Once the groom took his seat, the grandma brought him food. The bridegroom sat down to eat; but, he could not eat a morsel. Noting that his eyes were scanning the room for someone, the grandma said, 'I understand dear son-in-law! You will not eat alone.' Then, she looked at all the boys, girls, brothers and sisters-in-law and told them, 'You leave or our daughter will not eat with him out of bashfulness.' Saying this, she went out of the room in search of the bride. Now the brothers and sisters-in-law and all the young boys and girls focused all their individual attention on the bridegroom. They felt a little upset. The grandmother-in-law was very efficient: she almost dragged the bride, made her sit beside the bridegroom and ordered, 'Grandson-in-law! Now everything must be eaten.' She disappeared and re-appeared a little later with two cups of steaming hot tea. Presenting it she said, 'This old busybody will now vanish, so eat to your heart's content.' She bolted the door from outside and left. The bridegroom had not had any chance to take a good look at his bride. He pulled back the covering from her head and face and in eager anticipation, wonderstruck he muttered, 'Turn.' Shyly, the bride began drawing back her ghomta.[1] The groom held her hand down forcefully, and gazed at the beauty that came from the realms of the gods. He pleaded, 'Say something.' The bride hid her face in her lap, extremely shy. The groom having tried to raise her head with both his hands gave up finally. The bride drew her ghomta and sat with her back facing the groom. The groom was thinking of the ways in which he could possibly make her speak, ways of getting to know her. After straining his head for a very long time when the groom picked up his cup to sip the tea, the naughty bride, giggling, pushed the groom, and the cup fell from his hands and filled the room with tinkling sounds. The bride laughed aloud and uncontrollably on seeing the sorry face of the groom. In the meantime, the grandma came in to ask them to come for lunch, and having understood the whole situation burst out laughing teasingly and raised a commotion, '*Olo*![2] Come all of you and see what the new groom has done.' As soon as they heard the call, everyone collected from all sides and corners. Then, the sound of laughter filled the entire house. And an heavenly ecstasy filled the hearts of the bride and the groom.

Translated by Anindita Roy
Department of Comparative Literature, Jadavpur University

'Pratham Cha Khawa'; *Gulistan*, mid-December to mid-January 1933-34/Paush 1340 BS.

Also available in *Zenana Mehfil: Bangali Musalman Lekhikader Nirbachita Rachana, 1904- 1938*, edited by Shaheen Akhtar an Moushumi Bhowmik (Kolkata: Stree, 1998), pp. 180–82.

Notes

1 Ghomta meant covering the head and sometimes, a part of the face, with the loose end of the sari.

2 Colloquial way of calling people; commonly associated with women.

PART IV

'WORKING' FOR THE NATION

39

SWARNAKUMARI DEVI

Essay 17 offers a note on the author.

On Politics (1908)

Any act of murder breeds evil, and murder by throwing bombs generates its extreme form. On the one hand, the guilty and the innocent are simultaneously wiped out, and, on the other, the events planned with utmost secrecy arouse feelings of terror in people's minds and create a dangerous situation. We feel gravely remorseful seeing young men, dedicated to the welfare of the country, engaged in such acts. Now we hear that they also intend to loot and steal. If this is true, then whom will the country depend on, and on whom will our hopes be pinned? 'If injustice and oppression are the methods, then the country will not benefit, rather chaos will increase like an epidemic, turn into mindless delirium, rending apart the heart of the motherland in the effort to protect her.' These are Rabindranath Tagore's words.[1]

But it seems impossible to accept that those learned people who are the inspiration behind Narendra's act are so bereft of good sense that they will condone such torture of the helpless and innocent of our country.[2] Those who know Aurobindo also know that he is incapable of encouraging murder or theft.[3] But the actual truth of an event cannot be limited by what people think may or may not be possible. This is open to proof. However, Narendra, the culprit, will say anything now so that he may be freed, and none of this can be believed unless there is ample evidence. It is common sense, as according to English law, just as a famous barrister has been appointed by the government for Narendra's defence, similarly, an equally competent barrister must be provided for Aurobindo; only then will the judge be able to come to a decision when he hears the arguments of both sides.

Aurobindo's sister Srimati Sarojini has appealed to the public for monetary help in recruiting an able barrister for her brother. But I hear that many people are wary of donating for the cause. We do not understand the reason for this apprehension. As long as Aurobindo has not been proved a traitor to the government through a proper trial, we must consider him as innocent. This is exactly what English law says. Even when Kshudiram confessed that he was responsible for the assassination,[4] Judge Cornduff requested lawyers to fight his case.[5] When the person who murdered Judge Norman was caught red-handed, there was a counsel who stood in court on his behalf. Where the crime is punishable by death or exile, this is the law. We can see that English law is tempered to an appreciable extent by mercy and justice. No one is sentenced to death without the opportunity to prove his innocence. So if our countrymen's efforts to prove Aurobindo's innocence actually incur the wrath of the government, then this casts doubt upon the government's own principles of justice. At such a time, anyone who loves justice whether he is local or foreign ought to donate generously to Srimati Sarojini.

The newspaper *Umpire* has commented obliquely that people wish to donate anonymously because they think that Aurobindo is actually guilty.[6] Alas! Are these people so blind to truth? Even a child will understand that this wish for anonymity is nothing but the fear of antagonizing the government by helping a person whom the government thinks is guilty, even though that view is not shared by the citizens. But such cowardice is nothing more than shameful for the people of this country, as well as insulting to the government. When Narendra is trying to implicate other respected civilians, then if the truth of the allegations is not settled once and for all through the pointed questions of the defence barrister, people will assume that the government is partial. This is not desirable. It is because we are well-wishers of the government that we believe in this.

Since the occurrence of the bombing catastrophe, everyone in the land is submerged in a sea of sorrow. What sort of foolishness is this on the part of the youngsters! While taking the pledge to work for the benefit of the country, they have ironically undertaken the path of evil. By resolving to eradicate violent oppression, they have resorted to violence, which is truly unfortunate. The first consequence of throwing a bomb had caused the death of two innocent women. Whose wife and daughter were they? Mr. Kennedy, is a Congress partisan and especially sympathetic to the Indian cause. Who would not be devastated by such deaths? And who would not condemn the wrongful actions of the wayward youths? If they had stayed on the path of justice and given their lives for the country, their martyrdom would have had a meaning—they would have left the country with an example to emulate. ... From this incident, everyone ... must learn that our liberation will not come through such unjust, criminal means. Our liberation can be attained through unity. The secret criminal acts that these youngsters have performed are acts of treason which strike at the roots of that very unity. We have always lacked unity. Despite being human ourselves, our dharma has been to look down on other humans with hatred and disgust. Are not names and descriptions like 'chandal', 'yavan', 'mleccha', the untouchable who attends the crematorium, the foreigner, and he who does not follow true religion, indicative of disgust and hatred? ... It is through western education that we have now understood that unity is good for us. Now, Hindus and Muslims alike think that this is necessary. Recently in England, a branch of the All Indian Muslim Committee was established.[7] One of its aims is the fostering of unity and friendship among the different communities of India. The former judge of the Calcutta High Court, Justice Amir Ali,[8] as the president of the meeting said, 'I have been working continuously for the last few years to ensure that unity and friendship between Hindus and Muslims may flourish because in India, the benefit and prosperity of all people are connected to the common good of all communities.' This may be our desire, but we regularly perform actions contrary to this. Since the division of Bengal, the hope of unity between Hindus and Muslims has become even fainter.[9] Those who want the good of the country too are beset by feelings of division and are becoming divided from one another. The division between those who desire equality and those who resort to extremism has caused the Congress to degenerate and these adolescent revolutionaries have set out on the path leading to the destruction of the country.

British rule is not the reason for our poverty. If we are ever truly able to stand united like a strong wall, rejecting our differences, then we will be able to form a great nation, staunch in the face of sudden attacks. In truth, the British government is not our enemy, and this government is not indifferent to our welfare. We live in peace and comfort under British rule and the country has progressed on many fronts. But it is true that this government is not our ideal Ram Rajya.[10] Oppression occurs when there is a conflict of interest between the ruler and the ruled and takes place when the ruler and the ruled belong to the same race as well. Ireland, Persia and Russia are examples of this. In fact, such conflicts will always arise between the powerful and the powerless, the master and the slave, the ruler and the ruled.

If we work through legitimate means, through contemplation, intelligence, unity and firm resolve, we shall be able to overcome such oppression and injustice to some extent. Ability triumphs everywhere. As we have heard, some British banks refuse to lend money to swadeshi enterprises even when there is no chance of incurring loss. We can easily overcome such dependence by opening national banks. The people have now become aware of this to a great extent. But we see very few landlords coming forward. If the rich and the middle class, irrespective of their own selfish ends, come together in such endeavours then we will be able to feel the true taste of freedom even if we remain colonized. If we feel that working together in such a manner is impossible for us, then the desire for a unified nation is nothing more than a hopeless indulgence.

That we can achieve results even against the British if we are united has been proved by the boycott of Branson by the native attorneys and pleaders.[11] In many cases, even if united resistance has not yet yielded visible results, the final success of such endeavours is inevitable. Just as it is imperative for us to express our displeasure and opposition when we see injustice, similarly, it is not a wise strategy to express hatred towards the British. Good relations between the ruler and the ruled have always been completely desirable and each side must make efforts in this direction.

There is no unredeemable evil in this world. Some rays of hope appear even within that which we think of as unmitigated evil. We may hope that knowledge will open the eyes of both the ruler and the ruled due to this terrible act of throwing a bomb. Those of the ruled who harbour evil thoughts will realize the horror of such acts and the ruler will understand that the strategy of oppression alone cannot be the best way of ruling the country.

Many politically aware and thoughtful Englishmen are now of the opinion that the government is responsible for anarchy and misrule in the country. If there is a revolution of any kind, it is to be understood that some sort of unrest with the rule lies in its foundation. To understand this and take steps to remove it are the government's responsibility. The extreme unrest and dissatisfaction in the land that we see now is the result of Lord Curzon and the government's complete indifference to the wishes and the just appeals of the subjects.

India is a land of hundreds of thousands of people. If a small, insignificant number expresses its dissatisfaction in this way, then there is nothing to be surprised about, especially because almost everyone who has been a part of this is a young man who has not yet attained the maturity of mind and a true understanding of what is beneficial and what is not. Now, if the misguided exploits of one or two youngsters and statements like that of Narendra who wishes to be released from captivity, provoke the government even slightly, and it starts oppressing the youngsters in the country, causing needless repression of the subjects subsequently. Indians truly do not want the end of British rule—we do not want it, keeping our own interests in mind—we know that we are not yet prepared for self-rule; we shall suffer if this is given to us. So what is it that we want? We want justice, we want the highest political rights, and we desire from the British the kind of behaviour that one human being hopes to get from the other. Instead of a master and slave relationship, we urge for a friendship between the ruler and his subjects. The people of the country are satisfied with little. Those who say that this is not the case, make a mistake. Fletcher has fined Clarke a mere 500 rupees in the Brajendrachandra case,[12] but people are satisfied with that. Kshudiram has been given the death sentence, but Cornduff's impartial conduct of the trial has made him the object of everyone's praise. If everyone was as impartial and just like Cornduff, then we would have no cause for dissatisfaction or regret. Whether guilty or guiltless, everyone is now devastated. The land is seething with uncertainty and unrest and people have given up all hopes for justice. If now the government replaces its oppressive strategies with Lord Canning's sympathetic policy,[13] then alone can the hearts of subjects fill with confidence and gratitude; instead of the wails of agony that we hear today, there will be paeans of praise to the British Raj on all sides.

Translated by Ipshita Chanda
Department of Comparative Literature, Jadavpur University

'Rajnaitik Prasanga', Bharati, mid-July to mid-August 1908/Sravan 1315, khanda 32 (vol. 32), sankhya 4 (no. 4), pp. 189-92.

Also available in *Swarnakumari Devir Rachana Samkalan,* edited by Abhijit Sen and Anindita Bhaduri (Kolkata: Dey's Publishing in collaboration with School of Women's Studies, Jadavpur University, September 2000), pp. 288–92.

Notes

1 Rabindranath Tagore's views about militant nationalism and his critical representation of it is found in the novels *Ghare Baire* (1916) and *Char Adhyay* (1934). His critique of nationalism and the genesis of militancy is found in the essays collected in *Nationalism*.

2 Narendra Goswami and Indu Bhusan Ray had hurled a bomb at M. Tardival, the Mayor of Chandernagore (now Chandannagar). Narendra Bandopadhyay was the mastermind of this action. Narendranath Goswami, a prisoner who had been intentionally kept separate from the other prisoners confined in the European Ward, was brought to the Jail Hospital by a European Convict Overseer named Higgins. Narendranath was shot dead in the Hospital by two fellow prisoners named Kanai Lal Dutt and Satyendranath Bose. Attempting to arrest one of them Higgins was shot through the wrist.

3 Aurobindo Ghosh (1872–1950) was a freedom fighter and an Indian nationalist. From 1905–10, he was one of the most active leaders in the movements for India's freedom. However, later he turned to spiritual evolution and developed his own visions and philosophy on human progress. The central theme of his vision was the evolution of human life into a 'life divine'.

4 Kshudiram Bose (1889–1908) was one of the youngest revolutionaries in the history of India's independence movement. Aged sixteen, Kshudiram took recourse to terror, planting bombs near police stations and targeting government officials. The specific bombing for which he was sentenced to death in 1908, resulted in the deaths of three persons—Mrs. Kennedy, her daughter and a servant. On the night of 30 April 1908, Kshudiram and Prafulla Chaki approached the European Club at Muzaffarpur. They waited in the bushes for Chief Presidency Magistrate Douglas Kingsford to come out. Kingsford had gained notoriety for his harsh verdicts on nationalists. They saw a carriage coming and assuming it was Kingsford's hurled the bombs. The occupants, Mrs. Kennedy, Miss Kennedy and one of their servants, were killed instead.

5 It appears to be Justice Cornduff who heard the Muzuffarpur case where Kshudiram was tried. However, unlike most judges and magistrates, Cornduff did not pass a quick anti-nationalist sentence. He gave the accused a fair chance to present his case and hire a lawyer. His views on this particular case can be seen in a report he submitted to the Chief Justice Lawrence Jenkins regarding the *Barindra Kumar Ghose and Others vs. Emperor* on 23 November 1909. In the report, Cornduff stressed on

the necessity of adhering to the rules of evidence. He wrote that the verdict should be based not on what the court feels is right, but on the proofs that are coherently brought before the court. Cornduff doubted whether his colleagues on the several benches had at all been able to draw a distinction between this 'legal proof' and their own 'moral convictions' about the accused Indians.

6 The newspaper was founded in Manchester in 1884 as *The Umpire*. A penny newspaper, it was the first successful provincial Sunday newspaper in England. Owned by H. S. Jennings, *The Umpire* was subtitled 'A Sporting Athletic Theatrical and General Newspaper', and focused on sports and theatre news. In 1894 it absorbed the former daily newspaper, *The Manchester Examiner and Times*.

7 It seems to refer to the All India Muslim League, founded in 1906 by Syed Amir Ali (1849-1928) in Dhaka. He also established the London Muslim League in 1908. This organization was, however, an independent body and not a branch of the All India Muslim League.

8 Referring to Syed Amir Ali, who was an Indian Muslim jurist from the state of Oudh from where his father shifted to Orissa where he settled. He was a prominent political leader and author of a number of influential books on Muslim history and the modern development of Islam. He is remembered for his contributions to the formulation of Muslim Personal Law, as well as the formation of the political philosophy of Islam, during the British Raj. He was a signatory to the 1906 Quran Petition (see n 7).

9 The first Partition of Bengal was in July 1905, under the viceroyalty of Lord Curzon. It separated the largely Muslim eastern areas from the largely Hindu western area. Western Bengal was clubbed with Bihar and Odisha and Eastern Bengal with Assam. Indians recognized the politics of 'divide and rule' that were being played by the British, who denied this and declared it was for administrative efficiency. The Partition was cancelled in 1911, the capital shifted to Delhi. It could not however undo the growing polarization of Hindus and Muslims and ultimately the province was partitioned in 1947.

10 The just rule of Rama, the hero of the epic *Ramayana*, who is supposed to be the epitome of a great ruler. This was used as a metaphor for the ideal condition obtained under the greatest and best of rulers, and by Gandhi as a standard to be aspired for and achieved as an alternative to the rule of the colonizer.

11 In the context of the Ilbert Bill where it was proposed that Indian Judges could try Europeans, a mammoth meeting took place at the Calcutta Town Hall on 28 February 1883. J.H.A. Branson made a statement in the

meeting for which the native attorneys and pleaders staged a boycott against him.

[12] Brajendrachandra was a landlord or zamindar in Mymensingh in East Bengal. The case was *Loftus Otway Clarke* vs *Brajendrakishore Roychowdhury* (18 June 1912). Justice J. Fletcher on 29 January 1908 passed an order in Calcutta High Court for a decree of Rs 500 against Clarke in the Brajendrachandra case (1907–12).

[13] Charles John Canning (1837-59) was Governor-General of India during the Indian Mutiny of 1857. He dealt with the deep-seated discontentment of the Indians, established a more liberal policy, decried by the British and laid down a more efficient economic system.

40

SRIMATI SUFIYA KHATUN

There is a controversy about the identity of this writer. Someone who signed herself (himself?) as Sufiya Khatoon, was the editor of *Annesa* (1921), a journal published from Chattogram (present-day Chittagong), probably the first Muslim woman to edit a woman's monthly magazine. She was known to be the wife of Rashid Siddiqui who published the magazine. However, a Sufiya Khatun who appended the letters B.A. to her name, wrote many essays in Bengali periodicals published from Calcutta between 1922 and 1925. Searches for the identity of this writer have yielded no result; the records of Calcutta University which lists the graduates, does not include her name.[1]

The Hindu, the Muslim and Raja Rammohan (1924)

Just like Shishupal and Sri Krishna[2] could not stand the sight of each other, there is no love lost between the Hindu and the Muslim in present times. Here, Muslims demolish the temples of Hindus and the Hindus beat their musical instruments before the Jumma Masjid, while the foreigner claps in mockery. This is exactly what they have always wanted.

When a brother does a shameful act of inflicting pain upon his own kin, we are forced to shake off our sleep. And this is why I must stress that the idea of independence in this country will remain a far-fetched goal, as long as Muslims do not learn to live in harmony amongst themselves.

Almost a century ago, when the country was not even aware of the idea of *swadeshi*, a great visionary dawned upon the sky of Indian history—a man who dared to believe that to introduce Hindus and Muslims as one community, every person needs to rise above his identity of being a member of a particular community, and with this foresight he envisioned this unity as the only key to the country's necessary freedom. This man was Raja Rammohan Roy. But we had shunned him then; we had called him an atheist.

If I said that the Raja had no desire to publicize a new religion, I would probably run the risk of annoying certain orthodox Brahmos who belong to the 'I-am-not-a-Hindu' wing. The leaders who succeeded the Raja shared his desire. But the conservative Hindus had inflicted so much torture on these benevolent, great men, that they were forced to create a new society, and in order to procure legal rights to marry socially, they were compelled to pronounce, 'I am not a Hindu'. But the day this happened, an alliance, without even a formal registration, had come to pass in the Sadharan Brahmo Samaj.[3]

The Raja had absolutely no desire to sever ties with the eternally effeminate religion of the Hindu. His only intention was to cure this diseased religion. The religion of the Hindus was originally never idolatrous. The brahmins in the Satya, Treta and Dwapar ages[4] were selfless, keen in charity work; but brahmins in the Kaliyuga love only earthly pleasures and have a strong urge to procure wealth. Therefore, in order to earn a few paise, these hungry brahmins discovered the novel way of scribbling certain nothings as their *Puranas*. Herein, lay the root of the ruin of the Hindu religion. If one wrote even 'I am killing mosquitoes and I am killing fleas' in a few verses in Sanskrit, they became the highly revered sacred hymns.

In such *Puranas*, the ways of worshipping the devi far exceeded the outer pomp of following a thousand or five rituals and pursuing the exact rules of gift-giving to the priest. I think, such sad days dawned upon Hindusthan only after the death of the great Indian emperor Prithviraj[5] because many *Puranas* recount that the brahmins were barred from entering the territory of the non-Hindu *mlecchas*.[6] This is proved by the fact that Raja Adisur[7] of Bengal had to invite five brahmins from Kanyakubja.[8] The degradation of the Hindu[9] has also led to the degradation of his cultural language, so much so that it is almost a dead language today.[10] As a result, the Hindus are forgetting the real essence of the sacred religion. Manu had already decreed—if a sudra uttered the Vedas, cut his tongue and clog his ears with lead lest he hears them. So, the wretched sudra could not help but found his own religion and sense of duty upon the wisdom of the brahmin. On the other hand, brahmins happily exploited these helpless and poor people by quoting from the *Puranas*. However, only Mother Ganga can tell what astonishing words of wisdom poured from their sacred tongues.[11]

The flag of the Hindu religion first went aflutter in the Vedic ages.[12] However, figuring out the exact dates of this age has been beyond the calculative capacity of historians so far. But there seems to be no calculation error in that this age was definitely not around the birth of Hajrat Muhammad or that of Jesus Christ. Also, there is no error in the knowledge that the Eternal Voice of Truth had touched the Hindu sages first, several lakh centuries ago, much before it could reach the Hajrat Muhammad or Christ.

Many may even say that the Hindu Vedas are in favour of idol worship. Let us assume this is true; but let me also state that this was only during the pre-Vedic Ages. The Hindu's pre-Vedic age have been exactly like our pre-Islamic days. In the peak of the Vedic ages, sages had sung to their heart's content, '*Satyam gyaan manantam Brahma. Aanandarupaamritang khadvibhaati, shaantang shivamadvaitam shuddhampaapvidham*.'[13] This had been their prayer.

However, with the advent of the *Puranas*, the Hindus began to forget this essence gradually. They forgot the greatness of compassion and substituted it with petty class division. I will not be able to count accurately, the number of sub-divisions and their further classifications the Hindus branched out into, so it is difficult to enumerate how many new branches emerged out of the thirty-two main branches of Hindu communities across India. Raja Rammohan Roy appeared when such was the plight of India. He realized that the country could not be salvaged unless the Hindu was brought back to the path from which he had gone astray. Religion was not the only thing in the Raja's mind ... He was the first to speak of India's freedom simultaneously with her religious resolutions ... That was the time of the decline of Muslim rule and the ascendancy of British imperialism ... And probably, seeing this sorry cycle of events, the Raja had thought, 'Become human again, do not be sorry that the country is gone but at least become human once again.' The Raja was frantically looking for a way to raise his twin brothers (Hindus and Muslims). But raising them together was not an easy task. The brothers were uniquely different—one's shrine became impure if cow dung fell there, but the other's temple became sacred only if its floors were scrubbed with cow dung; one chanted: '*Namoh Brahmanya Devaaya Go-Brahmanaaya hitaaya c jagadhvitaaya krishnaaya govindaaya namoh namah*'[14] and the other sacrificed this same cow on his festival days. The Raja decided after much reflection that the only way to mix this wine and water was to remind the Hindu of the Real Supreme Soul, the *Param Brahma*, and disengaging him from his false attachment to the pride he took in the trivialities of class distinctions. This was the seed of the Brahmo Samaj. During this movement of breaking superstitions and blind beliefs, when the inter-dining question had arisen, the leaders had stood their ground and said it was absolutely not offensive.[15] But there was no need to eat together at all! I believe making this moderate statement is absolutely incorrect. On realizing that getting rid of the superstitions of the Hindus was no less than a '*swaraj*' in itself, the leaders of Bengal were forced to say, that there was no need of eating together at all.[16]

One community can never embrace another community until it can eat and mingle freely with the other. This is a historical truth—not my own words. Unity does not mean one would greet each other, '*Bhai saheb salaam*', or '*Ram babu namaskar*', on the roads. Unity implies a closer bonding. If one community does not associate itself with the families and festivals of another community, their unity is nothing but foppery. Love for another human being, dining together with him and a free exchange of everything must occur from a man's heart spontaneously.

Today, if a Hindu boy asks to be given food by a Muslim woman, there is no way in which she can stop herself from embracing this boy like her own son and serve him affectionately. ... I was extremely astonished on seeing such a Hindu boy in my friend's family. In the beginning, I did not even know that he was a Hindu. It was someone's marriage. And before I share this, I hope that my readers are aware of the strictness of the purdah. I think they know that even in these times Muslim women are veiled with a strictness that would probably be beyond the belief and imagination of any outsider. And, amidst such orthodoxy, I was taken aback to see the influence this Hindu boy had on this Muslim family. I was extremely surprised!

The boy was indispensable to the marriage arrangements. He took care of the money, arranged for the food; he was all over the place taking care of every possible detail. He even decided what clothes were to be given to the women in the family, even choosing the bride's and her groom's attires. How could I control tears in my eyes when I heard the children in this Muslim house call him, '*Bor-da*'[17]? How could anyone fight back the tears on witnessing such divine unity of the

Hindu and the Muslim? Who would not have rejoiced on hearing from this Hindu's mouth, 'O Mother, where are you?' This friend's husband is a staunch believer in the purdah, but strangely, when it came to this lad, he would say, 'He is our own son; so, why be veiled before him?'

Reader! Behind this unimaginable unity of the Hindu and the Muslim is this young boy's unbiased compassion. He has comingled with such love in this family that none can think of him as an outsider.

One of this friend's sons is an ICS, very *saheb*-like, extremely Anglicized, so much so that he would not tolerate one word against the English.[18] But the day this Hindu boy was imprisoned, shouting, 'Jai Mahatma', my friend's son was so hurt that he threw away his uniform in utter disgust and burnt it alongside a stack of all the foreign clothing he had ever owned.

Reader! Imagine that in every family in this country if there is such love between the Hindu and the Muslim, then the very words 'Hindu' and 'Muslim' will disappear.

No matter how much the leaders of my community, that is, the prominent Muslims try to convince us that 'Pan-Islam' does not exist in India, I do not believe it: it seem to be a distortion of the truth. We still dream, 'to build castles in the air' that one day this entire world will become Islamic and every church and every temple will sing '*Allah O Akbar*' instead of saying 'I am praying to Thee, O Lord Jesus' or '*Har Har Shankar*'.

That we still believe in such vague dreams has become even more evident as we feel the need to purify ourselves more than ever before. What obstacles have we not created to prevent Swami Shraddhanandaji from alleviating the fortunes of a deprived and lost community?[19] We have not been able to stand this because we are still clinging to our dreams of the 'Pan-Islamic' world. I have even heard some say, 'Swami Shraddhanandaji should have also taken others, besides the Muslims.' I ask if a Muslim missionary can try to convert a Hindu, what is so wrong about a Hindu missionary trying to say the same thing? Of course, the Hindu does not do this anyway. And this is only because the Hindus are disunited. Unlike us, the Hindu does not truly believe that people from his own community are his brothers. The brahmin does not accept the sudra or others as his brothers but treats them as slaves. . . . None protests when a Hindu converts to Islam.

Today, we may be extremely disheartened to find some Muslims converting into Hinduism, but this is only because of our disgust in our own community and our inefficiency in preventing such occasions. The ones that have become Hindu have not converted for nothing. We had forsaken them—cast them out socially—we could not embrace them like our own brothers, and we had turned away our faces from them. We were ashamed to call them our own. And feeling terribly hurt, our brothers left us. The fault is entirely ours.

Many of us still believe that this is not our country. Just like these Englishmen, even we had come to rule this land and spread our religion; that our places of birth are Arabia, Turkey, Egypt.

But even the Anglicized Bengali society just like us claims that their 'home' is actually abroad, whether or not the British accept this cannot however be stated conclusively. Now I see that there is no difference between them and us. Though I am ready to build a platform as high as the Qutub Minar so that one can use it to announce as loudly as possible about one's non-Indian ancestry, there is no mistake that if not fifteen and a half annas but fifteen and a quarter annas of each Muslim in this country has descended from Ram, Shyam, Jadu and none other.

These are the arguments of one side. But it takes two hands to clap. The Hindus are equally at fault. The Hindus hate Muslims a hundred times more than the Muslims hate Hindus. I have seen with my own eyes that in Bengal a Hindu washes himself immediately if a Muslim even touches him by mistake. However, this happens more in the countryside than in the bigger cities.

But, even in larger cities like Calcutta, a Hindu landlord is usually reluctant to lease his house to a Muslim tenant. All they say is, 'Oh Lord, shall I have to finally let this house out to a *Mucchalman*! Am I mad!' and so on. When the great freedom fighter, zamindar Khanpani Saheb of the Mymensingha district was released from jail, almost on the verge of his death, he was desperately looking for a house.[20] And during his house hunting ordeal, he heard similar responses addressed for a Muslim from a khaddar-clad famous zamindar who lived on one of the widest streets of Calcutta. I can even name and the street he lived, if need be: . . .

Let us not think about the past and feel worse about our present condition. Whatever had to happen has happened. Today, we must learn to say, 'Become human again.'

And this is why whenever I think of the unity between the Hindu and the Muslim, I am reminded of Raja Rammohan Roy who was treated like a mleccha, called an atheist and looked down upon by Hindu society; who had thought for the betterment of not just the Hindus, but also dreamt of a more developed Muslim community. This was the uniqueness of the Raja's religious teaching. He had never intended to convert anyone. He had never claimed like all the other religions of the world that his was the only path to salvation. He taught compassion: that could flow unhindered even if one chose to believe in one's own religion. He wanted to explain to us that there was just one essence, only its manifestations were varied—some called it God, some named it Ishwar, while others called out Allah. He wanted to show that even if a Hindu believed in Hinduism and a Muslim in Islam, they were but children of the same Mother India! The Raja believed he did not have to invent any new scheme to accomplish this. Whatever had to be known was already present in the Hindu Sanatan Dharma. But in those days, the tiger-cub named Hinduism had fallen amongst lambs and considering himself to be part of the herd, bleated along with them pathetically. Seeing the sorry plight of his community, Rammohan only tried to remind them of their true nature; that they were meant to roar and not bleat like sheep.

The Raja wanted his countrymen to understand that the only way Hindus and Muslims could ever unite was when the Hindu could shake off the false pride attached to the class distinctions he had once created, so that a Muslim is also able to freely pray to his God in the very place where a Hindu offers his prayers. And therefore, the Samaj Mandirs were built so that Hindu, Muslim, Buddhist, Christian and all others could come to a common place and pray together. A place, where at the end of the week a Hindu could meet his Muslim brother, and the latter could find out how the Hindu's children were; a place where all could meet freely. Even the '*priti-bhojan*' or communal feast organized by the Brahmo Samaj was precisely with the intention of getting the two brothers together at one place, a place where they would share the same food and reflect on cordially sharing their brotherhood, for their Father was one.

I sincerely believe and strongly proclaim that the salvation of this country lies solely on these views of Raja Rammohan. And, from the recent events I have witnessed, I am more certain than ever that this is the only way. The Muslims get upset when they see their brothers converting to Hinduism. It seems that doing away with caste differences or eating out of a Muslim's hand is not sufficient. The only way to the goal is when the Muslim remains a Muslim and the Hindu remains a Hindu.

The Arya Samaj is Hindu. They think that the Vedas are generated by human agency, and thus not divine. They do not believe in class distinctions either. Despite their progressiveness, why have they not been able to inspire unity between the Hindus and the Muslims? This is because they are quick to declave that anyone who joins their society should be Hindu, emphasizing the fact that there is no place for Muslims in their society. And for obvious reasons, no Muslim can ever take this insult. I strongly feel that nothing much can be achieved until the relationship between the Hindu and the Muslim becomes like that between the Rarhi-Barendra[21] or the Shakta-Vaishnav. I say Rarhi and Barendra because even the brahmins are divided into two classes—Rarhi and Barendra. The Rarhi and the Barendra eat together. They are even extremely fond of each other. But, they never allow a marriage alliance between the groups. As for the Shaktas and Vaishnavs, the Shaktas worship Shakti and the Vaishnavs are followers of Vishnu. Though their religious perspectives and the form of worship are entirely different, they intermingle with each other almost effortlessly. I have heard that in some places, they even marry amongst themselves. We must become exactly like them. . . . Or else, nothing else will ever work.

However, I think this country will benefit largely if we stay away from intermarriage. There is nothing good in it. In fact, it should be kept at bay, not only from a religious point of view but also from a scientific one, for it is scientifically hazardous too.

Translated by Anindita Roy
Department of Comparative Literature, Jadavpur University

'Hindu, Musalman o Raja Rammohan', *Bangabani*, mid-May to mid-June 1924/Jaishtha 1331 BS, barsha 3 (year 3), prathamardha (first half), sankhya 4 (no. 4), pp. 441–47.

Notes

1 For details see Sufiya Khatun, 1999, *Narir Adhikar o Anyanya*, edited by Sumit Adhikari, Sahitya Prakashani, Kolkata.

2 In an episode in the epic *Mahabharata*, Shishupal, king of the Chedis in central India, after insulting Lord Krishna several times in an assembly,

finally enrages him, who strikes his head off.

3 The Brahmo Samaj movement was started on 20 August 1828, by Raja Rammohan Roy and his friends by opening a place of public worship on Chitpore Road in Calcutta. It was duly and publicly inaugurated in January 1830 by the consecration of the first house of prayer, the Adi Brahmo Samaj. The Sadharan Brahmo Samaj is a religious division of Brahmoism formed as a result of two schisms in the Brahmo Samaj in 1866 and 1878, respectively. Differences between Keshab Chandra Sen and the Tattwabodhini Sabha which regulated the affairs of the Samaj, led to the creation of a separate ministry under Keshab Sen the Mahaacharya or Great Teacher of the Brahmo society, and finally, his expulsion in 1865. In 1878 the marriage of Keshab Chandra Sen's eldest daughter Suniti to the Maharaja of Cooch Behar, Prince Nripendra Narayan, when both bride and groom were minors, in violation of the Brahmo Marriage Act of 1872, became the cause of action for the first schism in the New Dispensation. Samadarshi party, led by Keshab Chandra Sen, returned to its Brahmo roots and reconstituted itself as the Sadharan Brahmo Samaj.

4 Satya, Treta and Dwapar are the three *yugas*, which means age or era—the astronomical cycle of four yugs. Kali Yug is the last of the four yugs named after its creator Kali.

5 Prithviraj Chauhan (1149–92 CE) was of the Chauhan (Rajput) dynasty of Ajmer and Delhi. Samyukta or Sanjukta, daughter of Jai Chandra Rathore, king of Kanauj, had eloped with him, the story of which was written as *Prithviraj Raso* by Chand Bardoi. He defeated Mohammad Ghori in the Battle of Tarain in 1191. Next year, he was defeated, captured and executed.

6 Referring to the Muslims.

7 The available facts on King Adisur are disputed. Some believe that Adisur was like King Arthur, more of a myth than reality. Some historians believe that King Adisur and King Jayanta are the same. Jayanta was king from 772-73 AD. In the *Bengal and Assam District Gazeteer* (vol. 4, p.15) Adisur is recorded not as king of Bengal, but of Mithila. Walter Hamilton (*A Geographical, Statistical, and Historical Description of Hindoostan and Adjacent Countries*, vol. 1, 1820) states that he was a man of the medical or Vaidya caste and obtained the governorship of Bengal subject to the rulers in the west. His wife had a son named Ballal Sen, fathered by the River Brahmaputra, in the form of a brahmin, which in turn regulated the caste system in Bengal.

8 Later came to be known as Kanauj.

[9] Degradation of the Hindu here refers to the excessive respect shown towards brahmins, to the extent that prompted them to exploit people. For example, earlier, there were places where brahmins were not allowed according to the author's readings (this is not corroborated by evidence and may simply be hearsay). Bengal was one such place. Brahmins were imported from elsewhere (for which also there is conflicting evidence), but thereafter they gained control over society.

[10] Referring to Sanskrit.

[11] River Ganga is considered as the holy river and is referred to as 'mother'. Brahma asked Ganga to flow from heaven to earth. Ganga started flowing with such force that Lord Shiva had to control her by holding Ganga on his matted hair. King Bhagirath satisfied Lord Shiva through his penance and succeeded in bringing Ganga to earth. The water of the Ganga is considered extremely auspicious during the performance of rituals, which again are conducted by brahmins; thereby being associated with their words of wisdom.

[12] The author refers to the Vedic religion. 'Hindu' as a term was coined much later, after the arrival of the Muslims.

[13] True knowledge dawns by meditating on the Brahma, the nectar of bliss that cleanses ... and the purest way (vidhi) of annihilating one's sins is in the peaceful form of the non-dual Shiva.

[14] I offer my obeisances again and again to Lord Krishna who is worshipped by qualified brahmins and is very dear to them. He is always concerned with the welfare of the cows, the brahmins and the whole Universe, and also brings pleasure to the cows, lands and the senses.

[15] The Prarthana Samaj, which was founded in 1867 under the influence of the Brahmo Samaj, devoted themselves to promoting interdining, intercaste marriage, widow remarriage, education of women and the uplift of depressed classes. The leaders of this movement were Mahadev Govind Ranade, a judge of the Bombay High Court and R.G.Bhandrakar, a Sanskrit scholar and historian. They drew their beliefs from the Sant poets of Maharashtra, Namdev, Tukaram and Ramdas.

[16] The interdining movement began in Maharashtra (see n 15) and was spearheaded by Keshab Chandra Sen. The Brahmo leaders of Bengal, who were at odds with Sen (see n 3) did not criticize the move, but did not emphasize its importance either. The writer thinks that they should not have taken a 'moderate' stand, but rather being extremist, insisted on interdining in practice and principle.

[17] *Bor-da* means eldest brother in Bengali.

[18] Indian Civil Service. Appointment as a civil servant was a great

achievement for Indians in British India. Though popularly known thus it was actually called the Imperial Civil Service, and begun in 1858. By 1905, only 5 per cent of the appointees were Indians, mostly from Bengal. In 1947 there were 322 Indians and 688 British.

[19] Swami Shraddhanand (1856–1926) was an Indian educationist and a missionary of the Arya Samaj. While propagating the teachings of Swami Dayanand, he also established educational institutions like the Gurukul Kangri University and played a key role on the *Sangathan* (consolidation) and the *Shuddhi* (re-conversion), Hindu reform movement in 1920s. In late 1923, he became the president of *Bharatiya Hindu Shuddhi Sabha*, created with an aim to reconvert Muslims, specifically 'Malkana Rajputs' in western United Province. This antagonized the Muslims and brought him into direct confrontation with Muslim clerics and leaders of the time.

[20] The Pani family controlled the Atia district of Mymensingha. Saiyid Khan Pani was the founder of the Karatia family, and it was he who got this pargana as a jagir from Emperor Akbar. Members of this family are referred to by Mohammad Ali Azam in *The Life of Maulvi Abdul Karim* (Calcutta 1939).

[21] Rarhi is a class of brahmins from the part of Bengal located at the western side of the Ganges. Barendra is a class of brahmins from the northern part of Bengal.

41

SRI SITA DEVI

Sita Devi (1895–1974) was the daughter of Ramananda Chattopadhyay and Manorama Devi, and thus sister of Santa Devi. She was admitted to Bethune School in 1908. In 1912, she successfully took the matriculation examination and obtained her B.A. Hons, English in 1916. She wrote her first novel, *Udyanlata*, jointly with her sister Santa Devi. Both sisters used the pen-name, Sanjukta Devi, when writing this novel. *Matir Basha, Matririn, Mahamaya* are some of her other well-known novels.

Bengal's Women Working for the Country (1930)

A written report published from the Centre of the great Conference of Asian Women[1] and a beautiful letter written by the Persian Women's Council[2] to the secretary of the above-mentioned Conference was published in the Kartik [mid-October to mid-November] edition of *Bangalakshmi's* 'Nanakatha'.[3] This was followed by a satisfying reply from the Women's Council in Java.[4] They remarked, 'You are trying to bring together the associations (of women) scattered (in Asia) and (make them) work in unison for the welfare of Asia and the world, hence we convey our heartfelt cooperation. Not only are we glad to receive this invitation, we also accept it as an answer to our own desires.

'We, the women of Indonesia, will be very glad to meet our other sisters from Asia. This will help us to understand the women's movement in other countries.

'We have selected a few representatives from our associations, who will speak for us. But unfortunately we cannot ensure that they will be able to meet you because their travel is largely dependent on the financial condition of our associations.

'Will you be kind enough to keep space for two representatives? We are hoping that by participating in a conference that wants the welfare of Asia and the world, we will be able to make some contribution.'

A Lahore-based newspaper, *Tribune*, published an article on this women's conference, a lot of which is worth considering. The writer says—

> During the last fifty years, the women's movement has been visible worldwide. In many countries women had to fight for gaining liberty from the bondage of slavery to men. They have shown ample evidence of their firmness in mind and fortitude and one by one their chains of dependence are being broken. Women's liberation has reached its height in Europe and America. The main reason behind this is that in the last World War, old customs and laws were mostly rendered useless. Those old laws which stated that women are to be subservient to men, have either been amended or changed, thereby emphasizing that equal rights are to be shared by women and men in every aspect of life and in every sphere of employment. As a result, India too is not silent. Although most women of our country are illiterate and superstitious, still there are many newly enlightened women in our country who are eager to overcome the old obstacles and follow the road to progress independently. As time passes, the revolt of women against oppression will gain momentum and become more widespread. As humanity gradually progresses, the extensive powers that men now hold will be proved inadequate, limited and foolish if they use these powers to stop this movement. It will be useful not only to women but to mankind in general if women are given a chance to blossom in their physical, mental and moral lives. If not today then tomorrow, women will gain their full rights and it will be futile to obstruct their path, as this will only increase and prolong the conflict between men and women.
>
> However, it is to be remembered that having equal rights does not mean gaining the same rights. As there are differences between the bodies and the minds of men and women, similarly there are differences in gaining control and behaviour. It is also to be remembered that old traditions and customs are not to be abandoned simply because they are old. That the traditions and customs

survived long enough to become old proved that they were needed in the human society at a certain time and place; otherwise they could not have withstood the ravages of time for such a long period.

The proposal of reconstructing society based on equal rights for men and women does not mean that all the norms of society will be done away with and the family will be destroyed. Those who support and are acting as leaders in this movement should prevent this danger in the first place. The problem has taken on huge proportions in Europe and America, hence participants in the women's movement in Egypt, Turkey, Japan, India and other countries should learn from their predecessors. For this reason, we gladly welcome the proposal from the Asian Women's Conference. They will give direction to this movement after deliberating on the pros and cons.

Nothing can be more extensive than the matters on which the organizers of the Conference have planned to deliberate. There is no doubt that the lectures, discussions and the proposals that are to be presented in the Conference will take forward the task of reforming society to a great extent. The importance of this kind of international conference is such that words are not enough [to express it]. We hope that the representatives of different countries will compare their views and judge the proposals that are placed in the Conference with their experience to form a new perspective. It is very appropriate that leaders of the Conference insisted on preserving the values of oriental culture in their proceedings. Their good intentions are shown through their refusal to imitate the West blindly.

It is a matter of great joy that a session of this Conference is to be held in Lahore. The natives of Punjab are ahead than their counterparts in other provinces in the field of social reforms. We hope that they will try their level best to make this Conference a huge success. It is a matter of great pride for Lahore to be the first centre for the Asian Women's Conference. The organizers of the Conference are assured of receiving full support from various countries in Asia. A reception committee has been organized for proper reception of the representatives. Applications are being invited for membership of this organization. We hope that the residents of Punjab will pay attention to this and join the association in greater numbers. Only three months are left for completing all arrangements. All those who want women to be emancipated should try their very best to make this Conference a total success.

We hope that the women of Bengal will not fall behind. It was this province that first announced women's education and women's emancipation. The Bengali women of today should not forget this honour. Not only do we have a duty to ourselves, we also owe it to the oriental civilizations and to the world at large. Interacting with women of various nationalities helps one to understand the world much better; and with the exchange of thoughts, the power to think increases. It is hoped that many Bengali women will participate in the Conference and enrich themselves and others. Different women's associations should try to arrange such conferences in Bengal in future. If they try, they certainly will succeed—one has no doubt about it at all. Bengal does not have fewer educated and progressive women than Punjab. But their natural urge to work has been overshadowed by centuries of habit and hindrance. No one thinks that the women of Bengal understand or love their country less than others. But one is sorry to admit that unlike the women of other provinces who come forward to work for social reforms and for demanding various rights for women without any misgivings, Bengali women cannot do this. The custom of purdah is greatly responsible for this.[5] However eagerly one might wish to, one cannot possibly do all types of work from home, and all women do not have the ability to afford vehicles (that will carry them around in a state of purdah). The question of transport arises the moment there is a proposal to do something involving women. This problem should be forcefully dealt with. It is not humiliating to walk, and one cannot possibly lose anything if people stare. One has no count of how much work is left unattended (because of this problem).

In preparation for Lahore, it is inevitable that a huge amount of money will be spent entailing a lot hard work. If such a conference is organized in Calcutta, there will be presumably no dearth of money. Bengal's hospitality in this regard is well known. The way money was spent three years ago in the Congress session in Calcutta has not been equalled at other session venues. My intention is not to say that it is a virtue to spend money unnecessarily. But I only wish that our apathy to work tirelessly should not make us apprehensive about our progress. The initiative of the Congress to form a group of women volunteers was very motivating. Not only enthusiasm, but also education is needed to work for the country and for other work (of a similar kind). That we are not inferior to men should not be propagated through lectures and newspaper articles [alone], it should also be practiced. Volunteers should be involved in activities like reception of guests in big conferences, decorating the pavilion, organizing, maintaining discipline and even controlling the traffic; no paid services are hired for these. Most probably the volunteers will do all this work in Lahore too. We should try to hold a similar session of the Conference in Calcutta by 1932. Thereafter, we all should prepare ourselves in such a way that there are no shortcomings in the arrangements. The guests should not have any cause to think that they have come to a province that is weak in education. Mahatma Raja Rammohan was born in this province; he was the first to raise his voice for women's emancipation in this country. We should not be considered unsuitable for this honour.

Translated by Debarati Chakraborty
Department of Comparative Literature, Jadavpur University

'Desher Kaje Banglar Meye', Bangalakshmi, mid-November to mid-December 1930/Agrahayan 1337 BS, barsha 6 (year 6), sankhya 1 (no. 1), pp. 68–71.

Notes

1 The All Asian Women's Conference, the preparatory stage of which is mentioned in this essay, was held in Lahore between 19 and 25 January, 1931. It was organized by the Margaret Cousins, who had also been instrumental in forming the All India Women's Conference. This conference of Asian women was attended by women from Afghanistan, Burma, Ceylon, Japan, Persia, where women from Britain, United States, New Zealand and Java participated as observers.

2 The Iranian Constitutional Revolution took place between 1905 and 1911. The early consciousness of women's rights (or rather lack of rights) which led to the establishment of societies and magazines started shortly after. In 1906, despite the parliament's refusal to allow organization of political societies, women created several organizations, including the society for women's freedom, which met in secret until it was discovered and attacked. The Jam'iat e nesvan e vatan-khah (Patriotic Women's League) was born around 1918; it published *Nosvan Vatankhah*. In 1922, Mohtaram Eskandari created the patriotic women's organization. She was arrested and her house was burned. Zandokht Shirazi, another women activist, organized the Women's Revolutionary Association.

3 *Bangalakshmi*, a women's magazine that carried photographs and biographies of western women who were successful in public life.

4 The modern Indonesian women's movement began in the early 1900s, hand-in-hand with the growing nationalist feelings in the country marked by the establishment of nationalist organizations which were initiated by a small number of educated Indonesians. Important events occurred in line with this nationalism, such as the Youth Congress on 28 October 1928, which resulted in the famous youth pledge, Sumpah Pemuda. The first women's congress was held the same year on 22-25 December in Yogyakarta. This marked the beginning of a more organized women's movement in Indonesia. The first women's congress in Yogyakarta was followed by other congresses in Jakarta (1929), Surabaya (1930), Jakarta (1935) and Bandung (1938). The Congress in Bandung decided that 22 December—the starting date of the first women's congress—would become Mothers' Day. As reflected in the Congresses' documents, the women's movement in the colonial era discussed contemporary issues, such as polygamy, discrimination against women at workplaces, women's limited access to education, child marriage and women trafficking.

5 A system of screening women from strangers; in early nineteenth century, women were not allowed to step out of their houses. Except their husbands, the women used to talk to all the menfolk in the house from behind the purdah.

42

SUKHALATA RAO

Sukhalata Rao (1886–1969) was the eldest among the six children of Upendrakishore Raychaudhuri and Bidhumukhi Devi. The film director Satyajit Ray was her nephew. She passed the entrance examination from Brahmo Balika Shikshalaya and was admitted to Bethune College but could not complete her Bachelor's degree. She wrote and translated extensively for children in Bengali. She was also a trained painter and illustrated some of her own books. After her marriage to Dr. Jayanta Rao, the eldest son of Madhusudan Rao and Padma Bai, she moved to Odisha. She was well known in Odisha as a zealous social worker. Her books include *Ali Bhulir Deshe, Galpa Aar Galpa, Nanan Galpa, Khoka Elo Beriye* in Bengali and *Behula* in English. She also wrote many primers in Bengali, English and Oriya. She received several awards for her writing, painting and social service including the Bhuvaneshwari award, Sir John Olfendon KCS medal from the Lieutenant Governor of Bengal and the Kaiser-e-Hind.

The Ideal Woman (1931)

If Indian women do not arise
This India will not wake up.

With women becoming more aware, India, today, has finally woken up. While some women are serving the country; some are selflessly engaged in stabilizing the home and the family. Some have even dedicated their lives for eudaemonia [human welfare/happiness] without any heed to their own well-being. Some have taken up the promotion of education as their life's objective. Others have devoted their lives to the welfare of women and society. In this last category, there is an eminent German social reformist and philanthropist Dr. Alice Salomon[1]—an ideal woman. She was born in a famous rich Jewish family. Having studied in school for nearly fifteen years she was ready for marriage. But the day this girl declined marriage and expressed her wish to promote education and remain single throughout her life, shocked her orthodox conservative family. Danger signals were sounded everywhere. Relatives arrived in hordes from all places. But her father's sudden death left the whole family in deep sorrow. So the issue of marriage remained buried for some time. Taking advantage of the situation Alice started to educate herself in many ways. She recollects that once as she stood in front of the mirror she thought to herself, 'What is the purpose of this life?' the answer that she received from deep inside her heart was, 'to remove sorrow and grief from this world and to dedicate one's own life to help in its development'.

Her struggle began in her adolescence, and as she became older her knowledge and intelligence blossomed. Alice came in contact with many women's organizations. At the age of twenty-one, she established a women's organization independently. Her endeavours and perseverance for women's education, their awakening, and overall development was exceptional. Subsequently she set up a 'serving group' whose objective was to serve the human world with all its heart. She was not only involved in these works, but her intense desire for learning also led her to Berlin University, thereafter to other countries where she learnt several important skills.

In 1908, Alice founded a school named Social Work for Women. Students there learned various subjects that would benefit society. This education was not restricted to book learning only; there was arrangement for everyone's practical training according to the work they wished to do. Even during holidays, they had to continue with their work. After they passed their examinations, they got certificates and salaries for the work they did during the training. Those who selected this as the mission of their lives knew that they were going to be poorly paid but even then they worked happily. They had to struggle to protect and helps in society's sorrow, grief and distress. They felt immensely satisfied by carrying out their work gladly and virtuously. Apart from this, Alice also helped other schools with various kinds of arrangements.

During the last war, this capable woman tried, to a large extent, to give shelter to the blind, crippled, hungry and homeless people. While sacrificing her entire life to serve humanity, she even managed to find time to write a few books.

Dr. Alice Salomon has established another school called the Academy of Social Work. In one part, child rearing, house maintenance, cookery, and so on, are the important subjects taught to mothers and wives of the country. Even after working for fifty-five years she remains active, energetic and cheerful. This woman, has been a pillar of strength, exhorting the whole world of women to awaken the dormant power within them—'Rise, awake, acquire the greatest treasure of all'.

A strange thing about this great knowledgeable and hard working woman is her charming personality. Her compassion, her love are not confined within the small domain of her family; this huge world is her household. That is why her work has been extensive. She has dedicated her life for the uplift of women.

Like this great woman of the West, a religious, compassionate and virtuous woman was born in this country; Saroj Nalini.[2] The terrible call of fate caused her to leave this world without completing her work. Let the enterprise of all those women who have accepted her as the ideal and have committed their lives to improve the condition of women be successful.

Translated by Jayeeta Bagchi
School of Women's Studies, Jadavpur University

'Adarsha Nari', Bangalakshmi, mid-May to mid-June 1931/ Jaishtha 1338 BS, barsha 6 (year 6), sankhya 7 (no. 7), pp.589–90.

Notes

1 Dr. Alice Salomon (1872–1948) was a German social reformer and pioneer of social work as an academic discipline. She joined the Federation of German Women's Associations and became its deputy chairperson.

2 Saroj Nalini Dutt (9 October 1887–19 January 1925) was an Indian feminist and social reformer. She was a well-known social reformer, educationist and a pioneer of the movement for the uplift of women in Bengal. She pioneered the formation of Mahila Samitis (women's institutes) in Bengal

and helped them receive vocational training to enable them to earn for themselves and support their families. She was particularly concerned about the plight of the Hindu widows. She dedicated herself to the cause of women both inside and outside the home as well as the community. She started her first Mahila Samiti in 1913 at Pabna (now in Bangladesh) with the object of developing friendly cooperation among the women in purdah. Subsequently, she started the Mahila Samitis at Birbhum (1916), Sultanpur (1917) and Rampurhat (1918). The Mahila Samiti she started in 1921 at Bankura dedicated itself to educate rural women and uplift their position in society. It started training midwives and established a maternity home. She also took the lead in introducing the charka in village homes. She reorganized the local girls school in Birbhum which was called Sir Rivers Thompson School. In recognition of her distinguished and dedicated service in the field of social welfare, she was awarded an MBE (Member of the Most Excellent Order of the British Empire) in 1918.

43

SWARNAKUMARI DEVI

Essay 17 offers a note on the author.

Our Responsibility (1908)

'Why were you accumulating these arms?' In reply to Norton's[1] question, Narendra Goswami replied, 'To declare war against the government.'

If those who collect three or four firearms to declare war against the English are not mad, what else are they?

When Prafulla Chaki[2] was arrested by Inspector Nandalal, the former committed suicide with this regret, 'You did this despite being a Bengali?'

What is to be understood from this? These misguided youngsters thought that the strategy of revolt that they had adopted for good government and for gaining independence was approved by their countrymen, and that as the general population would not be able to give their lives for this cause, they would sacrifice their lives on their behalf. These immature minds with uncontrolled imagination, and a passionate zeal abandoned the path of effective and constructive work and ran headlong on the wrong path.

When Curzon dismembered Bengal, the rich and the poor alike felt inspired and enthusiastic to pursue the ideal of national brotherhood; all were fired with the zeal of adhering to and spreading the principles of swadeshi.[3] For Indians, 16 October is a memorable day. On that day the vast gathering present contributed such an enormous amount towards the development of the textile industry that the donors and the collectors could not keep pace with one another. People who were held in respect by their fellow citizens went from house to house all over Calcutta, on foot, to collect donations, something they would not have done otherwise. The Technical College, National College, National Fund were the fruits of the enthusiasm. Besides these, the Bangalakshmi Mills, small weaving training centres and different industries were established, and people avowed to follow the path of swadeshi overwhelmingly.

We watch as the fire of enthusiasm, instead of gradually becoming more intense remained as it had been at the onset; rather than becoming more passionate towards constructive and productive changes in Bengal, the spirit seemed to be dampened and stagnant. The ebbing of enthusiasm on the part of the rich, the professionals or labouring classes was not surprising. But the group of youngsters who had taken a vow to give their lives for the country also seemed to have lost the zeal with which they had once dedicated themselves to the nation. Would they forget their real duties towards their nation, too, swayed by the politics of the time?

... We must now proceed towards, the development of different types of industries, the adoption of swadeshi goods and the rejection of foreign ones. Here, however, it is necessary for us to be patient. Forcing people to use swadeshi goods through the destruction of foreign goods in shops will yield no permanent result. On the one hand, we must proceed on this path by making people conscious of its need, and on the other we must make alternative swadeshi goods available. ...

Setting up spinning mills is very expensive. Instead of waiting until sufficient capital is collected, it is necessary to set up weavers' training centres in every neighbourhood. Small sugar mills could easily be established in every village. There is no dearth of intelligence amongst Bengalis. If someone studies science with the intention of contributing towards the growth of industrialization through new inventions, he/she will surely attain success. If the young could go abroad to learn how to make bombs, why should they not be able to do the same to learn the ways of industrialization? Their earnest desire must be directed towards their country's development. I hear that foreigners carry back to their own land crores of rupees by selling glass bangles in our country. This is not an essential commodity, like clothes, it is merely an item of luxury. Youngsters can convince people to forsake using such items and persuade the rich to set up industries that would produce such goods in our country itself. Countless options of commerce could be set up in this country even without establishing factories. Fish, fruits, milk are imported in tinned containers from abroad; if this technology could be learnt by us, then we ourselves would be able to export them and earn money for our country. If one concentrated, focused and strove patiently to do such work, the progress of our nation would inevitably lie on more secure foundations. ... I see no pertinent purpose of British rule in India. India needs foreign rule, so the British are here. When the need is over, they will leave. That is the law of nature. We do not know how they will leave, nor is there any need to think about it either. When it became unnecessary, Romans left Roman Britain and returned to their own country. Even after defeating the Boers,[4] the British left the land to them. Then Sweden unanimously declared that they would not continue to be ruled by Norway and regained independence even without using any arms, or shedding a drop of blood in 1905.

The law of nature does not function in one way for the western races and in another way for the eastern. If we are capable of self-rule, we will achieve it by any means. Everyone knows that in Holland the land is below sea level. The people of Holland have walled in the sea, formulating a strategy to make their country habitable. Because Europe and America are hardworking, they have made great strides in science, industry and trade. If we could acquire all the qualities of a great race, who would be able to keep us in thrall?

Our fault is at the source. We may as well accept that we do not make any real effort towards nation building. The rightful means of attaining it is by boosting the nation's character. ... The pupils of yore displayed legendary devotion to the teacher. But at present, in many instances, the youth, swollen with pride about their knowledge, display a kind of disrespect and indifference towards those who display wisdom, which is not at all conducive to national progress. The way in which foreign students attain strength of character traversing the steps of discipline must be a lesson for us. In every household and school in Europe and America, the sort of discipline and control that every child experiences helps them to inculcate a sense of responsibility. An American recounted that in every school children must learn the fire-drill. This is because in the eventuality of an outbreak of fire in the neighbourhood, each student is expected to fling himself into the rescue operations which is taught with iron discipline. ... In this country, however if anyone is in trouble, people just form a crowd and stand by as passive onlookers, afraid of being drawn into the trouble ... A proverb says, first take yourself to safety, and then think about your father.

It is not that volunteer groups are only doing something laudable by giving themselves up to the assistance of others; they are also truly helping in building the nation's character. But this only covers one aspect. Nation building must encompass all fields. Unless the women of the country are educated, the nation will not be able to progress truly. Despite this, how far has the education of females been able to progress in our country? I quote what someone has written about this in the journal *Gurukul:*

> Though the extremists are creating a lot of furore about democracy, freedom, brotherhood, and so on, the differences of caste and creed remain lodged deep in their hearts. They are against women gaining the minimum of freedom from the prison of the antahpur, the inner house, yet they do not feel hesitant to express their disgust for dependence and slavery. They are even hesitant about touching those who are in the service of the nation but belong to a lower caste, yet they demand rights equal to those of Europeans and when they see that a carriage is specially designated for the English in a railway train, they lose all self-control. They do not want to accept the mastery of the white race, but they announce with great conviction that only those born as brahmins are worthy of being counted in society. Reforms must be affected in all areas, not in selective ones alone. ... Despite the excess of imperial power, there was slavery in Rome. Those who are regulated blindly by the orders of the priestly class and who bow down before their orders unquestioningly are the ones who do not pay attention to the arbitrariness and control exhibited by their rulers but accept their mastery without hesitation. Hence, only political movements cannot bring the general mass to the beneficial path of emancipation and fraternity.

Translated by Ipshita Chanda
Department of Comparative Literature, Jadavpur University

'Amader Kartavya', Bharati, mid-August to mid-September 1908/ Bhadra 1315 BS, khanda 32 (vol. 32) sankhya 5, (no.5), pp. 229-32.

Also available in *Swarnakumari Devir Rachana Samkalan*, edited by Abhijit Sen and Anindita Bhaduri (Kolkata: Dey's Publishing and School of Women's Studies, Jadavpur University), September 2000, pp. 292-95.

Notes

1 John Eardley Norton (19 February 1852–13 July 1931) a barrister, politician and judge in Madras and Calcutta, was the chief prosecutor in the Alipore Bomb Case.

2 Prafulla Chaki was born on 11 December 1888 in the Bihar village of Bagna District now in Bangladesh. A freedom fighter and revolutionary, he shot himself in the head on 1 April 1908 when surrounded by the British police.

3 Swadeshi was a movement for India-made textiles, crafts and manufactured products to renew industries that had declined greatly because of foreign products imported cheaply under the British empire, adding to Britain's wealth and India's misery.

4 The Boer wars, 1880-81 and 1899-1902, were fought between the Dutch settlers in South Africa and the British empire which ruled South Africa and opposed the Boers' control over their territories.

44

SRI NIRAJBASINI SOM

She was the daughter of Nirmalabala Som and Jadunath Som, and received her B.A. Hons degree from Bethune College. She was also the co-founder of Women's Christian College.

A Brief Description of the Present State of Women's Education in Bengal (1931)

The tree that will yield the fruit of women's education in Bengal, as desired by us all, is still in an infant stage and its rate of growth does not meet our expectations. We have to rear this child with intense care in order to nourish it. For this reason, we require unwearied endeavour, undaunted spirit, unflagging perseverance and the constant display of compassion. As a result of several days of persistent endeavour and struggle, a favourable environment has been created. It seems that this young shoot will now grow into a large tree in the near future with its branches spread far across.

This meeting is an emphatic example of the new awakening of the spread of women's education in the country. Nowadays, women have become very vigilant regarding the proper education of their girl children. In the past ten years, whatever modest development that has taken place in women's education in Bengal can be proved from the list mentioned subsequently. It is indeed a source of great safisfaction that our perception about women's education has changed significantly. For this reason, the path for future development has opened up and become more easily accessible. Up to now, the leaders have worked extensively in tilling the field, the time for enjoying the benefits of the yield has arrived.

I present a list recording the development of women's education in the past ten years. According to the census report of 1921, the population of Bengal was 4,74,92,462.[1] Among them 2,45,28,365 were men and 2,29,64,097 were women. The number of educational institutions for women and the number of students in the year of 1921 have been listed in Table 1.

Table 1. Number of Institutions and Students 1921

	No. of Institutions	No. of Students
College	3	212
High School	25	4,805
English Medium	41	6,049
Bengali Medium	31	3,148
Primary	10,069	2,75,334
Other Institutions	275	8,230
Total	10,444	2,97,778

According to the present count,[2] the population of Bengal has been 5,05,65,667, out of which 2,64,95,375 were men and 2,40,70,292 were women.

Since the present census report is yet to be published, the number of educational institutions and students is enlisted in Table 2, as provided by the State's Annual Report of Department of Education.[3]

Table 2. Number of Institutions and Students 1931

College	4	375
High School	33	9,492
English medium	18	6,977
Bengali medium	12	1,354
Primary	16,743	4,76,573
Art and other educational institutions	56	2,439
Training college, etc.	3	52
Other educational institutions	241	7,125
Total	17,110	5,04,387

It is quite clear from Table 2 that in the past ten years, while educational institutions for girls have increased in number, the number of students has also doubled. Unfortunately when we compare the ratio of the number of educated women to the number of people, our spirits dampen. In the 1921 census report even women who could recognize the alphabet were considered to be educated but by that parameter the report showed that the educated women came to just above 2 per cent. And today, after ten years, it is still in doubt whether it has increased to 3 per cent. For this reason in order to change this situation we have to shoulder a huge task. Until primary education becomes compulsory for women we need to continue to struggle tirelessly. Today a thin ray of good fortune resulting from this awakening has been brought to our notice. Now it is our duty to illuminate this hazy evening into a sunny morning.

Thereafter the primary concern is to fulfil the country's needs and direct it properly, for which the most important and primary need is money . . . It has often been noticed that the amount of money adequate for the spread of education is never available. At present, the condition has worsened. For this reason, many a school is about to close. The government's help in this regard is meagre. If society does not come forward to help the uninterrupted progress of girl's education, then the good start of this nobel work will proceed towards an unavoidable end. As a result of this, women's education will again reach its lowest rung of degradation and our past endeavours will become futile. Much time will be required to return it to its present condition.

In order to solve this problem, I am sending a declaration to the representatives of the All India Women's Organization. I request you to find the correct path to emerge out of this serious condition so that we can save ourselves from this miserable downfall. Just like financial constraint, the absence of an eligible teacher is also an alarming problem. In order to eradicate this problem we have to make proper arrangements for the improvement of the standard of teachers in future, and at the same time, open up smoother ways for their higher education. In the absence of a suitable teacher how can a good school be made and the quality of education be improved?

Often there is difference in opinion whether girls' education is being directed by a proper ideology or not. Generally, the methodology of education is attacked. Describing it with various kinds of adjectives like unsuitable, harmful, and so on. Though I don't subscribe to this opinion fully, it must be agreed that the methodology practised has many faults. Realizing these faults, the Department of Education has tried to make a number of corrections and changes in the syllabus. The educational need of the country's future mothers and wives has been addressed to some extent. But further correction is needed in this field. So I request the representatives of the organization to design an ideal methodology which could eradicate the absence of education among girls and women of all classes and direct the student towards the manifestation of the ideals of womanhood, as wife and mother . . .

I want to briefly outline a few measures that the All India Women Organization has taken in order to solve this problem:

(*a*) Arrange a large amount of money for the spread of women's education. Half of the money given for primary education in Bengal should be used for the establishment and management of girls' schools and this needs to be implemented vigilantly . . . to spend one-fourth of the funds allocated for higher education on women's education.

(*b*) In each district there should be at least one girls' high school established. There should be a hostel for girls in each of them. It is necessary to have at least one English-medium school and corresponding hostel in each sub-division/sub-district.

(*c*) The newly formed law of primary education contains a statute that there should be one central educational committee and a district educational committee for each district. The provision of a suitable number of women representatives in central as well as each district committee is very necessary. Otherwise, the spread of education among girls will be obstructed.

(*d*) In order to have better arrangements for an adequate number of teachers, more training schools and colleges must be established.

This was read in the session of 1 July of the meeting of All India Women Organization.[4]

Translated by Srotoswini Majumdar
Department of Comparative Literature, Jadavpur University

'Bangladeshe Streesikshar Bartaman Abasthar Sankshipta Bibaran', *Bangalakshmi*, mid-July to mid-August 1931/Sravan 1338 BS, barsha 6 (year 6), sankhya 9 (no. 9) pp. 740–42 .[5]

Notes

1 The word used in the original is Bangladesh, which is a common term for the area known as Bengal before the partition of the sub-continent in 1947. It has been changed here to avoid confusion between what in India is known as West Bengal and the country Bangladesh that came into being in 1971 after erstwhile East Pakistan broke away from Pakistan.

2 Present count as mentioned in the original.

3 As the article was written in 1931; it may be assumed that the annual report pertains to 1930–31.

4 This refers to the meeting, held on July 1930, of the All India Women Conference on educational and social reform. Details are available from Annie Wood Besant in *The Theosophist Magazine* July 1931- September 1931.

5 In the original article, the writer signs off with the degrees B.A. and B.T. appended to her name.

45

ABALA BOSE

Abala Bose (1864–1951) was born into a distinguished family. Her father was Durga Mohon Das, a leading member of the Brahmo Samaj. Her older sister, Sarala Ray, was a keen supporter of women's rights and an educationist. Abala herself was an early feminist, educated at the Banga Mahila Vidyalaya and Bethune School. In 1881, she cleared the entrance examination with a scholarship of Rs 20 from the Bethune School. With a scholarship obtained from the Government of Bengal, she went to study medicine in Madras. She could not, however, finish the course because she got married to Jagadish Chandra Bose. In 1919, she established the Nari Shiksha Samiti in order to spread women's education and train widows to be able to earn a living. In 1925, she established the Vidyasagar Bani Bhavan to spread adult education amongst the womenfolk. In order to empower established women economically, she also set up the Mahila Shilpa Bhavan in 1926 and the Bani Bhavan Training School in 1935. Even before the Calcutta Municipal Corporation could come up with the idea of free education at the primary level, she set up many such schools in Ballygunge, Bhawanipore, Narkeldanga, Bowbazar. In 1930, she introduced for the first time, the concept of Montessori education at the Brahmo Balika Shikshalaya. She also founded the Sister Nivedita Women's Education Fund for primary education for adult women, with a starting sum of Rs 100,000, as contributed by her husband, Acharya Jagadish Chandra Bose.

Women's Cooperative Store (1932)

This store was established by the cooperative society of the Committee for Women's Education. This cooperative society was registered in the group of cooperative societies according to the laws of 1912.[1] This was the first collective endeavour of Bengali women. All the members of this society were thrifty, independent and their main aim was to propagate the principles of the cooperative and to achieve the economic welfare of women. The funds generated by this cooperative society were to be used in the following ways:

(a) Setting up cottage industries and other necessary industries by the members of the society, including provisions for the sale of goods produced by these industries.
(b) Providing loans or advances to the members of the cooperative society.
(c) Procuring raw materials and machines for the members.
(d) Arranging for the sale and distribution of goods manufactured by the members.
(e) Supervising the work of the members of the cooperative society regularly.

The women's cooperative store at 14 Cornwallis Street was opened by the Cooperative Society of the Committee for Women's Education[2] to encourage women, ensure the sale of homemade goods, propagate the Indian cottage industries and encourage the use of Indian goods and products made by women at home. The cooperative store was run by women for the welfare of women. The shares of this cooperative society were distributed at the rate of Rs 5 only to include women from various backgrounds. Anyone could buy the shares of this society by being a member and paying an annual membership fee of Re 1 only.

Some enthusiastic members of the Cooperative Society of the Committee for Women's Education established this cooperative store in a small rented house at College Street. The great patriot Acharya Prafulla Chandra[3] had always been enthusiastic about the welfare of women; he had graciously agreed to be the president of the inaugural function. Lady Mookherjee opened the store to the public.[4] We were able to open the store in the above-mentioned house with the help of the most efficient Ranjanbabu of the Calcutta Corporation's College Street market. Women workers were inexperienced though they had initiated it and came together just to propagate the use of indigenous goods and help women in producing and selling manufactured goods locally. In the month of April (Baishakh), I compared our store with the well-established store of Bombay and expressed my views about the Bengali women in *Prabasi.*[5] I hoped that the solidarity of the women of Bengal would definitely yield results. I was very upset when I heard the news of the closures of the Bombay store. The store was run by garment traders. Women from well-established families handled the sale of the products. In spite of this, the Bombay store shut down which induced a certain degree of apprehension amongst cooperative societies. The cooperative societies had little capital; the only hope was that the women of Bengal would stay true to their pledge of propagating native goods. With this belief the board of directors of the cooperative store shifted their base from College Street to 14 Cornwallis Street. Here, we had to pay double the money and the expenses of running the store also increased. Our only hope was the enthusiasm and support of Bengali women.

The stability and development of the store entirely depended on women who always remained alert and aware, looking out for ways and means towards their own welfare. The Cooperative Society of the Committee for Women's Education started their work on a very small scale but if they received help and encouragement from all it would become a source of pride. Indira Devi Chaudhurani[6] was the president of the organization and Mrs Purnima Basak was general secretary; Charu Mitra and Madhurilata Mahalanabish were the assistant secretaries. Surama Sen was treasurer and the Polish wife of the efficient chemist of Bengal Chemicals was the organizing secretary. Besides, there were nine women directors. There was no particular owner; the accounts were audited by the accountant of the cooperative society. As a part of the cooperative society, the organization received help and advice from them. The store was only a year old and very soon its annual general body meeting would be conducted. In this past year, we might not have earned major profits but I am satisfied that there have been no losses either, which is no mean achievement. If the store had earned profits, the money would have been used for the development of women. My humble request to the readers of *Jayasree* is that they inform their friends about this store, encourage the directors and help them in fulfilling their mission of the 'Women's Cooperative Store'.

Translated by Prajnamita Dasgupta
Department of Comparative Literature, Jadavpur University

'Nari-Samabay Bhandar', Jayasree, mid-August to mid-September 1932/ Bhadra 1339 BS.

NOTES

1 The Cooperative Societies Act, passed in 1912, was meant to amend the law on cooperatives, and covered the whole of India.

2 Abala Bose was very enthusiastic about women's education. In 1919, she started this committee to educate women and make them self-sufficient. Another intention behind starting this Committee was to educate widows and give them some vocational training. Krishna Prasad Basak, who was then headmaster of Brahmo Balika Sikshalaya helped Abala Bose to start this committee.

3 Academician, chemist and entrepreneur, Acharya Prafulla Chandra Ray (1861–1944) was the founder of Bengal Chemicals and Pharmaceuticals, India's first pharmaceutical company. He is the author of *A History of Hindu Chemistry from the Earliest Times to the Middle of Sixteenth Century* (1902). Ray had a doctorate in science from Edinburgh University. In 1896, he published a paper on the preparation of a new stable chemical compound mercurous nitrite. He started a new School of Chemistry in 1924.

4 Daughter of Phani Bhusan Adhikari, a professor of philosophy of Banaras Hindu University, Ranu, later Lady Ranu (1907–2000), was married to Sir Biren Mookherjee, who established the IISCO steel plant at Burnpur. She was a close associate of Rabindranath Tagore since her childhood days and later became a great connoisseur of art and culture. She founded the Academy of Fine Arts, Calcutta, in 1933.

5 The first Bengali monthly magazine published outside Bengal. Begun in 1901, it was edited and published by Ramananda Chattopadhyay from Allahabad, and received contributions from famous Bengali writers, including Rabindranath Tagore.

6 For details, see headnote on Indira Devi Chaudhurani, Essay 37.

46

SRI SWARNALATA BASU

She was a member of Bengal Provincial Franchise Committee, and the wife of Mr. P. K. Basu.

Women's Right to Vote (1933)

Many of us hear the word 'vote' and consider the casting 'vote' as an exclusive right of men. Nowadays, orderly elections are held everywhere—Council, school, college, playground. I want to mention my observations about the voting arrangements for women in the Bengal Council. Presently, the number of those women, who have received the right to vote in the Bengal Council, is very small. The reason is that men or women who do not have property that yields a specific income cannot caste their vote. There are not many female property owners of this type in this country. A new administrative system will be introduced in India very soon. So at the moment it is necessary to increase the number of women voters, as we women also have a claim over our country, we too have a duty towards our country, about which we have not thought till date. Apart from the spread of education we are gradually progressing in matters concerning household affairs, education and social reformation. In the process of executing this work, I realize that it is necessary for us to acquire the right to vote. If this right is acquired then the electoral candidates will not be able to consider women voters as completely insignificant or worthless. If there is a desire to hold the election following other 'civilized' nations in the Council, then they will not be able to go against our opinion easily. In almost all developed countries, election candidates have to depend on the voters. They have to remain alert about the needs and complaints of the voters. They have to construct their own view (to be presented in the election body) after considering voters' opinions. The candidates have to make a written proclamation where they need to describe the work they have done for the country and the type of work they are prepared to do after entering the Council. If all these promises are not kept, then they cannot expect to get elected the next time.

Even in our country, candidates have started to depend upon the support and consent of male voters. Women voters are so few in number that they do not depend upon their votes. That is why they are not burdened by a responsibility towards us. They do not have to produce endorsement for any progressive work that they have done for women and none forces them to do so.

The only remedy possible in this situation is to increase the number of women voters. Many are thinking about this subject now, and those who are associated with the welfare of women have given a petition to the government pleading for increasing the number of women voters. It is not that the attention of rulers has not been attracted towards this subject. The Simon Commission,[1] British Prime Minister MacDonald[2] and the Lothian Committee[3] have all expressed their opinions that it is necessary to increase the number of women voters. In our country many movements have been carried out on this issue. Now even men are supporting us . . .

We have thought deeply on this subject and have decided that for women the eligibility to cast a vote in the Council must not be restricted to those possessing property. It will be necessary to implement a different method to measure women's eligibility otherwise even after the introduction of the new administrative system the possibility of women getting elected to the Council will decrease. Moreover, we ourselves will not be able to nurture the inclination to differentiate the good from the bad, and the candidates also will not encourage or consider our opinions at all.

Besides being property owners, there are two other ways to make women eligible to vote: first, by imparting ordinary education; second, wives of those men who have been designated as voters because they own property must also be endowed with the right to vote.

It can be calculated that the number of those women who cast their votes in Bengal as property owners is 5,00,000. At present, the number of mature educated women is almost 6,75,000 and the number of women who can vote because their husbands are property owners is 8,00,000.[4] So the sum total of eligible women voters becomes 16,76,000. Among these, some women possess more than one of the above qualifications. However, they can only cast one vote. Therefore, the above-mentioned number will decrease and accordingly, the number of women voters is assumed to be not more than 15,00,000. Even if this is less, at present we cannot demand more than this; it can be hoped that this will gradually increase—the reason being that along with the spread of education among women, the number of educated women will also gradually increase.

By this arrangement, no particular class of women will be prevented from being able to vote. Those who are married, would either become voters for being educated or as owners of property or as wives of male voters who are property owners. Those who possess ordinary education, whether they are unmarried, married or widows, will not have to depend upon the education received in school or upon the ability to pass examinations in order to become voters. Even those women, who are minimally educated, living only within the inner apartments of their houses, will be counted as voters. Over and above, the Lothian Committee has instructed that before becoming widows, if women have been considered as voters for being the wives of male voters who owned property, then their names should remain in the list of voters even after their husbands' demise. In this way, the respect of the widows will increase further.

It is believed that women, who become voters because they are the wives of male voters, tend to get influenced by the opinions of their husbands. However, could it not also be said that even husbands might get influenced by their respective wives? That is why this statement does not have much importance. Women have expressed their liberal views in the field of education and about various types of social reform. So, there is no reason why this would not happen with regard to voting.

The Lothian Committee supports the two means that we have proposed earlier to increase the number of female voters. After discussing the Lothian Committee's views, the Select Committee,[5] which has been constructed by the Parliament, will take a decision. And, most probably, this decision itself will be endorsed by the Parliament. If any part of the Lothian Committee's recommendation advises a decrease in the number of women voters, then that will be perilous for the entire female society. According to the assessment of this Committee, the number of women who, as wives of male voters in Bengal, can themselves become voters, will be 8,00,000 approximately. However, if there are contrary opinions about this view then from the total of 15,00,000 female voters, 8,00,000 will be subtracted. But it has already been stated earlier that this objection is baseless. That is why the women must begin a movement immediately to make the Select Committee accept the recommendation of the Lothian Committee. If this number is made to decrease, then women's influence on election candidates will decrease.

A few days ago, all members of the Assembly and of Bengal Presidency Women's Association informed the Prime Minister by telegraph that if all adult women are not enfranchised then nothing less than the number determined by the Lothian Committee for women is acceptable to them.

Translated by Prajnamita Dasgupta
Department of Comparative Literature, Jadavpur University

'Meyeder Voter Adhikar', *Prabasi*, mid-June to mid-July 1933/Asarh 1340 BS, bhag 33 (part 33), khanda 1 (part 1), sankhya 3 (no. 3), pp. 389-90.

Notes

1 The Indian Statutory Commission was a group of seven British Members of Parliament that had been dispatched to India in 1927 to study constitutional reform in that colony. It was commonly referred to as the Simon Commission after its chairman, Sir John Simon.

2 James Ramsay MacDonald (1866–1937) was a British politician and twice Prime Minister of the United Kingdom. He rose from humble origins to become the first Labour prime minister in 1924.

3 At the close end of the Second Round Table Conference (September-December 1931), a White Paper recommending the increase in the number of the enfranchised women was presented in both the houses of Parliament of Britain. The complexity of the franchise question compelled the franchise sub-committee of the Round Table conference to

recommend setting up a committee to investigate the demands. Thus the Indian Franchise Committee, under the leadership of Marquess of Lothian was constituted in December 1931 and it started its work in 1932.

4 Cited by Geraldine Forbes, from Government of India Home Department file dated 25/3/1929, in 'Number of Women Voters in India', *Women in Modern India*, vol. 4, (Cambridge University Press, 1996), p. 101.

5 Select Committees are usually temporary committees established by one of the houses of Parliament, UK, to investigate or study a problem.

47

SRI MANORAMA BASU

Manorama Basu (1896–1976) was the wife of Satyendranath Basu and sister of freedom fighter Kalipada Sarkar. She was an active leader of the Jessore Congress. She was imprisoned a number of times. She participated in the 1942 Quit India Movement. She was imprisoned for four years. As the president of the Jessore Congress Women's Division, she worked for women's education, the welfare of the lower castes and abolition of the caste system. In 1938, a movement began across the country, demanding the freedom and return of all the freedom fighters imprisoned in Andaman Island. Manorama Basu participated in this movement actively with the leftists. After Partition, she came to West Bengal. She died in Belgharia.

The Position of Women in the New System of Governance in India (1936)

The Laws of 1935

Soon a new set of laws will be promulgated in India. Let me briefly discuss the rights of women under them. It has taken more than seven years to form this new system of governance (Government of India Act 1935). The Simon Commission stepped into this country in the winter of 1927. The Commission was set up with a view to discuss the state of India and to reform the ancient laws that had been prevalent in the country. Since then, there have been many movements within India and in places outside it too, demanding reforms. The people of this country have become aware of their rights as a nation—they have begun demanding their rights. Hence, before any laws could be permanently passed to determine the fate of India, many commissions were set up and many conferences held. The commissions have completed their tasks. The India Reform Bill has been passed into law.[1] And, our rights and the system of governance will be determined by this law itself.

Rights Women Possessed Prior to the Present Law

Before we can understand the rights given to us by this new law, we must know about our position in the past. So far, India has been ruled by the reformed laws of 1919.[2] It was in the year 1892 that elections were held in India for the first time, and people had voted. However, voting rights were very limited,[3] hence the number of people who could vote was also few. The Commission that was formed in 1917 had especially stressed in its report that the number of people eligible to vote must be increased. Nothing had been done to change this situation. Hence, only three out of every hundred people had been able to cast their votes. Irrespective of gender, only those who owned a certain amount of taxable property had the right to vote. Though there was no apparent distinction in voting rights between a woman and a man, yet, the number of women who cast their votes was visibly few. Throughout the country, only 15,300 women could cast their votes.[4]...

Rights Granted to Women in Accordance with the New Reform Bill?

The status of women in the new system of governance of India is very different from what it used to be. According to the new law, besides ownership of property, many other criteria will be included for determining the eligibility to vote. Even the qualifying amount of the taxable property that earned its owner the right to vote, has been reduced sizeably. Any man or woman who can show proof of having paid six annas[5] of *chowkidari* tax[6] or the Union Board's tax, or at least eight annas of cess or the municipal tax or the income tax, is eligible to vote. In this way, many villagers or the poor shall have the right to vote. Even the wife of the property owner will have voting rights. In case of the death of her spouse, the widow's voting rights will not be revoked. The aim behind all of this is to encourage a larger number of women to cast their votes.

Rights of Educated Women

In Bengal, women who are twenty-one years of age or above and have at least cleared Matriculation or any other equivalent government examination are considered eligible to vote.[7] Obviously, in its initial days, the number of female candidates eligible to cast their votes only after having cleared their examinations were to be few, if not negligible. There was a movement demanding that voting rights must be granted only if one could read and write. Many women's organizations and committees had also jointly petitioned the government appealing for such reforms. Even the India Secretary of State for India was briefed about this proposal made by women . . .

Means of Increasing the Number of Female Voters

There is no doubt that if the number of women who can vote expands sizeably, even their opinions will be duly considered by the governance systems. . . . The only way to expand the number of women who can vote and thus create a space for themselves in the country's governance is through women's education. Earlier, we had also demanded voting rights for adult females, but the excuse that there will be many problems in facilitating this prevented the implementation of this proposal. If all adult females could get voting rights, then the number of female voters would rise to several lakhs and not be limited to just a few thousands. . . . We must all pledge to educate and empower our sisters in every possible way. We will try our level best to establish schools in every city and every village, and even collect funds to support the spread of education financially. . . .

Number of Voters in the New System of Rule

If the right to vote is determined on the basis of what I have just mentioned, then, the number of voters will leap from 70,00,000 to 3.5 crore or 35 million and 60,00,000 among the 3.5 crore will be women. The number of female voters will stand at 60,00,000 from 15,300. If the entire population is taken into account, then, instead of 3 people in every 100, there will be 14 people in every 100 who will have the right to vote. Even this figure is not too impressive—and we have to put in our best efforts to increase the strength of the electorate. No government can be representative of its society if the male and female adults do not have the right to participate in the process of electing their representatives.

Importance of Women's Vote

Until now, I have discussed at length women's franchise and their eligibility as voters. But I have not discussed in exhaustive detail why a woman should vote at all. Let me say a few things about the importance of women's right to vote.

It is not possible to form in any country, a government, where every single citizen will be present to voice individual demands. It may have been possible once in the Greek metropolis but not any longer. The countries are vast and the population is so large that it is impossible to imagine that every single citizen will be present at a particular place, at any given time, to discuss some matter of great importance. The metropolis in Greece was small; hence, every citizen could easily participate in every discussion. In present times, the people who are eligible to vote are divided into many small groups called constituencies. Every constituency sends a representative to the council or the legislative assembly. The people of every constituency have the right to choose their representative. Every representative who is elected has some responsibility towards his electorate. The betterment of his constituency is always at the back of every representative's mind. If he fails to deliver any benefit to his constituency, the representative runs the risk of never being re-elected. This is why I stress upon women's right to vote. The greater the number of female voters, the more will be the influence of women on these representatives. Through these representatives acting as intermediaries, women will be able to influence the country's system of governance.

Functions of the Legislature

The legislature makes laws and is the most important institution in the government of any country. Representatives meet at the legislative assemblies and put their heads together over significant issues of current times, discuss them and find solutions to them.

The Legislature of Bengal

The Bengal Legislative Council[8] is entrusted with the implementation of laws in Bengal. Bengal has been divided into a certain number of constituencies. From each constituency, a representative was elected to the Bengal Legislative Council.[9]

Till today, no female representative has been elected to Bengal's Legislative Assembly. The lack of representation is not because there is a rule that bars women representatives or that they are not competent enough. Actually, there are no such hindrances at all. The real hindrance is the scarcity in the number of female voters. However, the new legislative assembly of Bengal will be a different picture altogether. According to the new law, Bengal shall have two legislatures—one will be the upper house and the other is the lower house or the Bengal Legislative Assembly. For any bill to pass into law, both these houses must vote in favour of the bill. Five seats have been reserved for women in the lower house. However, they can also independently contest against men for the general seats. Hence, the number of women in the legislative assemblies will never be less than five, in fact, it could be much more.

Various Communal Electorates amongst Women

Unfortunately, just like men even women have been divided on the grounds of religion. Amongst the five seats that are available, two have been reserved for the Hindu, two for the Muslim and one for the Anglo-Indian community. The voters of one community will elect a representative only from his community—meaning a Hindu can vote for a Hindu, a Muslim can only vote for a Muslim, and so on.

This mechanism of division has been sustained even in this new system of governance of India. Despite continuous protests against this system of distinction, there has been no fruitful outcome.[10] We do not want to call ourselves independent in this way. But sadly, we had no power to choose on this issue. This was one issue that was left undiscussed, this was one issue on which the British government had already made up its mind—and we had no other way of convincing them by our views. The system of division that was predominant amongst men was forced upon the women as well.

We continue to hope, however, that one day, every man and woman shall come together and demand the right to elect a competent representative from any and every community. Until that happens, we have to remain content with whatever we receive.

Influence of Women on the Legislative Assembly

Many important issues will be discussed in the new legislature of India—many significant laws shall be passed. And this is the time when the assertion of women's rights in the legislature is indispensable. What can five female representatives do amidst 250 general representatives? . . . If the number of female voters expands, then even the male candidates cannot dismiss women, because their candidature will depend on a large number of these women whose votes can win them a seat. Therefore, the men cannot neglect matters of comfort and necessity or the demands and hopes of women if they have hopes of winning their votes.

The Central Legislatures of Delhi and Shimla

It is not as if the legislature in Bengal solely implements laws in Bengal. The laws of Bengal which are connected with any part of India as a whole are framed according to the policy at the Central Legislative Council of Delhi and Shimla.[11] Even Bengal has to obey these laws.

Even the Central Legislature has two houses—a lower house or legislative assembly and an upper house or council of state. Presently, none of these houses have a female representative. There will be two similar houses even in the new system of governance in India. The lower house shall be called the federal assembly. Nine seats will be reserved for women in this house. One out of these nine seats will be kept for Bengal. In accordance with the new system of governance of India, the upper house will continue to remain as the Council of State. However, when the India Reform Bill was presented in the House of Commons, it was proposed and eventually agreed that six seats shall be reserved for women in the Council of State.

Duty of Women

In this crucial phase of change in India's system of governance, the fate of the country largely depends on her womenfolk. That we stand united—should be our uniqueness. We have been able to rise above trivial commotions and religious differences. Caste, community, religion, or differences in point of view have not been able to disrupt our harmony; so much so that even the Simon Commission has not been able to overlook this.

'The efforts put in by these women will throw open for India several channels for progress—the country will be salvaged by them. It will not be a lie on my part if I said that India will never be able to reach its coveted place in this world until her women are educated and take upon themselves the responsibility of their empowerment.'

The Simon Commission could not help but say these words about the women of this land. This is why I want to repeat that the power given to women in the new system of governance, the Government of India Act 1935, which is not negligible, and this we must all take to our hearts.

Even if this new system of governance is not to our liking, we must not trivialize it. Whatever powers we have, let us accept them and strive to make our presence felt. A certain organizational principle lies even in this variety. When we can say confidently

'Nana bhasha nana mot nana poridhan,
Bibidher majhe dekho milono mohan'.

(There are many languages, ways of thinking and dressing; in the midst of such variety there is great unity.)

Only then shall we know that our endeavour has been successful, only then can we try to achieve self-rule and only then will

'Dekhiya bharote moha jatir utthan
Jagojon manibe bishmay!'

and only then will we see in India the rise of the great race, and the world will watch with wonder ...

Translated by Anindita Roy
Department of Comparative Literature, Jadavpur University

'*Bharater Nutan Shasantantre Narir Sthan*', *Prabasi*, mid-April to mid-May 1936/Baisakh 1343 BS, bhag 36 (part 36), khanda 1 (vol. 1), sankhya 1 (no. 1), pp. 50-54.[12]

Notes

1 The Indian Councils Act 1909, commonly known as the Morley-Minto Reforms, was an Act of the Parliament of the United Kingdom that brought about a limited increase in the involvement of Indians in the governance of British India. The purpose, following the agitation over the proposal to partition Bengal, was to give concessions to a limited number of Indians, such that the loyal elements among the upper classes may remain faithful to the British.

2 The Government of India Act 1919 was an Act of the Parliament of the United Kingdom. It was passed to expand the participation of Indians in the Government of India. The Act embodied the reforms recommended in the report of the Secretary of State for India, Edwin Montagu, and the Viceroy, Lord Chelmsford. The Act covered 10 years, from 1919–29. It provided a dual form of government (dyarchy) for the major provinces. In each such province, control of some areas of government, the 'transferred list', were given to a council of ministers answerable to the Provincial Council. The 'transferred list' included agriculture, supervision of local government, health and education. The Provincial Council, enlarged though all other areas of government (the 'reserved list'), remained under the control of the viceroy. The 'reserved list' included defence (the military), foreign affairs and communications.

The Imperial Legislative Council was enlarged and reformed. It became a bicameral legislature for India. The lower house was the Legislative Assembly of 144 members, of which 104 were elected and 40 were nominated for a tenure of three years. The upper house was the Council of States consisting of 34 elected and 26 nominated members for a tenure of five years.

3 The Franchise Committee, a fruit of the Second Round Table conference, headed by Marquess of Lothian was set up in December 1931 and toured India in 1932. They recommended the expansion of franchise to more women. A wife over 25 could vote if her husband had property; a widow of over 25 could vote if her husband had been enfranchised at the time of his death, and graduates over 21 years could vote. Also see essays 46 and 57.

4 This figure was mentioned by the Franchise Committee on Indian Constitutional Reforms which was headed by Lord Southborough. He came to India in 1917 and the Franchise Committee's reports were published in 1918 and 1919.

5 One anna denoted one-sixteenth of a rupee.

6 Police tax introduced by the British.

7 For details on the entire debate and different provisions offered to women of different provinces, see essays 46 and 57.

8 This was the local legislative council, set up through the dyarchy system following the 1919 Act, consequent upon the Montague-Chelmsford reforms, in each province. For further details, see n 2. The Bengal Legislative Council constituted under the Act of 1919 was formally inaugurated on 1 February 1921 by the Duke of Connaught. A few years later, under the provisions of the Government of India Act 1935, two Chambers of the Bengal Legislature, the Legislative Council and the Legislative Assembly, were created. The life of the Assembly, consisting of 250 members, was to be five years unless dissolved sooner; while the Council, with a membership of not less than 63 and not more than 65, was made a permanent body and not subject to dissolution with the provision that one-third of the members should retire every three years.

9 The Act of 1919 gave Bengal 89 geographical constituencies out of which 39 were Muslim constituencies. Out of these, 33 were rural constituencies. The electoral constituencies were communal and of 'special interest'. Muslims, Sikhs, Eurasians, Christians and Europeans had separate constituencies. Where these communities were in a minority, wieghted representation was followed. The 1932 Communal Award also proposed separate constituencies for scheduled castes, which Gandhi opposed with a fast unto death.

10 The All India Women's Conference, National Council of Women in India and the Association of Indian Women resisted this move to split the constituencies on communal lines, as mentioned in the *Report of the All India Women's Conference* (1933-4, pp.18-19), *Stri Dharma* (16 September 1933, p. 549) and in the memorandum titled 'The Status of Women in the Proposed New Constitution of India' submitted to the members of the Joint Select Committee, June 1933.

11 Central Legislative Council was the result of dyarchy or dual system of government introduced by the Montague-Chelmsford reforms and the 1919 Act (see also n 8). The Central Legislative Council moved to Shimla in summer and remained in Delhi for the rest of the year. These are not two separate councils, but named after the two cities in which they met during the year.

12 In the original article, the qualification of the writer, M.A., was appended to her name.

48

RENUKA MANDAL

No biographical details about the author could be found.

Indian Women's Movement (1940)

The Indian women's movement took a definite form after the Second World War.[1] Even so, a women's movement ought to have started here much earlier. As the foreign rulers stood in the way of all social reform movements, the women's movement could not set forth. The form taken by our nationalist movement in 1905 did not accommodate women. The revolutionaries of 1905 had begun a movement inspired by nationalist zeal, in which radical social and economic reform was emphasized in rather ambiguous ways.[2] The revolutionaries of the time had a very hazy view of political freedom and did not feel the need for a revolutionary women's movement. Hence, women themselves needed to lead the women's movement.

It is historically seen from the most ancient times to the present that . . . women's joys and sorrows, progress and regress depend upon men. When the ancient socialist society broke down, women's position became lower; the ancient Greek society is an example. Since the time of Roman rule to the rise of Christianity, from feudal and medieval societies till the formation of industrial society, the status of women in society has been very low. Though many women were seen occupying the highest political position during these times, their number has been so few that their place in the pages of history may well be ignored. In India we see that at least two or three women were rulers, yet in the 2000-year-old history of patriarchal society, the philosophical rule and control of men remained supreme. India was no exception. It was not as if there were no interludes of matriarchal society in between patriarchal rule.[3] But such periods were very few and short-lived. . . . The main characteristic of patriarchal society is that there is very little acknowledged place for and the utility of women within it. Though science has helped the expansion of mechanical civilizations in all lands and in every society and material realism has taken root in national philosophical thinking, the world is still influenced by the philosophy of patriarchal [gender] organization, and in a sense, even regulated by it. Though capitalism has made available the labour of all classes for the benefit of one single class, yet its fundamental truth is that all progressive movements benefit by the structure of capitalist society. The Russian Revolution was an expression of the progressive nature of capitalist society. One of the main aims of this revolution was to give women emancipation. We have discussed this in the essay entitled 'Talking about Women' in the Falgun issue of *Mandira*, 1346 (mid-February to mid-March 1939).

. . . Any women's movement in this country of the *Ramayana*[4] and the *Mahabharata*[5] involves fighting against the philosophy of these texts. It is sad to note that though these days, in many public gatherings, long proposals about women's emancipation are adopted, and sometimes even equality with men is demanded, such gatherings do not understand the meaning of women's emancipation exactly, or realize that they taint the real, complex social problems that characterize women's lives by colouring them with their own views. Many women join the women's movement in India to keep up with fashion and to imitate the latest style in self-embellishment. Such movements generally provide space for daughters of well-placed bureaucrats. If we were to look at it from the point of view of actual social problems, there seems to be nothing in such movements, yet as they are against the custom of purdah, they still prove to be of some use. With regard to the demand for women's property, one may point out that as long as personal property is legal, these demands cannot be ignored completely. If we look at it from the point of view of women's freedom, then the Qur'an is much more progressive than the *Manu Samhita* or the Gita. The position of the Bible and the Hindu *Shastras* on the issue of women's freedom is very ambiguous. But the Qur'an describes women's emancipation in clear terms. If we have a minimum knowledge of the Bible and the Hindu *Shastras*, then we can well understand to what extent the Qur'an has taken human civilization forward from the point of view of women's freedom. But we do not wish to return to the Qur'an. We want freedom in clearer terms.

That freedom can be demanded and obtained, this view itself seems strange to us. Those women who frequent the large public gatherings in India demanding, 'We want women's emancipation' and those who support such demands understand nothing of women's freedom. Is it not a mockery of ourselves to remain economically and otherwise dependent on men within the family and then demand emancipation like beggars on the station platform? Women's emancipation will not happen suddenly just because we threaten someone with proposals of satyagraha. If we are to wrest women's freedom, then its foundations must be strongly laid, or else it will be extremely ephemeral because to get freedom as a gift from men is to strengthen women's bondage.

At present, many of the leaders of the Congress and the Muslim League are against women's emancipation. Those who are followers of Gandhi want to keep women in complete slavery because the first stage of women's freedom, that is, economic independence is total anathema to them. They think that wives are meant to beget sons. They are against industrialization. The civilization of the spinning wheel cannot give economic independence. Owing to industrialization, today, the differences between villages, disparities between provinces, conflict between nations, mutual hatred between religions, clash of civilizations and the inequality between men and women are removed and a new society, a new world, is created. Do we want to reject this civilization that is the result of ages of philosophical and scientific research and return to the civilization of the handloom where there is a colossal waste of human labour, where humans cannot provide food and clothing for themselves despite hard labour? The industrial civilization gives people better results and a better life in return for much less labour and a civilization that spreads knowledge equally among human beings and turns the human race into a civilized world where there is no violence or hatred. The village or spinning wheel society knows nothing other than violence, hatred, and the struggle to find food and shelter. We have to understand which one is better. Those who blame the fall of British capitalism and the rise of Nazism and Fascism on industrial civilization are either blind or are interested in self-aggrandisement.

By joining the Congress' women's wing or the Students' Federation's girl students' wing, one will serve to hinder the freedom of women. Real emancipation will come when the women of India will be able to feel the real shackles imposed upon them by their religion, society, customs, parents and 'apparently happy family lives' biting deeper into their limbs like links in gold chains more and more acutely. If emancipation is to come, we must rise in revolt against the world of the mind. If real emancipation is to come, then there must be revolt against all superstitious customs and blind beliefs. If we are to make this revolution possible, first we must join the movement that demands the rapid spread of industrial civilization. The national movement is a true weapon of industrial civilization. If industrial civilization spreads across the world, then a certain path of human progress will open up. The meaning of true human emancipation is where there is no difference between men and women; everyone is free. So, he who wishes to take the industrial civilization forward in India is the true devotee of freedom. Every Indian woman has the duty of taking this civilization forward.

We must think carefully that when world civilization is in crisis, our 18 crore or 180 million *devis* and *bibis*[6] are ensconced in a corner of their rooms, begging some godman or fakir for an amulet for their husbands or sons. The limits of their world are their parents, husbands and in-laws. If we are to make our freedom permanent and strongly rooted, we must break our golden chains. And the rest will follow.

Translated by Ipshita Chanda
Department of Comparative Literature, Jadavpur University

'Bharatiya Nari Andolan', Mandira, mid-November to mid-December 1940/Agrahayan, 1347 BS, barsha 3 (year 3), sankhya 8 (no. 8), pp.553–55.

Notes

1 In the inter war years, between 1917 and 1945, there were two main issues that the women's movement took up—political rights for women and reform of personal laws. The essays from this period in this book discuss the findings of the 1919 Franchise Committee led by Southborough and the Franchise Subcommittee led by Lothian in 1931-32, and the response of men in politics and of organized women's groups like AIWC, WIA, NCIW, and so on (see essays 46, 47, 57, 58 and 59). In 1938, the

Indian National Congress set up a National Planning Committee under the chairmanship of Jawaharlal Nehru. One of the 29 sub-committees established was on 'Women's Role in a Planned Economy' in which many prominent women's organizations and women Congress leaders were members. Political, economic and legal rights as well as participation in the freedom struggle were the main elements in the women's movement. Women's participation in the public arena and in politics legitimized their claim to a place in the governance of India.

2 This refers to the rise of militant nationalism in 1905 after Curzon's decision to partition Bengal. A section amongst the Congressmen turned against the moderate policy of the older members, and led by Bal Gangadhar Tilak, Lala Lajpat Rai and Bipin Chandra Pal they formed the extremist group within the Congress. Surendranath Bannerjea was one of the most important public leaders who protested against the partition of the Bengal province in 1905. Banerjea was in the forefront of the movement and organized protests, petitions and extensive public support across Bengal and India, which finally compelled the British to reverse the bifurcation in 1912.

3 Not in mainstream, but matrilineal societies were common among the Nairs in Kerala and in the North Eastern hill regions, like the Khasi and Jaintia Hills. However, generally the head was the eldest male, though succession went down the women.

4 The *Ramayana* is an ancient Sanskrit epic, ascribed to the Hindu sage Valmiki. It depicts the duties and ideals governing the roles of the father, servant, brother, wife and king. The word 'ramayana' means 'Rama's journey'. The epic consists of 24,000 verses in seven *kandas* (books) and 500 *sargas* (cantos) and tells the story of Rama (an avatar of Vishnu seen in Hindu scripture as the preserver), whose wife Sita is abducted by Ravana, the demon-king of Lanka. Thematically, the *Ramayana* explores human values and the concept of dharma. It is an important influence on later Sanskrit poetry and Indian life and culture. The characters Rama, Sita, Lakshmana, Bharata, Hanuman and Ravana are all fundamental to the cultural consciousness of India and Nepal (see also Essay 39, n 10).

5 It is one of the two major Sanskrit epics of ancient India, the other one being the *Ramayana*. Besides its epic narrative of the Battle of Kurukshetra and the fate of the Kauravas and the Pandavas, the *Mahabharata* contains much philosophical and devotional material, such as a discussion of the four goals of life or *purusharthas*. Among the principal works and stories that are a part of the *Mahabharata*, some like the Bhagavad Gita, the story of *Damayanti*, an abbreviated version of the *Ramayana* and the

Rishyasringa, are often considered as works in their own right. Traditionally, the authorship of the *Mahabharata* is attributed to Vyasa (son of Sage Parasara). The oldest preserved parts of the text are not thought to be compiled appreciably earlier than around 400 BCE, though the origins of the story probably fall between the eighth and ninth centuries BCE. The text probably reached its final form by the early Gupta period (c.a. fourth century CE). The title may be translated as the 'great tale of the Bharata dynasty'. It is the longest Sanskrit epic. About 1.8 million words in total, the *Mahabharata* is roughly ten times the length of the *Iliad and Odyssey* combined, or about four times the length of the *Ramayana*. It is divided into 18 *parvas* or chapters.

6 Devi means goddess; bibi is a respectable married Muslim woman; both are ways of referring to a lady.

49

SARALABALA SARKAR

Kishorelal Sarkar, the father of Saralabala Sarkar (1875–1961), was a practitioner in the Calcutta High Court. Saralabala was married to Saratchandra Sarkar. Her grandmother, Rasasundari Devi, was the first woman to write an autobiography in Bengali, which was named *Amar Jiban*. The members of the *Amrita Bazar Patrika Group*, Sisirkumar, Hemantakumar and Motilal Ghosh, were her maternal uncles. Saralabala wrote from a very young age. Her very first poem was published in *Bharati* in 1893. After the death of her husband in 1903, she immersed herself in literature. She contributed poems, essays and stories for magazines like *Sahitya, Pradip, Utsah, Jahnavi, Udbodhan, Antahpur, Suprabhat, Prabasi* and *Bharatbarsha* regularly. She received the Kuntaleen Puraskar in 1907 for her story *Smritichinha*. In 1953, she was appointed as the Girish Chandra Ghosh Lecturer by the University of Calcutta, and was the first Indian woman to get this prestigious post. During the Swadeshi movement she remained a support to her colleagues. Her main writings include *Arghya, Nivedita, Swami Vivekananda o Ramakrishna Sangha, Sahitya Jijnasa, Pinkur Diary, Pravaha, Manushatwer Sadhana* and *Chitrapat*. *Harano Atit* is her autobiography.

The Women's Satyagraha Movement (1947)

While the women's satyagraha[1] movement was taking shape, many political agitations were simultaneously in progress like a prelude to the movement itself. Some of these were the temperance movement, rejection of foreigners and their forms of education, challenging the laws and many other forms of protest. The whole of Bengal was set ablaze with these movements. The currents of these movements stirred every lane and alley, the rich, and poor, men and women alike, swayed with the fervor of nationalism.

On every road and in every shop, every man carried a loom; even those who used to run up and down the stations selling alcohol, now carried looms. Irrespective of whether one spun or not, the loom had become indispensable. In the huge wholesale markets of Burrabazar every tradesman who seated comfortably on a well-sprung mattress had with him a loom. And the credit for effecting such wondrous change went to the women satyagrahis in Kolkata.

At daybreak, groups of satyagrahi women would fill up the enclosures made for this purpose. Young girls between twelve and thirteen, Bengali, Marwari, Gujarati, Hindusthani, women from all classes and walks of life made up this group. Their duty was to ensure that no foreign goods were sold in any of the shops. They had to keep guard on the shops. Any suspicious smuggling of foreign items immediately ceased. However, the implementation of force was strictly prohibited, hence on seeing the transaction of foreign goods, the satyagrahis folded their hands and tried to win over the buyer and the seller solely through logical reasoning; such were the rules of the satyagraha. But it cannot be said that there were no exceptions to these rules. However, these groups of women were greatly respected by the tradesmen here; some of them were even feared. Whatever it be, the tradesmen would usually never argue or protest in response to the appeals of these satyagrahis.

The *katra* or wholesale market was the centre of much activity. Many vendors with their supplies of food, paan, dried fruits, fruits, and so on would come to sell here but if a woman satyagrahi bought any of their goods, they considered themselves so blessed, that they would not even accept a paisa for the items sold. In the torturous heat in the months of May and June (Jaishtha and Asarh), the soda-lemonade and ice-cream sellers helped the satyagrahis to quench their thirst, but absolutely free of cost, so much so that even the bus conductors would not take bus fare from the women satyagrahis who boarded bus no.11 to Burrabazar. The taxi drivers would also sometimes give a free ride. There was then an iron and fitting shop close to that of Manohar Das's; the owner of this shop was a Bengali. One day, he walked up to an elderly satyagrahi and with his hands folded requested her, 'Ma, we see that hundreds of young and little girls come to the katra with you every morning; if we arrange for their breakfast, will you accept it please?' His request was, however, not accepted.

In the godowns that were adjacent to the shops, the owners would invite the satyagrahis to come one at a time when the clothes were being packed, and having checked the bundles for suspicious items, the satyagrahis would put on them a signature stamp. Only with this signature stamped on them could the bundles be carried out without any problems.

At the doors of every katra was posted a woman satyagrahi. Of course, even the policemen were on guard outside, and they would sometimes inform the women about bales with foreign fabric in them. When these bales were seized by the satyagrahis, the policemen would do nothing to save the bales and in a way, they visibly helped the satyagrahis. Needless to say, only the Indians in the police force helped in this way.

The office of the women satyagrahis was at Raja Dinendra Street, the house number possibly being 144. In this house lived Santi Das[2] with her elder sister Priti Das and their mother Ashalata Das.[3] All the meetings, discussions and planning of strategies for further action were held in this house. The group leader of this committee was Urmila Devi.[4] Jyotirmoyee Ganguly,[5] Mohini Devi[6] and many others were present at the working committee. As far as I can remember, Jyotirmoyee Ganguly and Mohini Devi were also the co-group leaders. Santi Das and Bimalpratibha Devi[7] were the associate work managers and Jyotsna Mitra was their assistant. Presently, Santi, having married Professor Humayun Kabir, is Santi Kabir and Jyotsna having married Mr. Gopal Sanyal is Jyotsna Sanyal.

Often, upon a request from the surrounding rural areas, the committee sent one or two women to spread the message of the movement. These women had to spend three or four days, sometimes even more in the rural areas, because usually an invitation from one village led to another in the neighbouring one. Sometimes, even this writer has had to travel to Kushthiya-Kumarkhali and many villages that fell on the Howrah-Amta route. Purnadas was a part of this group, the first time we travelled to Kushthiya. The groups also had invocators who would summon people and many efficient male workers to join the satyagraha. At every station that we passed, whenever travellers gathered, the station reverberated with the cry, '*Vande Mataram*'—

and having travelled for long when we would finally reach our destination, our spirits would be recharged with an endless enthusiasm.[8] In fact, the intensity of nationalism in the city was flowing into the countryside and was being welcomed with compassionate and arduous zest. Even the *kulabadhus,* the women of the household, were inspired by the ideals of the movement. In every meeting, women gathered in such large numbers that arranging for a place to hold such a huge meeting was becoming a problem. Even women from farmers' homes became part of such meetings. There were provisions of food for at least ten to twelve workers who had devoted themselves to breaking the law or civil disobedience movement, including the withholding of taxes. In order to escape the police, the men had to be on the move constantly and in such a way that they could not be recognized. It was but obvious that in the darkness of the night whenever these men knocked at any door, their hunger and thirst would be quenched by their host with great affection.

The infancy of the women's satyagraha committee was not marked with too many impediments; however, with time the ruler became stricter in his ways and many were imprisoned. As far as I can remember, the very first to be jailed was Padmaraj Jain's daughter, Indumati Goenka.[9]

Though there had been arrests before this, the captive was usually released after a short while. I remember Indumati's case was heard by Rocksberg's bench at the Bankshall court. The accused was only a young girl. And this young girl had rebelled against the strong and glorious British Empire.

Only 100 women satyagrahis had been given permission to witness the trial in the courtroom; but the audience was much bigger than the prescribed number, because there was no way in which so many heads could be counted. It was a rule to stand when the magistrate walked in; but the satyagrahis refused to show respect to the court. Hence, the magistrate could not come and take his seat. Urmila Devi then explained to them that the gesture was not a form of respect to the British government, that it was common courtesy. But the satyagrahis remained reluctant to accept this logic. And amidst this discussion, no one knew when the magistrate walked in and took his seat. Indumati was jailed for nine months. No sooner was the verdict passed, the entire court room was brought down with the satyagrahis' slogans, 'Vande Mataram'. Santi Das went to Burrabazar immediately and declared a strike.

As a sign of protest, even the *Anandabazar Patrika*[10] remained out of print for six months. People would eagerly wait to hear from the countryside. *Anandabazar Patrika* then had its office at 171 Mirzapur Street. Chits of handwritten paper or typed sheets of news were pasted on the walls of the office. Hundreds and hundreds of people would gather to read the news. These were even circulated in the shape of very small pamphlets. The buying and selling of these pamphlets was a punishable offence in those days, yet their circulation remained unhindered. Stacks of pamphlets would disappear in no time, some paid one *anna*, some a *shiki*[11] and others would buy it for a rupee. What was paid was not important for the seller, keeping a track of what one paid was not possible either because the rapid buying and selling would take place under the strict scrutiny of the policemen. The money collected in this way was saved in the funds of the women satyagrahis; besides many volunteered to help with funds every day.

I am reminded distinctly of one of the many processions led by the women satyagrahis. It had started from the Shimla Vyayam Samiti. Possibly, this was their first procession. Many little boys and young lads had suffered the lathi charge of the police, yet the procession had remained fixed in its destination.

I also remember the procession at Raja Dinendra Street. After the arrest of Santi Das, a procession was proposed. Even the Marwari and Gujarati women, the Hindustani women, too, had approved of taking out this procession. There was great apprehension about the procession being allowed to move unchallenged, hence another proposal was made—that every single woman would carry the national flag and walk slowly in an organized queue, whatever the provocation be, no one would leave the rows of the procession or drop the national flag. This was unanimously accepted by the committee.

By the time the procession could begin, it was past evening. The procession had gone only a little distance, when a group of policemen came and barred its way; and the police superintendent ordered the procession to disperse. The women, not being allowed to advance, held tightly on to the national flags and sat in the middle of the road. It was getting darker, yet even when everything was completely dark, every woman in the procession remained sitting in the queue, barred by the policemen. Having understood that the procession would not disperse unless they were forced to, a group of white soldiers took charge, dismissing every Indian policeman in the troupe. So, there was a large audience that had collected at the windows of their homes and were staring down. The whites went about banging on their doors ordering them to shut their windows and doors tightly. Then, having combed every nook and corner with their searchlights for any source of potential assistance to the women, they ruthlessly fell upon the peaceful procession with all their might—kicked them, slapped them, pushed them, unleashing a storm of violence upon the women. In the face of this unanticipated attack, many women were seriously wounded, many even collapsed on the ground—and until the procession dispersed, the assault continued in full force. It was almost two in the night, when the whites left, having beaten the procession to dispersal and some kind supporters from around helped the women reach their homes.

Another procession was led to celebrate the National Day near the monument at the Garer Math [the maidan]. Around this time, many women satyagrahis were in the jail. Many policemen on horseback had collected to tame these women; but they had willingly surrendered after hoisting the flag unhindered. The police released all these satyagrahis after a night's imprisonment.

There was a procession led from Mirzapur Street in order to mark the *Deshbandhu Divas*.[12] The police had not granted permission for the procession initially. Later, they had approved on condition that only women would participate in the procession. Of course, only rows of women had led the procession with flags in their hands, but soon it was joined by men who kept coming in from all sides. Eventually, a few rows of women had turned into a sea of people in the procession, which was supposed to go towards the Deshbandhu Park, where an assembly had been arranged and speeches were supposed to be delivered. Accordingly, the sea of people surged towards the Deshbandhu Park. The police sergeants began charging with their lathis, and the horsemen tried to create chaos. Frequently, these horses would stumble upon the women; luckily, however, no one was crushed under their hooves, but many were seriously injured. On that day, this was how Deshbandhu's memorial assembly drew to a close.

Eventually, even the women sataygrahis were accused and arrested on charges of breaking law and order. Most of these charges were brought against the women satyagrahis because of the hindrance they created to selling foreign clothes in the market. It looked as if the foreign commodities had almost been wiped out of the trade arena. The satygrahis were not practising non-violence—that was the pretext used to imprison many groups of women at once. Around fifty women were imprisoned together and this case was judged at the Jorabagan Court.

That day many men charged with participating in the satyagraha movement were also presented at this court. The lawyers had tried to argue the case in their favour, but the sataygrahis were in no mood to defend their acts. So many flowers and garlands were brought that day that the courtroom was buried in flowers from the clerk's desk to the judge's desk. When the sentence was passed, the entire courtroom reverberated with deafening applause. It seemed as if the satyagrahis had already succeeded in winning Bharat from the hands of the foreigners.

This degree of punishment could not dampen the spirit of the women sataygrahis, in fact, it was fired anew and blazed forth. Women from every region all around came to join the women's satyagraha movement, and the government decided to ban the Women's Satyagraha Committee as illegal.The day the government made this announcement, how estatic Urmila Devi was. She said, 'Today we have triumphed and the British government has failed.'

Nevertheless, after the ban, large groups of women were not sent out for fear that they might be arrested and this might bring an untimely death to the satyagraha; hence, it was decided that only three or four girls would be sent at any given time in order to keep the fire of satyagraha burning.

In the meantime, the jails were being filled with satyagrahis. Urmila Devi, Mohini Devi, and many like them had been imprisoned. Ordinary women prisoners were inspired on being jailed with the likes of such mighty women. The women sataygrahis often tried to help bring comfort to these other women in jail. The food that was brought for the sataygrahis from outside the prison was shared equally with every prison-mate. Nirjharini Devi had the responsibility of dividing the food equally amongst all. She was an elderly satyagrahi, and was affectionately called pishima [paternal aunt] by her companion satyagrahis. The ordinary women prisoners and the jail authorities respected her immensely, and she was so closely attached to all the satyagrahis that she was the one to whom everyone would come with all their complaints and demands.

Once, two groups were divided in their opinion about hoisting the flag in the jail. It was probably to mark the *Jatiya Divas* or national day. One group was led by senior women like Urmila Devi, Jyotirmoyee Ganguly and Mohini Devi. Hoisting the flag under such conditions, they felt was not possible. The other group had the likes of Santi Das and Bimalpratibha Devi. The latter were adamant that they would have to hoist the flag.

In the courtyard of the jail there was a huge tree, its trunk had become extremely slippery owing to incessant rainfall over the past few days. It was decided that the flag would be tied to one of the tallest branches of the tree, so that it could be visible even from afar. A girl named Abha could climb trees, but the rains had made the tree so slippery that climbing one of its topmost branches and tying the flag around was a very tough task, it was dangerous, for she could have slipped any moment and hurt herself.

But Abha took the responsibility with a broad smile on her face. The tricolour was made in complete secrecy; stitched and sewed with borders of saris and whatever clothes was available. It was big and looked very beautiful. Very carefully, Abha started climbing the tree. Abha tied the flag. It unfurled and went aflutter and the groups of satyagrahis gathered at the feet of the tree burst out shouting, 'Vande Mataram'.

The flag could be seen from afar. The men outside had looked at the flag in amazement and by the time the jail superintendent Major Singh came and stood underneath the tree, Abha had not been able to come down. Fearing that she may slip and fall, trying to get down hurriedly, Major Singh alerted everyone, while be himself felt a little jittery. Anyway, Abha slowly climbed down unhurt, followed by an uproar of 'Vande Mataram'.

It was then punishment time. Who were the culprits behind such a misdeed, and who led the team. Major Singh's questions were answered with an unanimous: 'I'.

'Urmila Devi, Mohini Devi, you too?' Their silence was taken as assent, but Santi and Bimalpratibha had objected, 'No, they were not for this plan. How unjust! Those who had not agreed to be part of the act, what right did they have even in partaking the punishment?'

The buoyant Abha is no longer alive, but her cheerful face shall be ever remembered by her companions.

The Women's Satyagrahi Committee had existed for about a year and a half or two. The ones who were acquitted were arrested and imprisoned immediately after they were released. Many other groups had slowly become a part of it. Other rebellious girls also joined them in the prison. Santi and Suniti, even Bina Das, had become regular pilgrims to the jail.

Around this time, many incidents had taken place. The ruthless torture of the police in the countryside, burning Jhareshwar Majhi's barn and the murders in the Hijli Jail had all happened about this time. After this, many women satyagrahis went to Karachi and became members of the Karachi Congress.

The last assembly of the Women's Satyagrahi Committee was called for at the Albert Hall.[13] Santi Das had summoned the congregation. An unimaginable number of people had gathered. But just before the assembly could begin, the news of the death of Chameli Devi, one of the committee's most important member, filled the Hall. As a gesture of respect to this great comrade, Santi called off the assembly. The Women's Satyagrahi Committee did not call any more gatherings.

Only two Muslim women, who had joined this Satyagrahi group, were jailed. One of them was the fourteen-year-old Hasnara Begum and the other was Daulatenechcha Khatun.

Translated by Anindita Roy
Department of Comparative Literature, Jadavpur University

'Nari Satyagraha Andolan', Anandabazar Patrika, Sharadiya 1354 BS (1947).

Notes

1 The word *satya* (truth) is derived from *sat*, which means being; 'nothing is or exists in reality except truth' (M.K.Gandhi, *Young India*, 30 July 1931). Truth (satya) implies love, and firmness (*agraha*) engenders, and therefore, serves as a synonym for force. The most potent legacy Gandhi left to India was Satyagraha born of truth, love or non-violence.

2 Santi Das and Bimalpratibha Devi were entrusted with enrolling volunteers for the women's satyagraha.

3 She was the president of Nari Satyagraha Samity of Calcutta. Around fifty volunteers from the Bengal Pradesh Congress Committee picketed the foreign clothes and liquor shops from College Street junction up to Burrabazar in Calcutta. The movement also spread when volunteers

from the South Calcutta Congress Committee, led by Lavanya Prava Das, picketed cloth shops around Russa Road. Besides this, Mahila Rashtriya Sangh, led by Lotika Ghosh and the Ladies Picketing Board set up in 1931, were also active.

4 She was the sister of Chittaranjan Das, a Congress leader, and along with her sister-in-law, Basanti Das, they motivated the women's satyagraha movement in Bengal. In 1929, the Nari Satyagraha Samiti of Bengal was formed. In 1930, Urmila Devi was arrested for picketing foreign goods shops, thereby becoming one of the first women to be imprisoned for political activities in Bengal.

5 Referring to Jyotirmoyee Gangopadhyay. For biographical details, see Essay 29.

6 She was vice president of the Nari Satyagraha Samiti and a Congress worker of long standing. She was the oldest woman imprisoned for satyagraha. It seems that she refused her to be released from prison because she felt her presence would lessen the torture meted out to younger prisoners.

7 As secretary to the Nari Satyagraha Samiti, Bimalpratibha Devi also raised money for the defence of the accused in the Chittagong armoury raids. She was arrested in 1931 for her involvement in the Manicktala dacoity case.

8 A poem from Bankim Chandra Chattopadhyay's 1882 novel *Anandamath* which played a vital role in the Indian independence movement. It was first sung in a political context by Rabindranath Tagore to his niece Sarala Devi Chaudhurani's tune, at the 1896 session of the Indian National Congress.

9 Indumati Goenka (1914–1971), the daughter of Padamraj Jain (1882-1946) and daughter-in-law of freedom fighter Kedarnath Goenka, was among the first women in Bengal to be imprisoned in connection with the freedom movement. Her marriage to Keshavdev, in 1929, at sixteen was characterized as 'ideal' by the *Vishwamitra*, a newspaper of Calcutta because it reportedly broke with customs of purdah, dowry, jewellery and ostentation. She was a student at Bethune College and studied in the Bengali medium, which was unheard of for Marwaris at the time. She promoted khadi, participated in the Nari Satyagraha Samiti, picketed foreign shops and burnt foreign cloth. She supported women's education and widow remarriage and was an activist against purdah and dowry. Indumati was arrested and sentenced to nine months' imprisonment for being listed as the secretary of the Rashtriya Mahila Samiti on a pamphlet that called for the resignation of the police. Burrabazar shops closed for

a day to protest her arrest. To honour her, the girls in Bethune College did not attend their classes.

10 In 1922, the *Anandabazar Patrika* was started by Mrinal Kanti Ghosh, Prafulla Kumar Sarkar and Suresh Chandra Majumdar. The first edition of the paper appeared on 13 March 1922. The new daily at its very moment of birth was defiantly waving the banner of protest. Suresh Majumdar had been incarcerated by the British. In his early youth, Majumdar had been a follower of the armed revolutionary, Jatindranath Mukherjee (popularly known as Bagha Jatin). Prafulla Sarkar had been a participant in the Swadeshi movement but he was arrested and jailed in 1923 as editor of *Anandabazar Patrika* for publishing an article praising Jatindranath Mukherjee. Between its founding and 1947, the editor, publisher and printer of *Anandabazar Patrika* were jailed by the government innumerable times for fearlessly propagating nationalist views. Prafulla Sarkar's wife, Nirjharini, was jailed thrice in the 1930s for participating in satyagraha at the call of Mahatma Gandhi.

11 Sixteen annas used to make one rupee; four annas used to make one shiki.

12 The birthday of Deshbandhu Chittaranjan Das.

13 Albert Hall was inaugurated during the visit of Prince of Wales, Edward VII.

PART V

GENDERING PUBLIC SPACE

50

ANONYMOUS

The Strike of the Bombay Signalmen (1899)

Those who read newspapers know and those who do not have heard that the Bombay Railway's signalmen have called a strike. It is no longer possible for one part of India to remain unconcerned with the joy and pain of other parts. We sympathize with the sufferings of all Indians. Though *Bharati's* time and space are limited,[1] we cannot let slip the opportunity of helping the fever-struck strikers who will be in dire straits if they are not helped immediately. Thus without going into a lengthy discussion about strikes, I offer one or two comments to help readers understand that it is our specific duty to help the signalmen. In this situation, the points mentioned in favour of the signalmen need to be especially considered.

(i) There is no doubt that the signalmen have many genuine and just causes for grievance.

(ii) Having sent repeated petitions to the company explaining their tale of pain and suffering, they have seen that these have not been paid heed by the company.

(iii) Earlier, when the Anglo-Indian guards had called a similar strike, they had not shown this type of judiciousness; at the very beginning, they took hasty and intemperate actions.[2] In spite of this, the company took a few initiatives to combat them, which indicates that they had a connection with the government. That is, keeping in mind the problems faced by the public and the injustice meted out towards the railway guards by the company, the government considered it proper to bear down on the latter. In the present situation, that heavy power of the government

has weighed upon the weak. Taking advantage of the common people's lack of sympathy for the strikers, the government is helping the company against them.

(iv) The Anglo-Indian community is even trying to circulate this to the public as another example of conspiracy of the Pune brahmins so that people's views are shifted from the real causes of protest.[3] All Anglo-Indian newspapers have come together on this matter and are fighting against the poor Indian signalmen.[4]

(v) The signalmen had proposed an agreement with the help of a neutral mediator, but the company did not agree to this.

(vi) The company has concluded that crushing the strike is the only way towards a solution; that is, the signalmen are being unjustly enticed to betray their own groups.

(vii) It is clearly seen that this problem cannot be solved through fair means since strength has been taken to be the sole criterion. When it is apparent that the oppressor has been able to unite Anglo-Indian society to strengthen its oppression, then without any further discussion regarding this matter, for the time being at least, we too should wholeheartedly unite to strengthen our weak countrymen, and this is a definite responsibility.

(viii) The hope of victory in this face-to-face conflict is not so far-fetched as to make any endeavour in this direction seem insane. We have come to know from a reliable source that the company's bravado about its strength is without a base. The company is losing half a lakh of rupees every day, and they have to send back all those signalmen whom they have hired from other places; moreover, the skill and honesty of the new recruits is suspect. So if our signalmen can continue for a month or two then the company would be subdued.

(ix) Apart from this, if our people's sympathy is expressed, then it is needless to say that it would increase our countrymen's strength; the company can use it as a pretext to move towards a compromise.

It is needless to give any more reasons. It would be enough to say that Mr. Pherozeshah Mehta,[5] eminent and respected, in the past few days, had called for a meeting of a few well-known persons in Bombay to help the signalmen. Two and a half thousand rupees had been raised here; the next day it increased to five thousand rupees. They intend to raise ten thousand rupees very soon. But there are many signalmen and a huge amount of money is required. So they have written a letter requesting monetary help from Bengal. They have not only requested for money but also for sympathy. That is why if each one of us could spare a small sum of money and send it, then it will be accepted with a lot of love; and would inspire our countrymen in this hour of trial. Apart from this, those who want to test their strength against the Anglo Indians can go ahead. It is only by chance that one gets an opportunity to do so much by spending so little. I am confident that the readers of *Bharati* will not let this opportunity pass. Two-five rupees, ten rupees, whatever one can afford to give, should be sent to this address:

Hon. Pherozeshah Mehta, Esqr.
Bombay.

The Bombay committee has given Mr. Surendranath Tagore[6] the responsibility of raising funds in Bengal: 1, Rainy Park, Ballygunge this is the address at which money can be sent in his name, or it can be sent to the office of the editor of *Bharati* and it will be forwarded to the right place, and the donor will be acknowledged in *Bharati*. Those who do not want to publish their names will be acknowledged through pseudonyms. Help and sympathy have already been received from one or two respected and famous people.

Translated by Ritika Batabyal
Department of Comparative Literature, Jadavpur University

'Bombay Signalarder Dharmaghat', Bharati, mid-April to mid-May 1899/ Baisakh 1306 BS.

Notes

1 *Bharati* was founded by JyotirindranathTagore (1849–1925), elder brother of Rabindranath Tagore, and along with *Balaka* it was published by the Tagore family. Rabindranath Tagore was a regular contributor.

2 In 1897, the skilled Anglo-Indian members of the Amalgamated Railway Servants Society of India and Burma employed in the Great Indian Peninsula Railway struck work on the issue of fining and scrutiny. They were affiliated to the railway union in Britain, and their successful

agitation made the authorities fear the militancy of organized workers of European origin. In 1899, the Indian signalmen employed on the same railway carried out a strike for higher wages, which is referred to later in the essay. The authorities were wary of the Indian protestors.

3 The Indian press, Marathi newspapers like the *Mahratta* and the *Kesari* organized funds to support the Indian railwaymen (the essay is part of this campaign, too, in faraway Bengal). Because of the involvement of the educated elite (as newspapers were mostly read by them), the Anglo-Indian press took the view that this was a conspiracy of the educated Indians against the government.

4 The indigenous newspaper industry that Robert Knight thrust himself into in mid-nineteenth-century India consisted of a motley small-circulation daily or weekly sheets printed on rickety presses. Few extended beyond their small communities and seldom drew together the disparate mix of castes, tribes and regional subcultures of contemporary India. The media were more often dominated by the Anglo-Indian presses, which promoted purely British interests Knight, in impassioned fashion, recognized a void to be filled. Knight founded the *Times*, and later, the *Times of India*. Seven years later, he launched a new venture, a periodical called the *Indian Economist* (1869) that focused on financial news. Two years later, he founded the *Star of India* (which became the *Indian Statesman* in 1872). Knight's *Statesman* was a worthy rival of Calcutta's other Anglo-Indian dailies, the *Englishman* and the *Indian Daily News*.

5 Sir Pherozeshah Mehta (4 August 1845–5 November 1915) was a Parsi political leader, activist and a leading lawyer, who was knighted by the British Government in India for his service to law. His political ideology was moderate and not directly opposed to the Crown's sovereignty; however, he demanded more autonomy for Indians to self-rule. He became the Municipal Commissioner of Bombay Municipality in 1873 and its President four times—1884, 1885, 1905 and 1911. He was chosen the President of Indian National Congress in 1890.

6 Satyendranath Tagore (1872–1940) was the first Indian to become a member of the Indian Civil Service. He was an elder brother of poet Rabindranath Tagore. Surendranath Tagore (1872–1940) and Indira Devi Chaudhurani (1873–1960), Satyendranath's children were well-known figures. They had lived in England as children. Surendranath translated Rabindranath's *Four Chapters* in English. He had produced a condensed version of the main portion of *Mahabharata* in Bengali. He had certain links with the militant revolutionary organizations fighting for India's independence from the British yoke.

51

SWARNAKUMARI DEVI

Eassay 17 offers a note on the author.

Which Way Lies Our Responsibility? (1908)

The newspapers tell us that recently three boys have been arrested in Burdwan. It appears that learning that the Governor of Bengal would be passing through by train, they had made plans to assassinate him. There was another instance when a bomb was hurled at a train bound for Agarpara. That the youth have still not rid themselves of such wrong ideas is a matter of grave concern. If they dissipate all their energies in such anarchic activities, where will they find the energy to do any work that is truly beneficial for society?

How many people are capable of giving their lives for the country? Amongst the tens of millions of Indians, the number of such fervent patriots can be identified easily. But these people are only wasting their lives, sacrificing themselves and their enormous strength for some misguided beliefs. Labouring under the belief that they are doing something constructive, they are actually bringing the country to the brink of a catastrophe. Those who have dedicated themselves to the service of this country in such a fit of passion must ponder over the circumstances calmly. That is all that we request.

What does history say? What examples do we see in foreign countries? Even in independent countries, we have not seen that assassination benefits a nation. Furthermore, we are a weak, dependent and enslaved nation. In the given situation, doesn't killing a couple of Englishmen appear to be the epitome of stupidity? If they had been misled, then experience should have alerted them to their error of judgement. This kind of anarchy has spread terror in the whole country.

The policy of torture by the police, punishment of innocents, muzzling of the press, rigidity of the judicial system are increasing the oppression of the people regularly. Who can say that if this oppression becomes permanent, we would not be converted into a dormant and docile state? It is evident that this kind of violence is a thousand times more harmful to the subjects than it is to the rulers. If, today, the British rulers decide to blow all Indians away with cannons as a way of keeping their subjects under control, we do not have the power to resist. What happened to the protesters in Bombay? In truth we depend solely upon the sympathy of the rulers and their sense of justice. It will not do to pretend that this truth is false. There is no doubt that dying for the country is a holy act, but if that fails to achieve the desired end, if it is harmful instead of beneficial, then what is the point of it? If you jeopardize your countrymen for whom you are ready even to forsake your life by your actions, then such a death is surely not desirable.

A sailor is not expected to drown his ship by driving it into the face of a storm; similarly, to let loose a handful of soldiers to fight against a huge force of the enemy means that destruction is certain. Hence, in the context of such unequal power ratios, those who serve the country must rid themselves of their commitment to death and make the kind of sacrifice that will be most fruitful for the country. In other words, instead of forsaking their lives, they must live to work for their country. Even after attaining independence, a lot of work needs to be done to consolidate the foundations of the nation. This would require much labour and planning; it is doubtful whether one generation's life-long efforts will be enough to complete the task. Giving away one's life in a moment of excitement is an act of bravery easy to perform, but to struggle lifelong with dedication and discipline and sacrifice one's self for the cause of nation, needs greater courage. This should be the ideal commitment for an Indian. If the powerful party itself does not hope for success through violence,[1] then how can the weaker party hope for success? With calmness and patience, oppression must be borne, all obstructions overcome, and the path of progress must be followed with a staunch vow towards total commitment. Internal strife is the root of all our dilemmas, an obstruction to our progress. What more needs to be said? That great organization which had infused a new and vibrant life into the national body is today ridden with internal dissension, rendered weak and alienated, and is on the verge of extinction.[2] ... Acceptance of swadeshi and rejection of the foreign, spread of education and patriotism amongst the masses, collection of funds for the progress of industrialization and trade and, above all, strengthening ourselves as an unified entity should be the chief mantra for our success.

Regular exercise will benefit the body and increase strength, while mental endeavour will enhance the quality of thought and . . . nourish our minds for further development. Hence, if youngsters abandon the care of their minds and bodies for the cause of patriotism, then there will be very few in the next generation fit to work for the country . . . Besides, the rulers need to be taken into confidence, and their help enlisted, so that these efforts are not viewed by the government with suspicion. In fact, if something is achieved jointly by the Bengalis and the British such efforts will prove permanent. Some people say that if we take the help of the government in any work that would be of benefit, it would detract us from our own goal of seeking independence and harm our sense of self-respect. But this is completely untrue. First, there is nothing like complete independence; in some form or the other, one needs to depend on others' assistance; our country constitutes rulers and subjects, one dependent on the other; what we pledge cannot be completely dissociated from the ruler's perspectives. Hence, such views have no real value.

Second, if we remain in comfort and expect that the government will ensure that we get food, then we will become entirely dependent on them. Instead we need to strive tirelessly and enlist government support to bring our efforts to fruition so that our sense of self-respect or independence remain unharmed, and this is particularly applicable for those who are willing to endeavour and work, and seek the confidence of the rulers. . . . In practical terms, maintaining friendly relations with the rulers is just as necessary as maintaining amity amongst our own selves. I do not know how far the advice given in this regard by Sir Andrew in his farewell speech will be effectively implemented,[3] but the fact that the powers who rule are beginning to understand this arouses our hopes. It is true that the government does not desire evil for us; to demean and belittle the subjects is not part of their policy. It is because we do not know one another, . . . there is so much conflict. But 'salaambaji' or sycophancy is not the true relationship between the ruler and the ruled. That I am using 'salaambaji' in the popular sense in this case perhaps needs no explanation. The slavish expression of respect for self-aggrandizement is what we understand by 'salaambaji'. This may obtain favours, but does not result in equality or earn sympathy. Our misfortune is that the majority of those who mingle with the rulers do so in the hope of earning some meaningless title, or perhaps because they are unable to stand tall and assert their equality with the rulers for fear of being harmed in some way. They consider sycophancy as the only way to attain their mean selfish objectives. So the ruling class too has become used to this so much so that any deviation from such behaviour is considered by them as a form of disrespect shown to them. The fact that it is possible to establish relations between the ruler and the ruled does not occur to them at all. On many occasions, the sycophants do not hesitate to conceal the true sentiments and wishes of the subjects and convey the exact opposite of what is desired by the people, thus telling the rulers what they want to hear. What the raja of Kashi said against swaraj is one instance of this kind of mentality.

The fault does not lie in the ruling class but in us. We must understand this and correct our behaviour. Friendship of the great and the good can be acquired only by showing greatness and goodness. If they see that we behave like them, that we respect them not to win personal favours but in earnest desire for their friendship so that we can work together for the good of the country, that we are not insulting them by not behaving like sycophants, but respectfully, soberly and fearlessly, merely pointing out to them their responsibilities towards India, then gradually friendship and trust will definitely grow between us. Rammohan[4] and Vidyasagar[5] were respected friends of the highest rulers of the land as they showed character and expressed feelings of true friendship. Can any maharaja claim to have attained that level of closeness and friendship by being a sycophant to the rulers? The present advocate general has attracted the respect of the rulers through his fearless sense of justice and responsibility towards the country. But alas! Where will those whose deepest desire is to fulfil their own selfish ends find the courage to act similarly? . . .

The government is not an enemy of the people—we are our own enemies. Young men of today who are the hope and support of the country, who are perceived as selflessness personified, must not reject the government or antagonize the rulers but consider showing their strength of character and behaving in a manner which will win them their friendship. If we can win their confidence, as well as establish unity amongst the swadeshis on the one hand, and earn respect from the foreigners on the other hand, then we can establish sovereignty in India and make swaraj successful without spilling a single drop of blood. Now Cotton and Wedderburn are getting into disputes with men of their own race because they wish us well. If we are able to demonstrate some strength in character, then a hundred Cottons and Wedderburns will be aroused to consider our struggle as an act to earn self-respect and will be willing to give us the rights that are justly ours.[6]

There is nothing that cannot be achieved by making an effort. Who knew that the boys of Bengal could create a bomb factory in the midst of such surveillance? But let them understand that such acts are detrimental to our progress; instead they should concentrate their energy to craft a way towards sovereignty.

Translated by Ipshita Chanda
Department of Comparative Literature, Jadavpur University

'Kartavya Kon Pathe?', Bharati, mid-December to mid-January 1908-1909/ Paush, 1315 BS, khanda 32, sankhya 9 (no. 9), pp. 430-33.

Also in *Swarnakumari Devir Rachana Samkalan,* edited by Abhijit Sen and Anindita Bhaduri (Kolkata: Dey's Publishing and School of Women's Studies, Jadavpur University), September 2000, pp. 295–98.

NOTES

1 Refers to the Indian National Congress.

2 Refers to the Indian National Congress.

3 The official referred here cannot be ascertained.

4 Rammohan Roy, 1772-1833, was the pioneering social reformer of modern India, who persuaded the British Governor General Bentinck to pass legislation against the practice of sati. He also founded the Brahmo Samaj, a society that broke away from traditional Hindu worship to practice a rational form of Hinduism based on the Upanishads (see also Essay 40, n 3).

5 For details on Vidyasagar, see Essay 12, n 13.

6 Sir Henry Stedman Cotton, ICS, was sympathetic to Indian nationalist aspirations and was the President of the Indian National Congress in 1904. As Commissioner of Assam, he lent his name to Cotton College, Guwahati, founded in 1901. William Wedderburne entered the Indian Civil Service in Bombay in 1860, and retired when acting Chief Secretary to the Government of Bombay in 1887. He was concerned about peasant

indebtedness and suggested reform that was supported in India but was blocked by the India Office in Britain. He also supported the expansion of local self-government to include Indians and to give equality to Indian judges. He was seen as supporting the aspirations of Indians and was not appointed as a judge in the Bombay High Court. This led him to retire early in 1887. Along with Allan Octavian Hume he was a founder of the Indian National Congress and served as its President in 1889 and 1910.

52

SARALA DEVI CHAUDHURANI

Sarala Devi Chaudhurani (1872–1945) was the younger daughter of Jankinath Ghoshal and Swarnakumari Devi and perhaps the first woman nationalist. She topped her BA examination amongst the female candidates in the University of Calcutta and was awarded the Padmavati gold medal in the year 1890. She was fluent in Bengali, Sanskrit, Persian and English. She taught at the Maharani School at Mysore for almost a year. She threw herself into the swadeshi movement. She launched *Pratapaditya Utsav* and *Veerashtami Brata* to encourage the nationalist feelings of the people. She also founded *Lakshmir Bhandar* to encourage the use of indigenous goods. Her efforts helped in the formation of the Bharat Stree Mahamandal (the Great Assemblage of Indian Women). In 1930, she established the Bharat Stree Sikhshasadan. She also started a girls' school for older girls at the Albert Hall in Bhawanipore, affiliated to the Bharat Stree Mahamandala. She edited *Bharati* with her elder sister Hiranmoyee Devi and also on her own. In Lahore, she ran the paper named *Hindustan* with her husband, Rambhuj Dutt Chaudhuri. Among her major books are *Jeebaner Jharapata*, her autobiography, *Nababarsher Swapna* and *Shata Gan*.

Communion (1911)

(A summary of speeches delivered at different women's gatherings)

A prayer mentions:

'Where in communion with the world
You are struck with wonder,
It is there, that with me you bond.'

My mind seeks to know where this bond exists, and I realized that it exists in work. Be it a spiritual communion, a meeting, a committee, an association, or any kind of gathering, we develop our kinship with each other and with God through work. To which nation do we—the few women who have gathered to participate actively in the meeting and cordial communion—actually belong? . . . Our only identity is that we are Hindus and daughters of our country. But we represent only a small section of the several unknown, unseen and unnamed siblings of Calcutta as well as our country. Driven by a good cause, we have been able to come close to each other and bond with one another. Still, it must be kept in mind that in this enormous family of India, we are a handful of girls. There are tens of millions of girls like us in India's bosom. Perhaps another similar association like ours has been formed, inspired by some other novel idea that has not struck us as yet. Perhaps other Indian women, located elsewhere, are carrying out responsibilities that are beyond our capacity. Don't you feel curious to know where and what these other women of India are doing? For instance, in the family kitchen, if you are asked to prepare pulao, won't you feel curious to know then who among your sisters is responsible to cook the rice, who the lentils, or who is in charge of the provisions or laying the table? My desire might be to do everything single-handedly, but since my ability is limited, I might extend myself with love and affection to others. If somebody else completes my half-done work, then, in a way, it is done by me because the one who does it is a sister of mine. That is why one must have the curiosity and the indomitable desire to know what the other sisters are doing. One of our very primary aims of the great association that has been founded—the Bharat Stree Mahamandal or the Great Assemblage of Indian Women,[1] is to circulate among you the news of the activities of one another.

So many rivers, cutting across mountains, meadows, lands, are rushing towards the sea, merging in its heart in ultimate communion. The Ganga, Yamuna, Saraswati, Narmada, Cauvery and Tapti—all of them with their respective diversities merge with the sea rumbling the song of the sea in harmony. Similarly, in the symphonic rendition of the *ragas* and the *raginis*, what is audible is the movement of the seven basic notes: *Sa, Re, Ga, Ma, Pa, Dha, Ni.* But if there were no music, where would the notes harmonize? If there were no ocean, where would the eastern and western currents merge? The Bharat Stree Mahamandal is striving to establish the link between you and the others. Will you correspond with each other and like to share your experiences with each other? To initiate this process, at the onset, you need to let the secretary of the Bharat Stree Mahamandal know your name and address and that you are interested in participating in this association. If a group intends to on its own, it should send a write-up to this organization including the names of the members, mentioning its aims and the rules and regulations to which it adheres.

These are to be followed by half-yearly or yearly reports of its activities. These reports will be collected by the Bharat Stree Mahamandal at the end of the year. At the annual council of the Bharat Stree Mahamandal, where women from different parts of India and representatives of different groups will meet, the reports of all those women's groups and associations will be read out before the assembled audience. Let all of them be inspired by the depiction of each other's trials and achievements . . . let them learn and sympathize with others, and . . . let them dedicate themselves to their causes with redoubled energy. Overlooking our multifarious activities and interests, let us weave a web of mutual cooperation. It is through work that we would communicate with God. A prayer to Him implies asking for strength to execute those acts that He has chosen for us. Meditation and contemplation, austerity, service and philanthropy are all different forms of action . . . The Bharat Stree Mahamandal is the ultimate platform that connects my work with yours and others with that of mine . . .

The Bharat Stree Mahamandal not only becomes a meeting ground of diverse groups, but also a connecting link between one end of India and another, naturing many lives within its bosom. Every Indian woman, irrespective of race, religion, caste and creed will be a member of this great community. As you understand by the phrase 'Bharat Stree Mahamandal' or 'Great Assemblage', it implies a large community encompassing the whole of India beneath its canopy, thus spreading out a mat to encompass all. Bengali, Hindustani, Marwari, Marathi, South Indian and Punjabi women—all are invited here. Any woman from any nation, such as Europe, America, Iran, Japan or any other country, those who love India and want progress of women in India and are willing to befriend them, are eligible to join the membership of the Assemblage. With the help of its collective human and financial resources, the Great Assemblage will shower enlightenment on those who remain in the domestic confines in India, find a way of sustenance for the destitute housewives, facilitate the availability of medical treatment for the distressed women of India and make an attempt to promote the development of provincial literature. Any small group may take the responsibility of any of these services and be a part of the Bharat Stree Mahamandal too. It will try its best to help these groups either financially or physically, providing them with human resources.

What great service is done by the Young Women's Christian Association! The idea was initiated by a Scottish lady who in turn inspired a few more ladies and their mutual interaction created a driving force within them. They began corresponding with women of Scotland, England, Europe, America, Asia and all other countries, and this has yielded such beneficial services to women of all countries!

Englishwomen have the energy for doing so much work; then why would it not be the same for us? This might perhaps be due to the lack of camaraderie amongst our fellow sisters. The Bharat Stree Mahamandal is an instrument for establishing such communication and companionship. By means of this instrument we shall aspire towards driving the domestic engine, a powerhouse represented by the housewives. We intend to increase the availability of medical treatment among those who are unwell, and try to promote the development of provincial literature.

Almost as soon as Europe came in contact with Asia, different groups of Christian missionaries had taken charge of education in the domestic sphere among the Indians. None of the Scottish, English, Irish, French, Russian, Portuguese, Danish, Swiss, German or American missionaries could stay away from this venture. Because of their initiative, many of us have now become educated. Is not the time ripe for us yet to bear the responsibility of our education? In spite of the indomitable enthusiasm shown by the missionaries, most Indian families, being afraid of religious hostility, turn their backs upon them and are reluctant to let them enter their houses. Shouldn't we reach those houses of our country bearing the lamps of education? How long will you sit so passively immobile? Look at the biographies of those Christian women—what examples of self-sacrifice! How much physical hardship had they overcome! What strong resolution! . . . Do we not possess these qualities? Can we not perform these feats? Why can't we? Practice hardships as they did! Be austere! Resolve! Nurture a mission within your hearts and correspond with each other! The Bharat Stree Mahamandal has well established connections between women of different localities and of different towns—it will unite the women of different provinces with one another and will create a spiritual communion between the women of the Indian subcontinent and of other continents. You will be delighted to know that a letter has arrived from a Hindu lady, living abroad in England, where she has expressed her desire to be a member of the Great Assemblage of Indian Women and has sought our permission for launching a branch of it in England along with her English friends.

By setting up branches among the localities of this metropolis you can arrange for domestic education and organize a fund for the sustenance of destitute women. When you visit a suburban town, you can assemble the womenfolk and explain the purpose of the Assemblage, and continue serving by forming a branch. You must maintain a goal in your mind ... we ought to keep in our minds ... that we must keep spreading education among our sisters. We shall try and locate these women, who have little education but who struggle for their survival and appoint them to visit places and educate others, teaching whatever they know about any subject.

English ladies organize reading clubs. The members, at times, make a rule to read something serious every day for an hour, apart from plays and novels. She, who breaks the rule, records it in her diary and gives the club a fine for her violation of the rule. Suppose, instead of a reading club, you set up a teaching club and become its members. Each of you according to your limit of endurance, resolve to teach somebody something every week for an hour. If you are in a joint family, then at a definite time you may sit with the womenfolk of the family. If you know Bengali, you may teach a bit of it, if you know English, you may teach it as well. You may teach others music, embroidery, painting, or anything else that you know. If there is no learner at home, interact with the ladies in your neighbours' houses, meet them and teach them. If there is no locality nearby, teach the girls of your own domestic staff. The main point is if you have the resolve to offer, there will be no dearth of receivers. You have to maintain a diary about your mission. If there is any deviation from the rule or any lapse in your mission, you must record it in your diary and send the Assemblage a fine as your penance. Now the month of Baishakh—the first month of the Bengali solar calendar—is arriving. On its first day, Paila Baishakh or 15 April, thousands of Indian women across India will vow to partake in hundreds of rituals. Those who have been recently enlightened amongst you unite your minds and hearts with others and take a vow in the New Year ... My orthodox sisters, within your several rituals make space for another one, which is essential for your country and the time. Make people realize that educating others is a pious act and should be made a part of our daily rituals. Take a vow of educating and motivating others to do the same. The utility of a mission is perceived in a two-fold way: as a service to oneself and to others. The one who takes the mission, through restraint and discipline, attains self-elevation and from inert and bestial beings, one learns to progress towards a humane self, the mission-induced offering leading to the benefit of others.

Apart from that we will collect handicrafts from artistically skilled women and open sales counters in neighbourhoods on behalf of the Bharat Stree Mahamandal. Perhaps this will provide the means to provide refreshments for the child of some poor lady, maybe somebody will manage to get him warm clothes or somebody will provide his school fees in this way. The women of our country suffer but never speak out. If an arrangement can be made whereby none but the secretary would know who is sending what for sale, then many can be encouraged to find a means for sustenance by sending their wares here...

There is no other bond that is more enduring and more endearing than the bond of work. Where the goal and the action are same, there exists the same spirit and love. With the connecting thread of the Bharat Stree Mahamandal we must tie the knot of love with the women of other provinces. Only across this bridge of action can Indian women reach out to one another ... the Bharat Stree Mahamandal is that connecting bridge. To strengthen the power of this assemblage each of us has to become a member of it. Do not say, 'So what, if I am not a member, there are so many others, what does it matter if I am not one?'

A king, digging a large pond in his kingdom, sent commands to all the milkmen of his state that by that very night each of them should pour only a small pot of milk into it, for he wanted to see a sea of milk the following morning. At sunrise when the king along with his ministers came to see the sea of milk, what he saw was no sea of milk, but a water body spread before him with no sign of milk at all. A milkman from nearby was summoned. When he came, the king asked, 'You poured water in it, why not milk?' Trembling in fear the milkman said, 'Forgive me Lord, I thought thousands of my fellow milkmen will pour milk, and let me, a poor fellow, pour a pot of water into it that will do no harm to the sea of milk.'

The second milkman was sent for and he gave the same answer... As an explanation was demanded from each, everybody had the same thing to say . . . each of them failed to perform his bit of the duty and hence there was a mere pool of water. Had each one performed his respective duty there would have been a sea of milk.

If each and every educated Indian woman does her own duty, first of all, by participating in this assemblage, second by trying and helping it to achieve its goal, only then the Bharat Stree Mahamandal will become a sea of milk, or else, a pool of water will show up without doubt. . . . If we do not do that, whom shall we be depriving then? It will be our own selves, not the women of other countries.

Do not forget,
That you are not merely yourself,
That you are one among many others,
And that your honour lies
In the honour of those many others of your land.

Translated by Sudeshna Majumdar
Department of English and Other Modern European Languages,
Visva Bharati

'Jogajog', Bharati, mid-April to mid-May 1911/Baisakh 1318 BS, barsha 35 (year 35), sankhya 1 (no. 1) pp. 30–35.

Also in *Sarala Devi Chaudhuranir Nirbachita Prabandha-Samkalan* compiled by Abhijit Sen and Anindita Bhaduri (Kolkata: Dey's Publishing and School of Women's Studies, Jadavpur University), January 2004, pp. 123–28.

Note

1 Bharat Stree Mahamandal, the Great Assemblage of Indian Women, was founded by Sarala Devi Chaudhurani in 1910 in Allahabad. It is considered to be the first women's organization in India.

53

SRIMATI SARATKUMARI CHAUDHURANI

Saratkumari Chaudhurani (1861-1920) was born in Barrackpore. She completed her education at Lahore, where the first three years were spent in a Bengali school after which she was admitted in a European school. She was married to Akshay Chandra Choudhury in 1871. Many of her writings have been published in *Bharati, Bharati o Balak, Sadhana, Bhandar, Bangadarshan, Manasi, Dhruva, Sabujpatra, Manasi o Marmabani, Visva-Bharati*, and so on, and many of them were unsigned pieces. Her only book was *Shubho Vivaha* (1906), which was reviewed by Rabindranath Tagore and considered as a valuable work of Bengali literature.

Women's Education and Vocational Training (1914)

Many months ago, one evening, the three of us were chatting in the third-floor room. One lolled about on the bed and the other two were lounging on it. Srimati Jnanadanandini Devi said, 'Look, I believe that if we strive for it, we could do a lot for the country and its people.[1] Suppose your husband is a doctor, and some needy person is suffering from lack of treatment, you could appeal to your husband and get the person treated. Someone's husband may be a barrister and he may be able to attain justice for some hapless victim of injustice.' . . . We were so immersed in our discussion that we scarcely realized when the thick gloom of dusk was dispelled by the night as moonlight flooded the room. I have forgotten most of the other things we had talked about.

All that has stuck in my mind is the bright moonlight and the fact that a few days after that the Sakhi Samiti was established under the aegis of Srimati Swarnakumari Devi.[2]

The strangest thing was that Swarnakumari Devi was not present with us that evening. And yet, she had been thinking along similar lines of women's power, and our plans and ideas were brought to fruition by her diligent efforts. Sakhi Samiti was established in April 1886. Its goals were increasing interaction between women, spreading literacy and education amidst them, helping widows, aiding orphans, and so on.

For many years, Swarnakumari Devi had toiled away on these endeavours. In those years Hiranmayee Devi had come to her mother's aid by taking into her own home a few orphan girl children and looking after their education and well-being. This happened years ago and a chronicle of all the events would run into reams of pages. Neither do I remember each and every detail worthy of mention. But I do remember the handicraft fair—what a joyous event, what zeal and fervor! After working patiently and firmly through many hurdles Swarnakumari Devi retired and Sakhi Samiti met with an ultimately end. Then Hiranmayee Devi took up one of the causes of the Sakhi Samiti by establishing a women's vocational training school and she has put in a great deal of effort to make it a success. This school has been set up with an aim to improve the lot of Hindu widows. At this time, nearly thirty Hindu widows of varying ages live in her household, following their religious customs and norms and being educated and trained in various crafts at the same time. They produce dusters, towels, saris, silk cloth, socks, vests, lace and daily wear with their own hands.

These days even in our country most people—of high or low class—use socks, shirts, vests, and so on, for which one has to run to the shops. Those who have children at home or have daily dealings with tailors must be aware of the problems associated with these tasks. One has to keep an eagle's eye on the tailor so that he does not make away with the extra cloth; when they demand unreasonable fees, one can only stare at them dumbfounded; and last of all, one is not sure what the tailor will finally make and present, claiming it to be the greatest creation of all times! ... Most of you may say, 'Give up all these luxuries and life would be so much simpler.' Let us suppose that is possible in the case of the women. We may agree to emulate our great grandmothers and retreat happily singing, 'Let us go back, go back my dears.' But the daily clothing of men such as socks, vests, panjabi, shirts, jackets, coats and trousers will always be in demand. Therefore, it is quite obvious that if women learn the art of stitching, it would be very convenient for the household. . . . It is not only the widows who have access to this vocational training. Even housewives and young married women can enrol themselves and obtain an education and get trained in various skills. The women at this vocational training school manufacture hand-woven fabrics as well as beautifully made and embroidered handkerchiefs, jackets and dresses. . . .

The tender hands and compassionate heart of the married woman are eternally engaged in the act of providing. But in our country the moment she becomes a widow her value crashes meteorically. In that instant this auspicious woman is branded an inauspicious being. Owing to her fate, the caring woman's heart, full of good will, is freed of ties of domesticity and is made available to be engaged in the service of greater humanity. She is made to feel like the lowest of the low and an unwelcome burden on her relatives; she perceives her life as worthless and she passes her days somehow, trying to occupy as little space as possible. Very few people have truly appreciated the contribution that Hiranymoyee Devi has made to the nation by setting up the vocational training school and thereby establishing that the multitudes of widows are not worthless appendages to society. It is very unfortunate that because of the lack of funds the work is not progressing as it should.

Hiranymoyee Devi and her troop of workers are well aware how difficult it is to collect a simple monthly donation. It appears as if these widows, who do not have husbands or sons, are entirely *their* responsibility and have nothing to do with the nation and its people. How do I enlighten people that this is the vocation of one and all in the land? If society and its people can successfully lend a sense of purpose to an empty life, the hapless widow would consider herself blessed to be of service to them. If everyone realizes that these young women are preparing them to be of service to society, would they then hesitate to reach out and contribute to the welfare of these women? We, the married women, live in seclusion: our own home, our husband, sons, brothers and fathers, are our sphere of work. For the ill-fated women, if a close relative takes pity and provides shelter, it goes a long way in saving face, but life is burdensome nonetheless. Can anyone look upon these millstones kindly? This is the story of every household. Therefore, many such widows from decent homes are often seen eking out a living by doing work that is below their dignity. When they toil endlessly in a relative's home and yet are denied two square meals with any modicum of decency, then working as a maid in a stranger's home and earning one's living look like a better option.

When one does domestic work in a stranger's home, there is no distinction between dignity and indignity. Poverty bears the stamp of indignity and thus, with the rude behaviour one faces every day, one's heart and soul too sink to a nadir of despair. The woman, who could have gladly spent her days in endless toil and religious pursuits in her own brother's home, is instead preoccupied with thoughts of how she would polish off a little oil or a cup of milk when she works in a stranger's home as a cook.

In the West, so many women opt to stay unmarried and devote their lives to earning their living and serving society through charitable and missionary work. One hears of so many famous women, many of whom are spinsters. But in our country that cannot come to pass. And yet, there are many widows who have been married in name only, many girl children who can barely remember their wedding day (who became widows soon after) but of course, they are widows and not spinsters. This vocational training school has been established specially so that such young girls and women do not go astray and acquire a good education and handy skills.

Earlier, around nineteen or twenty young married girls used to come to this school for education and training. There were vehicles arranged to ply them back and forth. But where there should have been students in excess of hundreds, there were only these twenty or so. This makes it very obvious that there has not been much thought given to the betterment and education of women. When all the people of the country were working themselves up to a frenzy, talking of progress and improvement, they failed to grasp that if you take care of the sapling, the fruit shall be sweet. Since the Samiti faced severe shortage of funds, inadequate even to continue training a mere handful of students, there is now no provision for a vehicle to pick up and drop off the girls. But if they wish, they could go on their own and receive training at this school. Earlier the school was located within the city, but now it has been moved to Lansdowne Road. If you wish, you could go and see it for yourself.

Translated by Sreejata Guha
Translator and independent scholar

'Narisiksha o Mahila Shilpashram', *Bharati*, mid-February to mid-March 1914/Falgun 1320 BS, barsha 37 (year 37), sanhkya 1 (no. 1), pp. 1190–93.

Notes

1 Renowned for her innovations in Bengali women's dress reform and modernization of manners and etiquette. Jnandanandini Devi (1850–1941) was born in a remote village in Jessore. She was married at the age of eight to Satyendranath Tagore, the first Indian to become a member of the Indian Civil Service (1864) and elder brother of Rabindranath Tagore. She was one of the first to emerge from the strictest purdah into the public gaze of elite British officialdom by attending civilian parties and among the first handful of Indian women to cross the seas when she went to England for a long visit in 1877 with her children. See also Essay 37, n 3.

2 A handicraft fair was organized by the Sakhi Samiti (Society of Friends), the first Mahila Shilpamela, which was started by Swarnakumari Devi in 1888 with an aim to assist helpless orphans and widows. This was done to raise funds as the subscriptions from members were not sufficient to run the organization. Apart from saris from Dhaka and Santipur and handicrafts from Krishnanagar and Birbhum, there was a large collection of handicrafts from outside Bengal—Kashmir, Moradabad, Varanasi, Agra, Jaipur and Mumbai. Swarnakumari Devi's objective was to display indigenous products and sell them. The fair was quite a sensation in her days.

54

SRI SITA DEVI

Chapter 41 offers a note on the author.

The Duties of Women as Citizens (1931)

Even a few years ago, none in our country thought that other than their household duties women could have any work to do in the outside world. But nowadays, women are venturing into different activities and are successful in almost all of them, so our expectations from women are increasing day by day. Thoughtful people are acknowledging the fact that in social, civic and national issues, their help is needed. Although antagonism remains, it will continue till the time women do all this work successfully and show others that they are capable. To prove their capability, it is necessary in the first place to give them good and proper education and free them from the imprisonment of the purdah. Child marriage is now a punishable offence in the eyes of law, therefore, it can be hoped that we do not have to fall behind because of this abominable practice.[1] Although a fourteen-year-old girl is still not suitable for being a wife and mother, there has been some changes, which is better than none at all.

The women of Bengal have participated in social work, although their numbers are few. In recent times, they have been participating in large numbers with full encouragement on national issues, and have gained a considerably good reputation. This proves that they are able to work; in some cases, they are more suitable than men. They are by nature peace-loving as well as non-violent, so there is no chance of them causing any disturbance. Apart from this, they are not in the habit of leaving one job undone and running after another, their minds generally move in a linear direction. They rarely indulge in rumour-mongering. For all these reasons, they are especially suitable for non-violent nationalist work.

It is now important for women to participate in civic matters. In this regard, not much has been done by women until now. In Bengal, only one or two women's names are heard in this context, but they too, have not done much. Dr. Muthulakshmi Reddi[2] of Madras has written an article on this topic in a magazine named *Streedharma*. According to her, women are eminently suitable for civic work. They are accustomed to familial discipline and taking care of little children, old and disabled people. For these reasons, in order to implement the laws which are formed to safeguard these feeble and helpless people, help from the womenfolk is especially necessary. There are several laws for women and children, for instance, the Children Act,[3] Act regarding Child Marriage, Act against Prostitution, and so on.[4] If these laws are to be suitably used, then help from women themselves as well as from female law-enforcers is necessary. At first, people might be surprised on hearing this, because this proposal is novel. But then when women entered the medical or nursing or legal professions, there were many disagreements regarding this matter. Now, however, their value is recognized by all and nobody even thinks of removing them from these areas. For women criminals and young criminals, the employment of women police is absolutely necessary. In order to do justice to those women who are accused of several kinds of crimes, especially physical sins (prostitution), help from women is a special necessity. The anguish and misery of a woman can be best understood by another woman and criminals can confess all to them without any qualms.

Not many people know that women are employed in the police force in countries like England, Germany and Austria among others and they perform their duties ably. They are known as assistant police in Austria and they are given responsibility of young criminals. Apart from this, they take the evidence of women criminals, accompany them to the police station, keep an eye on little children so that they do not beg or smoke, investigate brothels and examine those women who are involved in the flesh trade. From the reports of the Austrian police, it is found that twenty-seven women work for the police force.

In the welfare department, the police chief wants to employ thirteen more women, since he is much in favour of women police. There are groups of people in every country who traffic in women. These assistant policewomen fight against such immorality. They are responsible for immature beggars and juvenile criminals whose health and morality are both adversely affected. They always stay with these criminals, are present when a woman testifies, and try to rescue drunken women. They try to save those women who suffer from the oppression of their drunken husbands. They work as wardresses in prisons and look after the police juvenile homes and hostels for women and girls.

Recently, a proposal for employing women police in the Liverpool municipality has been accepted. In favour of the proposal, it is reasoned that in order to help men and women, women police need to be employed by the police department.

I am not saying that women should be employed as police constables in the Indian police department at this very moment. It is now necessary to have well-educated women experienced in social reforms in this department. Those nurses who work as health inspectors can work here. Lady doctors too are necessary in this case. At times, it is necessary to examine girls in order to determine their age, and for other reasons too, women criminals and those women who lodge complaints have to be physically examined. All this should be done by lady doctors.

All laws should be used in such a way that the weak and the poor are not persecuted. The rich, most of the time, do not have to take refuge in law, and it does not matter to them at all even if they are threatened with strict laws. Many a time, the implementation of those very laws which are created to safeguard the weak and the helpless people leads to the ill treatment of the poor and the helpless. Often women criminals are unnecessarily mistreated. In these cases, the dishonoured women need help. Thus some women should be officially employed by the police department, or else they should have special powers in their hands. Women are not always arrested for involvement in sinful work or crimes. Highly educated women and women from respectable families too are arrested for national causes and are sent to prison. It will be a great mistake if the common police are given responsibility for them. Owing to this they are dishonoured in many cases.

The police in England are famous and said to be the best in the world, and now they too are frequently proposing to recruit women. Policemen might be efficient, but when it comes to matters regarding women criminals, they are not as suitable as women. In the judicial department, many women are working as jury members; in our country too, women are working as freelance magistrates. Crimes are committed by both men and women. Therefore, to render equal service to both sides, there should be equal representation in the legislative and judicial areas.

I have mentioned earlier the reasons behind the necessity for women doctors in the police department. Prostitutes and criminal women, too, might not want to be tested by men. It will be inhuman oppression to force them in this regard. A famous women's organization met the police commissioner of Vienna about this matter. They said that it was necessary that the police department should have more women. The police commissioner gave sympathetic consideration to their petition.

Women are best suited for taking the responsibility of maintaining a less exploitative society and rescuing prostitutes. The laws regarding eradication of prostitution and rescuing minor girls give the police the right to enter the rooms of prostitutes to search for minor girls. The permission of the police commissioner in this regard is enough. But when they are to enter these types of houses and search for the girls, then it is necessary that the women police or freelance women workers go with them. In the Madras Municipal Committee, much effort was made to get a bill sanctioned (on this matter), but the home member opposed it, citing reasons like lack of money and lack of women workers.

The educated and enlightened women of all the provinces should try to safeguard all types of rights pertaining to women. They can function as freelance workers till such time as suitable paid workers are available. Nagarik Hitashadhika Mandali or Women's Committees for the Welfare of Citizens should be started in all big cities. They are to keep an eye on the suitable implementation of the laws meant to safeguard women. They should also keep an eye on whether laws made for the minors are being suitably implemented or not. But for gaining this special power they should apply to the government. However, that should not be very tough. In Calcutta, this special power has been given to the representatives of the organization which works against cruelty towards animals. It is necessary to be watchful so that a human being is not in a condition worse than an animal's.

This is how civic duties should be performed with the help of legalized aid. Needless to say, legal help is necessary for checking corruption and redressing oppression. It is because those who are engaged in corruption are only interested in their own selfish needs. Hence, they are not going to heed anybody. In that case, the *hitashadhika* or the women who desire the welfare of the citizens should work with help from the law. But there are many other things which the volunteers can do by themselves, without taking help from the legal department. They can go from door to door and give advice on cleanliness, instructions on not to dump garbage in front of the main door or in the back alley, take suitable action so that the germs of contagious diseases do not spread, and so on. The women of our country do have some duties apart from the household ones—duties as citizens—but this cannot be easily understood by them. They might keep their houses neat and clean, but may well dump the garbage in front of someone else's house. They are responsible for spreading the germs of contagious diseases to a large extent. Very few women know how to clean a patient's bedding and clothes, how to clean the dirt and garbage of the patient's room. Sometimes they do not even remember that if they throw a banana skin on the road, someone might slip and fall. When travelling in a train or a steamer, other passengers get extremely harassed by the uneducated, uncivilized behaviour of these women.[5] Schools and colleges do not educate students on these matters, so some other measures must be taken. If pictures are printed through magic lanterns and lectures are given, then it might work. Much instruction must be given on taking care of children's health as well as the mother's health. There is a severe shortage of orphanages, homes for the distressed, and homes for the prostitutes in our country. Women should take the responsibility of creating these things. It is mainly their work to take care of the poor and the needy. In a family a woman holds the place of the benevolent mother and sister, a similar thing should happen in case of the city and the nation. They should come forward by themselves in this regard, without waiting for anyone else.

Translated by Debarati Chakrabarty
Department of Comparative Literature, Jadavpur University

'Narir Nagarik Dayitva', Bangalakshmi, mid-June to mid-July 1931/ Asarh 1338 BS, barsha 6 (year 6), sankhya 8 (no. 8), pp. 632–34.

Notes

[1] Child Marriage Restraint Act, 1929, popularly known as the Sarda Act after its sponsor Rai Sahib Harbilas Sarda was passed on 28 September

1929 by the British Indian Government. It fixed the age of marriage for girls at fourteen and boys at eighteen. It came into effect six months later on 1 April 1930 and it applied to all of British India, not just the Hindus. It was a result of the social reform movement in India.

2 *Streedharma* is ascribed to Dr. Muthulakshmi Reddi. Muthulakshmi Reddi (30 July 1886 Madras) was an eminent medical practitioner, social reformer and awarded the Padma Bhushan. She was the first woman legislator in India. She was appointed to the Madras Legislative Council in 1927. She was the first girl student to be admitted into a Men's College, the first woman house surgeon in the Government Maternity and Ophthalmic Hospital, the first woman legislator in British India, the first chairperson of the State Social Welfare Advisory Board and the first woman deputy president of the Legislative Council and the first Alderwoman of the Madras Corporation Avvai home.

3 The Maternity Benefit Act was passed in Bombay in 1929, but not until 1939 in Bengal. Nothing named the 'children act' can be found. There are details about the law on prostitution from the Hindu perspective in Essay 55. For details on the Children Marriage Act, see n 1.

4 Women were rarely allowed in public, hence their behaviour was allegedly not proper as they did not know the social forms of politesse or have the confidence that comes with education. Lower class women were visible and mobile, but their behaviour was seen as improper. The writer is being self-critical for a female audience, attempting to alert her readers to the consequences of their lack of education. The educated bhadralok who had middle-class standards, influenced by western modernity and education, seems to be the model for the women citizen.

5 In the original article, the term 'Sri' precedes her name. B.A. is appended to the writer's name.

55

KAMALA MUKHOPADHYAY

Kamala Mukhopadhyay (1913–2005) actively participated in the anti-British movements, right from her days in school. At the request of her older sister Tapasbala, who was a student at the Bethune School where a strike was observed to mark the dissatisfaction with the Simon Commission, Kamala, a student of Class 9, gathered the students of the Anandamayee School and observed a similar strike. In 1929, she was admitted to Scottish Church College and participated ardently in all political activities, including the Satyagraha movement. In 1931, after the murder of Stevens[1] when many women were arrested, Kamala also was put behind bars. She was the first put in the Siuri Jail before being moved to the Hijli Jail. After her release around 1938, she took upon the responsibility of editing the women's journal, *Mandira*. She became a member of the Communist Party in 1938. In 1943, she was selected as the leader of the Mahila Atmaraksha Samiti,[2] which carried out relief work during the Bengal Famine.

Law Eradicating the Profession of Prostitution (1933)

Not a long time ago, I asked an important gentleman who recently arrived from Bengal, 'Sir, there are so many educated and good women singers in Calcutta, so why does the radio play gramophone records of the songs of only two or four women? The women of our country too, just like American women, earn money for themselves as well as work for the country by lecturing, telling stories and singing.' To this he replied, 'You don't understand the situation in our country—those women whose songs and music are broadcast from Calcutta are all prostitutes. As a result, the women from respectable households can't visit the studio and perform their songs and music.' When I disagreed with him, he said that if the arrangements were such that the prostitutes and the girls from respectable families do not come into contact with one another, then the educated girls might go there and perform their songs and music. The gentleman was 'enlightened', and had stayed for a long time in foreign countries, he had heard of the several vices of the West, but he still retained the same mentality. Gentlewomen and prostitutes are not to stay under the same roof, let alone talk to each other for a few minutes. But if one delves deep into this matter, then one realizes that to some extent the cause of the downfall of these fallen women are these very gentlemen.

A few days ago, I noticed a great uproar in the daily newspapers and the monthly magazines of the country in favour of the eradication of the profession of prostitution. Everybody seems to be in favour of this movement, none against it. While reading the lectures delivered by the leading social reformers of Bengal one realizes that the time is ripe for the actual cleansing of our own houses. We do not want to forget the errors and vices of the society, nor do we want to leave them alone, we truly want to cleanse society inside out. In a newspaper, I saw that in the city of Calcutta alone there are 53,000 Hindu, 5,000 Muslim, 300 Japanese, Chinese, European, Jewish and Armenian prostitutes. Isn't the number of prostitutes large in proportion to the population of the city? If a law about the eradication of prostitution is implemented, then what is going to happen to them, and what is to be their position in society: these are some of the questions that came to my mind, and I cannot but write a few words regarding this matter.

Among the 58,300 prostitutes in the city of Calcutta, my primary concern is about the 53,000 Hindu prostitutes. The reason is not because I am Hindu myself; but because it is a problem for them. The other 5,300 do not face such a great problem because I believe that their social laws are more generous in comparison to the Hindu social laws. If the law regarding the eradication of prostitution is passed, then liberal Muslim society perhaps will not give a second thought before giving the 5,000 unfortunate women a place in the society. The Muslims are liberal in these kinds of matters, and they do not harbour the fear of being made outcastes, neither do they fear going to hell for such matters, therefore, I think that there might be something that can be done and arrangements made for the Muslim prostitutes. And for the remaining 300 prostitutes from various other countries, they too can secure some place or the other in their respective communities, and hence it is not that much of a problem in their case either.

In Bengal, the Muslim population is greater in number than the Hindu, but if in the city of Calcutta alone there are about 53,000 Hindu prostitutes, then their number (in comparison to the Muslims) in the whole of Bengal can easily be guessed. Who are these Hindu prostitutes? Are they different from any other woman in any other society? Aren't they like any other woman with regard to their birth, physical features, inclinations, hopes and desires, tenderness and love? The reasons behind the greater number of Hindu prostitutes in comparison to their Muslim counterparts could be due to three major reasons—child widowhood, accidental degradation and poverty. In other societies the women might be severely punished for these reasons but once they fall[3] they are not cast out of society; if they still want to lead a decent life in society, then society does not push them away. But that is never possible in a Hindu society. Someone who has done wrong even once is not forgiven by society. The Hindus will address the women as mother in their religious books and scriptures—but they are not going to forgive this mother. The woman becomes a worm from hell, but the person who is responsible for pushing her onto this path may well be (or become) a great leader in society! He is hailed by shouts of triumph everywhere; and innumerable garlands of victory are seen to be hanging around his neck.

Let it be—I do not have the courage to speak about the prostitutes of Bengal, let alone India, they are uncountable in number. I am thinking about the 53,000 unfortunate women in some dark corners of Calcutta. If these 53,000 'women soldiers' are forced to stop their 'business' because of the law, then what are they going to do? How are the food, clothing and shelter of these 53,000 women to be arranged, and who is going to do what is necessary for them? This responsibility is not for one day or for one month; but for many days. Where will the Hindu accommodate these women? What will be the arrangement? Many people doubt that it is possible to remove all the prostitutes from society by making laws. This problem exists in no uncertain terms in the West. They too have been and are still thinking about this problem. True, prostitution has been termed illegal and has been [legally] stopped in many countries, but in reality, prostitution has not stopped, and according to many, it has increased. In this regard, I cannot help but say a little about America. All across America, there was a great agitation to make laws against alcohol and the profession of prostitution and later such a law was passed.[4] Therefore, legally, there should be no alcohol and prostitutes in that country. But if anyone wants either one of these or both, there is no dearth of them, rather they are found in sufficient quantity—this fact cannot be denied by anyone. This situation can be seen in any small or big town in America. In many towns, several neighbourhoods, irrespective of [the inhabitants being] black or white, are immersed in this 'profession'. Although in many towns there are no 'prostitute localities' as there used to be in the past, now they are scattered in such a way that they can be found by those who want them. The evidence can be found in the streets and cinemas. Many people might wonder why, in a country like America where women are not cast out of society time and again, and have ample opportunities to earn an honest living, there are so many prostitutes. This question is hard to answer, but looking around me I think that those women who are in that profession are there because of the fascination for affluence and because of the hardships of poverty rather than their own free will. Apart from this, in India, those who have money have more than enough; and this class of people are few in number—those who do not have money are greater in number, although the fascination and desire for wealth is there on either side.[5] In order to fulfil this need, one is forced to earn some 'extra' money without any shame.

In this country, a decent living is becoming impossible for common people as time passes. The poor are becoming poorer day by day; and during periods of unemployment, like this year, the rich are not willing to spend their money as they used to do earlier. Therefore, it can be seen that society is not doing enough for these uneducated, barely educated and half-educated women. The law tells them to 'be good' but they are not able to be so because society is not able to provide the women with essentials, like food, warm clothes, powder, rouge, cream, a warm room, furniture and other things; therefore, they are forced to explore other routes. This profession is abominable, but its essential requirements include nothing other than beauty and youth ... The police and the common people know how to abide by the national religion, that is, they love to take bribes, and as a result, this profession is gradually increasing with little or no resistance at all. But no one should think that these women are evading the law while they continue to carry on this profession. That is not wholly true, sometimes the police catch them in earnest ... They are punished according to their age and the degree of the crime. Those who are young are sent to the 'Reformatory' and are given education according to their respective taste so that in future they are able to earn sufficiently for themselves. Apart from this, there are several women's welfare organizations which educate these women in various things, but it is unfortunate that these are not sufficient in number.

In America women have equal opportunity. If they wish, they can work in many places where men do, and they can claim their place in society, but still they do not do any such thing! Therefore, I wonder whether it is possible to remove all the prostitutes from our society all of a sudden! Although it may not be possible to remove all, what problem can there be in giving the woman the right, if she wishes, to earn a living independently or to marry? I understand perfectly that there is a great stigma attached to these women and that the men are, to a large extent, responsible for this, but again, I was thinking about the law. What is going to be the result of this law? If it is really possible to reform all the prostitutes , then I would be overjoyed, but we still have not learnt to forgive the 53,000 prostitutes in Calcutta, whom we have given no opportunity to become good, whom we did not educate when there was still time. If today, all of a sudden, by implementing some laws, we stop the only means of livelihood of those whom we have taught nothing but how to be prostitutes, then, I wonder, where will they go? How will they survive? Again, I wonder how many men in Hindu society will be willing to marry a prostitute and raise a family. Or, suppose these women stop being prostitutes and earn their livelihood as daily maids working in houses: are we going to accept prostitutes (working) in our houses? One should not think that I do not want prostitutes integrated into society. I want this to happen and because of this I eagerly ask the social reformers, can we not forgive these women? If we do not forgive them then what is going to happen to them? And, if nothing can be done for them then what use will this law be?

Social reform is no doubt needed, and everyone wants that this law should eradicate this profession, but what happens after that? Will the Hindus still stick to their orthodox stance and keep them away, or will they give these women the right to be equal with the others? The Muslims never cast out a member of their own religion from society; therefore, perhaps the Muslim women will not lack a place in society, but where is the place of these women in Hindu society? There is a special necessity for a change in mentality in Hindu society, otherwise these sorts of reforms would not do any good to society. Rather, in many cases, they would promote evil. If Hindu society wants to remove all the prostitutes, then it too will have to be more generous, more fair and reasonable, and more forgiving. If this profession is stopped only by implementing laws, while these women are not provided for by society, then I think social promiscuity will increase rather than decrease. Society will be engulfed by perversity and ugly disease.

But should this law be suspended? Never, and besides, arrangements should be such that other laws to reform society could be made. The problem is great, the solution is even a greater problem, and this cannot be done in one day. The faster this law is passed, the better it is for society, but simultaneously, social and mental change among the Hindus is more necessary. Not only should this be propagated by speech and writings, but also brilliant examples should be set by working for this cause. We should first understand that we wish to cleanse our house of filth and this should be shown through deeds. We must realize that education rather than any law is necessary to keep women within the bounds of their social roles, and it is this education, and not law, that will enable a woman to choose a suitable place for herself.

Translated by Debarati Chakraborty
Department of Comparative Literature, Jadavpur University

'Bar-Banita-Britti Daman Ain', *Jayasree*, mid-March to Mid-April 1933/ Chaitra 1339 BS.

Also in *Pather Ingit: Nirbachita Samvad-Samayikpatre Bangali Meyer Samajbhavna: 1927-1967*, edited by Sarmistha Dutta Gupta (Kolkata: Stree, 2007), pp. 219–23.

Notes

1 Mr. C.G.B. Stevens, District Magistrate and Collector of Comilla (East Bengal), was shot dead on 14 December 1931, by two Bengali girls (thirteen years old) Shanti Ghosh and Suniti Chowdhury of Comilla.

2 Literally means women's self-defence, it was founded in 1942. The members were predominantly communist women. In 1942, the year of the Great Famine, the organization's main activity was to mobilize women to demand food for the famine-affected people.

3 'Fall' is the literal translation of the Bengali word used to describe an

encounter that may be construed as sexual. It would generally suggest the loss of virginity, but what exactly that may connote to people of different groups and classes appears, at least from literary evidence, is fluid. The description 'fallen woman' in this context was commonly used.

4 There was a national ban on the sale, production and transportation of alcohol, in place from 1920 to 1933. The dry movement (Prohibition) was led by rural Protestants in both political parties, and the ban was mandated by the Eighteenth Amendment to the Constitution.

5 The word used is 'shaukh': which captures the subtlety of both desire and fascination, translating generally into 'inclination', which seems to be too mechanical here.

56

SUDHAMOYEE DEVI

Starting her education at Shantiniketan in 1917, Sudhamoyee Devi (1896–1982) completed her B.A. from Bethune College. She was married to Prabhat Kumar Mukhopadhyay, the biographer of Rabindranath Tagore. She was also the founder of the Bolpur Girls' High School and its principal from 1935–54. Amongst her major literary achievements is the publication of the *Rabindra Rachanar Ingreji Anubad-Suchi (Kabita o Gan)* in the form of a book. She also translated many songs written by Tagore into English.

Birth Control (1933)

For some time now, in this country we have been debating on the issue of birth control and its importance. It is natural for women to think more about this because it is essentially a matter concerning women, though, indirectly, it applies to the entire nation. There is need for birth control—first, from the perspective of health; second, education; and third, economics.

Needless to say, a mother's health suffers serious setbacks if she gives birth to too many children. In our country we do not seem to be much concerned about the mother's health. . . . The physical strength that a mother needs to give birth to a child takes a long time to be replenished. If she has to give birth to another child before she regains that strength, it is like being tortured, and affects the child as well. Would it be possible for that child to be born healthy? Moreover, the mother needs to give time and attention or the proper care of the (unhealthy) baby. When there are short intervals between the births of siblings, whose needs will the mother fulfil and give priority? In addition there are family duties. A mother, who can properly take care of all her household responsibilities, after taking care of her babies, deserves great praise for her stamina. But it is very tough for most mothers to maintain such a balance. In such cases, children suffer the most. They do not get timely food and baths, let alone the mother's affection. Besides, owing to her fatigue and consequent lapse in concentration, the mother is unable to inculcate good habits in the child from a tender age. ... whatever she does with the child is often done in haste. As a result, often a relation of disrespect and obstinacy develops between the mother and the child ... A mother who wants to do justice to both family and childcare often puts such strain on both her health and mind that it becomes difficult for her to survive for long. ... Those who remain live with fragile health, only increasing the burden on the family. Every day numerous such instances occur before our eyes, yet we refuse to see them. Several children need basic education and the ambience of the home to gain lessons of courtesy and etiquette, ethics and morality from the parents which can be attained by developing a close mother–child relationship based on dialogue ...

It is the duty of the parents to decide the number of babies they would like to have depending on their financial strength. Else, it will be an injustice towards the children. We have already mentioned that lack of proper care is harmful for both the child and the mother's health. Also, mother needs leisure, both physically and mentally, for the proper education of her children. In middle class or poor families, such leisure for mothers is hardly available. Not everyone can afford domestic help. Responsibility for all domestic chores falls upon the woman of the house. Besides, there is the responsibility of her children's education and well-being. So, it is virtually impossible for her to perform all her duties properly if there are too many children. Apart from this, looking after the husband and his entertainment is another duty of the woman of the house. ... The husband after returning from his day's work, expects uninterrupted peace of mind and happiness, care and companionship of the woman. A chaotic house makes the man's heart turn against his home and he starts visiting other places for entertainment. Old age catches the woman quite early in life in the absence of leisure for youthful enjoyments.

Keeping in mind all these disturbances and the limitations of money, many men these days are averse to the idea of marriage. ... The darker side of marriage also comes to the fore for several educated women. This disturbing situation may be managed through birth control.

God has bestowed humans with something called intellect. That people will be guided by the blind forces of nature is not God's will. It is the duty of every couple to give birth to only that many children as they can take proper care of without any financial or other problems.

It is a gross mistake to assume that financial strength gives one the license to have as many children as one wants. It is true that a rich person can afford to employ servants who can also take care of the children. But is giving birth to many children such an easy affair? Despite all the comforts of a rich household, it requires a long time to regain the strength that one loses in the process of giving birth to a child. Hence, in several instances, we see that even a rich person's family goes wayward as the health of the woman breaks down after giving birth to several children.

It is equally true that none has the right to decide on not having any having child merely to protect one's selfish interests and suit one's convenience. We should not forget that marriage is a social affair; the primary objective of marriage is procreation. It is the duty of every couple to gift society with good children.

It is important that the couple have deep respect and love for each other. Only then can the children be good and virtuous. . . . raising the issue of divorce on every pretext is very disturbing for society. Divorce does not seem to be a good option when a couple has one or two children. The couple can restrain themselves and not express their problems before the children. . . . and other members of the family. A temporary separation often helps in wiping out the differences between the two.

It is not a bad idea to delay taking up the responsibility of children for a certain period after marriage. This time may be utilized by the couple to assess the honesty and depth of love towards each other. It is very common that immediately after marriage, the couple has a tremendous desire to be with each other as much as possible. This desire eases out with time. If the woman has to take the responsibility of children before that period has passed, it often disturbs the man, unconsciously creating a distance between them. Often this leads to broaching the question of divorce, there is an . . . inability to understand each other's circumstances and mental states. So, it is not a matter of pride to allow the question of divorce to surface so easily. Rather, it is important to sort out the reasons for such temporary conflicts and arrive at solutions.

It is really dangerous for the society to allow divorce on petty issues. But one should have the right to opt for divorce if there are no children and one finds something wrong in the other person's character. These days it is absurd to think that the wife will have to worship the husband even if he has a bad character. But it is important to be certain enough before openly opting for divorce. One should give the other person the time and chance to rectify the faults. Under no circumstance is divorce a joyful outcome. If there are already one or two children, divorce sets a very bad example before them. In that case, both the husband and the wife have the right not to stay with each other until the other person sets things right. Perhaps this could also reduce adultery? ...

Even without discussing divorce at great length, we can conclude that birth control should remain in our own hands. ... controlling creation according to need is not wrong.

Many fear that laws about birth control will result in gross licentiousness in the society. No one has so far been able to rid society of licentiousness. Are those lower-class people, who know nothing about birth control, less licentious? They, on the contrary, take even worse measures and engage in grotesque deeds. It is the innocent children who suffer the most in the absence of birth control laws. ... If we really want to curb licentiousness, it is important to search for means to restrict people's desire to commit adultery through education, efforts to increase work opportunities and work force, and channelizing people's minds towards different avenues.

If parents or elders discuss the importance of the practice of restraint as well as the beauty of sexual union with adolescents, it might help in solving several critical problems easily. If young boys and girls realize by themselves what harm the abuse of this union may cause to their own health as well as to society, there will perhaps be no need for stricter codes to restrict licentiousness. In order to cure the disease, it is better to treat it internally and not keep one's attention restricted to the external injury.

Translated by Suvradip Dasgupta
Department of Comparative Literature, Jadavpur University

'Janma-shasan', Jayasree, mid-March to mid-April 1933/Chaitra 1339 BS.

Also in *Pather Ingit: Nirbachita Samvad-Samayikpatre Bangali Meyer Samajbhavna: 1927-1967,* edited by Sarmistha Dutta Gupta (Kolkata: Stree, 2007), pp. 225–29.

57

BEGUM SHAMSUN NAHAR

Though primarily tutored at home, Shamsun Nahar Mahmud (1908–1964) successfully completed her B.A. in 1932 and M.A. in 1942. She was largely involved with issues concerning women throughout her life. In 1935, the British passed the Government of India Act. Women had no voting rights. Shamsun Nahar Mahmud was one of the chief pioneers who on behalf of the Nikhil Bharat Mahila Andolan principally struggled for the voting rights of women. In 1939, she was the head of the department of Bengali at Lady Brabourne College. In 1933, under a dual editorship with her brother Habibullah Bahar, Nahar published a magazine called *Bulbul*. Post-Partition, she went to Dhaka and joined the All Pakistan Women's Association.

Political Rights of Women (1935)

It is very fortunate that the political rights of women have been acknowledged to a small extent in the forthcoming amendment.[1] The women of this country are awakening—they are moving forward on the road to progress. In this journey forward, at a time when the mind is split between hope and joy on the one hand and fear and doubt on the other, this new administrative amendment has created a new chapter in the history of our awakening.

There is widespread awareness amongst us, but still we have to admit that in matters concerning education and social affairs, we have miles to go. Where matters relating to education happen to be in such a sorry state, it cannot be hoped that women will be aware of their political rights. One cannot say that we have thought about our rights and responsibilities regarding the governance of the country deeply. Despite this we have got the rights that are due to us.

In this regard, I thank our providence when I think about the women of England. Their free way of life is perhaps something that many women desire. But we are astonished when we hear that they had to strive so hard even to gain those rights that we have got so easily. It is not yet twenty years since they have gained the primary political right: the right to vote . . .

From the mid-nineteenth century, a group of Englishmen and women started an agitation for voting rights. Slowly this agitation spread throughout Britain. Many groups organized various types of movements and several associations were built throughout the country. The signatures of thousands of women were collected and an application was sent to Parliament. Among the women who signed were famous women like Miss Florence Nightingale[2] and Miss Mary Carpenter.[3] But the amazing fact is that nothing came of these associations and meetings and applications. The granting of voting rights to English women still did not seem imminent.

Gradually, another group was formed which thought that they would force the attention of the government towards them by violating laws and disrupting peace in any way possible, or else their goals would not be fulfilled. Therefore, they disobeyed the government's laws and tried to create unrest and disquiet throughout the country. Groups of women were imprisoned. There, too, they did not let the authorities rest in peace—they went on hunger strikes, disobeyed laws and embarrassed the authorities relentlessly. Sometimes it was felt that this might succeed. But several times the bill regarding the voting rights of women (came up but) was not passed by Parliament because men, apart from a very few, were all against it. The thought that women would have equal rights with men regarding matters of nation and politics was unbearable to them. Starting from Gladstone[4] including Lord Curzon,[5] Lord Birkenhead,[6] Lord Asquith[7] and several famous politicians—all were against this bill. At last women emerged victorious; in 1918, English women gained voting rights. The overall victory was achieved in 1928. In this year, they were given equal rights in voting like their male counterparts. For this outcome they had suffered day after day, made many sacrifices.

One or two matters are worth mentioning in the history of their struggle for rights. First they had to fight for these. Second, they were not disheartened by failure . . . it is our good fortune and a matter of joy that the rights, which were gained by the Englishwomen with such difficulty were obtained by Indian women without much endeavour.

The women of India have only recently gained voting rights; now they have the power to participate in matters concerning the nation-state.[8] But the struggle is not yet over. In this matter, we have something to say regarding the women of Bengal. Political rights depend on various eligibilities [which form the criteria for voting]. We see that wives, whose husbands have voting rights can vote too, and so can the women who have property in their name. The upcoming constitutional amendment has lessened the amount of property required (for eligibility to vote)than that prescribed presently by law.[9]

Apart from gaining voting rights through property-related matters, the eligibility criteria for voting has been extended in other areas too. Women can have voting rights by dint of their education. There seems to be some discrepancy, however, between the women of Bengal and other provinces regarding this eligibility through education. Women from provinces like Madras and other places are eligible to vote if they can just read and write, but for the women of Bengal and two or three other provinces, the standard of eligibility has been raised further. It has been settled that they will not be able to vote unless they have passed the Matriculation, which displeases them. Among them are Hindu and Muslim women who have made further progress in education and experience than many women who hold university degrees. But they are unable to cross the demarcation line of the Matriculation because of lack of opportunity. Though for some women of this group, the primary goal of their life is women's education and movements for their progress, owing to such an arrangement they are unable to have voting rights based on their educational qualifications!

But the women of Bengal are not indifferent to this significant matter. Numerous protests through associations and meetings were conducted. Different Hindu and Muslim women's associations even petitioned together in the court of the Indian councillor in England.[10] Therefore, it has been settled that after implementing the new constitutional amendment from the second election onwards, the educational qualification would be lowered, and those who could read and write could vote.

Besides this, there are complaints from the women of Bengal which are more serious in nature. In the *Bangiya Byabasthapok Sabha*,[11] there are only five seats for women—one for Anglo-Indian, two Muslims and two Hindus. The approximate number of councils in Bengal is nearly 250. Although the number of councils in Bombay and Madras are fewer than in Bengal, the number of women's seats there are eight and six, respectively. The political rights of women have been acknowledged in the new constitutional amendment made by the government, thereby showing its open mindedness, but undoubtedly justice has been gravely flawed in the case of reservation of women's seats in Bengal.

This injustice reached its peak on matters regarding seat division. It has been decided that among the four Hindu and Muslim seats of the Bengal Council, there will be two constituencies—one in the city of Calcutta, the other cities being Dhaka and Narayangunj. As a result, the whole of Bengal, apart from Calcutta, Dhaka and Narayangunj will lack the advantage of the rights granted to women by the impending constitutional amendment.

Responding to these complaints, the authorities say if the constituencies are spread beyond Calcutta, Dhaka and Narayangunj, they will be very large and it will be impossible to carry out the election procedure. But depending solely on this pretext, it is meaningless to deprive all the women voters of Bengal of their fundamental rights.

One remembers a funny story in this regard. The renowned scientist, Newton, once received a small rabbit from one of his friends as a gift. He used to keep rabbits as pets. But incidentally, all of them were bigger than the new one. While contemplating about where the new rabbit should stay, he thought that the entrance of the cage where the bigger rabbits stay is big, so the new rabbit will need a smaller entrance. Therefore, the existing cage will not do. How will the small one pass through the door that was meant for the bigger ones! The mind which solved many complex scientific problems effortlessly was not able to find a solution to this problem!

In this world so full of diversity, there is no dearth of funny things. The same happened in this case of voting rights of Bengali women. There has been a great commotion among the powerful heads of the British empire regarding the Indian political amendment, but no one had any solutions about how the unfortunate women of Bengal could enjoy their justified rights equally with men. The entire political machinery of this country has become topsy-turvy—numerous complex problems have been solved; despite having so many brilliant minds with a vast knowledge on diverse election procedures it was impossible to fashion some sort of arrangement (to enable) the women of Bengal (to vote)!

The only thing that the women of Bengal now trust is the Hammond Committee.[12] It is not wrong to assume that they will do provide the required justice and help women's education and progress. Otherwise, the voting rights will have no meaning for the women of Bengal. When women in every part of the country will be able to express their views in political matters, a new era will begin in the history of the country.

Translated by Debarati Chakraborty
Department of Comparative Literature, Jadavpur University

'Narir Rashtranaitik Adhikar', *Saogat*, mid-October to mid-November 1935/Kartik 1342 BS.

Also in *Pather Ingit: Nirbachita Samvad-Samayikpatre Bangali Meyer Samajbhavna: 1927-1967*, edited by Sarmistha Dutta Gupta (Kolkata: Stree, 2007), pp. 154-57.

Notes

1 The writer perhaps is referring to the Government of India Act 1935.

2 A celebrated British social reformer and statistician, and the founder of modern nursing; she came to prominence while serving as a nurse during the Crimean War.

3 An English educational and social reformer, Carpenter publicly supported women's suffrage in her later years and also campaigned for women's access to higher education.

4 William Ewart Gladstone (29 December 1809–19 May 1898), was a British liberal statesman. In a career lasting over 60 years, he served as Prime Minister four times (1868–74, 1880–85, February–July 1886 and 1892–94), a record.

5 A British conservative statesman who was Viceroy of India (1899–1905) and foreign secretary.

6 He was the Secretary of State (1924–28), a post created after 1858. The Secretary of State was the political head of the India government.

7 He was the Prime Minister of Britain (1914–18). Though he opposed women's suffrage, later, when he was forced into a coalition government with pro-suffrage conservatives, he had to support women's suffrage in 1917.

[8] In 1919, Indian women got the right to vote. This was implemented in the Madras and Bombay presidencies by 1921, the United Provinces in 1923, Punjab and Bengal and Assam in 1926, Central Provinces, Bihar and Orissa in 1930.

[9] For details on what is prescribed by law, see Essay 46.

[10] Probably V.K. Krishna Menon, member of the Commonwealth of India League, Labour Councillor for the Borough of St. Pancras from 1934–39 and again from 1939 and from 1944–47; he was also the independent councillor from 1940–44.

[11] Bengal Legislative Assembly, following from the Government of India Act, 1935.

[12] The delimitation committee was chaired by Sir Lauri Hammond (1935) and the report was presented in three volumes.

58

SALMA RAUSHAN-JAHAN

We are unable to find any biographical details of this author.

What We Have to Say (1936)

The article 'Indian Muslims' was quite good as are Mr. Lilamoy Roy's writings generally.[1] His discussions are so clear and the way he puts them forward attracts us and makes us want to know him. But why does Mr. Roy avoid problems easily? Had an equal proportion of good intention been added to his knowledge and his intelligence, then the beautiful pages of Bengali literature would not have been filled completely with so many half-truths. His mind is especially that of an elite Hindu. This may be unintentional, but he sees the Hindu–Muslim problem through the eyes of a moderate Hindu. Probably we too, unknowingly, see through the eyes of a Muslim. Yet it seems that he has the capacity to see more if he wants to. When he talks about Muslims, he is looking at only those Muslims who are barbarians intellectually. 'Muslims think they are foreign conquerors like the English.' 'Muslims think of themselves as outsiders, colonial conquerors, and we are all aboriginals, natives conquered in this country.' I found this ridiculous but still did not become angry because it is a part of such a warmly written article. But even for the sake of civility could he not have said 'some Muslims think' instead of 'Muslims think', since in reality only some of the Muslims think, and that too only the office-going Urdu-speaking Muslims? It is difficult to say the same about the other Muslims. Did Mr. Roy totally neglect people like us? To talk about Hindus and Christians in general he has selected the opinions of a few Hindus or Christians.

Likewise, we can also close our eyes and say all Muslims think of India as their own country just as Hindus do. Do I lie completely in that case? Which Hindu loves India more than you or me? According to Mahatma Gandhi's yardstick, Mr. Roy's *Hinduism*[2] does not even survive. Let Mr. Roy answer this—even when someone like Mahatma Gandhi promotes India as 'Hindustan' where in his mind does he place the Muslims? Can we treat Rama as god? We trust him as a good ruler and a calm, dedicated, respectable person. We don't believe in the *Ramayana* as a religious text but see it as an excellent epic. Will Mahatmaji agree to this? It is not our wish that Hindus should perish. But had they vanished, then Mr. Roy believes that Christians would have saved Indian culture and tradition from the hands of the Muslims. I do not oppose his attitude towards the Christians. Christians are talented. But where in the thousand-year history of India did he get this picture of the Muslims? In these thousand years, how many copies of the Vedas and the Vedanta have been burnt to ashes by the Muslims? His idea about today's Muslims is not very clear either. Like blood, Indian culture is enmeshed in the Muslims' every nerve and muscle. Yet why do our appearances seem so different in his eyes? Are Muslims to be solely blamed for thinking of the Hindus as the other? Even a few days back, it was seen that the Sikhs have taken a unique step to save the Harijans from the clutches of the Muslims. Will Moonje embrace Sikhism or does he even believe in the religion?[3] Must a goat be beheaded with a knife even after it has been eaten by a tiger? Mr. Roy might say: This is politics. To us politics is not beyond society. Its current reaches social life. Social life has not been spared. Let me offer an example. My anonymous Hindu female friend fell in love with an anonymous Muslim male friend. My female friend was not underage. My male friend was handsome, well educated and belonged to an elite family who were overt nationalists. But due to a ploy by a powerful nationalist leader of the time my friend had to leave the country. My female friend sacrificed her happiness to remain an Indian!

Whatever the relation is between a Hindu individual and a Muslim person, I want to say something to Mr. Roy, and that is, even if Hindus vanish from this country, one day, their sculpture, paintings and monuments will remain dear to us as cultural heritage. We will not worship idols but will carefully protect them as Indian artifacts –this I firmly believe. We will still read the *Ramayana* and the *Mahabharata* with as much interest as we do today, not as religious texts but as epics.

It is not true that we do not think of Kalidasa[4] as our own: who loves *Meghdoot*,[5] *Shakuntala*[6] more than us?

It is true that our culture, that is, the culture of the Indian Muslims, is somewhat Indo-Iranian and not totally ancient Indian. We love Hafiz.[7] Is it merely because Hafiz is non -Indian? Hafiz talks about our hearts, he is our contentment. Our desires and grief find resonance in Hafiz's verse. That is why Hafiz is so cherished by us. We love *sharab*[8] more than *somrasa*,[9] we love *saki*[10] more than *tambulkarankabahini*.[11] Mr. Roy will have to pardon us for this. It won't harm India; on the contrary, this is essential for the 'diverse flourishing of the national spirit'. We love Kalidasa but enjoy Hafiz a little more because we love him. But we love Tagore more than all of them not merely because he is an Indian. The climate, the water in which the poet's mind bloomed is so much known to us that without mixing Indian philosophy with Tagore's poetry our heart sings out to him: 'How do you sing, you who are endowed with all qualities! We listen enraptured!' We feel proud to call Tagore our own. And then, we do not disrespect Ajanta. Our culture is related to Saracenic architecture like Al Hambra.[12] Can't one look simply at that? Taj Mahal is more precious to us than Al Hambra!

We do not judge common Hindus by the yardstick of the leaders of the Hindu Mahasabha. We request Mr. Lilamoy Roy to expand his vision when talking about Muslims in general. Irrespective of what happens to the Hindu–Muslim problem, will our friendship not sweeten if the vision is expanded?

Translated by Jayeeta Bagchi
Department of Comparative Literature, Jadavpur University

'Amader Katha', *Bulbul*, mid-January to mid-February 1936/Magh 1342 BS, barsha 3 (year 3).

NOTES

1 Annadashankar Ray (1904–2002) wrote under the pseudonym Lilamoy Roy. Born in Dhenkanel district of Odisha, he started his literary career

by writing in Oriya. He was one of the renowned poets belonging to the 'Sabuj' group of Oriya literature. Later he started writing in Bengali and wrote several stories, novels, essays, travelogues, and so on. His first book was *Tarunya* (1928). Among his other famous works are *Agyantabash, Kalankabati, Ratna-o-Srimati, Agun niye khela, Na, Kanya, Rakhi, Basanta,* and so on. He was also famous for his *Rhymes*.

2 This refers to 'Hindu' religious beliefs as opposed to Islam or Christianity, though no single uniform form of belief or practice can be considered to encompass the range of beliefs and practices which are derived from the Vedas or later the *Puranas* and are commonly clubbed together under the misleading term 'Hinduism'. It does not refer to the aggressive brand of brahminical practice that is currently espoused as a political agenda by some parties in present-day India.

3 Dr Ambedkar met Dr B. S. Moonje, spokesman of the Hindu Mahasabha, in Bombay in 1936, and again in Rajgriha, the same year, in June, to discuss the conversion of 'untouchable' Hindus to Sikhism. Moonje and the other Hindu Mahasabha leaders were convinced, but M. Rajah, a leader of the 'untouchables or Harijans, as they were named by Gandhi, decided to inform the Congress about this conversion. The internal debate about this in the Congress and the different opinions expressed regarding both 'untouchables' and conversion were exposed. Moonje proposed that the Hindus would not object to the conversion of 'untouchables' to Sikhism, would support the neo-Sikhs' benefits under the Poona Pact, provided none of them converted to either Christianity or Islam, and the drawing of lower-class coverts to these religions back into the Hindu fold. Ambedkar's correspondence showed that from this conversion to Sikhism, it was economic prosperity rather than political or social benefits that he expected for the depressed classes. Also, if the 'untouchables' converted to Islam or Christianity, they would go out of the fold of Hindu culture completely, which would be difficult for them in terms of adjustment. See D. Keer, *Dr Ambedkar: Life and Mission* (Popular Prakashan, 1990), pp.277–80.

4 Kalidasa (most likely fourth century AD) was a renowned classical Sanskrit writer, widely regarded as the greatest poet and dramatist in the Sanskrit language. His plays and poetry are primarily based on the *Puranas*. According to some scholars, Kalidasa may have lived either near the Himalayas or in the vicinity of Ujjain or in Kalinga. He wrote three plays: *Malavikagni-mitram* (Malavika and Agnimitra), *Abhijnanasakuntalam* (Of Shakuntala Recognized by a Token), *Vikramorvasiyam* (Pertaining to Vikrama and Urvashi), *Abhijnanasakuntalam* being his masterpiece. He

is the author of two epic poems *'Raghuvamsa'* (Dynasty of Raghu) and *'Kumarasambhava'* (Birth of Kumara, narrating the story about the birth of Kartikeya, son of Lord Shiva and his wife Parvati). Among his lyrical poems are: *'Meghdoot'* (Cloud Messenger) and *Ritusamhara* (the Exposition of Seasons).

5 It is the story of a *yaksha* (created by Lord Brahma in a state of extreme anger and in darkness; as a result they were extremely ugly) trying to send a message to his lover through a cloud. Kalidasa set this poem to the *mandrakranta* meter, known for its lyrical sweetness. It is one of Kalidasa's most popular poems and numerous commentaries on the work have been written.

6 *Abhijnanasakuntalam* tells the story of King Dushyanta, who while on a hunting trip meets Shakuntala, the adopted daughter of a sage and marries her. A mishap befalls them when he is summoned back to court. Shakuntala pregnant with their child inadvertently offends a visiting sage and brings on herself a curse by which Dushyanta will forget her completely until he sees the ring he has left with her. On her trip to Dushyanta's court in an advanced state of pregnancy, she loses the ring, and has to come away unrecognized. The ring is found by a fisherman who recognizes the royal seal and returns it to Dushyanta, who regains his memory of Shakuntala and sets out to find her. After more travails, they are finally reunited.

7 A Persian poet of the fourteenth century, Hafiz was very famous in Bengal. His poems were appreciated by many members of the Brahmo Samaj. Among the translations of his works, the most famous ones are '*Divan*' translated in prose form in Bengali by an unknown author in 1893 and in verse form by Girishchandra Sen, named *Hafiz Bachan* in 1898. Among other translations, *Rubait-e-Hafiz* (1930) by Kazi Nazrul Islam and *Rubait-e-Hafiz* (1935) by Kanti Charan Ghosh are famous.

8 Refers to wine.

9 A drink made from some kind of leaf which causes intoxication.

10 The person who pours wine.

11 Women carrying boxes containing paan which are served to the guests.

12 Islamic calendar.

59

ARATI MUKHOPADHYAY

There are two writers of this name both connected to the Tagore family.

(*a*) One married Anandabhushan Mukhopadhyay, who was the son of Swarnakumari Devi's daughter Hiranmayee Devi.
(*b*) The other one was married to Irabati and Nityaranjan Mukhopadhyay's grandson, Arunranjan. Irabati was Saudamini Devi's daughter and thus Hiranmayee Devi's first cousin as their mothers were sisters.

Women's Movement and Educated Women (1938)

Of late, in our country women have also begun to awaken. For this, one should be grateful to the entire women's liberation movement because it has aroused the woman's mind and heart. For many years, women of various provinces in India had allowed themselves to remain powerless and weak under the pressure of social norms; they did not have any value as human beings, nor did they have any identity. Society in those days did not even have the time to consider women as human beings and acknowledge that they too have minds of their own. Therefore, for all these years, women were treated like domestic animals.

In such a situation, when women, the lifeblood of society, were brutally neglected and insulted, we encountered Rammohan Roy and Vidyasagar carrying the lamp of hope in their hands.

When women were put up on a pedestal, treated as goddesses and sent to accompany their husbands to heaven, Rammohan, and later, Vidyasagar, acknowledged the necessity of women's education and condemned celibacy which girls who were widowed as children were made to practise, thus announcing a new era. As a result, people gained some sense. Long after this came the swaraj movement, which infused new life to female society. Women and men realized that in this new age no one can do anything alone. In the last wave of the swaraj movement, many women left the inner quarters and stood beside their fathers, brothers and husbands. It was the dawn of women's awakening.

After that, whenever the Congress started a movement, women joined in. Another thing to be noted is that in the last movement, most of those who joined were ordinary women from ordinary households. Those women whom we call educated were so few in number that one feels ashamed to write about them. But these are the women who should have come forward first. Perhaps it was here that women's education yielded an unusual result. This may be because they perhaps could not understand the relationship between their education and the movement. Therefore, despite their education, they could not strongly feel the necessity of joining the liberation movement. The importance of education does not lie in gaining some degree from school and college if one returns thereafter to the life of dull leisure.

Perhaps everyone will admit that lack of education is the main obstruction in our national movement. Therefore, why do we not use education for a good purpose? What would be the cause, nature and outcome of the women's movement? Our country is in an extreme crisis at this juncture, not women alone but men too are daily suffering under the pressures of colonialism. And, if the condition of the two groups is compared, the condition of women appears to be more miserable. Men can balance the outside world and their lives. They get opportunities to educate themselves. But women are still confined within the household because of the social structure that dates back to the age of the *Shastras*. The girls in schools and colleges look as if their guardians had sent them outside their homes to roam around for a while, only to return home later. Nobody has any desire to learn the truth. Nowadays, it appears that a girl's only aims in life are clothes and cinema or theatre. Therefore, should we understand that book learning is failing to bring any good sense into stagnant female minds? What can be asserted is that there has been as yet no women's movement in our country which has been effective in changing the stagnant minds of women. Perhaps it was here that things went wrong. Women trod the same path as the Congress movement did. But this movement did not have an impact upon women's society as it ought to have. At present this lack has been much discussed, but it remains evident that educated women are still silent. People may say that many men have not participated in the freedom movement—if seen from this perspective, even if we do acknowledge that men did not participate [in as large numbers as they ought to have], the question [of the movement's lack of impact upon women's society] still remains! Nowadays in various places, cities and villages, organizations are created for propagating reform movements among women, who, in turn, have not the slightest bit of interest or willingness (to participate) in them.

One is astonished when one witnesses the mentality of educated women. The entire country is crying for a fistful of rice, oppression and illiteracy are at an extreme—knowing all this, if our fellow women still remain silent, then it is best for them to turn their faces away from contemporary times. A large number of women in this country are powerless and silent; if sensible women do not step forward, then will the orthodox society ever take responsibility for the enlightenment of women? Several people think that the girls' journey from school to college is an important part in her education and reflect upon the progress of women's education. But when one delves a bit deeper into this matter, one realizes how shallow this view really is. Different people have different opinions about women's liberation and the distorted image that they present is not (always) acceptable. Moreover, when even educated women think that Hitler's 'Go back to the kitchen' is the final word in the matter, then one feels truly sorry. One is tempted to retort that for an eternity the woman has been in the kitchen, and after being educated if you still think you must return there, then truly there is nothing to be said. No one can ever set aside domestic life, and one never has done so, but is that the beginning and the end of life? Are there no other problems [to be tackled] in society?

This might seem to be distorted image of women's liberation. But we have to understand that women's liberation is directly linked with the freedom of our country. Therefore, no one should ever think that the women's movement is a movement against men. This will be a movement of both men and women against colonialism. Educated women should not remain silent if women are to be included in the movement. As time goes by, we may begin to notice that women are gradually removing themselves from [this sort of] work.

Women of the West are so lively. The girl students are equally interested in games, fun and socio-political movements. And, the women in this country strive only to ease the sins accumulated through daily living. Are the innumerable voiceless and illiterate women required to look up to such women for direction? If so, why are the educated women still silent? In other countries, women take a firm step forward in the nation's freedom movement. Evidence of this can be found in history and in the present workings of public life. Women in Russia today are completely liberated and govern the state effectively. But if one looks at history, one can see [that they were subjected to] brutal oppression, illiteracy, poverty and sorrow. A handful of women who got the chance to be educated then used this opportunity effectively. They would spread out in groups in villages and factories. Is it not possible to do something similar in this country? If every college girl makes up her mind to do something and is firm on this matter, then the movement can progress effortlessly. The educated women are keeping their education confined within a small circle. But this mentality will only bring back the dark age that we have already crossed. One can hope that the inertness of the female mind will diminish and educated women will come forward to establish real freedom and liberation and participate in the freedom movement of India. After all, education is considered the main objective all over the world.

The women's movement should not be limited only to the middle class, and for this it is necessary for women of all classes to work in unison. This depends on our educated girls. One can hope that in the near future, the women of our country, especially the women of Bengal, will be able to broaden the scope of their education and their minds to include wider areas than before.

Translated by Debarati Chakraborty
Department of Comparative Literature, Jadavpur University

'*Nari Andolan o Sikshita Meye*', *Mandira*, mid-May to mid-June 1938/ Jaishtha 1345 BS, pp. 83–85.

60

SUDHA RAY

After the death of her father, Sudha Ray (1911–87) was forced to earn a living for her family. She had already completed her I.A. by this time and came to Kolkata in 1931 to find work. She was admitted to the B.A. course in Asutosh College and taught at the Kamala Girls High School to meet her expenses. During this time, she associated herself with the Labour Party and worked very closely with the labour unions in the jute mills and the dock areas. She even helped the likes of Sishir Roy, Vishwanath Dubey, Pramod Sen, Nirmal Sengupta and many others from the Bolshevik Party of India. She was a member of the politbureau of this party, secretary of the Dock Labour Union and Jute Mills Labour Union. She was one of the strongest influences behind the formation of the Mahila Atmaraksha Samiti. She also formed the Lokshiksha Parishad with K.D. Ghosh to help spread adult education among women. She facilitated the formation of many trade unions across the country. She was the leader of the Women's Federation ever since it was formed in 1954. She was also a member of the group that had represented India in the World Women's Congress at Copenhagen in 1955. She was the president of the United Trade Union Congress and established a Mahila Sanskritic Sammelan in the 1960s which contributed immensely to the development of women and children.

The Issue of Freedom and the Women's Movement (1938)

A few years back when the Civil Disobedience movement was at its peak, women's movements had carved a special place for themselves. But then, when the entire nation was wounded by the tormented reaction and reeled under its shock, the significance of the women's movement could not be seen completely. Today, once again, the daughters of India and Bengal have taken a step towards participating in movements.

In October 1936, this resulted in the formation of a regional organization of Bengali girls called the Nikhil Banga Mahila Karmi Sangha, comprising women workers of Calcutta. The reason behind forming this organization was the development of a few permanent principles in the organization of women's work in Bengal.

Many groups of girls had participated in the Civil Disobedience, but there were no separate forms of participation for women when these political agitations were taking place. However, the best part about these women's movements today is that the women have realized their strength in working as a team.

Jayasree[1] and *Mandira*[2] are but forms of these women's movements. These two monthly journals are being entirely run by the endeavours of women. *Jayasree* had been embraced by Bengali women a long time back, and now even *Mandira*—with its new message and progressive thinking—has earned for itself a unique identity of its own.

But all of this is dimmed by the memories of the 'Andaman Diwas' when the police struck the women on their heads with lathis. When groups of political prisoners in Andaman had gone on a hunger strike demanding freedom, the labourers, farmers and students of Bengal had responded to the agitation in large numbers. What had the daughters of Bengal done then? Groups of girls, though very few in number, participated in this agitation and not only demanded the freedom of the prisoners in Andaman, but added their voice to this demand made by the whole of Bengal. With bowed heads, they suffered the ruthless blows of police lathis on the fourteenth of a particular month.

Against what wrong has this women's revolution been inspired? Our revolution is against shackles and slavery. Hence, from our broad perspective, from the subtle scientific and historical perspective, one has to analyse and understand the reasons for women's dependence, the significance of women's freedom and the reasons for the relevance of the women's movement.

The most important contributor in making women dependent is their financial dependence on men. In primitive days, when men and women had worked equally hard gathering food for their survival, there was no dependence of one upon another. The women were equal with men, as an integral part of society. No one then had the strength to appropriate women's freedom.

But the day the idea of private property was introduced—that is, the day private possession over forces of production was claimed—that was the day when women's position started to regress slowly and they became dependent. From the day this primitive man prepared land for agriculture and formed settlements, the tools of agricultural production and the bows and arrows for hunting were snatched away from her hands. The woman was sent into the inner house. She became the bearer of the prospective heir to the man's private property, the nourisher and the nurturer, and nothing more than an object of man's insatiable desire for graitfication. For all her needs, she was forced to depend on her man. Our future became dependent on man's mercy. We were fettered then, and we have still not been able to break away from these fetters.

... Many ask questions like what exactly do you think is the meaning of women's freedom? The meaning of women's freedom is that like men, women also want equal participation with men in the systems of social production. Having earned financial freedom in this way, we can extend it not only to the political arena, but also change the social norms and conditions, where we can function with utmost freedom. Hence, the issue here is that for equal participation in social production we need absolute freedom and competence. This is our general demand.

What is the form of the women's movement? If this is what we desire, then what shall be the structure of our movement? We have noticed that individual rights to the forces of production led to the formation of nuclear families, thereby causing a division in the society. And, in this division, every woman became crystallized as an object possessed by the family—the dependent.

This system of personal property makes a dependant out of not just women, but innumerable labourers and farmers. The owners of these properties shackled uncountable men and women into slavery. Society was divided into two classes. One group had absolutely nothing—and there was the other group which possessed everything. This class division became eminently clear after the establishment of modern factories.

Of the women of these two classes, women of the deprived class suffered even more. Their enslavement was even more heart-wrenching. On the one hand, there was the oppression of poverty, and on the other, bondage at home. Then, when in present times, capitalism spread massively to engulf this huge planet, there was no longer any familial bonding amongst them. The husband, brother, father, and so on, went away somewhere in search of work—the wife, daughter and mothers went away to some other place. Capitalism began to exploit both men and women alike. Unemployment had begun to raise its ugly head. The deadly fangs of unemployment pushed many a young man to suicide and forced many women to prostitution, sometimes even suicide. The spread of capitalism and the exploitation it subsisted upon now began giving birth to a corrupt society.

On the other hand, it is not as if the women of the rich households and those of the middle class were very independent. Apart from a comfortable way of life and a little freedom to travel here and there, they were entitled to no other freedom. The wealthy men believed that women were only objects of pleasure, nothing more than the womb that would give birth to the heir to their private property. They make lofty remarks about respecting women, but forcing them to remain ever dependent on another; the owners of the forces of production have disrespected women like no one else ever has.

Hence, our revolution is not against men, it is against the class of affluent owners who possess the forces of production. The crusade against the capitalist class has already gathered force in many quarters. Oppressed men and women have come together today, forsaking their lives to grind the mastery of the capitalist into dust. If their ownership can be ended, if the woman is allowed equal participation in the process of social production, then none can stop women's freedom. Look at Russia, where millions of women were shackled at home like pawned goods. After the private rights on social means of production were abolished their freedom has flowered beautifully. Their women do not trail behind politically, economically or in terms of equal participation in the social means of production. When millions and millions of women in the so-called 'civilized' capitalist countries are compelled to sell their bodies in order to fill their bellies, I see in Russia innumerable women, who were once forced into prostitution under the reign of the Tzar, now risen to become political analysts and engineers, making contributions of great worth to society.

This clearly states that our crusade is against capitalism and that our target is the capitalist class.

All of India is ablaze with the idea of independence. Unless India is free, her women can never be free to participate in the equal distribution of the nation's social means of production. Hence, those who segregate India's freedom from women's freedom and talk only about the latter are either pretentious or disillusioned. The movement for women's freedom is not, and cannot be, set apart from the movement for the country's independence.

What is the duty of the women workers in Bengal? The ideal of the handful of women in Bengal who have taken steps to begin the movement afresh should be to bring together every woman worker in Bengal to one forum, form one group, irrespective of individual units, organizations and opinions, in order to try and stir up a massive women's movement.

Hence, confining the women's movement to the middle class will not help at all—we have to spread it even amidst the labourers and the farmers. We must never forget the consolidated strength and the unimaginable sacrifices that the women exhibited in the state of Manasa. Keeping in mind the instance of the Satyagraha movement against the Forest law in Jhansi, small groups must now be really moulded into a tangible women's organization.

Our work must be to hear out the grievances of the oppressed and exploited men and women, to spread awareness amongst women and also introduce to every person the real significance of the women's movement—spreading the message far and wide. Our intent about the women's movement must be crystal clear and immensely solid. ... and larger number of women must be encouraged to become a part of this mission. Hence, to make this dream come true, women have to take charge and come to the fore.

This truth has been exemplified in the satyagraha at Delhi. Whenever a woman has politically led any movement—she has always emerged with great respect. Pages of history testify even today the significance of the Rajput queen of Jhansi;[3] and Pasionaria,[4] the leader of the labourers in Spain, the symbol of a democratic Spain and the leader of Spain's Communist Party, have found deep respect and acknowledgement in every heart.

Keeping these goals before us all the time, we must proceed in this revolution for freedom. We have to try—so that hundreds of thousands, millions and millions of groups of oppressed women can come and join this crusade of ours. Our focus must be on a massive upsurge of women's enlightenment.

Translated by Anindita Roy
Department of Comparative Literature, Jadavpur University

'*Swadhinata o Nari Andolan*', *Mandira*, mid-September to mid-October 1938/Ashvin 1345 BS, barsha 1 (year 1), sankhya 6 (no. 6), pp. 292–94.

Notes

1 A monthly magazine published in Dhaka, edited by Leela Nag. The name of the magazine was given by Rabindranath Tagore. Its first issue was published in April 1931. Its main aim was to arouse patriotic feelings among women. The contributors were mostly women.

2 A monthly magazine published from Saraswati Press, 1, Ramanath Majumdar Street, Kolkata, edited by Kamala Chattopadhyay. It was first published in April 1938. The magazine starts with a few words of blessings by Rabindranath Tagore. It also had the encouragement of Subhas Chandra Bose. Its main aim was to highlight political, social and economic changes and the freedom movement which started at that time.

3 The queen of Jhansi (1835–58), a princely state ruled by the Marathas situated in north-central India. She was one of the leading figures of the Indian Rebellion of 1857 and a symbol of resistance to the rule of the British East Indian Company in the sub-continent.

4 La Pasionaria, real name Dolores Ibárruri (1895–1989), a Spanish Communist leader, who lived in exile in the Soviet Union (1939–75).

61

LEELABATI ROY

Leelabati Roy (1900–70) was the pen name of Leela Roy (née Nag). She was a freedom fighter, a radical Indian politician, a reformer, a journalist, a philanthropist and a close associate of Netaji Subhas Chandra Bose. Born in an upper middle-class Bengali Hindu family in Sylhet (now in Bangladesh), she graduated with honours in English from Bethune College, Calcutta, in 1921 and was awarded the Padmabati Gold Medal for her academic performance. She was the first woman student at the University of Dhaka and a pioneer in the history of women's education and women's movement in East Bengal. She obtained an M.A. in English from the University of Dhaka in 1923.

She was involved in the activities of secret organizations such as Jugantar and Anushilan Samiti during her student life. She was the joint secretary of Nikhil Banga Nari Votadhikar (All Bengal Women's Franchise Association) and arranged various meetings to form public opinion about social and economic rights of women. In 1923, she established Dipali Sangha, an association for women with the main objective of enhancing women's militancy against the Raj. She founded Dipali School and twelve other free primary schools. She made an important contribution to Muslim women's education. One of the schools emerged as the Qamrunnessa Girls' School in Dhaka. She also established an institution known as Shiksha Parishad (Association for Mass Education) for spreading female education in a mass scale.

In 1925, she joined Anil Roy's revolutionary group Sreesangha, a Dhaka-based institution for female students and extended its branches in many places in Assam and Bengal. Leela took part in the Civil Disobedience Movement and was imprisoned for six years, one of the many bouts of being arrested.

In 1931, she started publishing *Jayasree*, the first magazine edited, managed and wholly contributed by woman writers on women's issues. In 1938, she was nominated to the National Planning Committee of the Congress. In 1939, she married Anil Roy. After the resignation of Subhas Chandra Bose from the Congress they joined him to form the Forward Bloc. In 1940, she went to jail again and after her release she accepted the editorship of *Forward Bloc*, the weekly mouthpiece of Netaji's party. During the Quit India movement, both she and her husband were arrested and her magazine banned. On her release in 1946, she was elected to the Constituent Assembly of India and contributed in the drafting of the Constitution of India. During the Partition of India, she joined Gandhiji in Noakhali and participated in the relief work.

Which Is the Ideal Sphere for Women's Work? (1940)

Which is or which ought to be the ideal sphere for women's work is a question that has been discussed and researched upon by common people as well as the learned from time immemorial and thus one cannot trace the moment when this discussion began. Recently, Mahatma Gandhi's comment on this issue in the *Harijan* brought it once again to the limelight.[1] In the *Harijan*, Mahatma Gandhi said, 'In my opinion it is degrading for both man and woman that woman should be called upon or induced to forsake the hearth and shoulder the rifle for the protection of that hearth ... The sin will be on man's head for tempting or compelling his companion to desert her special calling.' Here, Gandhiji has pointed out the 'special calling' or a specific workplace for women ... The question is whether there is or there should be a special workplace for women. In the present social structure, the primary workplace for women is within the four walls of the house, taking care of their children and doing household chores. Let us find out whether this is the ideal workplace for women or not and if they can move towards their self-development and self-realization taking this as their proper sphere. One cannot say that in the present social structure, the woman's self has developed. Hence, in society, country and at home, there is a difference between what Gandhiji has called women's work like taking care of children and doing household chores and man's work like running a state, protecting the country, creating new social structures, regulating the country's economy and politics. The former set of activities has never been given the status of the latter and these two groups of activities do not belong to the same class. Thus, for the complete development of an individual, the coexistence of both these sorts of work is important for both men and women.

In present times, women are not suitable for the public activities mentioned, thus their personalities are not holistically developed and they do not hold respected positions in society. Many believe that there is a difference between the male and female brains and mentalities and thus, the differentiation of the workplace is not only necessary but inevitable. About this, Gandhiji said, 'As fundamentally, man and woman are one, their problems must be one in essence. The soul in both is the same. The two live the same life, have the same feelings.' Modern psychology and sociology have also proved that there is no difference between the intellectual levels of men and women. There is a difference between the emotions of men and women but this cannot logically substantiate the artificial separation of their workplaces. In fact, their workplaces should be the same because of the similarity in their intellect. Self-confidence and self-fulfilment are important for men and it is not different in the case of women.... In the creation of the mental structures of men and women, there is a difference; men and women are different and this difference is needed in home as well as in the outer world, to make the home, society and nation suitable for man and woman, with their unique essences. Hence, by limiting what is meant by 'household work' within narrowly defined boundaries is not healthy for the society, as the welfare of the community depends on the complete development of both men and women. Some say that men and women should not be crowded into the same field. In fact, if they choose different work areas, then there will not be any useless competition and wastage of ability. Women often have to face certain obstacles in working outdoors mainly due to pregnancy, and due to this inability their connection with the outer world often gets disrupted and results in major problems. Thus, household chores are thought to be best for women. We have seen when women workers demand equal wages for equal work, their employers find it better to appoint male workers with the same salary as (in the case of men) the fear of facing obstacles during the course of their work does not arise, and employers do not even have to pay maternity benefits. Hence, appointing male workers appears easier. So, if women demand equal rights they will have to move away from the sphere of outdoor activities.

If socialism is established then everything cannot be measured according to individual interests and there will be a change from the policies that have been undertaken by capitalists in the present society. Thus, for the welfare of the community, those policies will be implemented which are best for social progress. But at present, many use this argument to prove that household chores are best for women. In our opinion, society and nation are all for the good of human beings. Thus, we have to change a system where the complete development of individuals is not possible; we need to create a new society. It is totally meaningless to think that this unchanged society will remain as it is, and in order to adjust with this society we have to curtail the sphere of women's work and stunt their individuality. Mahatma Gandhi said, 'There is a vital difference between the two [men and women]. Hence, the vocations of the two must be different. The art of bringing up the infants of the race is her special and sole prerogative and without her care the race must become extinct.' If any work causes physical or mental damage to the prospective mother then such work should be discarded, and if required, alternative means and methods must be introduced in different work spheres [to accommodate women's special responsibility of child bearing].

Like Gandhiji, many feel that the tension and excitement of hard labour in the public world destroy the tenderness and natural beauty of women. All such outdoor activities are harmful for potential mothers and thus they should be abandoned. I agree that women do not have the right to do anything that is harmful for children, who are the future citizens of the nation, but it is necessary to judge whether certain things are actually harmful for children or not. One cannot measure how much physical work is harmful; we have seen that there are differences not only in different communities but among different classes of the same community. The English or American women, or those residing in the hill areas, like Khasia or tribal women will be able to work harder in comparison to Bengali women, hence certain types of labour are not harmful for them. Again, among the Bengali women, the poor women can work much harder than the rich delicate ones, but this does not mean that the children of the latter are less healthy than those of the former. ... We have no proof to justify that extreme physical work lead to the birth of unhealthy children, and vice versa. This completely depends on customary practices. If someone who is used to doing less work starts undertaking hard work on a regular basis, then I don't see any reason why this should be harmful for her child. ... In the primitive ages, human beings, for their survival, had to fight with untamed nature. During the earth's infancy, primitive women had to suffer much in order to protect their children but this did not disturb the evolution of human beings. English and American women are much more involved in the so-called public activities than their Indian counterparts but owing to this their respective children are not inferior to Indians in terms of health and mental development. Thus, we cannot agree that doing any kind of work outside the house will harm the women physically and mentally which in turn will harm the future citizens (their children).

We feel that any kind of artificial division between the home and the outer world is unnecessary, all work spheres within and outside the home need to be open for both men and women. Men and women irrespective of their sex should choose their work spheres according to their tastes and necessities. Due to years of lack of practice if a sudden opportunity to work in a new field results in some ill effects, these effects will be temporary and applicable in the case of both men and women. Women have to bear children, and naturally, they have to remain confined within the house for a brief and temporary period. We cannot go against the course and the rules of nature. There is no question about that. But just because women have to be temporarily confined within the house for child birth, it does not mean that they have to deprive themselves of any connection with the rise and fall of the vast universe which is always dynamic and reside in a totally vacuous artificial space of peace and contentment alienated from the actual world. This is because what women will lose in terms of character and community solidarity will not be their loss alone but an entire society and community will be deprived. Women have to save themselves as well as the entire community from such crippling fate.

Translated by Swagata Bhattacharya
Department of Comparative Literature, Jadavpur University

'Meyeder Upajukta Karmakshetra Ki?', Jayasree, mid-April to mid-May 1940/Baisakh 1347 BS.

Note

1 Literally meaning the Child of God, it was a term used by Gandhi for the dalits. Gandhi said it was wrong to call people 'untouchable' and called them Harijans. Today the term 'Dalit' is preferred and 'Harijan' is seen as patronizing.

62

SUPRITI MAJUMDAR

No biographical details about the author could be found. Her contributions have been found in *Mandira*.

India's Women Workers (1942)

Although India lags far behind other countries of the world in the realm of industrial competition, yet the number of female earners in India is higher in comparison to the number of female earners in the industrialized countries of the world. In the international scene, given India's total female population, the number of female earners is 25.3 per cent. In comparison to this, the sum total of female earners in an advanced and industrialized country like Britain is 26.3 per cent. The majority of Indian female workers come from the lower strata of society and they primarily work in mines, factories and tea gardens. According to the 1931 census, 48.8 million women earn, that is, 31 per cent of the total female population is engaged in earning their livelihood.

The number of female workers is highest in the tea, coffee and cinchona plantations. According to the 1921 census, 47 per cent of the total number of workers were female. The census of 1931 revealed that this number has come down to 36 per cent. The reason behind the large number of female workers in the plantations is the fact that only here are the workers permitted to live with their families. The nature of work in these plantations is agriculture-based and can be done easily. The women of the lower strata of Indian society are familiar with such work and they get the chance to work side by side with men. As women are paid lower wages, the employers consider (recruitment of) female workers to be advantageous.

Though work in the mines is not suited to women, earlier, owing to the scarcity of other jobs, many women used to work in the mines. Many female workers were even engaged in the interiors of mines. In mining, women were employed in greater numbers in coal mines. In 1936, the available figure of female workers working in the mines was 78,497, that is, 30.2 per cent of the total number and in 1924 this figure was 60,375, that is, 69 per cent worked inside of the mines. In 1929, with the intention of curbing different types of accidents and socially unacceptable consequences, the Indian government implemented an Act to reduce the number of female workers working inside the mines. This Act of 1929 compelled a reduction of female workers by one-third of the total sum of women working inside the mines, within a span of ten years. By 1939, engaging female wage earners inside the mines was completely banned. The total number of female workers working in different factories was 43,592.

By 1922, this number had gradually increased to 236,887 and in 1933 and 1936, it became 254,905 and 237,933 respectively. This steady rise in the number of women wage earners in factories not only implies the industrial growth of the country but also a simultaneous abundance in female workers. These figures include only those female workers who work in registered factories. Apart from these registered factories, there are many small-scale labour-intensive unregistered factories. Hence, we do not have the correct figure of female workers employed. In the case of women workers engaged here, rules and norms of factory laws regarding duration and condition of work are not implemented properly. No effort has been made to protect and safeguard the interests of these labourers through the creation of laws. Only in Madhya Pradesh has this been achieved to some extent. The number of female factory workers is greater in jute mills and cotton mills. The data available in 1937 shows 62,899 female workers in cotton mills and 38,899 in jute mills. The daily income of this huge number of female workers is remarkably less than that of the male workers. For instance, women wage earners cannot earn more than 8 annas daily in jute mills whereas men earn 1 rupee daily and sometimes even more than this. The income level of female workers in cotton mills is no better; they get paid daily but not more than 12 to 18 annas.

In 1891, the Government of India, for the first time, tried to improve the working conditions of female workers. The Indian factory law tried to give certain opportunities to women wage earners. This law ascertained that female workers will work for eleven hours per day.

Further, women cannot be engaged in any form of risky or life-threatening work; employing female workers after seven in the night and before five in the morning was also prohibited. According to the present factory laws, the maximum working hours for women wage earners is eleven hours a day in seasonal factories and ten hours a day in perennial factories . . .

Seventy-five per cent women in India are earning their livelihood. But this huge group of female workers leads a miserable life. Due to lack of education, poverty and inhuman conditions, these women have lamentable and helpless lives. Since they do not have any labour union. They are neither able to place their demands before their employers through a well-administered union, nor are they capable of persuading the employers to accept their demands. No law has been passed to protect the self-interest of the female workers. Generally, in factories, women and men work together. Since the machines of these factories are fit to be manoeuvred by men, women who are often forced to run these same machines, find themselves becoming ill. There is no scope for engaging women in vocational training; thus in spite of their abilities many a time they fail to prove their skills or are deprived from earning a better salary.

Apart from working strenuously in factories, women wage earners in India have to carry out their household duties and even during times of pregnancy they have no respite from their daily schedule of work. After the Maternity Benefit Bill was approved in 1924 at the Washington Conference it was decided that it would be introduced in India, but till today, the bill has not been effective in our country.[1]. Although the Bill was passed in the Union Cabinet last November, the provisions of the Bill are not adequate to mitigate the problems of women wage earners. Within a short span of time, after childbirth, these women have to resume work in the factories out of sheer necessity and during their absence from home they fail to manage any proper care for their new-born babies. The government can change this situation only with the help of employers. Almost all industrialized countries of the world have made arrangements for nurseries or dormitories for the convenience of women wage earners. India also requires this facility; the government needs to be aware of the situation and introduce the nursery system in the country.

Employers in India pay their workers according to the iron law of wages, that is, their main purpose is to provide the workers with the minimum subsistence and thereby maintain a free flow of workers.

They do not consider it worthwhile to give the matter any more importance than this. The government has taken a neutral stand regarding this policy. Therefore, any norm introduced by the workers' welfare union or human rights organization does not become mandatory for the employers.[2] In many countries Family Allowance System, Mother's Pension or Mother's Aid Fund Law are in vogue and because of this the workers do not have to depend entirely on their salary.[3]

Through the introduction of laws, extra emoluments in addition to their wages can be given to the workers according to their needs. New South Wales has passed a law providing a family allowance.[4] According to this law, the amount of expenditure that the worker's salary cannot meet will come from the Family Endowment Fund, which in turn will be replenished by the employers. This system provides an allowance to provide for the husband, wife and one child. Each of the other children of the worker is given an allowance of five shillings per week.

In 1932, the French government made the Family Allowance System mandatory in France. In Belgium too this system has been accepted. In the United States, though the Family Allowance System is not in vogue, yet Mother's Pension or Mother's Aid Fund have been implemented. This law helps the widows and pregnant women who have been abandoned by their husbands. Almost all countries of the world have taken steps to look after the worker's family and helpless pregnant women workers. It is only in India that no such measures have been taken yet. But the unavailability of skilled labour prevents industrialization in India. Skilled and competent labour is not easily available in India and the miserable living condition of the workers prevents them from providing a healthy environment to their children. If no measures are taken to curb the serious problems of women wage earners, then the progress of India's industrialization process is bound to be seriously affected.

Translated by Ritika Batabyal
Department of Comparative Literature, Jadavpur University

'Bharater Nari Shramik', Mandira, mid-March to mid-April 1942/ Chaitra 1348 BS, pp. 789–92.

NOTES

1 The Maternity Protection Convention of 1919, held at Washington, DC called for paid maternity leave before and after delivery. The convention was proposed for adoption by all members of the International Labour Organization at the first session of the general conference. First Maternity benefit legislation in India was introduced by M.N. Joshi, a private member of the Bombay Legislative Council, in 1924. Though this measure was rejected, the Bombay Legislative Council passed an Act related to maternity benefits in 1929, followed by the other provinces. The first central legislation in this area was the Mines Maternity Benefit Act of 1941.

2 About 1916 a body of British and Indian sympathizers formed the Workers' Welfare League of India, independent of all political aims or movements, advocating the provision of workers' welfare measures on the same lines, with that granted to the UK workers.

3 In the USA, the first state-wide mothers' pension law was passed by Illinois in 1911, and passed in seventeen states. Public fund's had been made available in some states to board children in their own homes or to assist the mother so that children might remain in school. Family allowances were one of the items proposed by the Beveridge Report in 1942. The Labour Party briefly debated pressing for allowances during the Second World War, but a party conference resolution to this end was opposed by the trade unions for fear that the amount paid would be taken into account in wage negotiations, leaving workers no better off.

The UK Family Allowances Act 1945, it came into operation from 6 August 1946, the first law to provide child benefit. Public aid to single mothers had been discussed as early as 1898 when the New York state passed a bill to provide grants to widows with dependent children in New York City. The take-off point for the mothers' pensions movement was the 1909 White House Conference on the Care of Dependent Children.

4 New South Wales passed the Family Endowment Act on 11 April 1927, setting up a family endowment fund to 'make provision for benefit of children by means of an endowment payable to mothers'.

63

ANWARA RAHMAN

Anwara Rahman signed herself as Anwara Rahman, M.A. In the women's issue of the magazine *Saogat* published in October-November 1936 (Kartik 1342), her name is prefixed as Kumari, denoting her unmarried status. This particular essay, written in 1936, does not have this indicator, so we may assume that she was married by this time.

Women's Freedom and the Ulema (1946)

History proves that in this world, priests and preachers are the greatest stumbling blocks to progress. Our unfortunate Muslim world is no exception, especially with regard to women's emancipation. Hence, it is the ulema who is most vocal in preventing us from demanding our rights to participate freely in social life.[1]

It is surprising to find that though holy Islam grants more rights for the freedom of women than all other religions in this world, the ulema tries to undermine these precepts of the Qur'an *Hadith*,[2] in spite of its acquaintance with it!

The revered prophet Hajrat Muhammad was the last preacher of Islam. What was his perception about women? How did women live under his rule? Is the ulema aware of that? Can any historian maulvi[3] assert that the strange veiling system, which is maintained within the *sharif*[4] in our country, was also present in Hajrat's era? According to Islam, the veil is equally important for both men and women. The society built and sanctioned by Hajrat decreed this system for both men and women. Men donned veils and dressed according to the rules before going to work. Similarly, women dressed themselves according to the Arabian custom to perform their daily duties. We can bravely assert that our Prophet Hajrat never forbade any innocent woman from leaving home in ordinary clothes, and our respected ulema cannot give any proof to the contrary. Rather, reliable sources of history show that many Arabian women went to the battlefield as volunteers in Hajrat's time and in the succeeding *Sahaba*'s era,[5] they looked after the wounded soldiers. When endangered, they took up weapons and inspired soldiers. They also went to the markets and joined meetings and conferences in a domestic atmosphere. At the time of Prophet Hajrat and Hajrat Abu Bakr, women participated in the gathering of Id held in the open. The only difference between men and women was that the men's rows were followed by the women's rows. There was a special significance in this arrangement of rows; but that is not our point of discussion. We just want to emphasize that at the time of Hajrat and the first Caliphate, women had the right to participate in the gathering at Id in the Idgah. The messenger of Allah did not consider snatching away this right from women; but his followers did. Hence, to call such acts righteous would mean to accept that the followers of Hajrat understood Islam better than Hajrat himself. Rather what we want to emphasize is that none should try to deprive us from what has already been granted to us by Hajrat's Islam.

In an important event like marriage, it is worth considering the extent of freedom granted to women in Islam. The main and clear intention of Islam is to allow women choose their life partners independently. In special circumstances, supposedly a girl's parents are absent and it becomes obligatory for the relatives of this teenage girl to marry her off, the girl still retains the right to deny it, and enter into marriage when she becomes an adult and choose her husband independently. If we analyse this Islamic custom, it is evident that Islam allows adult women to choose their life partners from many suitors; otherwise the practice of seeking their approval or disapproval at the time of their marriage does not seem to have any meaning. If the groom's selection by parents or others is not at all considered adequate, then to appoint lawyers and witnesses to get the bride's consent at the time of marriage is downright hypocrisy. But Islam cannot propose such a meaningless proclamation. If this is not the real purpose, then we should accept that there is a particular significance of the bride's consent to the marriage. But under what condition is such a consent really valuable? If the bride cannot meet the groom even in the presence of her guardians or close relatives, and even after maintaining the necessary protocol, can she have the liberty to choose the groom after considering his merits and demerits in comparison with others?

We earnestly request the ulema community to consider this question impartially. At the time of marriage, a lawyer asks the bride whether she agrees to marry someone from a particular village and of a particular descent in exchange of a specific amount of *meher*.[6] The bride is asked this question thrice to get her answer. But how can she answer it as an individual with a clear opinion in the matter if she does not have some prior familiarity with her would-be husband? With our limited understanding of the matter, we realize that there is a noble purpose behind this question. It means that we don't know your [would-be bride's] opinion. After meeting ten suitors, your father or some other guardian, possibly after discussing the matter with you, has approved of this groom who is present in today's marriage ceremony. Now, you must say whether this groom is really selected by you, and since he proposes marriage to you in exchange of this amount of dowry, do you accept his offer? What else can be the meaning of the lawyer's question to the bride on behalf of the groom? And if it is so, is it in accordance with the fundamental idea of marriage in Islam?

Here we are not asking the ulema to give out a *fatwa* in favour of the Christian idea of courtship or open love affairs between men and women before marriage.[7] We are just saying that when Islam's purpose is to grant one the independence to choose one's life partner, then according to the basic Islamic marriage rules, should there be any reason to oppose a woman who refuses to be guided by other's opinion and takes her own decision in marriage? She meets the suitors with proper respect and tries to know them. Then she takes her own decision after consulting her own relatives. We don't know whether our respected ulema will give any value to the reading of the Qur'an by some amateur like us; but does not the Qur'an really address women and say that even if you like a non-Muslim man more than a Muslim or a *momena*, you should accept a Muslim as your husband?[8] Here the only matter of concern is that if the Muslim woman does not get a chance to know any [Muslim or] non-Muslim men before marriage, how can she like or dislike any one of them?

That Islam grants rights to the teenage girl to reject her husband when she reaches adulthood is a debatable fact. This means that an adult Muslim woman is not compelled to accept any man chosen by her father or other relatives as her husband even after her marriage has been ceremoniously performed with him. Until the particular age is reached, the man to whom she has been married is only her probable husband, not an accepted husband. If after meeting him, while maintaining the natural respect and distance, and knowing all his positives and negatives, she thinks, when she comes of age and before beginning her marital life with him, that she cannot accept him, she can openly deny the marriage.

This does not seem to be an illogical arrangement. While on the one hand this entails that the approval of the guardian or the father is completely dependent upon the girl's consent, on the other hand, the circumstances (of society) have been made such that the girl can naturally interact with a man only after she begins to live with him as his wife. So it is our request to the ulema that they should agree to the intermingling of men and women in an atmosphere where respect and proper behaviour is maintained, so that they can get a chance to know and understand each other. With this, the ulema can support the cause of women's independence as upheld by Islam.

We have already mentioned that women went to the battlefield as volunteers at the time of Prophet Hajrat and the succeeding *Sahabas*. From this instance it is understood that they had the opportunity to know men other than their husbands closely. Without much close contact, it is not possible for them to nurse the soldiers and to take up arms to assist the men, if needed. Here intermingling does not imply physical interaction, which it never actually means. Physical relations can anyway be discreetly established between men and women without the necessary level of social sanction. Rather it can be accepted as a general fact that the possibility and the chance of such relations are almost non-existent in open, social and formal meetings.

Our religious teacher Karim also had the same opinion and we can assume this from an instance in the life of Bibi Ayesha Siddiqua, the mother of all believers.[9] Bibi Siddiqua once lost her way and was separated from Hajrat and his companions while returning from a battlefield. A young Muslim soldier found her and brought her home with him; but that long journey included one night. This provoked some murmurs about Bibi Ayesha and that youth. The religious Karim got disturbed by this; but an *ayat* [verse] of the Qur'an in this context became apparent which consoled him.[10] This also silenced the gossip.

So the Qur'an proclaims that if after questioning a woman's moral character one can't give proof to support these claims, the accuser will be subject to a certain number of lashes. That means the Qur'an dictates that in any condition, one should think of a woman or a man as having an indisputably pure moral character until some proper witness or proof discloses any information to the contrary. But this attitude of the Qur'an to see both men and women as naturally pure and noble gets completely ignored when it is assumed that if they get a chance to meet, even with propriety, they become involved in sexual indulgence. Actually, if we analytically discuss the Qur'an, Islam and the conditions in the age of Prophet Hajrat, we can clearly understand that Islam does not assume that human beings are naturally promiscuous. Had it not been so, the rules would have been different.

And when we actually analyse various classes or social conditions, what do we see? Though it is not possible to display any statistics, it is apparent at least in our country, . . . that the more intense the strictures of prohibition imposed upon a class or community, the greater are the resulting sexual perversions. There is a psychological dimension to it. Man is more drawn towards a forbidden fruit or a denied object than to anything easily available. We can conclude from this that if the interaction between men and women is unnaturally prohibited, this unnecessary obstacle put between them will excite their desire to know each other and may lead them to physical bondage, even before they come to know each other well. Any insightful, socially conscious observer can substantiate this.

So I appeal to the ulema (to accept) that granting freedom to women is not to be seen only as a means to protect life's basic demands, but also as an inspiration granted by Islam to eradicate the custom of prohibition and accept respectful communion between man and woman to make society healthier and purer.

If this system is implemented, women will require lesser effort to progress in all spheres of life and will be able to enjoy a freer existence. This can increase the importance of both humanity and Islam. Do the ulemas not intend that?

Translated by Dhritiman Chakraborty
Department of English, Maldah Women's College

'Nari Mukti o Ulema Sampraday', Saogat, mid-April to mid-May 1946/ Baisakh, 1353 BS.

Also in *Pather Ingit: Nirbachita Samvad-Samayikpatre Bangali Meyer Samajbhavna: 1927-1967*, edited by Sarmistha Dutta Gupta (Kolkata: Stree, 2007), pp. 230–34.

Notes

1 Muslim scholars having knowledge about Islam and the Islamic law.
2 The Prophet's words are termed as *Hadith*.
3 Learned person or a professor.
4 Respectable; of aristocratic lineage.
5 People who were the direct disciples of Prophet Muhammad and lived and worked for the cause of Islam during the first blessed era.
6 An amount of money promised in the *nikahnama* (wedding contract) at the time of marriage.
7 Ordinance, religious prescription.
8 Literally meaning to believe a faith, the feminine gender of *mumin*, an Arabic term frequently occurs in the Qur'an denoting a believer. Also means a Muslim weaver.
9 Ayesha , daughter of the first Khalifa Abu Bakr. She was one of wives of the Prophet. She is commonly known as *umm-al-muminin*, or the mother of all *mumin*, i.e., believers.
10 The story of accusation of adultery levied against Ayesha can be traced to Chapter 24 in Surah al-Nûr in the Qur'an.

64

SARALA RAY

Sarala Ray (1861–1946) was the eldest daughter of Durga Mohan Das. He was a distinguished member of the Brahmo Samaj. Her sister was Lady Abala Bose. Sarala Roy and her friend Kadambini Ganguly were the first women not only in India but in the whole of the British Empire to be allowed to go up for a University Entrance Examination. She was married to Dr. P. K. Ray at the age of sixteen. He became the first Indian principal of Presidency College. Sarala Ray was particularly concerned with improving the position of women through proper education. She was the first woman to start a Mahila Samiti in Dhaka. Later, she started a similar samiti in Calcutta. She spent a few years in London during which she started the Indian Women's Association (1912) with the purpose of providing scholarships for the training of Indian women teachers in the UK. It was due to her efforts that Gokhale Memorial Girls' School came into existence in 1920. As a member of the Senate of Calcutta University, she strove to establish a separate training college for women teachers. In 1931, she was elected President of the fourth session of the All India Women's Conference held in Madras.

A Few Thoughts on Women (n.d.)

While thinking about ourselves, so many ideas jumble up in my head, and some of them are so obviously true that I am hesitant lest I happen to say something offensive. If I do injustice to anybody or anything, I hope you will please point it out and correct me suitably.

I come to you after about a year. While abroad, I tried to keep up with women's schools, women's meetings, clubs, and so on. Sometimes it is useful to observe others in order to learn about one's own merits and demerits. Today I have decided to say a few words about our limitations. Over the past years, Indian women have made considerable progress. Apart from their household problems, various activities, worries and anxieties, and arduous labour, they have started paying attention to other things as well. While ensuring social progress—keeping their families and households in order, bringing up the children with care and looking after their welfare, as well as instilling the right spirit in their husbands' work, being helpful to them—women today are also mindful of their country, family and neighbours at the same time. Set any demanding task before them and they will apply themselves with enthusiasm. Now in the context of this new spirit and inspiration, we have to be careful about certain things. Some aspects about the foreign women favourably impressed me. It would be nice if we could imbibe some of those things in our work. Today I wish to bring to your notice briefly the following four things:

First, the real value of education in home life—this concerns the importance of education in our domestic life completely. Second, considering others to work with united effort; this means showing mutual respect in collective work and the belief that all work is respectable. Third, instilling method, order and punctuality as aid to domestic life and outside work. This is to emphasize on the importance of systematic order and punctuality within the home and outside. Fourth, reading literature for the improvement of both domestic and collective work.

Nowadays, we all love to be concerned with studies. Often we are made to believe that education means reading novels, newspapers, writing letters to husbands, keeping laundry accounts, distributing household duties and such things. Some people retort that we have become fashionable for this purpose alone. This may not be totally wrong—a fascination for the superficial veneer, an attraction for newly designed dresses, slothfulness at work, inclination for lazy gossip are often noticeable. We tend to forget that the real importance of education is much deeper and its effectiveness must be felt in our daily work. We do not keep in mind that my husband and my children along with all my relatives constitute a great empire; I am its leader and I am to guide this entire collective. Do we ever think of the fact that the well-being and happiness of those who are dependent on us are linked to our intelligence and discipline, to our cleanliness and thrift, to our ardent effort and acute sense of justice? We forget that education is not merely writing letters or reading books—nor does it simply mean gossip or back biting, nor does it mean going out in new clothes every time—education is helpful for organizing our family life—and the home is a place of attraction for our husbands and a place of learning for our children. There are complaints galore—I don't have this or that thing, my child is not serious about his studies, my husband is not quite eminent enough nor does he earn adequately, my daughter is going astray—such things occur in every family. But I ask: how many books have we read that deal with child rearing? Have we really spent a few moments of our spare time in the evenings thinking about what a child's natural inclination may possibly be? Have we ever thought about the kind of work he likes or what can make him open up to his mother? How many people have we consulted on these questions? How many times have we begged our husbands to buy us a few books on these subjects? The daughter goes astray—I couldn't bring her up the way I desired. Well, how many times have we had frank exchanges with her or made efforts to draw her on to the right path? Can rebuke and reproof alone make a good boy or girl?

We have to find out ways to keep children on the right path—everyone has to be led on to the right course suitable to his or her aptitude. How many times have we tried this? We groan about not having the husband's attention, but for that we need to be of assistance in his work! Even if it is not asked of us, we need to create a space for him where he may have relaxed transactions with us on his achievements and failures and despair, where he may have our sympathies—this is how we may prepare ourselves to rise to his expectations. Have we ever spared a thought for this? This needs a lot of reading and understanding and consideration—that is not possible only with an ornament or through some sweet nothings—but do we take it seriously or make an effort? Education is not simply about passing examinations—we have made education merely formal and instrumental for negotiating our daily cares and anxieties, mundane problems and to get over the challenges we face in our daily lives. Perhaps that is why we do not get its full benefit. We have not yet been able to make education a part of our ordinary life in a sustainable manner and because of this others misunderstand us, and our education remains useless in our daily lives.

In England, they have introduced a system of compulsory education. That is a system where, whether you are rich or poor, you must admit your child to a school; the poor do not have to pay for their children's education. The police would find the children between eight and fourteen years of age and take them away from their families to put them into schools where they are taught till they are fourteen at the state's expense. Let me tell you something about how good this has been for these children. I am not taking account of the children from wealthier homes as they have many other advantages. I shall tell you about a poor family that I have known.

My maidservant lived in a rented room in a baker's house; the maidservants there are educated, they know about the affairs of the nation. One day, she told me about the baker's wife. Hearing many good things said about her by my maid I once called upon her, introduced myself and visited her place twice or thrice in order to become acquainted with her mode of work. The more I saw her the more I was convinced of how much could be achieved through the spread of education. The frail woman, mother of eight children, had a husband who left home at night for his profession, came back at 8 o'clock in the morning and slept for the whole day only to leave again at around 7 o'clock in the evening, and could not afford to spend more than a couple of hours or so in the home. His relations with the family were rather distant. The elder son and daughter after their school hours worked as waiters in a hotel. They too were at work from seven in the morning till ten in the night. The rest except the youngest child went to school—the mother of the family began her chores at four in the morning and worked till midnight—of course she could not afford to employ a helping hand—and so she did all the work herself. Cleaning floors and utensils, lighting the ovens, cooking, serving food to all, cleaning the rooms and courtyards, doing the laundry, mending old clothes, stitching the new ones, helping the children with their school work, giving piano lessons to the second daughter—there was really no end to her duties. In addition, she attended mothers' meetings on Sundays and learnt a few things on weekdays at the working women's night classes. Reading books and newspapers, singing songs to her husband on Sundays, pushing the pram to take the baby out—there was nothing that was not her duty. Even to turn out the rooms, which she performed so routinely that each room was scrubbed once every week, and doing the laundry, which is also another big job in that country! That is done every Tuesday regularly despite this packed routine. She is a happy person—the sons take part in theatre and other recreational activities, each one of them has some money deposited in a savings bank account.

I was so surprised seeing her daily round of duties. She had invited me to tea and talked about so many things like a well-educated woman. Amidst all this, I learnt by chance that one of her young boys had met with a tram accident that caused his arm to be amputated. She took him to a hospital. I wondered how she could possibly leave that child back in the hospital and come home, to which she replied, 'Mrs Ray, beggars have no choice—the poor do not exercise their options. I couldn't afford to get him treated at home, had I shed tears for this inability, it would give my husband a sense of guilt. It was better that I took the boy where he could at least be given some care.' I asked her another day, 'Well, how can you make both ends meet with only this small amount of money?' She replied, 'Look, my husband gives me this much on Saturdays, my son and daughter give me this amount. I first send a certain amount to the savings bank accounts opened in everybody's name. Then I set aside a certain amount every week to buy new clothes for Christmas. Thereafter, I deduct the required amounts for the children's milk and for coal and house rent and tax. Then I divide what remains by seven to spend equally over the week, from Sunday to Saturday. I purchase as much bread as possible with the amount left and also some meat and vegetables, which I distribute among the family members, a little more given to the children, the grown-ups being given a little less.'

Seeing this poor woman keep her house in order with such rare foresight and methodical care for everything, I thought, what miracles education can achieve. If we can combine education with good health, then our lives may become ideal. True, we have begun rather late and no wonder, there are some faults at the outset, but we must be careful from the start so that our education may not degenerate into mere external frill, but that it may be useful for our daily lives. Our own households are like small kingdoms. It is our responsibility to administer them well. There we have to manage judiciously with a basic sense of natural justice, with consideration and meticulous labour. We must keep in mind that with patience and tolerance on the one hand and hope and incentive on the other, with all our physical and mental abilities drawn together, we have to bring up good children for the community and the country. In England, the labour the women undertake, their striving, their concern for the welfare of their own societies would make you think that whatever has been achieved here has been due to these women.

Unless the mother is noble, the child will not prosper. This is an old adage but it gives you a genuine sense of truth. If we cannot make our home great, how can we keep our mind and body clean and how, without proper physical and mental strength and without taking proper care of one's body, do we expect to give birth to children who are beautiful and strong? From where do our menfolk gather enthusiasm for the nation's work if we fail to transmit to them our strength of mind and our lives' vitality from childhood? Our education will be futile if we cannot use it with ease for our domestic duties. Brahmo women, especially, may never escape this allegation. We have failed to realize the greatness of those whose sacrifice and efforts have caused us to acquire education. To some extent, even today, we do not exactly comprehend what it means to be thus educated and how much greater our responsibility becomes after being educated, as compared to others. Every woman of the Brahmo community should keep in mind that because she has received education, she needs to excel in everything. She should remain calm and composed in trying situations of shock and mourning and should be able to organize her domestic space in such a manner that it may prove to be a place of comfort and true shelter for her husband and children and also for other relatives and friends.

Let alone following the path of our esteemed predecessors who were so lofty in their ideals that they reached almost divine proportions we are not even worthy of sitting at their feet. May we pray that we should remember not to do anything that will be an insult to their memories? . . . Let us not shy away from labour. Women have a great job to do in this society; with that in mind, let us try as much as we can, as much as we are capable of; with a cheerful spirit, with the memory of the noble men alive, with the strength they have instilled in us, let us unite to fulfil their hearts' desire.

My second point is the dignity of labour and considering others in our united efforts at work. To put it clearly, we need to remember that we must have respect for each other in all our work and realize for ourselves that all labour is respectable and worthy of pursuit. Today, we all believe that intense physical labour is no cause for shame. All work is worthy and a matter of pride; it is a sign of human dignity and we perform it applying all the potential inherent in us. . . . Yet even a poor widow does not wish to be dependent on others if she can help herself earning something by dint of her own physical strength. No one is ashamed to maintain herself through her own labour—independence is always better than dependence on others . . . Today, we are gradually learning the merits of collective work; it is slowly dawning upon us that it is good to take collective decisions to work for the welfare of our neighbours or for the community as a whole. It is a novelty for our women to come together irrespective of kinship relations or family ties, to build up something or to apply ourselves as best as we can to some common cause. To work for somebody else or to serve our neighbours or to sacrifice our own interests for our own people is nothing unusual for the Hindu women, yet to do so in a united manner, through collective decisions, is something new and it is necessary for us to be cautious about it because of its novelty. We must be careful to ascertain that the self is not projected . . . I shall undertake so much labour, I will work so much, I will think about it so carefully and still I will have no say in it! It is my work and my organization, it is I who will have to convince everybody to concur in my plan of work and still when we meet to discuss things it should be made to look as if it were all our collective thought and action.

This is not a very easy thing to accept. It needs to be cultivated, and we must note that it is also true that unless you are able to forget yourself and get immersed in it, the work doesn't seem to be a noble one. As long as we do something for our own benefit, the horizon becomes narrow and the work seems somewhat devalued. The moment we think we are chosen by others, we are labouring for others' welfare. We experience a keen sense of added enthusiasm. Besides, the 'I' itself is a great impediment to any kind of collective effort. For collective work, it is ideal if everybody feels that it is a common responsibility. Presently another evil has crept into us. Why should somebody else be doing what I have been striving for? I have gathered this group together and look she has also formed a rival one; I have organized a meeting and she has just raised the bogey of a parallel meeting. These are narrow 'womanish' things, so narrow that you feel ashamed to recognize that such things are really there within us. Is any bit of work my monopoly? Or, does the country solely belong to me? . . . Isn't it good that we thus cooperate in our common endeavour? Let us all go together, you, me and any third person. . . . Not all of us are fit for all kinds of work—one may sing well, one has an aptitude for teaching, one excels in stitching, one writes well, one tells stories beautifully, one may have a knack for entertainment. Amidst this diversity, is it fair to think that I am ignored or insulted if my name doesn't feature in any of these efforts or that the job isn't done well unless I directly participate? We suffer so often from such unnecessary self-projection.

Then the next thing is confidence. We do not really have confidence in anybody and this is mutually true. Believe me, it is perhaps true even for myself. But without mutual trust and confidence you cannot continue any collective work. There is a whisper there, 'Well, this is merely one of her ploys to collect funds'; or maybe an insinuation, 'That is a rumpus created to make a name for herself' . . . the real thing will be trivial. These are things that are always being said about us . . . We seem to be always in a hurry to reach a conclusion. We make one-sided judgements and charge somebody as guilty, and then slip away from the project she is associated with. We may even urge our friends not to cooperate with her or warn them of grave consequences that would follow from such collaborations. This is the state of our mutual confidence! Let me narrate an incident in this connection. In England, the patriot Richard Cobden is a renowned person. His daughter is the wife of the publisher Fisher Unwin. She is a great leader of the Suffragist Party.[1] Once I asked her, 'Look! The women of this Suffragist Party (perhaps all of you know about this group) are in different ways teasing and torturing the men folk in the street. Do you support them?' She replied, 'Mrs Ray, let me tell you. I do not really like these things at all but since I myself cannot put in my labour and find alternative ways for them I do not think I have any right to criticize their actions. Those whom we have made members of the council will find out the best ways to go about the job. Though I cannot agree with them in their present course of action, I have faith that my leaders are doing what they honestly feel is best and if they realize there is some mistake somewhere they will rectify it and change their course of action. I can only make contributions to their fund, and as I don't have any time for their work I am not entitled to criticize their method. I feel bad, but I keep quiet.' It was as if I was awakened by what she said. It seemed that we here were plunged in trivialities. Can you really do any collective work unless you feel like this? If you have to say something say it as one party to the matter. Merely saying abusive things from outside is to discourage people in their work.

I will make brief comments on the third and the fourth point, following method and order at home and outside . This is to show how important it is to observe order and punctuality in domestic life and in work outside the home. First, Tea Party: Scheduled time 4:30, we arrive at 6 o'clock. Well, the hostess cannot afford to sit and talk. She has to spend all her time in serving food to the guests whenever they may choose to come and when she has almost finished this job, our time is up and we are about to leave the place. We, the guests, seem to have come only to drink the tea she served, and for the hostess, her only duty seemed to be to serve us tea! Well, we are not short of tea at home and she who invited us is also used to pouring tea every day in her own home. We came together, we met so that we could exchange a few pleasantries, but that goes in vain and why? If on the contrary, we could be a bit more orderly and we would all come at 4:30 or say 5, then we would have tea, and proper conversations and social exchange too, and we would come back happy. The hostess too would feel relaxed through this entertainment of congenial conversation. To honour invitations punctually is not frightfully difficult. If we are a bit careful about it, these things become easy and reasonable. Then think of wedding and *sradh* ceremonies or after a death—these go on from morning till night—back-breaking labour. The guest comes only just to register his presence, but for the hostess, however, her daily schedule gets topsy-turvy. For days together, she cannot maintain any regularity neither in her meals nor even in bathing or sleeping. . . . It is true that these are glorious practices in the indigenous tradition but suppose we maintain at least some semblance of routine within this ritualistic framework. Suppose these receptions are limited to say eleven or twelve in the daytime and between six and ten in the evening.

Maybe with some adjustments depending on practices in particular families, one has equal opportunity for relaxation on the one hand and maintenance of social norms on the other. Then, for daily chores in every household, especially in large families, the woman of the house is perhaps in her storeroom or kitchen for the whole day. Soon after the morning tea, it is time for the office-goers to depart. With that over, the children come back from schools. When it is over with them, you have to take care of the tiffin for the babus back from their offices. And, hardly is that done when you have to organize things for dinner. This may continue well into midnight, till eleven or twelve at least; well, if the mistress of the house spends the whole day thus, then it boils down to the fact that her entire life is spent planning and managing food and meals. I do not say that women should not work, they will of course put in their labour, but within some limits and with some regularity. Everything must be taken care of; labour and relaxation should be compatible with minding the storeroom and other sundry jobs. As it is said in Bengal, 'Doesn't she who cooks also dress her hair?', so we must say, cook we will, but will do other things as well, and think about many other issues too.

Everything is possible, women of other countries also perform sundry odd duties; but we spend the whole day in a quagmire, simply because we cannot do the right thing at the right time. We need to organize our work better, keep things properly and in their respective places. In most of our work instead, we seem to follow that unseemly model of the unplanned headlong plunge, which is expressed in the idiom, waking the bride up to inform her firstly that she is about to get married and that the auspicious moment is passing. We do not think today of what is to be done tomorrow; do not even care to remember if all the sundry necessities are at home. Suppose we need an ice bag. Well, once when somebody fell ill we had purchased one but do not remember now where it was dumped. Today we have to give the child some castor oil, but cannot find the bottle right now. The child tumbles and bleeds profusely, we scamper around for a bandage. There are so many old clean clothes in the household, but at this hour of need not a single one can be located. The wife has an invitation to attend a social occasion, but the husband has taken the car to his office. He was not told anything, so heaven knows when it will be back! There is not a drop of cooking oil in store, and it has totally escaped notice, so nobody was asked to bring it. I offered to give you some money, but have not taken it from my husband! The husband comes back from office after a gruelling day's work. Then I bring to his notice a whole list of complaints and he is to give judgement on each issue. I have even seen a wife who would go under a quilt when she hears the husband's car arriving, because once he comes into the room, he would pay great attention to her. This is the silly way in which we conduct ourselves within our households. This is childish. It does not need a great deal of learning to organize the household to a reasonable extent; a bit of care to avoid major lapses is more than enough.

My fourth point is literature as aid to improvement. This is to say that we need to read books on every subject to improve upon our household as well as our collective work. The women of other countries have advanced so much because they read all the possible literature on a subject that they wish to improve upon. What not only the women of our own country but also women of other nationalities have thought about a particular subject may teach us some useful lessons. We may not absorb everything but still it may, on the whole, be of some use. Many of us are now aware of the deficiencies. Today we find time to think about the deficiencies and also look for books that are useful to overcome them. There are books about almost anything, about women's work, about their household work, about how to raise children, how to manage within limited means, how to wash clothes, how to keep the rooms clean, and so on—it is rather easy to read about these things.

I have taken much of your time today, but have not been able to present anything systematically. I have left many things out of my discussion, but if you kindly give me your opinion on these matters, it will be of immense help to me. One can learn so many things through mutual discussion. We wish to talk among ourselves in our club sessions on such topics of routine domestic interest. If we may choose the subject beforehand, then we can perhaps help each other through these exchanges. My purpose today is to suggest using our studies for our domestic duties—to try to remove our deficiencies, to erase from everybody's mind that studies are merely a formal thing and are not meant for practical purposes.

Let us rise to the occasion to strengthen our women's association as a place to discuss our domestic world: our home, household work, work for the country and efforts towards collective work. Come, and let us join hands to do these things well.

Translated by Sourin Bhattacharya
Formerly Professor of Economics, Jadavpur University; recipient of the Sahitya Akademi Reward for Bengali Literature, 2009.

'Meyeder Sambandhe Gutikatak Katha' (n.d.), *Sarala Ray Centenary Volume* (Calcutta Sarala Ray Centenary Committee), 26 November 1961, pp. 58–68.

NOTE

1 The National Society for Women's Suffrage had been founded in 1867 in the wake of the 1866 'Ladies Petition'. The person referred to here is Jane, daughter of the Victorian statesman and liberal John Cobden, and wife of the publisher Fisher Unwin. She joined the National Society's finance committee, and by 1880 was serving as its treasurer.

65

SANTISUDHA GHOSH

Essay 15 offers a note on the author.

Women and Employment (n.d.)

In our country, even today, women's activities were restricted within the four walls of the household. In other words, their only duty was to look after the well-being of their husbands and children. Recently, some women have begun to earn. Much earlier, in Europe, women were given the opportunity and right to earn; again recently, some countries like Germany have tried to snatch away this right and force women to re-enter the vicinity of the kitchen. In Russia, not only have women the complete right to earn but it is mandatory for every man and woman to earn. Different rules are prevalent in various countries; but overall it can be seen that no society has been able to decide whether it is proper and lawful to allow women to earn or not. Regarding men this has been decided from time immemorial, that is, every man will have to earn in order to sustain himself or he is in some way or the other, the possessor of some property (there is no problem even if he is the worthless son of a zamindar). There has never been any question in people's minds about this.

But the same thing cannot be said in the case of women. So it would not be a bad idea to discuss the new trend in our country regarding women's employment. Though we say 'human society', it needs to be clarified that this problem does not relate to the entire society; it is specific to genteel society or those who try to imitate upper middle-class society. Poverty-stricken people, who are not concerned about their status and gentility, do not care about this and both men and women work together to increase their earnings. As we have seen, in society, the structural disparity between man and woman is more explicit and pronounced within the upper social strata in most countries. So we will discuss this matter from that point of view.

Recently, it seems that women are earning for two reasons: either to overcome the condition of economic want or, in the case of unmarried women, out of choice, using their leisure hours properly by starting work. These are the two primary reasons for which their male guardians permit them to do so. Women, whether married or unmarried, well-to-do or poor, have rarely been known to earn from a general conviction that earning is a responsibility for both men and women in all cases, and men also have not supported this idea.

There are mainly two reasons why men do not consider it worthwhile to allow women to earn. According to the difference in their way of thinking, two classes of men become influenced by these two reasons; or generally, in most cases, every man is controlled by either of these two reasons, and hence, they tend to prevent women from earning. The first class thinks that women are weaker than men. Due to natural reasons, every woman becomes incapable of working from time to time. Hence, women would not be able to endure the hardship of work and should be given respite from the responsibility of earning. Since men are free from every obstacle, they should take the onus of earning upon themselves. Women on the other hand, should remain within the household and do comparatively less strenuous work. Since our world comprises both the interior and the exterior, it would be better to divide the work between the two for the smooth running of society. (This attitude has not only kept women out of the purview of earning but it has also led to the perpetuation of the idea that if wives and daughters earn, then their status will be at stake, in other words, society will think that the male members are incapable of earning and this will be humiliating for them.) The attitude of the second group is far more degraded. They consider women to be their own property, hence they are afraid that if women become financially stable then they can become independent, this will then change the social order wherein women always have to remain dependent upon men for the bare minimum subsistence. So men are always afraid that the right to earn will make them lose their rights of possession over this property called 'woman'.

In reality, these two reasons behind restricting women within the four walls of the household and depriving them of the right to earn serve the self-interest of men. Through the essays of many writers, one gets the feeling that one accursed day all the men decided to snatch away the right to earn from the hands of women with the aim of stealing women's independence. We do not think it reasonable to accuse the entire male fraternity in this manner. On the other hand, it is also wrong for the pundits who have announced that men, desirous of releasing women from all difficult responsibilities, have situated them within the comfort of the household, because their main intention is to put women on the pedestal of goddesses and worship them with devotion. The real reason is a combination of the two. Some men have really sympathized with women's gentle nature and have approved of this arrangement without thinking of its far-reaching repercussions. Another group of men was only guided by their own interests and hence have confirmed to this arrangement. There is still another group of men who love women, but consider them as their property. There is a tradition among affluent people of keeping pets like dogs and cats. In reality they love them, take good care of them, they even shed tears when they die, but these pets need to remain within their control, comply with their desires, graciously wag their tails when they are loved.

Let us discuss first the group of men who love women but do not want them to earn since they are against women's freedom. The fear that women would not listen to their husbands and brothers if they get an independent source of income is ridiculous. This is because nobody thinks of depriving a son or a brother of the right to earn using the same logic: that the latter would not obey his father or elder brother (if he became financially secure). In reality, respecting or obeying elders is a social custom and is independent of earning. But at the same time, it is impossible to impose unjust orders and whims upon any person who is earning, be it a man or woman. Also, it would be safe and desirable not to impose such orders upon an earning member. Those men who do not believe in such illogical prejudices would discard the idea that women should always remain under the control of men. On the contrary, if women have economic independence they would be able to protest against the unjust claims of their fathers, husbands, sons, and this would necessarily benefit society. Men who are afraid that independence would make their wives go wayward and not remain devoted to their husbands (this fear arises surreptitiously in the minds of the majority of men), must be asked whether it is possible to arouse love forcefully and what the real worth of such love is. A husband who thinks that his wife loves him only because she does not get the opportunity to interact with other men has no respect and faith in his wife and has lost faith in himself too (in our country most men do not respect their wives and the female species in general). In other words, he believes that he himself does not possess the love in his heart which is adequate to acquire and sustain his wife's affection.

One of the findings of psychology states that in affairs of love, the more a person's mind is vitiated with desires, the more he unreasonably suspects others. A cultured man who believes that his wife complies with his wishes because she depends on him for the bare minimum subsistence, who tries to satisfy his desires not out of love but because she wants to live in luxury, can never be satisfied with his wife's love. Can we not see a similarity between these wives and those women whom society calls prostitutes? When love between two individuals becomes true and divine, only then can it remain unblemished, despite there being innumerable chances of being separated. So it is shameful for those men who give such reasons to justify their view that women should not be given the right to earn.

The above reasons are in support of women's right to earn but in a negative way, that is, they show the apprehensions, which could be avoided if women are allowed to earn. People are completely unaware of the harmful effects a society faces if women are prevented from earning. This is what we intend to reveal now since it is significant from society's point of view. This leads to the spiritual degeneration of women as a group, which in turn cripples society. Man is her protector, therefore, he is the lord and master. She has no other option but to surrender herself to men, this is what she has learnt from her very childhood. From the very beginning she has seen the lives of her mother and grandmother and has been conditioned in such a manner that she believes there is no alternative to this rule in her life either. This prejudice has left such a deep impression that not only externally, but also in her innermost self, she feels that she is weak and frail. This false ascription of weakness has enmeshed her spiritual self in such a manner that she is unable to think of any higher goal in life. Even if she is inspired to achieve something higher, she is afraid to act since she knows it is beyond her ability as she is weak. We all know that the highest goal of the spiritual self is the attainment of moksha or salvation but the opposite idea has enmeshed the entire self of a dependent woman. Spiritual selfhood cannot be attained by the weak but in our country the spiritual self of women has been engulfed by feebleness and powerlessness. This degeneration of the individual self is dangerous for humanity. The worst effect of this is that women have unhesitatingly placed their lives in charge of men and this has resulted in a carefree attitude on the part of women. Since women remain unaware of the toil and hardships of earning, they start quarrelling with their husbands if the latter fail to give their wives a luxurious lifestyle. Thus in most cases, men consider women to be a burden. This irresponsibility and lackadaisical attitude are a woman's shortcomings as a human being. By depriving women of the right to earn and compelling them to depend on men for bare subsistence, the terms 'wife' and 'servant' have become synonymous in our society. Preventing women from taking responsibility for maintaining their own lives has created a serious predicament, which has been reflected in subjugated India's present social and moral poverty.

We commend highly those sympathetic people who have willingly taken the responsibility of enhancing [the quality of] the lives of women. Although their intention is noble, there is something amiss in their judgement. Taming or domesticating animals and birds is not the same as domesticating human beings. This is primarily because birds and animals do not have any mental or psychological requirements, what they require is the satisfaction of their physical needs. But human beings belong to a different category, combining the essence of both animals and gods; the mind and *atma* have not only combined with the body but have also played very important roles (as essentially human qualities). Therefore, human beings need to be treated in a different manner. They can never remain content with the fulfilment of their physical needs. In order to make the life of a human being meaningful, one has to give importance to the unfurling of the inner essence of the self. I have already shown how depriving them from the rights of independence has ruined the psychological and spiritual lives of women. Therefore, the well-wishers of women as a group will never try to restrict women from becoming self-sufficient. The logic that women are physically weaker than men and they have to face various health problems related to motherhood is not quite baseless. Those who feel from the bottom of their hearts that women should be released from all hard work and should engage in doing light jobs should try to mould and control social norms in such a way that through marriage every woman gets the right to enjoy her husband's income and becomes the owner of half of her husband's property. If women are men's better halves and child rearing is important for society, then married women's demand for wages is absolutely reasonable. If married women were paid for doing household chores then they would have never tried to look for jobs, rather they would have remained devoted towards their household duties. Further, this system would keep their freedom and self-sufficiency intact. Though the present legal system has entitled a woman to have rights over her husband's income, yet it is different from her own income. Only if the wife can prove the extent of torture meted out to her by her husband in a court of law, can she get a meager amount of compensation, which she can spend as she desires. Otherwise she has no right over her husband's income in her in-laws' house.

Apart from such violence as can be proved in a court of law, women regularly experience indifference and ignorance, and the two mouthfuls of food given to her out of kindness lead to her spiritual degradation. There is no remedy for this. Our proposal for the wife's rights over her husband's property and income can prove to be an easy way of remedying the wife's plight. (This is not an essay about women's right of succession; we have tried to give only an indication of it). Those people who out of sympathy have restricted women from becoming self-sufficient will not have any problems with this arrangement because on the one hand it takes care of women's delicate nature and on the other hand it does not prevent women from thinking that they are self-dependent. Otherwise, the wife has no alternative but to search for a job. This is the situation only of married women. In case of unmarried women since there is no question of the responsibility of motherhood, one fails to see any logical reservations against their earning a living. Rather it can be said that working and earning is a meaningful way of utilizing their time until marriage. Instead of idly squandering their father's or brother's income and yearning for a luxurious life, it gives them work experience and increases their sense of responsibility. Second, those people eager to save women from physical labour fail to notice the kind of physical exertion that middle-class women in our society do from morning till night, which is far greater than teaching in schools, colleges or jobs in offices and courts, or in the medical and legal profession or tailoring and even working in roadside eating stalls. There are many jobs in today's world where the amount of physical labour required is less than that required for household chores. Therefore, one cannot forcefully impose this idea. Further, in the name of women's frailty they are privately and carefully being pushed inside the narrow confines of the household where again the cowering qualities of timidity and bashfulness encompass their lives in such an unnatural manner that women become more weak and feeble.

There is another class of men with little vision who try to posit a different reason against women's endeavour to earn. They claim that in an age of decreasing job opportunities throughout the world, if women begin to enter into this competition (for jobs), then matters will become even worse. This contention at a glance sounds flawless. But if one ponders a little then one can argue that it is not only men who people this earth, the same number of women or even more, also live here. It is not men alone who require money to sustain themselves, women also have the same needs. Therefore, the problem of unemployment and dependence on others for sustaining oneself needs to be viewed from the perspectives of both men and women. In the name of social norms, those who are forcefully compelling women to remain unemployed are in reality not simplifying the problem but are out of ignorance cheating them.

Prevailing social conventions have made such strong imprints upon people's minds that they fail to think differently. They consider it a heinous crime to rearrange social rules. So, one cannot think differently in the context of women's employment. We are certain that if today a law making earning mandatory for women is passed, then a huge protest against the law would be voiced not only by men but by the majority of women too. By placing the responsibility on the shoulders of men, women have developed the habit of leading a life of comfort, evading responsibilities. They do not realize the mental and spiritual degradation that they are undergoing. Further, the mental strength required to challenge and reject conventional practices is also missing in most women. Well-wishers of society need to remember that men and women are not tools created for the age-old manoeuvring of the machine called society; rather society has to be changed and regulated in the right manner for the psychological, physical and spiritual evolution and well-being of every man and woman.

Translated by Anindita Roy
Department of Comparative Literature, Jadavpur University

'Nari o Uparjan' (n.d.), *Santisudha Ghosh: Nirbachita Rachana-Samkalan,* edited by Sarmistha Dutta Gupta (Kolkata: Dey's Publishing and School of Women's Studies, Jadavpur University), June 2008/Asarh 1415 BS, pp. 35–40.

A Note on the Bengali Periodicals

The essays in this volume are from the following periodicals:

Anandabazar Patrika (weekly), Sisir Kumar Ghosh, ed., Kolkata, mid-March to mid-April 1899/Chaitra 1306 BS.
Antahpur (monthly), Banalata Devi, ed., Kolkata, 1898/1305 BS.
Bamabodhini Patrika (monthly), Umesh Chandra Dutta, ed., Kolkata, mid-August to mid-September 1863/Bhadra 1270 BS (in circulation for sixty years, from 1863–1922/1270 BS–1329 BS).
Bangabani (monthly), Dinesh Chandra Sen and Bijoy Chandra Majumdar, eds, Kolkata, mid-February to mid-March 1922/Falgun 1328 BS.
Bangla Samayik Patrikapanji: 1931-47 Geeta Chattyopadhyay and Bimal Chandra Chattyopadhyay, eds, Kolkata: Bangiya Granthagar Parishad/Bengal Library Association, 20 December 2001.
Bangalakshmi (monthly), Kumudini Basu, ed., Kolkata, mid-November to mid-December 1925/Agrahayan 1332 BS.
Bangamahila (monthly), Kolkata, 1875/1282 BS.
Bangamahila (Navapraya) (monthly), Abhilash Chandra Sarvabhaum, ed, Kolkata, mid-April to mid-May 1915/Baisakh 1322 BS.
Bharati (monthly), *'Masik Somalochana Patrika'*, Dwijendranath Tagore, ed., Kolkata, mid-July to mid-August 1877/Sravan 1284 BS. Succeeding editors:
Dwijendranath Tagore, ed., mid-July to mid-August 1877–83/Sravan 1284–90 BS.
Swarnakumari Devi ,ed., 1884–94/1291–1301, BS.
Hiranmayee Devi and Sarala Devi, eds, 1895–97/1302–04 BS.
Rabindranath Tagore, ed., 1898/1305 BS.
Sarala Devi, ed., 1899–1907/1306–1314 BS.
Swarnakumari Devi, ed., 1908–14/1315–21 BS.

Manilal Gangopadhyay and Sourindra Mohan Mukhopadhya, eds, 1915–23/1322–30 BS.
Sarala Devi, ed., mid-October to mid-November 1924–26/Kartik 1331–33 BS.

Bharati o Balak (monthly), Swarnakumari Devi, ed., Kolkata, 1887/1293 BS.

Balak (monthly), Jnanadanandini Devi, ed., Kolkata, mid-April to mid-May 1885/Baisakh 1292 BS. (After two years of its publication, *Balak* merged with *Bharati*. From 1887–93/1293–99 BS *Bharati o Balak* was published. In 1893/1300 BS, the monthly was published again as *Bharati*.)

Bulbul (monthly), Habibullah Bahar Chowdhury and Begum Shamsun Nahar, eds, Kolkata, 1340–45/1933–38 BS.

Gulistan (monthly), S. Shamser Ali, Shiekh Mohammed Ali, and later C. Abdur Rauref, A.H.M. Faqarull Islam Khan, eds, Kolkata, mid-November to mid-December 1932/Agrahayan 1339 BS.

Jayasree (monthly), Leela Nag (Roy), ed., Kolkata, 1930–31/1337–38 BS.

Marmabani (weekly), Jagadindranath Rai and Amulya Charan Vidyabhusan, eds, mid-July to mid-August 1915/Sravan 1322 BS., no. 13. (*Marmabani* existed stably for only six months, but in order to keep the magazine from an untimely death, it was merged with the eighth edition of *Manasi*.)

Manasi (monthly), Fakir Chandra Chattopadhyay, Subodh Chandra Bandopadhyay, Induprokash Bandopadhyay, Shivratan Mitra, eds, Kolkata, mid-February to mid-March 1903/Falgun 1315 BS.

Manasi o Marmabani (monthly), Jagadindranath Rai and Prabhat Kumar Mukherjee, eds, mid-February to mid-March 1915/Falgun 1322 BS.

Mandira, Sachitra Masik Patrika, Kolkata, mid-April to mid-May 1938/Baisakh 1345 BS.
Editors:
Kamala Chattopadyay, mid-April to mid-May 1938–mid-March to mid-April 1939/Baisakh 1345–Chaitra 1346 BS.
Kamala Dasgupta, mid-April to mid-May 1940–mid-July to mid-August 1942/Baisakh 1347–Sravan 1349 BS.
Snehalata Sen, mid-August to mid-September 1942–mid-November to mid-December 1945/Bhadra 1349–Agrahayan 1352 BS.
Kamala Dasgupta, mid-December to mid-January 1945–mid-March to mid-April 1947/Paush 1352–Chaitra 1354 BS.

Arun Chandra Guha, mid-March to mid-April–mid-April to mid-May 1948/Chaitra–Baisakh 1355 BS.

Matrimandir (monthly), Akshay Kumar Nandy and Surbala Dutta, eds., Kolkata, mid-September to mid-October 1923/Ashvin 1330 BS.

Nabajiban (monthly), Kunjbehari Dev ed., Kolkata, mid-August to mid-September 1921/Bhadra 1328 BS.

Nabanoor (monthly), Syed Emdad Ali, ed., Kolkata, mid-April to mid-May 1903/Baisakh 1310 BS (regularly published till mid-December to mid-January 1906/Paush 1313 BS).

Prabasi (monthly), Ramananda Chattopadhyay, ed., Allahabad, mid-April to mid-May 1901/Baisakh 1308 BS.

Saogat (monthly), Mohammed Naseeruddin, ed., Kolkata, mid-November to mid-December 1918/Agrahayan 1325 BS.

Swadesh (monthly), Abhinash Chandra Das, ed., Kolkata, mid-October to mid-November 1905/Kartik 1312. BS.